EVALUATION IN ACTION

EVALUATION IN ACTION

Interviews With Expert Evaluators

Jody Fitzpatrick
University of Colorado Denver

Christina Christie
Claremont Graduate University

Melvin M. Mark
The Pennsylvania State University

Los Angeles • London • New Delhi • Singapore

For information:

SAGE Publications, Inc.
2455 Teller Road
Thousand Oaks,
California 91320
E-mail: order@sagepub.com

SAGE Publications India Pvt. Ltd.
B 1/I 1 Mohan Cooperative
Industrial Area
Mathura Road, New Delhi 110 044
India

SAGE Publications Ltd.
1 Oliver's Yard
55 City Road
London EC1Y 1SP
United Kingdom

SAGE Publications
Asia-Pacific Pte. Ltd.
33 Pekin Street #02-01
Far East Square
Singapore 048763

Printed in the United States of America

Library of Congress Cataloging-in-Publication Data

Evaluation in action: interviews with expert evaluators/edited by Jody Fitzpatrick, Christina Christie, Melvin M. Mark.
    p. cm.
Includes bibliographical references and index.
ISBN 978-1-4129-4974-3 (pbk.)
   1. Social sciences—Methodology. 2. Evaluation research (Social action programs)—United States. 3. Educational accountability—United States.
I. Fitzpatrick, Jody L. II. Christie, Christina A. III. Mark, Melvin M.

H61.E913 2009
300.72—dc22   2008003526

This book is printed on acid-free paper.

08   09   10   11   12   10 9 8 7 6 5 4 3 2 1

Acquisitions Editor:	Vicki Knight
Associate Editor:	Sean Connelly
Editorial Assistant:	Lauren Habib
Production Editor:	Astrid Virding
Copy Editor:	QuADS Prepress (P) Ltd
Typesetter:	C&M Digitals (P) Ltd
Proofreader:	Joyce Li
Indexer:	Kathy Paparchontis
Cover Designer:	Candice Harman
Marketing Manager:	Stephanie Adams

CONTENTS

———•◦•———

*SAGE Publications gratefully acknowledges
the contributions of the following reviewers: Julie D. Cushman,
University of Michigan; Andrea K. Rorrer, University of Utah;
and David A. Squires, Southern Connecticut State University.*

PREFACE

I n 1997, while serving as Associate Editor of *Evaluation Practice*, which later became the *American Journal of Evaluation*, I began a column of interviews on evaluation. The idea for the column emerged from my concern that we didn't know much about how people actually *practiced* evaluation. Journal articles and books were written about *how* to conduct an evaluation, describing purposes, steps to be taken in planning, and methods for collecting data and facilitating the use of results. Other articles presented results of evaluation or discussed a particular methodological approach. But we didn't have a real understanding of what evaluators *did* to carry out the evaluation. How did they identify the purpose of the evaluation? What stakeholders did they involve in that decision? In other parts of the evaluation? How did they make decisions concerning which constructs to measure? How to collect data on the constructs? Did they involve stakeholders or others in interpreting results? What strategies did they use to encourage use? I knew what I do in my own practice, influenced by reading others and my own years of practice, but I wanted to know more about what others, exemplars in the field, did when they conducted an evaluation.

In addition to wanting to "get under the hood" and learn more about the choices exemplars made in conducting evaluations, I wanted to know more about the extent to which evaluation theory, personal proclivities, and program context influenced evaluation choices. Evaluation theories were, and remain, a major area of interest in evaluation. Huey Chen and Peter Rossi advocated using theory from social research to guide evaluations in their writings on theory-driven evaluation. Other approaches or theories were concerned with involving stakeholders for different goals. David Fetterman developed and argued for empowerment evaluation as a way to involve stakeholders in the process to improve evaluations and the knowledge and understanding of those stakeholders. Brad Cousins, with others, described models for participatory evaluation. Jennifer Greene wrote about new approaches to Robert Stake's original responsive evaluation model. I was interested in the extent to which evaluators' practice was influenced by these different theories. When conducting a particular evaluation did exemplars adhere to a specific theory? How did they adapt to the context? To the needs of stakeholders? To the stage and characteristics of the program? How did their past training and orientation to evaluation influence their choices? In addition to *describing* evaluation practice, I thought the interviews could tell us more about the contrasting influences of theory and program context on evaluators' choices in the field.

I will add that the interviews were not intended as a research project in which each person is asked the same questions to compare responses. Instead, each interview was intended to illustrate one experienced evaluator's actions in one particular setting. After reading the evaluation reports and related articles, the interviewers, generally myself, developed questions around general stages of the evaluation, but often specific to the particular choices the evaluator appeared to have made. Furthermore, the evaluator's responses are his or her own interpretation of the program, its context, and the evaluation itself. Although the interviewer read the evaluation reports produced from the project to prepare the interview questions, and thus had knowledge of the evaluation as it was reported, others involved in the evaluation were not interviewed to corroborate the evaluator's remarks. As evaluators know, there are multiple perspectives on reality and truth. In these interviews, in order to learn about evaluation practice, I was interested in learning the evaluator's truth, his or her views of the evaluation process, and the contextual and theoretical factors that the evaluator believed influenced the choices made in the evaluation. The evaluator, as opposed to other stakeholders in the process, was familiar with evaluation theories and the contextual factors that influence stakeholder involvement, methodological choices, and possible efforts to encourage use and, thus, could describe what he or she saw as the influences on his or her choices. These issues are, in fact, what we want to learn about practice.

From 1997 to 2001, the *American Journal of Evaluation* published eight of my interviews, in a new section entitled "Exemplars" because we chose to interview exemplary evaluators about their practice. In 2002, Tina Christie began the column. The interviews aroused much interest, comment, and, occasionally, surprise. So we decided to put them together in a book that, as a whole, would help students and others learn more about how evaluations are actually conducted and permit comparison across interviews. We conducted three new interviews for the book to address areas—international evaluation, cultural competence, and capacity building—that had not been sufficiently covered in the existing set of interviews.

The book is intended for many audiences, including students in evaluation courses, new and seasoned evaluation practitioners, and those who conduct research on evaluation. For students and practitioners, the interviews provide insights into the different choices that evaluators make in defining their roles and conducting the evaluation. For evaluation theorists and researchers, the interviews can suggest ways in which evaluators may use and adapt evaluation theories to the context of a specific evaluation. As such, they may provide ideas for further research.

ORGANIZATION OF THE BOOK

The interviews are organized under four categories: evaluations with the purpose of determining the merit or worth of a program, evaluations concerned with description, evaluations with a focus on organizational development or capacity building, and evaluations with special concerns around cultural competency. Each category includes two to four interviews that illustrate practice in this category. However, each interview illustrates many other aspects of practice as well as the category under which it is placed. The categories are not all-inclusive and the interviews could be organized in many different ways. The Appendix lists the interviews under other categories. Thus, if a professor or reader is interested in learning more about evaluations that measure impacts or outcomes, the Appendix lists all the evaluations that take that focus. Similarly, if the reader is interested in interviews that make use of observation or randomized control trials, or evaluations that provide insights into use or involving stakeholders, the Appendix can serve as a useful tool. (The categories in the Appendix were selected to correspond to sections in many evaluation textbooks to permit faculty using such texts to identify interviews that may be useful for their students when reading a particular chapter.)

Each section begins by providing the reader with a brief introduction to the section title—that is, determining merit and worth, cultural competency in evaluation—and to questions the reader might consider when reading interviews in the section. Each interview then begins with an introduction to the evaluator and some of the issues illustrated in the interview. This introduction is followed by a summary of the evaluation written by the evaluator. The summary is intended to give the reader a context for reading the interview. Those readers who wish to read more on the evaluation can consult the further reading and reference lists at the end of each interview chapter. For most interviews, a more detailed description of the evaluation is available through either a report in the public domain or an article written about the evaluation. (This reference is listed as the first entry under Further Reading.) Thus, faculty may choose to have students read the entire evaluation report and, then, the interview. Each interview then closes with a commentary by the person who conducted the interview, Tina Christie in two cases and myself in ten. Finally, the interview closes with discussion questions for students and other readers to consider about that interview.

The book includes other chapters to assist the reader in understanding and interpreting the interview. The first chapter provides the reader new to evaluation with some insights into the field of evaluation practice and issues that are of concern to evaluators today. Analyses of the interviews are presented in the two closing chapters. In Chapter 14, I describe some of the conclusions I reached, by examining trends across interviews, about how skilled evaluators practice evaluation. In Chapter 15, Tina Christie, who has conducted research on the connections between evaluation theory and practice, discusses what we can learn about evaluation theory from these interviews.

We hope these interviews will stimulate discussions about practice—the challenges faced in practice and the choices evaluators can make. Finally, we hope the interviews will help evaluators reflect on their own practices and, ulti-mately, improve their evaluation practice by helping them make more con-scious, informed choices.

I would like to thank the 14 evaluators, who agreed to share their craft and their expertise in these interviews. I thoroughly enjoyed talking with each person I interviewed. Their delight and love of their work, their energy and caring about evaluation and social betterment came through in their voices, their words, and their work. They were refreshingly candid about the chal-lenges they faced and the efforts they undertook to produce useful studies. As professionals, they were willing to share their successes and failures in helping others learn.

Jody Fitzpatrick

ONE

EVALUATION AND ITS PRACTICE

Some Key Considerations and Choices

Evaluation covers a broad spectrum of activities, and different evaluators emphasize different kinds of evaluation activities. As a result, evaluation can be difficult to define. The traditional definition of evaluation involves judging the merit or worth of something—for example, a program, a policy, or a product (Scriven, 1967, 1991).[1] An evaluation might help teachers or school administrators determine whether a new curriculum or textbook is improving students' ability to write essays. Or it might help therapists at a mental health center determine whether a new approach to treating eating disorders is helpful for the types of clients they serve. Parents may use school "report cards" to judge the merit and worth of their children's schools or to select schools for the future. Congress or state legislatures may use the results of an evaluation to decide whether to continue, expand, or reduce funding for a program. All these examples illustrate stakeholders of different types, using the results of an evaluation to judge the merit or worth of a program or policy.

Fitzpatrick, Sanders, and Worthen (2004) expanded this original definition of evaluation to include identifying, clarifying, and applying defensible criteria to judge the object. This emphasis encourages evaluators and stakeholders to consider the criteria they will use to judge the product; such consideration can prompt useful dialogue between evaluators and stakeholders concerning their different views of program goals and how they are achieved.[2]

Others have defined evaluation more broadly. Daniel Stufflebeam (1971, 2001) and many in the related field of policy analysis (Heineman, Bluhm, Peterson, & Kearney, 2002; Lerner & Lasswell, 1951; Weimer & Vining, 1999) define evaluation and policy analysis in the context of making decisions.[3] Thus, Stufflebeam defines evaluation as "the process of delineating, obtaining, and providing useful information for judging decision alternatives" (1973, p. 129). Lerner and Lasswell (1951), who helped create the field of policy analysis, wrote that policy analysis, like evaluation, is "decision-oriented," "value-conscious," and "client-oriented." Heineman et al. (2002) discuss policy analysis as a means of improving government decisions to increase the public good. In evaluation and in policy analysis, many authors have emphasized evaluation's link to traditional social science research methods (Lindblom & Cohen, 1979; Rossi, Lipsey, & Freeman, 2004; Weimer & Vining, 1999). Thus, Rossi et al. (2004) define evaluation as "the use of social research methods to systematically investigate the effectiveness of social intervention programs in ways that are adapted to their political and organizational environments and are designed to inform social action to improve social conditions" (p. 16). The first part of their definition, and much of their book, focuses on the use of traditional, scientific research methods to conduct evaluations. However, the remainder of their definition illustrates the change in views of evaluation over time. They recognize that methods must be adapted to the characteristics of the environment for the results to be used to improve social conditions. The interviews in this book will illustrate how exemplary evaluators adapt their methods to the context and characteristics of the program and to stakeholder information needs.

BEYOND DEFINITIONS: IMPORTANT DISTINCTIONS ABOUT EVALUATION

One gains a better understanding of what constitutes evaluation by considering a number of distinctions that have been made about the types and functions of evaluation. Evaluation scholars have offered several different ways of mapping the variation that exists in evaluation practice. These include discussions of evaluation purposes, uses of evaluation, and alternative evaluation theories, models, or approaches. These different sets of distinctions are not completely independent. Rather, they constitute alternative ways of mapping the same territory. But it is useful for evaluators to understand these different mappings because each mapping highlights somewhat distinct and important features of evaluation.

Evaluation Purposes

One distinction that contributes to a better understanding of what constitutes evaluation is a consideration of its purposes. Building on previous ideas about evaluation purposes, Mark, Henry, and Julnes (2000) identified four different purposes for evaluation: assessment of merit and worth, oversight and compliance, program and organizational improvement, and knowledge development. The first purpose, judging merit and worth, reflects the traditional definition of evaluation. Alternatively, government and private foundations often use evaluation, not for judging the merit or worth of a program they have funded but for oversight and compliance, to determine if the program they funded has conducted the proposed activities or served the targeted client population. The delivery of the program may be compared with certain standards, but evaluation's purpose is to determine whether the organization *complied* with certain agreements or standards, rather than to judge the merit or worth of the program. States may ask whether county departments of social welfare provided services only to clients who met the criteria for service and what proportion of those clients in need they did, in fact, serve. School boards and state departments of education may examine test scores, graduations rates, and attendance patterns to monitor school performance. Foundations receive and study evaluations of those they fund, at least in part, to learn whether the funds were spent as the foundation intended. The public and the media demand that government be "accountable," and that accountability often focuses heavily on oversight and compliance.

Evaluation theories and models have expanded most recently in the area of Mark et al.'s (2000) third purpose, program and organizational improvement. Michael Scriven (1967) was the first to identify two types of decisions evaluation could serve: Summative evaluations (Mark et al.'s, 2000, assessment of merit and worth) were used to make decisions about program adoption, continuation, or expansion. In contrast, formative evaluations were used to make decisions concerning improving a program or policy. Of course, program and organizational improvement are a type of formative evaluation. But the idea of program and organizational improvement covers a broad array of evaluation activities, including needs assessments, empowerment evaluations, some participative evaluations, and appreciative inquiry. A director of an English language program for immigrants may use a formative evaluation to learn more about the factors that prompt students to drop out of the program and obtain recommendations to improve retention. A group of high school principals may conduct a descriptive study to learn whether teachers are able to implement a block schedule with the intended types of instruction. The results of this study will help them to determine what is feasible, whether more training of teachers is needed, and to identify teachers who are implementing the program in intended or innovative ways in order to mentor or train other teachers. Again, the intent is to improve a program, not to judge its merit or worth. In terms of broader organizational improvement, any organization might conduct studies of new employees and their impact, positive or negative, on organizational culture. The results of such studies might be used to change employee recruitment and hiring, orientation programs, or training of supervisors and other employees on needs for change in the organization. The idea of program *and organizational* improvement implies that evaluation's purpose can be to enhance an organization itself rather than a program within the organization. The focus on the organization will presumably improve the delivery of programs within the organization. For example, an evaluator might try to increase organizational capacity to make data-driven decisions by involving program staff in an evaluation.

Many evaluations also add to knowledge about the subject matter being studied, Mark et al.'s (2000) last purpose. As such, evaluation can also be research, adding to knowledge in a field. While the primary purposes of evaluation are to serve judgments of merit and worth, facilitate decisions about program continuation or improvement, and monitor or improve program or organizational performance, the data collected through evaluations can, and often do, add to knowledge in a field by testing a particular theory or intervention or by describing a condition or performance. The information or data evaluators collect may not have been available in that context, with that population, or with that particular type of intervention in previous research, and thus, knowledge is increased, and theories of behavior, motivation, or organizational performance may be enhanced through evaluation. Various kinds of knowledge can be enhanced. Evaluations can increase people's understanding, for example, of the nature or scope of a social problem, of the range of possible solutions to a problem, or of the feasibility of implementing a new kind of intervention.[4]

The purposes of evaluation refer to the intended use of the evaluation. That is, evaluations are conducted to help determine the merit and worth of a program or policy, to oversee organizations and learn if they have complied with certain agreements, to improve the performance of programs or organizations, and to add to our knowledge. However, often evaluations are categorized by the types of questions the study addresses or the focus of the evaluation. As such, evaluations may be considered needs assessment studies, process or monitoring studies, and outcome or impact studies. Many people new to evaluation consider evaluation to be focused on outcomes. Certainly, many evaluations examine program outcomes, but evaluations can also include descriptive studies of program actions or processes (Who attends or participates in the program? Is the program implemented as planned? What changes are made in the program model once it is implemented in the field? How do participants react to the program?). Evaluations may also include needs assessment studies to help policy makers, program managers, and other stakeholders in the process of planning a program (Does the prospective program or policy serve a real need? What types of clients have the problem the program is intended to address? What are some of the contributing factors to the problem? Which factors should the program address? What types of program activities might be successful in bringing about the desired changes in future program participants? What knowledge and skills would program staff need to bring about these changes?). The type of evaluation conducted often depends on the stage of the program and the information needs of critical stakeholders, but all are genuine evaluations that help in determining merit or worth, in monitoring program activities, or in bringing about program or organizational change and improvement. Multiyear evaluations may involve many of these types of evaluation as the nature of the program and the information needs of stakeholders evolve. Such changes in focus can be seen in many of the interviews in this book.

Uses of Evaluation

Research on the use of evaluation has shown other facets of evaluation. Early conceptions of evaluation and policy analysis focused on direct, or instrumental, use of the results. That is, the expectation was that results of evaluations would be used directly to make decisions, either formative or summative ones. For example, it was presumed that, based on disappointing evaluation results, policy makers would decide to discontinue funding of a program or program recruitment staff would change their methods of recruitment and criteria for admission to a program. Some research, however, suggested that the results of evaluations and policy analyses were rarely used in this direct way (Cousins & Leithwood, 1986; Hird, 2005; Patton, 1986; Stone, 1997). Others (Chelimsky, 1991; Cook, 1997) have argued that direct, instrumental use is more frequent than has been suggested and recent evidence suggests that it is so. In fact, the reader will learn of much instrumental use of results in the interviews described in this book.

Nevertheless, the oft-reported incidents of ignored evaluation results prompted others to explore the manner in which evaluation results *were* used. Many other uses have emerged, including *enlightenment*—that is, changing individuals' knowledge, beliefs, or views about something, whether those were characteristics or needs of clients or students, views of citizens or other stakeholders, relationships between factors previously not considered, or other evaluation findings. Enlightenment may simply awaken a user to an issue that has not previously been of concern. Alternatively, it may prompt the user to doubt, question, or even reconsider a previously firmly held belief. These uses do not necessarily lead to immediate action but, nevertheless, have influence over the long term.

Kirkhart (2000) has suggested that our focus on *use* has caused us to ignore the actual *influences* of evaluation. She believes that much of the power of evaluation lies in its unintended influences. The very idea of use seems to imply a conscious and intentional act by the person or group using the evaluation. In contrast, Kirkhart suggests that evaluation often makes a difference in more subtle ways, such that people can be affected by evaluation indirectly. For example, a policy maker may be influenced, indirectly, by an evaluation he or she does not even know exists, because the evaluation caused a key staff member to make a different recommendation about how to vote on pending legislation. Kirkhart also notes that the *process* of participating in an evaluation can influence the stakeholders who participate, a possibility that has come to be called process use. Michael Patton (1997) has defined process use as "individual changes in thinking and behavior, and program or organizational changes in procedures and culture, that occur among those involved in evaluation as a result of the learning that occurs during the evaluation process" (p. 90). Thus, individuals, managers, program staff, policy makers, or clients may begin to think of programs and policies in different ways as a result of their experience in an evaluation. These changes may have an effect on their future decisions or choices regarding program adoption, continuation, and development.[5]

Mark and Mills (2007) define a different type of indirect use of evaluation, procedural influence. This concept recognizes that people who do not participate in an evaluation may be influenced by the procedures or methods of an evaluation. For example, if evaluations of welfare reform very frequently include measures of children's well-being, this feature of the evaluation could increase the salience of this outcome for decision makers and other stakeholders.

In a departure from the focus on use, Mark and Henry (2004) have developed a generic model that outlines potential pathways to describe the effects or *consequences* of evaluation. Their model specifies three different "levels of influence" for evaluation: individuals, interpersonal interactions, and/or collective actions through organizations. The identification of these levels helps us describe different pathways and the ultimate route to use or change. An evaluation can initially have influence at one of these levels, and the change at that level of influence can then lead to changes at another level of influence, with a series of processes leading to the final type of use or influence that may occur. Furthermore, different types of change processes can occur at each level of influence. Thus, if an evaluation's influence is initially at the individual level, this influence may emerge as an attitude or a behavioral change, such as raising the salience of an issue or elaborating on an issue (akin to enlightenment). For example, reading an evaluation of a bullying prevention program for middle schoolers may prompt parents to consider the severity of the problem in their child's school or lead teachers to think extensively about the bullying in their own school. Evaluation's effects at the individual level will sometimes lead to changes at the interpersonal level. Evaluation effects or consequences that occur at the interpersonal level include attempts to persuade others, justifying something to others (continuation of a program, changes in a program), or persuading others to become change agents or to join in a movement for change (by demonstrating the positive or negative impacts of a program or demonstrating a strong, unmet need). Thus, the PTSA president who has read an evaluation of bullying programs may organize other parents and teachers to pressure for such programs in their school district. Organizations, on the other hand, may be influenced to use evaluation for instrumental purposes, changing policies or programs. In the case of organizations, the most familiar form of influence occurs when evaluation findings have overt instrumental consequences, when policies or programs are changed, expanded, or ended. However, organizations may also be influenced by evaluation in terms of agenda setting, that is, the raising of new topics to the table for consideration. Organization-level evaluation influence can also involve the initial decision to develop programs or policies, or diffusion, the spreading of programs or policies from one place to another. Changes at the organizational level can also lead to subsequent influence within individuals or in interpersonal interactions. In short, Mark and Henry suggest that a variety of pathways exist whereby evaluations can be influential.

These models and theories of use expand our views of evaluation and its purposes. In the interviews that follow, the reader will see many different types of use, from instrumental use for formative or summative purposes to enlightenment, agenda setting, and process use. The cases illustrate the myriad uses that evaluation can have, as well as the influence of the evaluator and the context of the evaluation on use.

Evaluation Theories, Models, and Approaches

In evaluation, "theories," "models," and "approaches" are often used interchangeably to refer to a set of formulations or principles concerning how evaluation should be conducted. These theories or approaches address different issues but may concern epistemology, purpose, assumptions, evaluation procedures, intended users, and other issues (Christie, 2003; Fitzpatrick et al., 2004; House, 1980; Owen, 2007; Shadish, Cook, & Leviton, 1991; Stufflebeam, 2001; Stufflebeam, Madaus, & Kellaghan, 2000). In essence, evaluation theories, models, and approaches describe how evaluation should be conducted. The interviews in this book demonstrate that, in practice, evaluators often adapt to the context to make decisions on how to conduct an evaluation. However, evaluators and evaluation practice are *greatly* influenced by models and theories. They influence the types of evaluation questions evaluators tend to pursue, the methods they use, the stakeholders they involve, and the types of influence or use they hope to achieve. As such, readers of this book should have some introduction to these different theories or approaches and their implications.

In its early years, most evaluations followed an objectives-oriented model or approach, in which evaluations were designed to determine whether a program's goals and objectives were achieved. In the absence of other models, and in response to government demands, such an approach seemed to be what evaluators did. Many evaluations, often prompted by funding sources or governmental mandates, continue to be objectives oriented, evaluating the accomplishment of the program's stated objectives (Stufflebeam, 2001). Such evaluations are not particularly concerned with program actions or process or in explaining *how* goals are achieved, but they simply (and it is usually not so simple) determine whether the program achieved its stated goals and objectives. Standards-based testing in schools is a prominent example of an objectives-oriented evaluation tool. Such testing is concerned with whether children have obtained the intended knowledge, not necessarily with *how* they have obtained it or *why* they have not. The focus is on outcomes even more than on an identified program. Accreditations for hospitals, mental health facilities, or institutions of higher education are also objectives oriented in their approach. Such accreditations generally focus on whether these institutions have achieved their goals and objectives (sometimes those of the accrediting society, other times those of the individual institution). Federal government agencies in the United States, through the 1993 Government Performance Review Act (GPRA) and the subsequent Performance Assessment Rating Tool (PART), have focused their evaluation efforts on whether goals and objectives are achieved. Today's term, *performance monitoring*, is very similar to the older term, *objectives-oriented evaluation*. In such evaluations, it is relatively easy to know what to evaluate: the objectives or outcomes. Nevertheless, even in such evaluations, important choices are made concerning *which* outcomes to measure and how to measure them.[6]

Other approaches and theories to evaluation evolved from the objectives-oriented focus as stakeholders realized that such evaluations often did not provide the information that they needed. Daniel Stufflebeam's CIPP[7] model based evaluations on decisions to be made at different stages of a program (Stufflebeam, 1971, 2001). By focusing on decisions, rather than objectives, Stufflebeam was one of the first to recognize that stakeholders' information needs may concern issues other than program objectives—for example, assessing needs, describing program activities or clients, measuring more immediate outcomes than those reflected in objectives, and so on. In further response to objectives-oriented approaches and to what he saw as inflexible, quantitative approaches, Robert Stake (1967) introduced participant-oriented evaluation. Participant-oriented evaluation, along with Guba and Lincoln's (1981) responsive evaluation, encouraged evaluators to become involved with a variety of stakeholders, not simply managers or policy makers, in planning an evaluation and, as the evaluation is conducted, to be responsive to what they are learning about the program. Their theories of evaluation emphasized the importance of observation and dialogue, qualitative methods to gain a greater understanding of the program, and flexibility in evaluation designs and measures, so that the evaluation could adapt and change as the evaluator learned more about the program. (See Green & Abma, 2001, for current views on responsive evaluation.)

These models influenced many of our contemporary evaluation theories. Theory-driven evaluation, developed by Huey Chen (1990), Len Bickman (1987), and others, drew from these original approaches but argued that evaluators should work with stakeholders and review existing research to develop models or theories to explain how the program actions should bring about the intended changes in program clients or participants. Program theories or logic models are used frequently today both to clearly delineate program approaches and intentions and to assist in identifying areas that the evaluation should address (Donaldson, 2007; Rogers, 2000). Although theory-driven evaluation involves engagement with stakeholders to develop program theory, unlike responsive evaluation, theory-driven evaluation is often paired with quantitative methods, primarily because its originators were quantitatively based.

Other models have evolved more directly from the early, participant-oriented approaches. These include participatory evaluation (Cousins & Whitmore, 1998) and empowerment evaluation (Fetterman, 2000). Participatory evaluation is a direct outgrowth of Stake's earlier work encouraging evaluators to "collaborate in some way with individuals, groups, or communities who have a decided stake in the program, development project, or other entity being evaluated" (Cousins & Whitmore, 1998, p. 5). Cousins and Whitmore (1998) identify two streams of participatory evaluation that serve different purposes: (1) practical participatory evaluation, which occurs as evaluators involve stakeholders to foster use of the results of the evaluation, and (2) transformative participatory evaluation, which involves stakeholders to "democratize social change" in order to empower groups or individuals (Cousins & Whitmore, 1998, p. 7). Empowerment evaluation, a type of participatory evaluation, moves on to "empower" stakeholders, particularly program staff and clients, to use the tools of evaluation and to actually become evaluators, making decisions and judgments, empowering themselves with evaluation information. Variants of these models include building evaluation capacity in organizations and mainstreaming evaluation. James Sanders (2003) has advocated for mainstreaming evaluation, which he defines as "the process of making evaluation an integral part of an organization's everyday operations" (p. 3). Many organizations today speak of themselves as "data-driven" organizations, reflecting some success in achieving this culture change.

Other contemporary models are derived from the early approaches of Stake (1967) and Guba and Lincoln (1981), but they are more concerned with values. These models are concerned with understanding the program in depth, being responsive to the context, and considering the values of different stakeholders and the impact of evaluation on those values. When the values are concerned with bringing about social change and democratization, these models might be considered as part of Cousins and Whitmore's (1998) transformative participatory stream. For example, House and Howe (1999) made evaluators aware of their potential to create and stimulate dialogue across groups that may not communicate and to stimulate democracy by permitting the voices of less powerful groups to be heard through evaluation.

Marvin Alkin and Christina Christie (2004) have developed an "evaluation theory tree" that is intended to illustrate the connections among evaluation theories. In essence, the tree provides a model, or mapping, of the relative relationship among major evaluation theories. Alkin and Christie's three major branches are methodology, values, and use. The branches are illuminated by a listing of individuals on each branch, and along different stems of the branches, based on their approaches to evaluation. Thus, the methodology branch is strongly influenced by Donald Campbell, a founder of experimental and quasi-experimental design in social psychology. The focus of many on this branch is on determining causal connections in programs using quantitative methods. The use branch is reflected in the participatory, empowerment, and mainstreaming activities described above. The goals of these evaluators are to maximize the use and impact of evaluation on organizations, decisions, groups, or individuals. Finally, the values branch reflects the original philosophical work of Stake (1967) and Guba and Lincoln (1981), now emerging in Greene and Abma (2001) and House (2001), in recognizing the diversity of values across different stakeholders and within a program and the political role of the evaluator in representing and depicting those diverse values.

Evaluation in Action: Choices

In spite of all the writing on evaluation theory, we have little idea of how evaluators actually practice. Many (Alkin & Christie, 2005; Henry & Mark, 2003) have called for research to examine more closely what evaluators actually do. Christie's (2003) original research surveyed practicing evaluators and theorists concerning their approaches to conducting evaluation using the three branches of methodology, values, and use. Her results showed that items reflecting the extent to which evaluators involved stakeholders and their preference for methods were the strongest factors in distinguishing the ways in which evaluation theorists practice evaluation. Practitioners' responses were

quite different from those of theorists. Only a little over a third of practitioners reported practicing in a way that was close to a theorist's model. In general, practitioners reported less stakeholder involvement than theorists and a
more quantitative methodological orientation. Christie's results are important
in that they are the first to systematically examine what theorists and practitioners actually do when they are conducting an evaluation. However, Christie's
study was based on respondents' self-reports concerning their practice.
Although self-reports are useful in learning what individuals believe is important in their practice, they may fail to reflect actual practice.

More recently, Alkin and Christie (2005) moved to a case approach,
asking four prominent evaluators, chosen to represent different theories, how
they would evaluate a particular case. This work provided more depth on these
individuals' approach to evaluation, but the case was still a hypothetical one.
The evaluators' responses to the case provide a means for comparing evaluators and, as such, give us a sense of the different ways they would approach
the same evaluation.

This book will continue using a case approach, but instead of asking each
evaluator to respond to the same case, we have interviewed each evaluator on
an actual evaluation he or she conducted. The interviewer first read the evaluation report and related articles.[8] The interview questions were then designed
to learn more about the choices the evaluator had to make in conducting this
evaluation and the underlying approaches he or she took to conduct the study.
As the theories above only begin to illustrate, evaluators face many different
choices in an evaluation: What is the purpose of the evaluation? How should
I define my role? What questions should the evaluation answer? How should
the evaluation be planned? Which stakeholders should be involved? How
should they be involved? Should the evaluation change as it moves along, and
if so, how? What should prompt a change in direction? What adaptations
should the evaluator make to the context of the program? To the needs of various stakeholders? What methods should be used? How should the evaluator
communicate results to the stakeholders? How often? Which results? To what
extent should the evaluator encourage use? Collaboration? Empowerment?
Logic models? Capacity building? What should the evaluator do when stakeholders disagree with the evaluation's methodology, approach, or results?
When ethical challenges arise, what choices does the evaluator face, and how
does he or she decide how to respond?

These interviews are designed to provide the reader with answers to these questions. The primary question, however, is "How do expert evaluators actually conduct an evaluation?" As such, the interviews reveal what Thomas Schwandt (2007) has referred to as "practical knowledge." Schwandt has argued that evaluators, and others in practice-oriented fields, "are often limited by an intellectualized theory-practice distinction, from which it is difficult to shake loose" (p. 29). Schwandt and others note that practical knowledge, the things one does in practice, is often difficult for practitioners, in fact, to articulate. It is this practical knowledge, what skilled evaluators actually *do*—which they may not be able to describe in the abstract or even be conscious of doing—that is of interest here. While we are not able to watch them in action, we can hear their stories. Just as qualitative interviews provide "thick descriptions" of programs or clients' experiences of these programs (Guba & Lincoln, 1989), these interviews provide a useful counterpoint to Christie's (2003) quantitative work in providing us with an in-depth description of what evaluators do in the context of one single evaluation. They illustrate the decision processes employed in a real practice setting by a range of skilled evaluators.

Fortunately, the people we interviewed were quite candid about the evaluations they conducted and the choices they faced, the problems they encountered, and, in their view, what worked and what did not. Through these interviews, readers can "get under the hood" and see what evaluators really do. We chose evaluators to represent different theories and approaches and, to a large extent, they do. So the reader will see an array of different practices. A related benefit is that the interviews provide reader-friendly examples of different approaches to evaluation.

With the case analyses, then, the reader learns more about how each evaluator acted in this particular case. The case may not be representative of his or her practice in general[9] but is useful in providing the reader with a sense for the particulars of how skilled evaluators make choices, and compromises, in an evaluation they view as important.

The 12 interviews are organized into four sections: (1) evaluations to judge merit and worth, (2) evaluations with a focus on description, (3) evaluations concerned with planning and organizational development, and (4) evaluations with cultural considerations. Interviews were organized by the key issues they demonstrated. However, each interview addresses many different issues in evaluation practice, and hence, the interviews could be organized and read in different ways.[10]

Notes

1. Determining *merit* concerns judging the quality of something, either overall or using specific criteria. *Worth* refers to the value of something in a particular context (Mathison, 2004).

2. The interview with Katrina Bledsoe illustrates a program for which stakeholders (managers, caseworkers, volunteers, and parents) have quite different views concerning its purposes and goals. Discussions during the evaluation permitted these differences to become apparent.

3. This book's primary focus is on program evaluation. However, policy analysis and program evaluation are related, and the authors will occasionally refer to references in the field of policy analysis to expand the reader's knowledge of this relationship. Evaluators and policy analysts, and others involved in applied research intended to inform stakeholders, can learn from each others' work and, as a result, enrich practice. At the risk of great oversimplification, policy analysts, as compared with evaluators, focus on policies more than programs; rely more heavily on quantitative methods as opposed to the mixed methods often used by evaluators; and have origins in the disciplines of political science and economics rather than psychology, sociology, and education, which have served as the foundational disciplines for evaluation.

4. As an example, see Len Bickman's evaluation of a systems approach to treating children's mental health. This system, which was an important theory being discussed by practitioners and researchers, had not previously been tested on a large scale in the field. His evaluations added to the field of knowledge concerning the systems approach. Similarly, the interview with Debra Rog concerns an evaluation that added to researchers' knowledge of homeless families. Because homeless families were new, there was relatively little research on the issue. Her evaluation showed that some of policy makers' assumptions concerning homeless families were incorrect.

5. See the interview with Jean King. This evaluation of a special education program had a primary concern with changing how stakeholders who are intimately involved in the evaluation view evaluation and use it in the future.

6. For example, amid some controversy in the evaluation community, the federal Office of Management and Budget with PART emphasizes randomized control trials (RCTs) to clearly establish that the program achieves its desired outcomes.

7. CIPP delineates four different types of evaluation: context, input, process, and product.

8. In this book, a brief summary of the evaluation is presented at the beginning of each chapter. Further readings at the end of the chapter list complete evaluation reports and articles on the evaluation. In a few cases, reports were not available for wider distribution.

9. In some cases, the evaluation is explicitly different from the evaluator's usual practice. See, for example, David Fetterman's case, where he does not use empowerment evaluation, the approach for which he is best known.

10. See the Appendix for a listing of the interviews under other categories.

REFERENCES

Alkin, M., & Christie, C. (2004). An evaluation theory tree. In M. Alkin (Ed.), *Evaluation roots: Tracing theorists' views and influences* (pp. 12–66). Thousand Oaks, CA: Sage.

Alkin, M., & Christie, C. (Eds.). (2005). *Theorists' models in action* (New Directions for Evaluation, No. 106). San Francisco: Jossey-Bass.

Bickman, L. (Ed.). (1987). *Using program theory in evaluation* (New Directions for Program Evaluation, No. 47). San Francisco: Jossey-Bass.

Chelimsky, E. (1991). On the social science contribution to governmental decision-making. *Science, 254,* 226–230.

Chen, H. T. (1990). *Theory-driven evaluation.* Thousand Oaks, CA: Sage.

Christie, C. C. (Ed.). (2003). *The practice-theory relationship in evaluation* (New Directions for Evaluation, No. 97). San Francisco: Jossey-Bass.

Cook, T. D. (1997). Lessons learned in evaluation over the past 25 years. In E. Chelimsky & W. R. Shadish (Eds.), *Evaluation for the 21st century: A handbook* (pp. 30–52). Thousand Oaks, CA: Sage.

Cousins, J. B., & Leithwood, K. A. (1986). Current empirical research on evaluation utilization. *Review of Educational Research, 56,* 331–364.

Cousins, J. B., & Whitmore, E. (1998). Framing participatory evaluation. In E. Whitmore (Ed.), *Understanding and practicing participatory evaluation* (New Directions for Evaluation, No. 80, pp. 5–23). San Francisco: Jossey-Bass.

Donaldson, S. I. (2007). *Program theory-driven evaluation science: Strategies and applications.* New York: Lawrence Erlbaum.

Fetterman, D. (2000). *Foundations of empowerment evaluation.* Thousand Oaks, CA: Sage.

Fitzpatrick, J. L., Sanders, J. R., & Worthen, B. R. (2004). *Program evaluation: Alternative approaches and practical guidelines* (3rd ed.). New York: Longman.

Greene, J. C., & Abma, T. A. (2001). *Responsive evaluation* (New Directions for Evaluation, No. 92). San Francisco: Jossey-Bass.

Guba, E. G., & Lincoln, Y. S. (1981). *Effective evaluation.* San Francisco: Jossey-Bass.

Guba, E. G., & Lincoln, Y. S. (1989). *Fourth generation evaluation.* San Francisco: Jossey-Bass.

Heineman, R. A., Bluhm, W. T., Peterson, S. A., & Kearny, E. N. (Eds.). (2002). *The world of the policy analyst: Rationality, values and politics.* New York: Chatham House.

Henry, G. T., & Mark, M. M. (2003). Toward an agenda for research on evaluation. In C. A. Christie (Ed.), *The practice-theory relationship in evaluation* (New Directions for Evaluation, No. 97, pp. 69–80). San Francisco, CA: Jossey-Bass.

Hird, J. A. (2005). Policy analysis for what? The effectiveness of nonpartisan policy research organizations. *Policy Studies Journal, 33*(1), 83–105.

House, E. R. (1980). *Evaluating with validity.* Beverly Hills, CA: Sage.

House, E. R. (2001). Unfinished business: Causes and values. *American Journal of Evaluation, 22,* 309–316.

House, E. R., & Howe, K. R. (1999). *Values in evaluation and social research.* Thousand Oaks, CA: Sage.

Kirkhart, K. E. (2000). Reconceptualizing evaluation use: An integrated theory of influence. In V. J. Caracelli & H. Preskill (Eds.), *The expanding scope of evaluation use* (New Directions for Evaluation, No. 88, pp. 5–23). San Francisco: Jossey-Bass.

Lerner, D., & Lasswell, H. (Eds.). (1951). *The policy sciences.* Palo Alto, CA: Stanford University Press.

Lindblom, C., & Cohen, D. K. (1979). *Usable knowledge: Social science and problem solving.* New Haven, CT: Yale University Press.

Mark, M. M., & Henry, G. T. (2004). The mechanisms and outcomes of evaluation influence. *Evaluation, 10,* 35–57.

Mark, M. M., Henry, G. T., & Julnes, G. (2000). *Evaluation: An integrated framework for understanding, guiding, and improving policies and programs.* San Francisco: Jossey-Bass.

Mark, M. M., & Mills, J. (2007). The use of experiments and quasi-experiments in decision making. In G. Morcöl (Ed.), *Handbook of decision making* (pp. 459–482). New York: Marcel Dekker.

Mathison, S. (Ed.) (2004). *Encyclopedia of evaluation.* Thousand Oaks, CA: Sage.

Owen, J. M. (2007). *Program evaluation: Forms and approaches.* New York: Guilford Press.

Patton, M. Q. (1986). *Utilization-focused evaluation* (2nd ed.). Beverly Hills, CA: Sage.

Patton, M. Q. (1997). *Utilization-focused evaluation* (3rd ed.). Thousand Oaks, CA: Sage.

Rogers, P. (Ed.) (2000). *Program theory in evaluation: Challenges and opportunities* (New Directions for Evaluation, No. 87). San Francisco: Jossey-Bass.

Rossi, P. H., Lipsey, M. W., & Freeman, H. E. (2004). *Evaluation: A systematic approach* (7th ed.). Thousand Oaks, CA: Sage.

Sanders, J. W. (2003). Mainstreaming evaluation. In J. J. Barnette & J. R. Sanders (Eds.), *The mainstreaming of evaluation* (New Directions for Evaluation, No. 99, pp. 3–6). San Francisco: Jossey-Bass.

Schwandt, T. A. (2007). The relevance of practical knowledge traditions to evaluation practice. In N. L. Smith & P. R. Brandon (Eds.), *Fundamental issues in evaluation* (pp. 30–41). New York: Guilford Press.

Scriven, M. (1967). The methodology of evaluation. In R. E. Stake (Ed.), *Curriculum evaluation* (American Educational Research Association Monograph Series on Evaluation, No. 1, pp. 39–83). Chicago: Rand McNally.

Scriven, M. (1991). *Evaluation thesaurus* (4th ed.). Newbury Park, CA: Sage.

Shadish, W. R., Cook, T. D., & Leviton, L. C. (1991). *Foundations of program evaluation: Theories of practice.* Newbury Park, CA: Sage.

Stake, R. E. (1967). The countenance of educational evaluation. *Teachers College Record, 68,* 523–540.

Stone, D. (1997). *The policy paradox.* New York: W.W. Norton.

Stufflebeam, D. L. (1971). The relevance of the CIPP evaluation model for educational accountability. *Journal of Research and Development in Education, 5,* 19–25.

Stufflebeam, D. L. (1973). An introduction to the PDK book: Educational evaluation and decision-making. In B. R. Worthen & J. R. Sanders (Eds.), *Educational evaluation: Theory and practice* (pp. 128–142). Belmont, CA: Wadsworth.

Stufflebeam, D. L. (2001). *Evaluation models* (New Directions for Evaluation, No. 89). San Francisco: Jossey-Bass

Stufflebeam, D. L., Madaus, G. F., & Kellaghan, T. (2000). *Evaluation models.* Boston: Kluwer.

Weimer, D., & Vining, A. (1999). *Policy analysis: Concepts and practice.* Upper Saddle River, NJ: Prentice Hall.

PART I

TRADITIONAL EVALUATIONS

Evaluations With the Primary Purpose of Judging Merit and Worth

This first section begins with three interviews concerning evaluations designed primarily to determine the merit or worth of a program. As such, we have defined them as "traditional evaluations" because they serve the traditional purpose of evaluation. A few other interviews in this book also address the merit and worth of the program they evaluate, but these three interviewers were the most clear in articulating this purpose for their evaluation. One can judge the merit or worth of a program in many different ways, using a variety of methodological tools, but in each of these three interviews, the evaluation is undertaken and the results are intended to be used to judge the quality of the program at hand.

Evaluations to determine merit and worth often examine whether the program is successful in achieving its goals or objectives. Thus, there tends to be a focus on outcomes. Each of these evaluations measure outcomes, but they make different choices concerning which outcomes to measure and how to do so. You will also see that determinations of merit and worth need not be based entirely on stated goals or outcomes. Most evaluators would consider it bad practice to study program outcomes without some sense of what is being delivered. Such studies are contemptuously called "black box" studies—outcomes are described without any sense of what went on in the "box." These evaluators examine the process of the program to learn how natural variations occur in program implementation, to gain a greater understanding of the program, or to learn whether the program model was actually implemented as planned.

The first interview with James Riccio concerns an evaluation of the Greater Avenues for Independence (GAIN) welfare-to-work program, implemented before welfare reform became a national initiative. Riccio's evaluation is commissioned by the California state legislature as a compromise in the midst of political turmoil over the directions such a program should take. He spends several years examining the implementation and outcomes achieved by the program in six California counties, using a randomized design and extensive data collection to describe program implementation and variation across counties. Riccio's results ultimately are used by the state legislature to encourage other counties to implement the variation that Riccio found to be most successful.

In the second interview, Jennifer Greene describes an evaluation on a much smaller scale with a different methodological focus. Greene's evaluation of a leadership program for environmental managers and policy makers in five states in the Southeast makes use of an intensive case study design, observations, interviews, surveys, and an in-depth study of selected participants' use of the skills they had gained in the field. She and her colleagues on her evaluation team share expertise to gain an in-depth understanding of the program and the values and concerns of the people involved in the program. She makes use of a continuing cycle of analysis, reflection on what they have learned, and responsiveness, or adaptation, to the program and the values of stakeholders.

The final interview with Len Bickman concerns his evaluation of the Ft. Bragg and Stark County systems of mental health care for children and adolescents. Like Riccio, Bickman makes use of a randomized design to study outcomes. But unlike Riccio, the program he is evaluating is not new; it is one that has matured and is ready to be tested for its effects. As a result, Bickman's role and audiences for the study are different from those of Riccio. His description of program activities is more concerned with whether those activities are faithful to the model. Bickman wants to know if the outcomes he examines are, in fact, a result of the systems of care model. The audiences for his study are not state legislators but people who make policy and fund programs nationally in the area of children's mental health.

These cases are placed together because they each consider the merit and worth of the program they evaluate, but they differ in many important ways—in the methods used, the stakeholders involved, the evaluator's interactions with those stakeholders, and the ways in which results are disseminated and used. The interviews address these and many other issues in addition to the determination of merit and worth. As you read them, consider how these evaluators are alike and how they differ in both methodological and other ways.

In reading these cases consider the following:

- What is the purpose of each evaluation? To what extent is the purpose concerned with judging merit and worth?

- How do the evaluators decide to determine merit and worth? What factors are most critical to each in judging the success of the program? Why are these factors important to them? To their stakeholders?

- Who are the key stakeholders for each evaluator? How do they differ in the ways in which they work with their stakeholders?

- How do they disseminate their results? Do they differ in how their results are used? Do you think those differences are related to their dissemination strategies or to other factors?

TWO

THE EVALUATION OF GAIN: A WELFARE-TO-WORK PROGRAM IN CALIFORNIA

An Interview With James A. Riccio

Introduction: At the time of this interview, James Riccio was a senior researcher at MDRC.[1] He now heads the organization's Low-Wage Workers and Communities policy area. Since the GAIN evaluation, Dr. Riccio has conducted research on a variety of other employment and poverty-reduction initiatives for low-income populations. He recently directed a nine-year, six-site evaluation of a comprehensive employment initiative in public housing (Jobs-Plus). Riccio is currently directing several large-scale randomized control trials, including tests of a conditional cash transfer (CCT) program that is part of Mayor Michael Bloomberg's antipoverty strategy for New York City and an employment retention and advancement initiative for welfare recipients and low-wage workers in Britain (UK ERA). He is also a principal advisor on a major MDRC study of community change in Chicago sponsored by the MacArthur Foundation. In 1996, Dr. Riccio conducted research on welfare reform in Britain as a recipient of the Atlantic Fellowship in Public Policy.

This interview was the first conducted for the "Exemplars" series published in the *American Journal of Evaluation.* James Riccio had won the American

Evaluation Association award for the best evaluation in 1997, and as Associate Editor of the *American Journal of Evaluation*, Jody Fitzpatrick proposed conducting an interview with him so that readers could learn more from Dr. Riccio about how he conducted the evaluation. In this interview, he discusses this multiyear evaluation, which was the first rigorous study of elements of welfare reform. He describes how he worked with the California legislature, which had commissioned the study, to help them make decisions on the contentious issue of welfare reform and with numerous other stakeholders, including state and county departments of social service, case workers, welfare recipients and welfare rights groups, and interested citizens. His evaluation was comprehensive: describing varying types of program implementation in different counties, using an experimental randomized design to examine the effects of GAIN on work and income over a five-year period, and studying the economic costs and benefits of the program. Through their work in describing variations across counties in implementation and focus, the evaluation was able to link specific strategies to successful outcomes. The results have been used by other counties and the state to implement new welfare reform initiatives.

Summary of the GAIN Evaluation

James A. Riccio

MDRC

GAIN was created in 1985 by the California legislature as California's main welfare-to-work program for recipients of Aid to Families With Dependent Children (AFDC). The program was designed to provide welfare recipients with job search assistance, basic education, vocational training, postsecondary education, and unpaid work experience to help them prepare for and find employment. Welfare recipients assigned to the program were required to participate in these activities. Those refusing to cooperate without "good cause" could have their welfare payments reduced as a penalty. Child care and transportation subsidies were available for those who needed them to participate. The primary goals of the program were to increase recipients' employment and earnings, reduce their use of welfare, and reduce government expenses for these individuals. State guidelines were developed for the county-based implementation, but counties had some flexibility in implementing the program.

MDRC won a contract to conduct the evaluation, which had four main goals: (1) to learn about the counties' experiences in turning this ambitious legislation into an operating program and welfare recipients' participation and experiences in it; (2) to determine GAIN's effects, or impacts, on recipients' employment, earnings, welfare, and other outcomes and whether positive effects could be achieved in a variety of settings; (3) to assess how different program strategies influence those results; and (4) to determine the program's economic costs and benefits. Implementation issues were studied in 13 counties, and the full evaluation was concentrated in a subset of 6 of these counties, representing diverse areas of the state.

The evaluation made use of an array of quantitative and qualitative data, including employment and welfare administrative records, program case file data, staff and recipient surveys, field research, and fiscal data from a wide variety of agencies. The impact analysis was set up as a large-scale field experiment, through which over 33,000 welfare recipients were randomly assigned to GAIN or a control group. The control group did not have access to GAIN services and was not subject to a participation mandate as a condition of receiving their full welfare grants. However, they remained free to enroll themselves on their own in any services normally available in the community. Program impacts were analyzed using data from existing administrative records on employment, earnings, welfare receipt, and food stamp payments (for all sample members) and the recipient survey (for a subsample). Finally, a cost-benefit analysis was used to estimate the overall financial gain or loss caused by the program for welfare recipients, government budgets and taxpayers, and society as a whole.

The study focused primarily on single-parent AFDC recipients, who head most welfare cases in California and the nation. It found that the program did increase recipients' employment and earnings and did reduce their reliance on welfare. These effects grew over time and were continuing even at the end of the five-year follow-up period. These enduring effects contrast with the findings on welfare-to-work programs of the 1980s, which were mostly low-cost, short-term job search programs. Evaluation results for those programs showed that the differences between the program and control groups tended to fade before the fifth year—largely because the control group eventually "caught up" with the program group (Friedlander & Burtless, 1995).

A county-by-county analysis in the GAIN study showed that each county achieved some impacts on either earnings or welfare payments for at least some groups. However, one county (Riverside) stood out because of the breadth, magnitude, and consistency of its effects, combined with its lower average costs. Over five years of follow-up, the program group in Riverside earned, on average, $5,038 more than the control group. This represents an increase in earnings of 42% over the control group average. AFDC payments were $2,705 lower, on average, for the program group, which is a drop of 15% from the control group mean. (Across all six counties, earnings in the program group increased by an average of 23% over the control group mean, and welfare payments dropped by an average of 7%.) Riverside was unusual in that it consistently achieved employment and earnings gains and welfare payment reductions for many different types of recipients, including those with substantial employment barriers. Moreover, it was cost-effective from the perspective of government budgets: For every dollar invested in the program, an estimated $2.84 was returned to government budgets. It is important to note, however, that even in this best-performing program, job turnover remained high, overall family income was only somewhat improved, and 31% of recipients were on welfare at the end of five years. In short, the results suggest that the program was well worth investing in but was limited in what it could accomplish by itself.

MDRC's implementation studies showed that Riverside's program emphasized a strong and pervasive employment-focused message that encouraged program participants to move quickly into the labor market. Although it also placed many participants in basic education activities, it typically encouraged school dropouts and graduates alike to search for work first. It enrolled them in job clubs that taught them how to look for work, prepare resumes, and conduct themselves in job interviews. In addition, through the active use of job developers, it helped many participants identify job openings in the community. It did not routinely direct recipients into vocational training programs or postsecondary education. The program also demonstrated a strong commitment to (and had adequate resources for) securing the participation of all recipients who were required to be in GAIN and relied on the program's penalty process to reinforce the seriousness with which it viewed recipients' participation obligation. This constellation of practices was not found in any other county and may have contributed to Riverside's broad success. This success has motivated other counties and states across the country to adapt their strategies to a more rapid-employment approach.

One example of such an adaptation comes from Los Angeles County. In the original GAIN evaluation, this county had stressed an education-first approach and showed little evidence of success. The county subsequently switched to a quick-employment approach, renamed its program Jobs-First GAIN, and submitted itself to a new random assignment test. That second evaluation found much better results. For example, during the two-year follow-up period for that study, Jobs-First GAIN increased the program group's employment rate by 10 percentage points and increased earnings by $1,627, or 26%, relative to the control group levels (Freedman, Tansey Knab, Gennetian, & Navarro, 2000).

The main GAIN evaluation, along with other studies, helped set the stage across the country for further testing of alternative ways of helping welfare recipients succeed in the labor market. The largest such initiative was the National Evaluation of Welfare-to-Work Strategies (NEWWS), which included additional tests of 11 mandatory job-search-first or education-first programs in seven states. It also included several multigroup randomized trials that directly compared these two different strategies. In general, that evaluation found that the education-first strategies, which focused largely on basic education and were considerably more costly, did not produce better labor market outcomes than the rapid employment approach. It also found that programs that adopted "mixed approaches" that included both job search and educational opportunities seemed to work best (Hamilton, 2002).

Also noteworthy is an unusual effort to get further inside the "black box" of such programs to understand what factors drive success. In a secondary analysis of 59 local program offices and over 69,000 people involved in either the GAIN or NEWWS evaluations or a similar evaluation in Florida (of Project Independence), MDRC researchers combined experimental and non-experimental methods to assess how certain features of welfare-to-work programs, implementation and management practices, types of clients, and local economic conditions influenced program effectiveness. Controlling simultaneously for office-level factors and individual-level client characteristics using a hierarchical linear model, the study showed that the degree of emphasis on quick employment had the largest independent effect on an office's earnings impacts. It also found that, other things being equal, more emphasis on personalized attention increased short-term program success, while high client caseloads, a strong emphasis on mandatory basic education instruction, and high local unemployment rates reduced it (Bloom, Hill, & Riccio, 2003).

Other welfare-to-work strategies evaluated in yet other post-GAIN studies included financial incentives or wage supplements to help make work "pay" better than welfare. These programs were found to increase family income more than mandatory service programs that did not offer such incentives.

Dialogue With James A. Riccio

Jody Fitzpatrick

Fitzpatrick: Jim, tell me how you first became involved in this study.

Riccio: I was involved from the beginning, back in 1986, when MDRC staff first began meeting with California officials to decide on the nature and scope of the study. I took the lead on the implementation and benefit-cost analyses and on the attempts to integrate these with the impact analysis. Dan Friedlander was the main impact analyst and Steve Freedman managed the connections between the collection of administrative and survey data and the impact and benefit-cost analyses. The project was a huge undertaking and involved many people at MDRC who brought expertise in diverse areas—quantitative and qualitative social science and evaluation research, public policy analysis, program management, computer programming, and management information systems. Even MDRC's most senior management staff, including Judy Gueron, its president; Barbara Goldman, its research director; and John Wallace, the manager of its San Francisco office, played key roles from the earliest planning and design work right through to the intensive, line-by-line review of the final report. It was a team effort in every sense.

Fitzpatrick: Your study won the American Evaluation Association award for the best evaluation in 1996, so obviously, it is outstanding in many ways. But all evaluations have their strengths and weaknesses. What do you see as the greatest strengths of your evaluation?

Riccio: I think we were able to go further than any preceding welfare-to-work study in integrating implementation and impact research and in trying to "get inside the black box" to learn how different program strategies might influence program impacts. Because this was a multisite study designed to provide us with reliable, site-specific impact estimates from a variety of GAIN offices, and because program philosophies and practices varied across those offices, we were able to test some different assumptions—theories, really—about what approaches worked best through systematic site comparisons. These were not perfect tests, by any means, and site comparisons are always tricky because so many factors other than program practices vary across settings and might contribute to differences in impacts. Nonetheless, we could show whether the observed patterns of variation in practices and impacts tended to support or challenge some of the prevailing assumptions about what works best in welfare-to-work programs. I think we've made a useful contribution to a larger, still emerging body of knowledge on this important topic.

Fitzpatrick: Let's begin now with reviewing the process of the study. What was the impetus for the evaluation? Many large, costly programs are implemented without much investigation of their success. Why was your study initiated? Who pushed for it, and what questions did they want answered?

Riccio: The legislative debate leading up to the passage of the GAIN legislation helped to sow the seeds for an evaluation. The legislation that was finally enacted reflected a political compromise between groups with competing visions of welfare reform. Liberal and conservative legislators were advocating reform bills that pushed in different directions. At the risk of over-simplifying, liberals advocated a voluntary program with a heavy emphasis on human capital development that was to be achieved through substantial new opportunities for education and training. Conservatives wanted a tough, mandatory program that would stress job search and workfare activities. The compromise was to mix these different elements into a single program. The model that emerged gave a priority to up-front basic education for those who lacked basic reading and math skills or English language proficiency. But job search activities would come before other education and training activities. The program would be mandatory, but a multistep penalty process would be included to insure that recipients' rights were being protected and opportunities for another chance to comply with the rules would be given before anyone's welfare check would be reduced. Workfare was also included, but later in the sequence of activities, and it took a variety of forms. All in all, it was a quite complex model. But was it feasible? Would it work? How much would it cost? Would it be worth the price?

A few important legislative staff pushed for this new program to be evaluated so that these questions could be answered. In fact, they argued—successfully—that the GAIN legislation itself should require that the new program be subjected to a rigorous independent evaluation. They did this because they cared about making good public policy. They, and some key lawmakers, apparently came to appreciate that reliable evaluation research could be a valuable tool in this process. During the legislative debate, they had used findings from earlier MDRC evaluations of welfare-to-work programs in formulating their views and in trying to shape the debate. They wanted to insure that, in the future, the legislature would be in a position to decide whether GAIN was worth continuing, or how it could be strengthened, on the basis of facts and not have to rely just on ideology and anecdotes.

Fitzpatrick: Whom did you see as the primary audiences for your study? And how were they involved in the planning stage?

Riccio: The California legislature and governor, who authorized the study, were obviously key, but they were not the only audience. Our contract was handled through the California Department of Social Services. We hammered out the specifics of the study with staff in that department, but only after consultation with many other groups that had an important connection to the GAIN program. Those stakeholders included legislative staff, representatives of welfare rights organizations and children's advocacy groups, representatives of schools and other agencies that were to provide services to GAIN participants, and officials from the counties involved in the study. MDRC and CDSS consulted with these groups to learn how they viewed the goals and challenges of the GAIN legislation, what they hoped to learn from the evaluation, and how the study could be most useful for them. They were all stakeholders in the GAIN program, and we wanted them to become stakeholders in the evaluation as well.

Fitzpatrick: How did you involve these stakeholders as the study continued? Did the legislators remain interested in the evaluation?

Riccio: Welfare reform remained high on the state and national political agenda throughout the period of the evaluation and, without a doubt, this helped sustain interest in this study. At the same time, MDRC staff expended tremendous energy keeping the various stakeholders in GAIN involved in the study as it unfolded. We routinely briefed each of the stakeholder groups and invited their feedback on the evaluation work plan, research design issues, questionnaire design, and, eventually, on the findings and draft reports, right through to the end of the study. We did all of this in person so they would have a direct, personal connection to the evaluation and the evaluators.

Fitzpatrick: What changes occurred as a result of these interactions?

Riccio: The interaction helped ensure that the questions we addressed were of interest to a broad range of stakeholders and built a broad base of support for and understanding of the evaluation. It also helped guard against hidden biases or politically charged statements creeping into our reports. I have no doubt that we produced better and more influential reports because of these extensive communications.

It was also worth the effort because it increased the use of the study in the policy-making process even before the final results were in. One story illustrates just how seriously state officials were taking this study. Part of the way through the evaluation, the California economy went into a recession and severe cuts were being made in the state budget. Understandably, there were also calls to cut GAIN program funds dramatically and to make major changes in the program model. However, early impact findings had recently been made available and showed promising effects. Some legislators used these early results to argue successfully that big changes in the program should be put off until the final evaluation results were in. Others agreed, and the program survived largely intact.

Fitzpatrick: Which audience had the most influence on the questions you chose to address?

Riccio: State legislative staff and California Department of Social Services staff set the priorities. However, everyone agreed pretty much on the basic questions: Did the program increase recipients' earnings? Did it reduce their use of welfare? Was it cost beneficial and for whom? How well was the program implemented, and did local conditions and practices influence the program's success?

Local implementation turned out to be very important. Although it was expected that the counties' programs would vary somewhat, no one quite anticipated the ways in which they would vary. Perhaps most striking was how the counties could all operate the same basic program model yet provide such different messages to recipients about work and welfare. Thus, recipients in different counties had different program experiences. This kind of variation became an important focus of the implementation study and, as we later discovered, had important implications for understanding the cross-county variation in impacts.

Fitzpatrick: Did these questions remain your primary focus throughout the evaluation?

Riccio: Yes, however, this was a long-term study, and we had to remain flexible. We modified our work plan several times to ensure that the information we produced would be as relevant and as timely as possible for the legislature and state staff. A number of times, we had to change some of the research questions we would address, the data we would collect, the selection of reports we would produce, and when these reports would be completed.

We didn't anticipate at the beginning just how important it would be to tie our report schedule to the annual legislative budget cycle. Almost every year, the state staff would come back to us and ask, "What information can you give us to share with our legislators?" Every year, GAIN funding, like funding for all state programs, was on the table, and of course, it was much more vulnerable when the state budget was being cut. There was a hunger for any useful information we could provide to help legislators understand the progress of the program even before the final results were in. We had to be responsive to state officials' very real need for information quickly while at the same time protecting the integrity of the evaluation and not releasing findings before we were absolutely certain they were right.

Fitzpatrick: Why did you select the particular six counties you studied?

Riccio: We wanted the counties to reflect the diversity of California—in terms of the size and demographic characteristics of the local population, the characteristics of the labor market, and other local conditions. This diversity would help us with external validity and in determining whether GAIN could be effective in a wide variety of settings.

Fitzpatrick: Did any counties refuse to participate in the study?

Riccio: Some did, particularly because of concerns over random assignment. We devoted considerable effort during the site selection process to trying to convince counties that random assignment was both feasible and ethical and an extremely valuable tool for determining the effectiveness of their programs. However, many county staff were rather confident that their GAIN program would work, and they were uncomfortable denying recipients services just for research purposes. Some were also concerned about the potential distractions of implementing random assignment procedures and complying with other research demands.

Fitzpatrick: How did you persuade some counties to participate?

Riccio: GAIN was not an entitlement, in contrast to AFDC. It was not funded at a level that guaranteed a slot for everyone it was designed to serve. Consequently, the counties had to deny many welfare recipients access to the program anyway. They could only enroll a portion of the eligible caseload. It was, therefore, reasonable to argue that random assignment—akin to flipping a coin—was as fair a way as any, if not more fair, for choosing who would get into this limited-slot program.

We also stressed that the program was unproved. No one really knew what the effects of the participation mandate would be or whether the enriched services and opportunities would actually help recipients get and keep jobs.

The program would be costly, and it promised to change significantly the terms and conditions for poor people to receive a full welfare check—for better or worse. High hopes were being pinned on it. It deserved to be carefully tested. Some counties cared about the answer and wanted to be part of the evaluation. Some did refuse. In the end, however, more than enough counties agreed to be in the study, and I believe the six that were finally included learned a lot from the experience and were glad to have been part of it.

Fitzpatrick: Your study included a descriptive component to examine implementation. The implementation results were eventually quite important in interpreting program impact. How did you collect data on the counties' style of implementation?

Riccio: We used a variety of methods, both quantitative and qualitative. We sent field researchers to the counties to observe GAIN orientation sessions, job search workshops, staff-recipient meetings, and other aspects of day-to-day program operations firsthand. These researchers also conducted in-depth interviews with staff at the welfare department and GAIN program offices and with staff at various schools and agencies that provided services to GAIN participants. We tried to learn from these qualitative efforts how these different players in the system were interpreting and operationalizing their functions. We also administered a formal survey to GAIN case managers to collect more standardized, quantifiable information on program practices and staff-resident interactions. We had to proceed on both of these tracks at the same time. We didn't have the luxury of doing field research first and surveys next. However, the results of the two different methods did produce consistent findings.

In addition to describing the styles of implementation, we examined participants' experiences in the program. For example, we collected quantitative data on their patterns of participation in GAIN activities. Teams of MDRC researchers went through folders that caseworkers kept on recipients to determine who participated in which GAIN activities, when, for how long, and whether they were excused from participating or penalized for noncompliance. Also, the recipient survey included a number of questions concerning recipients' views of the program. Together, all of the different sources of data provided us with a rich picture of GAIN in each of the counties.

Fitzpatrick: Tell us a little bit more about how the qualitative and quantitative methods used in the implementation study informed your understanding of the program and its results.

Riccio: The staff surveys gave us an opportunity to compare counties more rigorously and systematically than we could have with field research data alone. We could explicitly compare counties on a variety of dimensions of program practices and examine how these rankings correlated with recipients' participation patterns and program impacts. And we could do this not only across the six counties but also across the more than 20 different GAIN offices that were set up in these counties. The field research complemented the survey data in important ways, though. It helped us understand better what we thought we were measuring with the staff survey and allowed us to illustrate some of the important differences in staff practices across the counties that gave rise to the quantitative rankings that were based on the staff survey data.

Fitzpatrick: You described some of the differences you found in Riverside County in the summary. Tell us a little bit more about how it differed from other counties.

Riccio: Recipients in Riverside County received a very different message from staff about work than did recipients in other counties. In other counties, if you failed the math and reading test administered at the start of the program, you were typically directed straight into basic education activities, even though the program officially gave you the option of trying job search first. In Riverside, staff might say to these same people, "Why don't you try looking for a job first? If that doesn't work, we can then talk about education." The goal was to move people quickly into the labor market, and people were encouraged not to be fussy about the kinds of jobs they took. The motto was, "Any job is a good job and a potential stepping stone to a better job." This is not to say that Riverside was just a job search program; it wasn't. Lots of people there got basic education, and some—though not many—participated in training activities. But clearly the emphasis was on "quick employment."

As part of this strategy, Riverside hired special job developers to help recipients locate job openings in the community. It also established job placement standards for case managers to make them feel directly accountable for getting recipients employed, but to avoid "creaming," Riverside required that case managers work with everybody on their caseload, not just the most job-ready. Like all of the counties, Riverside provided substantial amounts of case management and closely monitored recipients' participation. However, other counties offered residents much more personalized attention and were slower to invoke GAIN's formal sanctioning process when confronting noncompliance. Although the Riverside program was more expensive to operate than the simpler, primarily job search programs of the early 1980s, it turned out to be much cheaper than the other counties' GAIN programs, according to our cost analysis, so it could serve many more recipients for a given amount of money.

Fitzpatrick: A recent article in the *Wall Street Journal* (January 30, 1997) argues that evaluation research of welfare is so politicized that no results are credible. Do you think that is true?

Riccio: That's a gross overstatement. Some studies may be politically biased in the sense that they selectively report findings that support a political agenda and suppress findings that don't. It's not accurate or fair to put all welfare evaluations in that category. In MDRC's case, a few factors help us guard against our studies becoming politicized. First of all, when we're able to use a random assignment research design, as in the GAIN study, it's hard to dismiss the evidence as simply "political." Almost anyone can look at the basic results of the study and see whether the program group did better in terms of employment and other outcomes than the control group. It's difficult to run from that kind of evidence, and you don't need to be a statistician to understand it. Moreover, the impact data are made available to other researchers on public use files, so they can check to see if they get the same results.

That does not mean that all results can speak for themselves. Interpretation is always necessary, and that raises the possibility that political biases will creep in. Therefore, MDRC has a policy of subjecting our draft reports to excruciatingly detailed internal and external reviews by people of different political persuasions. This is a good way to help authors keep any political biases they may have in check. Furthermore, all of the incentives for us as an organization are to remain as objective as possible. Our reputation is at stake. We're not a political advocacy group, and we would only weaken the organization if our studies were to become politicized.

Fitzpatrick: Do you think you were credible to the stakeholders you served?

Riccio: We've been fortunate in that our results have been trusted by people on both sides of the political aisle and who represent the many different stakeholders in the GAIN program. We tried to stay very close to the data we collected and back up our conclusions with evidence. Not all the stakeholders liked the news we brought. For example, not all counties were successful, or as successful as they had hoped to be. We told the bad news as well as the good news. Also, using randomly assigned control groups helped us enormously in establishing our credibility. In particular, control groups make it difficult for anyone to exaggerate the effects that the counties' programs can rightly take credit for. Over time, the control groups' earnings grew and their welfare payments fell. A county can claim credit only for the margin by which its experimental group's outcomes exceeded those of its control group.

I think another part of the reason why our research is trusted is that we tried to be clear on what we knew with a lot of certainty and what we knew with less certainty. A good example can be seen in the way we handled the county comparison and attempted to identify the factors causing the differences in the counties' effectiveness. Because we conducted random assignment within each county, we could speak with greater certainty about the effectiveness of each county's own GAIN program than about why program effects varied across counties. We offered an explanation of the county variation and some evidence to support it but also acknowledged that the evidence was not definitive. (See Riccio & Orenstein, 1996, for further discussion of these issues.) Being honest about the level of certainty that different findings and observations enjoy is critical if evaluators want to maintain their credibility.

Fitzpatrick: What aspect of the results did you find most useful? What did you find most surprising?

Riccio: The county variation spoke explicitly to a debate in the field of welfare reform and has influenced that debate: How much should programs invest in education and training activities to increase welfare recipients' human capital? And how valuable is a big, up-front emphasis on basic education? Many of us were surprised. Like many people following the welfare reform debates, we didn't think the Riverside approach, which gave less emphasis to education and training, would be the one that performed better. But that's what we found, and it changed opinions. None of our results demonstrate that basic education or other education and training can't work in some circumstances or for some people. Even Riverside placed some recipients into basic education. And evidence from other counties suggests that vocational training might have helped some recipients with high school diplomas or GED certificates get better jobs. However, the findings clearly cast doubt on the value of pushing recipients en masse into education as their first activity and assuming that for most recipients education and training must precede any efforts to find work.

Fitzpatrick: How did you disseminate the results of your study?

Riccio: First, key state and county welfare administrators and legislative staff reviewed draft copies of our reports. Their input helped increase the accuracy and fairness of reports, and in that process, they became intimately familiar with the findings. To get the word out more broadly, we adopted a two-pronged strategy—one for California and one for the rest of the country. Within California, we briefed state and local government officials and representatives from important state-level agencies, welfare rights and children's advocacy groups, and other stakeholders on the results of each report soon after it was completed. We also mailed copies of all reports to the welfare departments in each of the state's 58 counties, as well as to the key government and non-government agencies. Similarly, to reach a national audience, we mailed copies of the report to welfare departments and independent welfare professionals and scholars around the country whose names were on our extensive mailing list. We also arranged a series of briefings in Washington, D.C. on the major findings, including briefings for White House staff, Senate and House of Representatives staff, and the staff of major national organizations—liberal and conservative—who work on issues relating to welfare reform. In addition, we issued press releases to the national as well as California press to announce the findings of the major reports and spent hours working with reporters who wanted further details as they prepared their stories. Finally, many of us have presented the evaluation findings at numerous research and policy conferences.

Fitzpatrick: How have your results been used?

Riccio: In several ways. Within California, state policy makers took inspiration from Riverside's success and revised the GAIN regulations so that the program throughout the state would emphasize more rapid employment and focus less on up-front basic education while still including education and training as part of the program model. Even before that, however, Los Angeles County took steps on its own to revamp its program. Disturbed that their "education-first" approach had no statistically significant impacts on recipients' earnings, and, like others, impressed with the Riverside results, they overhauled their GAIN program to incorporate elements of the Riverside approach. They now operate a very different type of GAIN program and have witnessed a dramatic improvement in their job placement rates. However, they recognize that placement rates can be a misleading indicator of a program's ultimate success and, therefore, chose to fund a new random assignment study to determine the effectiveness of their new approach. This study, which MDRC was selected to conduct, is very important because it provides a chance to learn whether a Riverside-style approach can work in a big city, where many welfare recipients live in high-poverty, inner-city neighborhoods—a very different environment than is found in the more suburban Riverside County and more like the conditions in which much of the nation's welfare population lives.

We also learned that officials in many other states were familiar with the findings from the GAIN study—thanks, in part, to our intensive dissemination efforts—and many were influenced by those results to shift their program practices, more in the direction of rapid employment—although, again, not to the exclusion of education and training. So the study has been influential across the country. I think this, along with the Los Angeles experience, is fascinating testimony to the power of evaluation to influence public policy as it is practiced on the ground. In other words, evaluation findings can be influential and consequential even if they don't find their way explicitly into new laws and regulations.

At the same time, the evaluation did not have much direct influence on the development of the new federal welfare legislation enacted in 1996. Had programs like GAIN produced truly dramatic impacts on employment and the welfare rolls, rather than the more modest though positive effects it had, perhaps the welfare reform movement might not have gathered such strong support for enacting time limits on welfare receipt. The five-year limits in the federal legislation did not grow out of a solid base of knowledge from which we can predict their impacts on employment.

Fitzpatrick: How did you try to convey the policy importance of effects that may be statistically significant but small or modest in magnitude?

Riccio: Modest success is not the same as failure—unless the explicit goal of a program is to achieve dramatic change. Ultimately, of course, it's policy makers who must decide whether a program's effects are big enough to matter from a policy perspective. However, in presenting the results from any study, evaluators can and should set the proper context. When the Riverside results came out, some people thought they were big and others thought they were small. In some respects, the results clearly were disappointing: Many of the people whom the program helped to find jobs did not work continuously, which limited the program's overall earnings effects, sizable as they were, and many recipients were on welfare at the end of the follow-up period. At the same time, Riverside's overall effects happened to be the most impressive impacts of any large-scale welfare-to-work program that had been subjected to a careful, controlled experiment. And the program was cost-effective for the government. Clearly, the program accomplished a lot compared to past efforts, and we tried to make sure this was understood when we discussed our findings. Still, even this best-performing program was no miracle cure, and we were explicit about that as well. But no one has yet discovered any miracle cures in the welfare-to-work field. That's not to say that we should be content with modest victories. We should continue searching for more powerful approaches and putting them to a careful test. Careful evaluations can help keep us all honest about what we can accomplish and about how much further we have to go in solving tough social problems.

Fitzpatrick: Let me close with asking you what you learned about evaluation from overseeing this evaluation. If you had to do this study again, what would you do differently?

Riccio: I think managing the budget for a long-term impact evaluation is a tremendous challenge. As I mentioned, in this kind of project there's a constant—and quite reasonable—pressure to report on the initiative's progress early on. It's also inherently difficult to predict with real precision—and, therefore, to budget accurately for—all the up-front work that has to get done in order to get this kind of a study off the ground. For example, it's difficult to anticipate the amount of time and energy that must be spent explaining and building local support for random assignment, adapting random assignment procedures to the particular circumstances of many different welfare offices, training welfare department staff on those procedures and on other parts of the research, and so on. Lots of guesswork is involved, even for a highly experienced research organization. The challenge is how not to spend so much of your evaluation budget up-front and on intermediate reports that you end up being squeezed at the end and perhaps unable to analyze all the data you collect as fully as you'd like. At the same time, failing to lay the proper groundwork up-front or to accommodate the very real political pressure to share what you're learning quickly and throughout the project could seriously undermine, if not doom, an evaluation. I think we managed this tension reasonably well in GAIN, but I wish we could have found a way to conserve even more resources than we did for the final stages of the project.

Fitzpatrick: Thanks very much, Jim, for helping us see more clearly into the heart of this fascinating evaluation. Your comments have been most informative.

Fitzpatrick's Commentary

This exemplary MDRC evaluation of welfare reform in California exhibits many of the characteristics we write about in evaluation: attention to and involvement of stakeholders, examination of program implementation to help explain differing program impacts, flexibility and adaptation of evaluation questions and design during the course of the study, use of random assignment to examine critical outcomes when resources are scarce, and some combination of qualitative and quantitative methods. While this evaluation would hardly fit Kidder and Fine's (1987) description of "big Q" qualitative research, the primarily quantitative focus was appropriate for the legislative audience and the questions to be answered. The field observations served as a critical component in identifying the different messages being delivered to recipients by the counties. On the other hand, as Riccio notes, the experimental design used within counties proved important in establishing the credibility of their findings to their audiences. As noted by Cook and Campbell (1979), experimental designs can be implemented in the field when fiscal constraints do not permit delivery of a program to all recipients. Such was the case with the GAIN program.

Another strength of the GAIN study was its examination of many outcomes over a relatively long period: earnings, welfare payments, and employment. Given this, the variation in results across counties, across measures, and across time is complex, and conveying that complexity can be difficult. Often, effects were statistically significant but modest. Measures of effect size could have been useful in conveying the magnitude of these effects, but they were regrettably lacking. However, Riccio's primary stakeholders are not statisticians, and effect size can be a complex concept for nonstatisticians. One of the challenges evaluators face is communicating sometimes complex results to people who are not familiar with research methods. In such cases, relying on data about change can be more readily understood.

Moving people off of welfare into the workplace is an incredibly difficult task. No program can succeed in getting everyone employed. Nevertheless, welfare reform remains an important issue for all 50 states in the United States. Thus, the emphasis on finding messages that had some effect is important. The question being addressed is not whether or not "welfare reform" works but what aspects of it work, with what types of recipients, and in what kinds of settings. MDRC did an excellent job in helping California address these issues and, in so doing, helped other states as well.

Note

1. MDRC was originally founded as the Manpower Demonstration Research Corporation, but in 2003, it became registered as MDRC, the name by which it was best known.

DISCUSSION QUESTIONS

1. Is Riccio's primary purpose determining merit and worth? If so, what criteria does he use to judge the merit and worth of the GAIN program?

2. MDRC chose to use an experimental design with random assignment to conditions that are quite critical to recipients—that is, AFDC payments and work. Some counties were reluctant to participate in random assignment. Why were they reluctant to participate? Do you agree with their reasons? Or do you think MDRC and Riccio were correct in using this design? Support your argument.

3. Which part of Riccio's evaluation do you think was more labor intensive: the studies of the implementation or the studies of outcomes? Why?

4. Riccio indicates that MDRC established credibility with many important audiences and, thus, their findings were more readily accepted. What factors contributed to establishing this credibility?

5. Riccio says that "modest success is not the same as failure" and that "in presenting the results from any study, evaluators can and should set the proper context." He notes that some people saw the Riverside results as big and others saw them as small. This is not an uncommon situation in evaluation. Some evaluators advise setting standards so that outcomes can later be judged as successes or failures. But sometimes standards are unrealistic. What is the role of the evaluator in helping stakeholders judge the results? The issue of welfare reform has parallels to educational testing today. What do stakeholders in your community consider to be successful test scores? How can evaluators help stakeholders consider these scores?

6. Riccio is comfortable and straightforward with acknowledging that the work-first strategy that yielded the best results was a surprise to him and others in the welfare reform field. His discussion of the results represents the kind of integrity one hopes for in evaluation work. Have you ever faced results that are surprising in that way to you? Think of a specific example. How comfortable are you, or your organization, in accepting something that is counter to your experience or prior beliefs?

FURTHER READING

Evaluation report: Riccio, J., Friedlander, D., & Freedman, S. (1994). *GAIN: Benefits, costs and three-year impacts of a welfare-to-work program.* New York: Manpower

Demonstration Research Corporation. Retrieved April 22, 2008 from www.mdrc
.org/publications/175/execsum.html.

Bloom, D., & Michalopoulos, C. (2001). *How welfare and work policies affect employment and income: A synthesis of research.* New York: Manpower Demonstration
Research Corporation.

Freedman, S., Friedlander, D., Lin, W., & Schweder, A. (1996). *The GAIN evaluation.
Working Paper 96.1. Five year impact on employment, earnings, and AFDC
receipts.* New York: Manpower Demonstration Research Corporation.

Riccio, J., & Hasenfeld, Y. (1996). Enforcing a participation mandate in a welfare-to-
work program. *Social Service Review, 70*(4), 516–542.

REFERENCES

Bloom, H. S., Hill, C. J., & Riccio, J. A. (2003). Linking program implementation and
effectiveness: Lessons from a pooled sample of welfare-to-work experiments.
Journal of Policy Analysis and Management, 22, 551–575. (This paper won the
Association for Public Policy and Management's 2003 Vernon Prize for the best
article published that year in the association's journal.)

Cook, T. D., & Campbell, D. T. (1979). *Quasi-experimentation: Design and analysis
issues for field settings.* Chicago: Rand McNally.

Freedman, S., Tansey Knab, J., Gennetian, L. A., & Navarro, D. (2000). *The Los
Angeles Jobs-First GAIN Evaluation: Final report on a work-first program in a
major urban center.* New York: Manpower Demonstration Research Corporation.

Friedlander, D., & Burtless, G. (1995). *Five years after: The long-term effects of
welfare-to-work programs.* New York: Russell Sage Foundation.

Hamilton, G. (2002). *Moving people from welfare to work: Lessons from the national
evaluation of welfare-to-work strategies.* Washington, DC: U.S. Department of
Health and Human Services, Administration for Children and Families, Offices
of the Assistant Secretary for Planning and Evaluation and U.S. Department of
Education, Office of the Under Secretary, Office of Vocational and Adult
Education; New York: Manpower Demonstration Research Corporation.

Kidder, L. H., & Fine, M. (1987). Qualitative and quantitative methods: When stories
converge. In M. M. Mark & R. L. Shotland (Eds.), *Multiple methods in program
evaluation* (New Directions for Program Evaluation, No. 35, pp. 57–75). San
Francisco: Jossey-Bass.

Riccio, J. A., & Orenstein, A. (1996). Understanding best practices for operating
welfare-to-work programs. *Evaluation Review, 20,* 3–28.

THREE

EVALUATION OF THE NATURAL RESOURCES LEADERSHIP PROGRAM, 1995 THROUGH 1998

An Interview With Jennifer C. Greene

Introduction: Jennifer Greene is currently a professor in the Department of Educational Psychology at the University of Illinois, Urbana-Champaign. She has held former academic positions at Cornell University and the University of Rhode Island. Jennifer Greene has been an evaluation scholar-practitioner for more than 30 years. She is well known in the evaluation field for her perceptive and thoughtful writings on mixed methods design and on the importance of evaluation that serves democratic values and ideals. Her work focuses on the intersection of social science methodology and social policy and aspires to be both methodologically innovative and socially responsible. Greene's conceptual work in evaluation has concentrated on advancing the methodologies of qualitative and mixed methods approaches to social and educational program evaluation, as well as participatory and democratic commitments in evaluation practice. Her evaluation practice has spanned the multiple domains of formal and informal education and community-based support programs for families and youth. Greene has held leadership positions in the American Evaluation Association and the American Educational Research

Association. She has also provided considerable editorial service to both communities, including a 6-year position as a coeditor-in-chief of *New Directions for Evaluation.* Her own publication record includes coeditorship of the recent *Sage Handbook of Program Evaluation* and several articles highlighting her work on an "educative, values-engaged approach" to educational program evaluation, an approach consonant with that featured in this example.

In this article, I interview Professor Greene about the three-year evaluation of the Natural Resources Leadership Program (NRLP) to learn more about her style of evaluation and the choices she makes. She selected this study, conducted with her colleagues Camille Tischler and Alan Hahn, as one that is typical of her work. In it, she makes use of an intensive case study, observations, interviews, and surveys of participants to gain an understanding of the program and make a judgment about it. A major goal of the program is to change the way in which disputes are resolved among those involved in making decisions about environmental policy. In an attempt to determine whether that goal was achieved, she and her colleagues conducted mini-case studies of selected participants' work in the field, interviewing not only the people who participated in the program but also those who participated with them on disputes and observed their work. She discusses these mini-cases, her teamwork with her colleagues and with the stakeholders, some of the values that entered into the evaluation, and her ultimate conclusions.

Summary of the Evaluation

Jennifer C. Greene

University of Illinois at Urbana-Champaign

The Natural Resources Leadership Program (NRLP) brought a new vision of leadership and new approaches to the resolution of environmental conflicts to natural resource leaders in three southeastern states. These new ideas focused on reframing conflicts as opportunities for progress, rather than as fights to be won or lost, and on re-envisioning leadership as facilitating a consensual agreement rather than as persuasion to a claimed position. This leadership program was offered to approximately 150 leaders from the public and private sectors, and from environmental activist groups and industry alike, from 1995 to 1998. The program aimed to improve the management of natural resources and to enhance rural economic development while maintaining or improving environmental quality. Specific objectives for the participants were

> (1) to understand and apply collaborative, win-win approaches to problem solving; (2) to become skilled in working with people who have different interests, values, and philosophies on issues involving natural resources; and (3) to understand natural resource policy and decision-making processes, and take into account the biological, economic, social and political implications of natural resources management decisions. (curriculum materials)

The program was implemented as a series of five two-and-one-half-day sessions of residential instruction—in communication and conflict resolution skills, leadership development, and government and public policy processes—complemented by a trip to Washington, D.C., and a follow-up, year-long practicum. In the practicum, participants aimed to infuse the lessons of the leadership program into their own practice. The program's five instructional sessions were spaced out over a 6-month period; the practicum was to last another 12 months, followed by a final concluding session. After a pilot run of this leadership program in one state in 1995, the program was implemented for the next year in three southeastern states and for a third year in two states. Each program had approximately 25 participants. Thus, during the time span of this evaluation, the program was implemented a total of six times, with some variations across both years and states.

Our evaluation of this leadership program was framed by the evaluation priorities of the funder, the W. K. Kellogg Foundation, and of the visionary developers and primary implementers of the program. These priorities called for data gathering on program context, implementation, and outcomes. We responded with an evaluation design organized around case studies of each of the six leadership programs. We first conducted an intensive case study of the initial pilot program. This included reviews of all program materials; observations of all instructional sessions; interviews during the observations with most participants; repeated interviews, on site and over the phone, with program staff; attendance at Advisory Board meetings; and, in later years, follow-up surveys and phone interviews of participants. This intensive case study enabled the evaluation team to develop considerable understanding of the leadership program, as designed, implemented, and experienced. It also enabled grounded development of later instruments such as annual participant surveys. It therefore functioned as intended to anchor our evaluation in the lived experiences of those closest to the program.

The case studies of the remaining five leadership programs were less intense, as our evaluation resources needed to be divided across states and time. In addition to gathering information on each leadership program, we needed to continue to track the practicum experiences and longer-term program outcomes for the participants in earlier programs. Thus, in these other case studies, we observed two instructional sessions; interviewed some of the program participants on site; conducted subsequent follow-up surveys and interviews; and maintained ongoing communications with the program staff in that state.

These case studies enabled the evaluation team to develop reasonably thorough portrayals of this program as designed and implemented and to offer meaningful feedback thereon. Furthermore, near the end of the evaluation period, we sought additional data, and data beyond participant self-report, on program outcomes. We did this because we agreed with the program funders and other decision makers that the meaningfulness and value of this particular leadership program lay in the ability of its graduates to engage differently in "real-life" environmental disputes. Toward this end, we surveyed all Advisory Board members, conducted mini-case studies of selected participant practicum projects, and also surveyed supervisors or other key individuals in participants' work sites. We asked general questions of Advisory Board members regarding their views of recent trends in environmental problem solving in their state or locale. We sampled the "best" of the participant practicum projects and endeavored to understand how the leadership program had contributed to their success. And we asked work site supervisors for their views on relevant participant attitudes and behaviors upon completion of the leadership program. These additional efforts to gather outcome data—especially the analyses of practicum projects—significantly aided our efforts to draw important conclusions about the value of this leadership program.

The three members of the evaluation team had collaborated before on evaluation studies and had a strong, respectful working relationship with each other. Expertise in leadership development and in conflict resolution was also featured on the team. Furthermore, we had worked with some of the key program staff before and had a strong, collaborative working relationship with them. One mark of this relationship, and of our evaluation practice, was to engage in open, ongoing communications about evaluation progress and findings throughout the study. Each evaluation activity was an occasion for review, reflection, and analysis. And on each occasion, our descriptive and analytic-interpretive reflections were both shared back with program staff. This strand of ongoing analysis and discussion was a key contributing factor to the overall success of this evaluation.

Our evaluation indicated that the NRLP was generally successful in realizing its learning aims. Most program participants reported that they changed their conceptual understanding of environmental conflict, changed their ideas of effective leadership in conflict situations, and learned new skills and techniques for organizing people and information toward the resolution of conflicts they encounter. In terms of effects on practice, only a few participants were able to enact the new lessons learned in the field, in terms of actually facilitating a consensual decision in a conflict situation—for example, rewriting a state's nuisance wildlife regulation to meet requirements for *both* animal protection and efficiency. A number of others were able to use the project ideas to make important progress toward mediated solutions that respected multiple interests—for example, holding an open symposium on hog farm regulations so that farmers, public health officials, economic developers, and county residents could all voice their views. The reflections of the evaluation team thus highlighted possible ways in which this promising leadership program could meaningfully influence actual conflict resolution activities and strategies for more of the program participants.

With respect to evaluation approach, the emphases evident in this evaluation on (a) learning about and understanding the complexities of this leadership program as envisioned and as experienced in context, (b) foregrounding the value dimensions of the program's intentions and enactments, and (c) using a diverse mix of methods well capture my current work, as represented in the references that follow the interview.

Dialogue With Jennifer Greene

Jody Fitzpatrick

———•◦•———

Fitzpatrick: Jennifer, in your writing on evaluation, you have contributed much insight to the issues of both values and methodology. Can you tell us a little about how this evaluation illustrates some of the methods you advocate in evaluation?

Greene: Some of my work has highlighted the intertwining of values and methodology. Let me say a little bit more about my general thinking about methodology in that context, the ways I think about methodology that make explicit the value dimensions, and then the ways this study illustrates that intertwining of values and methods. This study had many of the characteristics that I try to implement in evaluations. But let me talk more generally first. My approach to evaluation is responsive, in Bob Stake's sense of the word, in that the evaluation tries to become attuned to the issues and concerns of people in the context of this program. And these issues are always ones about values. Second, my methodology is inclusive in that multiple, diverse perspectives, stances, and concerns are included in the evaluation. Finally, and I want to underscore this, the methodology is reflective. That is, in this particular evaluation, throughout the process of the three-year study, there was a continuing cycle of reflection and analysis. What have we learned? What does it mean? What do *we*, as evaluators, think about this? This reflective, iterative cycle was not only one that we as an evaluation team did, but was one that we shared with key stakeholders so we were able to say, "Here's what we're learning. What do you think about it?" So we used an ongoing process of writing up what we knew. We had a partnership, a collegiality with the stakeholders. We were not members of the program team, but we were not outsiders. We actually sought to be collegial with the program staff.

This particular study attained these qualities through the following kinds of approaches. It was primarily a case study approach, where the case was each institute in each state in each year. The institutes changed from year to year and there were variations across states. So the case study approach allows responsiveness to those changes. We also intentionally used a mix of methods.

The evaluation team had worked together before. One member of the team had expertise in leadership, another in conflict resolution. We used a process where we would meet and talk substance first, rather than get tangled in logistics. We had a good working relationship with the program people before this evaluation began, and this was very helpful. We wrote up everything, each evaluation activity, that is, each observation, each set of interviews, each survey. We didn't wait for the end. We shared the data and our thoughts with each other and all the stakeholders. We wrote annual reports, where we were a little more reflective. We had an ongoing exchange of information, an ongoing evaluative conversation. Staff in each state received information about the overall findings for that evaluation activity and about the findings for their state.

Fitzpatrick: Thanks. That gives me a real sense for how this study reflects your priorities as an evaluator. Let's talk about the start of the evaluation. What prompted this evaluation? Who initiated it and why?

Greene: This was a leadership program that was funded by the Kellogg Foundation. So the evaluation was a requirement of the funding. We had worked with the program people before on other evaluations, and they asked us to do this evaluation.

Fitzpatrick: Who did you see as the primary users or stakeholders? What were their concerns?

Greene: The program people—the developers and implementers in each state—were the primary stakeholders. There were two or three in each state. They were the ones with whom we developed the collegial relationship. We were mindful of the Foundation and their philosophy, and that did influence, to some degree, the way we framed the evaluation. We did, in the larger vision, see the program participants and their organizations as stakeholders; however, we didn't communicate with them throughout the process. But we certainly thought of them as important stakeholders.

Fitzpatrick: What did you see as the primary purpose of this evaluation?

Greene: I think we saw our job as to develop a good understanding of, and to make some judgments about, the quality and effectiveness of the leadership institute. We saw the evaluation as helping to do things better in the future. We hoped our work might inform the institute but were probably more oriented to developing a good description of how this institute was implemented, the ways it succeeded, and how it fell short.

Fitzpatrick: How did these purposes emerge? Is this purpose common to many evaluations you do?

Greene: Yes, it's probably pretty typical. The key challenge is determining the basis or criteria for making the judgment. In addition to criteria informed by team expertise, we were trying to be responsive to stakeholders' criteria and to what we understood of the Foundation's priorities. They were very interested in not just proving but improving. That was their slogan. They were also interested in outcome information. We used the program proposal that we got to develop a draft evaluation plan and shared it with our key stakeholders. They provided some feedback, and there we were!

Fitzpatrick: In any evaluation, there are generally more questions that we would like to answer than resources permit. Or some of the questions we think should be primary may be vetoed by the more immediate information needs of the stakeholders. Were there other evaluation questions that you would have liked to have added?

Greene: No, I attribute some of the smoothness of the initial process to the fact that we had worked with some of the key developers of the institute before. They liked our prior work and expected something similar to what we proposed. They already had a familiarity with how we worked.

Fitzpatrick: In your summary, you mentioned the strong collaborative relationship you developed with program staff, the ongoing communications about the evaluation progress and findings, and your use of these discussions for reflection and analysis. Can you tell us a little more about how this worked? How often did you meet with the program people? Did you meet with ones from each state separately?

Greene: Each member of the evaluation team had primary responsibility for one of the three participating states in the program. Phone calls, e-mail, site visits were all used as communication channels in these relationships. At least twice during the program period, these key state leaders convened, along with program developers, and at least one member of our team also attended. And, as I said, we worked hard to establish and nurture an ongoing evaluative conversation with these key staff.

Fitzpatrick: How did the users vary in their openness to using the evaluation for reflection and analysis of the institute?

Greene: All seemed quite open. The variation was more in their ability or willingness to make changes in the program.

Fitzpatrick: Can you tell us a bit more about that? What do you do when program staff are reluctant or unable to bring about needed changes? Is it sufficient to bring about reflection and analysis or to what extent should we push for change?

Greene: While our relationship with program staff was highly collegial, we did not have authority or responsibility for the program design and implementation. So when we provided feedback or stimulated reflection and discussion on some particular issue and then the program staff decided to keep the program as it was, we respected that decision. In this evaluation, we kept the issues alive in the ongoing evaluative conversation, because we wanted to encourage repeated and ongoing reflection and analysis. But we did not push for any particular program change. We did not believe we had authority to do that.

Fitzpatrick: This is, essentially, an evaluation of a training program, albeit an interesting and unusual one. Did you make use of any of the literature on training evaluation, such as Kirkpatrick's model for evaluating training or Brinkerhoff's writing? Were there any other models that influenced your approach to the evaluation?

Greene: A good question. What happened in this evaluation was that one of the team members—this was definitely a team effort—was an expert in leadership development in this kind of setting—that is, adult education, cooperative extension, rural farm, and agricultural issues, so we all just deferred to him. The meaning of leadership became a pretty important issue because the institute was trying to advance an alternative way of thinking of leadership, leadership as helping groups resolve conflicts and reach consensus, as opposed to advocating for, or even mandating, a certain position. But it did not do so explicitly; so many participants fell into old ways of thinking of leadership. And there were conflicts between the new way of thinking about leadership and certain activities in the program. For example, the program began with a team-building activity, often using a ropes course. Generating this sense of camaraderie in the group was somewhat in conflict with the emphasis on understanding and accepting difference that was central to the new concept of leadership. So the concept that we anchored our work around was more leadership than training.

Fitzpatrick: Yes, you can see the focus on leadership in your report. Let's move to discussing your methods of data collection. You make use of a combination of observations of the institute sessions, telephone interviews with a sample of participants, interviews with staff and advisory board members, surveys of participants and supervisors, and mini-case studies of some practicum projects. Tell us about how you decided to use this mix of methods.

Greene: I came up with three criteria that influenced our choices. Maximizing the depth of our understanding was primary and this led us to qualitative methods. All things considered, qualitative methods would be our preference. We needed to spend some time there, we needed to have a sense for what these institutes looked like and felt like. We wanted to know what it was like to be a participant in this program. What was the character and quality of the experience? But we simultaneously wanted to make sure we heard from a lot of people. Inclusion was another important criterion. The people you talk to when you're at the institute may not be the silent people, so the surveys helped us be as inclusive as possible. The Advisory Board was a group we could more easily survey than talk with everyone. The third criterion for our decisions about methods and samples was to ensure that we captured the experience and effects of this leadership program at its "best." This criterion is perhaps best illustrated in our selection of participant practicum projects for mini-case studies. We worked hard to select the very best practicum projects for these mini-case studies. (This issue is discussed further below.)

Fitzpatrick: Which methods were most informative to you? Or what insights did each add?

Greene: The mini-case study was the most important for outcomes. In terms of the broader goal of developing an understanding of the program and its accomplishments, there is no substitute for being there. The surveys were always ho-hum. Surveys yielded pretty much what we thought we would get back, but we wanted to use them for inclusiveness and perspective. The surveys were also important in documenting consistency in certain findings across site and time.

Fitzpatrick: Let's talk a bit about the mini-case studies. You used these to portray what participants have accomplished in the field; this focus corresponds to Kirkpatrick's Level 3 focus on outcomes or applications of training on the job. You made use of telephone interviews, surveys, and examinations of the practicum projects themselves to describe these applications. Tell us a bit about how the mini-case studies came to be a focus and how you selected them.

Greene: The emphasis on practical program outcomes was an intentional focus of the evaluation from the outset. Not only did our stakeholders want this information, but we thought it was important too. What we all know about training is that the real question is the "so what" question. Do people actually realize the intentions of training in the field? This institute, like much training, experienced a shortage of time. Also, participants had limited positional authority. Many didn't have the authority to go back to their work sites and make things happen differently. That is, there were many factors about the program's implementation that undermined the real prospect of conflicts being solved in a different way out in the field. But we still believed that whether and how participants had been able to actually resolve conflicts differently in the field was the question to pursue. And we decided to pursue this significantly through mini-case studies of selected participant practicum projects.

We deliberated a lot about the sampling of the mini-case studies. They were resource intensive and difficult. It was not just a matter of interviewing the participant but also tracking down others involved in the dispute resolution and learning more about what the participant had contributed. We wanted to examine the institute at its best. If this program really had the potential to change how people think about environmental disputes, then we should be able to see program effects in the field. And doing the mini-case study was the best way to approach it—to really see if the institute was doing what it hoped to do. You can learn a lot in training but not be able to put it to practice or not have the opportunity to do so. The idea was not to be representative but rather to purposefully sample the best cases. We wanted to learn if, at its best, the institute had the potential to make a difference.

We identified the best practicum projects through nominations, primarily from program designers and staff. We didn't just ask one person, we asked several. We defined "best" as meaning closest to the vision of the designers of the program, or most likely to demonstrate the value of resolving environmental disputes through mediation processes and concepts. The mini-case studies of the practicum projects were the most significant for the outcome question, but we also built into the methodology some tracking of all participants over time. So we were differentiating shorter-term and longer-term outcomes. Some telephone interviews were of people who had participated three years previously. We tried to make use of as much of the time span as we could, with some participants having been trained a few years before, to allow us to see whether further applications had occurred and how.

I don't think we were blindly following the outcome mania of today. We just agreed with program developers and funders that the outcomes were the important question.

Fitzpatrick: Sometimes it can be more difficult to engage people, particularly strangers, on a telephone interview than it is face-to-face. I noticed your telephone interviews with participants about their application of the content were about 30 minutes in length. What kinds of things did you ask, or do, to establish rapport and stimulate reflection and interchange?

Greene: Well, they weren't strangers; we already knew them. We had met almost all of them during our observations of the institute. But because one member of the evaluation team conducted most of the phone interviews—and this team member had not personally met all respondents before, we tried to do a variety of things to develop a relationship further before the interview. We sent an advance letter to describe the purpose of the interview. Then, the person who was conducting the interview made an advance phone call to set the appointment and to answer any questions, as well as to advance rapport and perhaps chat a little. So these two advance contacts furthered rapport for respondents the interviewer had met before and helped establish some rapport for those the interviewer had not met.

Fitzpatrick: I liked some of the reaction items that you used to obtain participants' feedback to the sessions on the survey. They tapped more than the typical reaction survey often does. (The survey made use of Likert-scale items, tapping particular issues such as "I wish we had spent more time during the institute engaging with each other on the natural resource issues we really care about," etc.) How did you decide which "sensitive" issues to tap with these items? Sometimes trainers are resistant to such items.

Greene: We decided to use the surveys after the first institute. By that time, we had already spent a lot of time in the institute talking with participants and staff. So the issues we wanted to pursue came from our interviews and observations. We changed them a bit as the institute changed, but many items remained the same throughout.

We did share survey drafts with the program staff. They had a chance to object to a particular question, but there was not a concern about probing into possibly sensitive areas because these were issues that were already part of the conversation. We had a constant flow of data write-ups and sharing of issues and questions.

Fitzpatrick: Finally, let me ask about the observation of sessions. Did you observe all the sessions? What kind of guidelines did you use to observe the sessions?

Greene: The first year, the institute was just in one state as a pilot institute. At least one of the three team members observed each session. We felt we needed to be there for the whole thing. We didn't have as many resources for the remaining institutes when it spread to two other states. So after the pilot, we picked sessions that we thought might be most revealing about what was going on in that institute.

We had a very open observation process. We had a one-page observation guide that listed the areas we would like to have information on. As with any observation, the actual process of observing is often very overwhelming. So the guide helped focus us. We were also all very experienced observers.

Fitzpatrick: Do you think you observed the same kinds of things? Or did your different areas of expertise lead you to note different issues?

Greene: The person with background in conflict resolution would note things that the other two didn't. The other two of us would see the degree to which participants seemed to be engaged, but we would not be able to discern relevant aspects of the program content that might have made it more engaging. So, no, we didn't see the same things, but there was reasonable consistency.

Fitzpatrick: And the inconsistency was good?

Greene: We didn't have the resources to have two of us there very often. But in the first year, in most of those observations of the five sessions, there were at least two of us there. And there were times when one of us would say, "Boy, I thought that session was great!" And the other would say, "*You did?*" Then we could talk and sort out our different perceptions: "Was it you or the participants who thought it was great?"

Fitzpatrick: What role did the stakeholders play, if any, in helping you determine the methods you would use?

Greene: They were active—the core group of program developers and implementers. Those people were part of our evaluation design process. We did have changes in design as we went along. In fact, each year we updated our evaluation design and shared it with them for their review. These key stakeholders were invited to comment on all the instruments. We sent them drafts. They were heavily involved in that. We consulted with them on sampling issues as I discussed. We asked them who was the best, among others. I would say it was a collegial relationship, like we were on the same team though doing different things on the team.

Fitzpatrick: I would like to spend some time on your findings. In your Executive Summary, you state your primary finding: that the NRLP's aim was "to improve the management of natural resources and to enhance rural economic development while maintaining or improving environmental quality" and that "the program was successful in realizing its aims." Tell us about reaching that conclusion. How do you feel you were able to tap those aims in your evaluation?

Greene: We were not trying to claim that this program changed the whole environmental decision-making process in the southeastern states but that in the cases we looked at, we felt it was the institute experience that led to a change. Did the institute do this for more than a handful of people in a handful of situations? No. We were trying to say that this institute, as designed and implemented, has the potential to bring about such change. We were trying to answer the question, "At its best, can the institute achieve this, bring about a change in how people make decisions on contested environmental policy?" And the answer was "yes." Those instances of success were the exception. Most participants did not experience those kinds of situations. Even so, what we're saying in the final report is that this program is worth doing again. If we had found no such instances of change, we would have been a lot less willing to say this is a good idea. We, as evaluators, personally believed it was a good idea, but our personal opinion wasn't enough. Rather, we anchored our judgment in the observed instances of meaningful success.

Fitzpatrick: But how much change is enough for success? What if you just found one instance of change?

Greene: I think we found enough. How many is enough? I don't know. This is clearly a values question. In this evaluation, we could portray change as almost a continuum, with most participants demonstrating some progress toward the goal of resolving conflicts differently. But we felt we saw enough evidence regarding this ultimate goal to say this leadership program is a good idea, and it was implemented well enough to have some impact. We had strong evidence of knowledge, skills, and attitude change, but the outcomes in the field were the main criteria we wanted to use to judge the institute.

Fitzpatrick: What did you see as the major impacts of the institute?

Greene: As I've noted, we did find evidence of people actually resolving conflicts differently, but the major impacts were much more modest. The impacts for most participants were the predictable individual changes in knowledge, skills, and attitudes. There were pretty consistent changes in attitudes and world view, notably participants' understanding of a different way to think about resolving environmental issues. People developed a lot of conceptual knowledge. They didn't develop as many conflict resolution skills as they wanted to, but they did report developing some—enough to make small changes in their work and personal lives. It was much more about individual changes in people rather than changes in environmental policy making.

Fitzpatrick: How did you measure the changes in attitudes and skills?

Greene: Mainly through self-report collected in the interviews and annual surveys—that is, through participants' own views of their changes. The practica also provided some evidence. There was consistency in these reports.

Fitzpatrick: Did you think about using more traditional paper-and-pencil measures of skills or attitudes?

Greene: I think only for about a second. We would have had to develop them and pilot test them. I don't think there are appropriate instruments out there. There may be, but it just was not the appropriate assessment for this context. It would have felt like a test—very off-putting and not consistent with the climate that the workshop was trying to establish.

What we did think about was the possibility of identifying, in each state, a current environmental policy area of considerable debate and trying to almost track it backward. This would have to be an area where there had been some recent action. Our intent would have been to see if there were any ways that the participants in this workshop had been players in this issue. But on reflection, we thought that was well beyond the reach of the workshop. It would have been hard to do for us. We were pretty sure we would not find very much. People told us we wouldn't. So we did think beyond self-report, but more in terms of examining other impacts in the field.

In regard to the self-reports of knowledge and skill change, there was no reason why people would want to report knowledge gains that they did not have. We got a real clear statement from many participants that they developed different ways of thinking and acquired another whole set of knowledge but that they did not develop their skills to the extent they wanted. They felt free to say that. Their comments were a reflection on the workshop. Other kinds of measures, tests, would have been insulting.

Fitzpatrick: Returning to your findings, I would like to talk about one of the sections of your final report because I think it might illustrate something about your approach to evaluation. You devote about one third of the report to a concluding section entitled "Evaluator Insights and Analysis." This section provides some clear and direct suggestions for change (articulating their different idea of leadership, adapting content and expectations to the fact that many participants were not in positions of power). It also contains some fascinating philosophical discussions of the nature of conflict vis-à-vis the goals of the institute, the contribution of extremists, and the role of self-knowledge. These latter sections appear to reflect some of your own writings in evaluation. I am thinking particularly of the section on self-knowledge, but also the section on extremists.

On self-knowledge, you write,

> We need to be able to reflect on how and why we react the way we do in our lives, what core beliefs and assumptions govern our actions, whether or not our processes are helpful to ourselves and others, and how they fit into what we know about the world we live in. The more fully we can trace the meaning we ascribe to situations and the improvements we prefer to our particular experience, feelings, emotions, attitudes, beliefs, morals, tastes, and talents, the more we will be able to legitimate the same in others.

These remarks are given in the context of the balance between teaching techniques, or the mechanics, of resolving conflict and the concomitant need for self-knowledge to resolve conflicts productively. On extremism and advocacy, you challenge the view presented in the institute that advocacy and extremism are to be avoided. You write, "Making conflict go away is not always the goal" and note that "they [extremists] see things we don't see . . . panning extremists puts a damper on free expression in any group. We are all extremist about something."

I was intrigued by these sections and wanted to ask more about them. First, how did these conclusions emerge from your evaluation? That is, some stakeholders might very well ask your source for these recommendations or reflections. Is it legitimate for an evaluator to raise these sorts of issues—that is, ones which are based more on our own values, judgments, and personal experience than on the data we have collected?

Greene: I want to first note that these particular insights and views came from the evaluation team member with expertise in conflict resolution, with unequivocal support from the rest of the team. It is also important to note that these comments took place in the final evaluation report. We did not claim the same extent of evaluator voice in all the other reports. We actually made an intentional decision, after considerable discussion, to include such a section in this final report and to clearly label it our thoughts and ideas. Most of these issues discussed in this section—all of them really—had been brought up before in previous reports—for example, the meaning of leadership. That is, these were issues that had been part of the evaluative conversation the entire time. We had not kept them secret. What was different in this final report was the extent to which we stated our own views on these issues, views that were embedded in broader discussions, especially within the field of conflict resolution. In the past, we would say, "We *wonder* if the issues of leadership are consistent with the workshop?" or "We *wonder* if advocacy for a position is always wrong?" In this final report, we not only said "we *wonder*," but "*here's what we think about this issue.*"

Fitzpatrick: But is it appropriate for you to do that? What are people hiring you for?

Greene: Our debate was not so much whether we had a legitimate right to do this. It was more over how it might be received. We wanted to present it in a way that was supportive.

But to answer your question, we claimed voice and legitimacy of voice because we had spent three years working in a collegial fashion with the institute and its developers. Another reason we felt we had the legitimacy to make these comments was the expertise on the team in conflict resolution and leadership. If we had not had that expertise, we would have felt less secure. So the team's expertise, experience, and familiarity with this issue gave us not just impressions over the year but also access to a broader set of contexts to draw from, so it was almost like sharing these broader contexts with this group. I am quite certain that it was the experience and expertise of the team in these domains that gave us the sense of legitimacy.

Fitzpatrick: I also was struck by putting these issues on paper. That is, I sometimes raise such issues in discussion with stakeholders, but not in such a direct way in the final report. What are your thoughts on how to communicate such issues? What was your goal in this communication?

Greene: I don't know how this final report was received. The report itself was reasonably short. Key people involved in the development of the institute retired just about the time we completed this report. Things got a little scattered. I never heard anything bad about it. By the time the final report came about, the opportune moments for engagement had passed.

Fitzpatrick: Do you think these suggestions had an impact on any of the stakeholders?

Greene: By the time this report came out, the moment for meaningful engagement with these issues had passed, which is one reason not to wait to do your important evaluation reporting until the end. So the report may have had some influence on people who were still involved, but the actual program activity had pretty much wound down. But as I mentioned, we had not kept totally mute the entire three years. By raising these issues during our conversations throughout the evaluation, we had drawn attention to the issues themselves. What we deferred until the end—and perhaps should not have— were discussions of these issues in their broader contexts. Such discussions, as illustrated in our final report, can illuminate multiple facets and dimensions of the issues that are of possible relevance to this program.

Fitzpatrick: How did stakeholders respond to the evaluation results during the evaluation? Did they use them in ways you had anticipated?

Greene: I think it was a real good communication flow. Those we knew and worked with most closely read the reports. If they had questions, they would ask. They would sometimes disagree and say, "Well, I see your point here, but I think the team building exercise is really important and here's why." We would respond, "But you're trying to deal with diversity here and you're pushing it to one side." And they would disagree. But there was some shuffling of the curriculum over the years. We provided a role in the project that was seen as valuable to the people.

Fitzpatrick: And the shuffling dealt with issues you raised?

Greene: Yes, to some degree. The program included a trip to Washington and a trip to the state capitol. We wondered, given the time and expense involved, what the value of these trips was. We wondered especially if the time might not be better spent giving participants more time to practice their new mediation skills or to observe skilled mediators in action.

Fitzpatrick: Did they continue the trip to Washington?

Greene: Yes, they continued the D.C. trip because this was new for many of the participants. And they did these trips very well. They arranged visits with policy people in the participants' area of concern and with representatives from their state. It was perceived as valuable by participants. The state capital visits, however, were not all continued, perhaps, in part, because we questioned their value.

Fitzpatrick: Most evaluations encounter some ethical challenges. What ethical dilemmas did you find most challenging in conducting this study?

Greene: There were no problems with field relationships, access, or betrayal of confidentiality. Nothing like that. I do think that finding the appropriate role for our own stances was a continuing challenge, and that was the issue we deliberated for the final report. Where is the place for the evaluators' viewpoint? You know you have a viewpoint and that your data are colored by your own lens. So I think the ethical challenge was being mindful of our own particular way of doing things. We just gave ourselves permission in the final report to not filter that. The evaluation team people were typical northeastern liberals who believe in environmental issues. Now this is a program that probably shared that philosophy, but they were trying to be more open to other stances and sides.

Fitzpatrick: In what areas did you find your personal stances on environmental issues presented the greatest challenges?

Greene: I think it had to do with particular environmental disputes, the woodpecker, the hog farm, the landfill. When the workshop people engaged with a particular situation, they brought these panels in, featuring people with different points of view. When they engaged with actual issues, my own views on these issues were often different, even extreme. Someone would ask, for example, "How much pollution is OK?" I would think none, a view shared by only some participants. So because this program dealt with contentious environmental issues, the personal stances of the evaluation team members on these issues were ever present. Our job, however, was not to engage in the substance of the environmental disputes but rather to understand how this program was advancing a different process for resolving them. Although actually, this content-process tension was another issue of ongoing attention in our evaluative conversation.

But there were no serious ethical dilemmas. Our evaluation team was interested in the public good. And we perceived this program as sharing that commitment. While this program was not exactly what we would do, it certainly was taking a step toward serving the common good.

Fitzpatrick: We all learn from evaluations. If you were to conduct this evaluation again, what would you do differently?

Greene: It is not going to be a long list, but there is one thing that I might do differently, but it is only a "might." As I highlighted before, throughout our work, we tried to stimulate issue-based conversations about the institute. But we deferred to our final report a fuller engagement with these issues in their broader contexts and as we understood them. Perhaps we should not have waited until the end for these broader conversations. Perhaps during the evaluation, we should have tried to bring into the conversation other people who had some expertise in conflict resolution, others with expertise in leadership, and others with expertise in environmental policy. It might have broadened the conversation and made it more substantive all along. But the hesitation here is turf. The people who developed and designed this program would never say they were the only experts in conflict resolution, but they probably felt they knew enough and especially knew what made the most sense for this context. But perhaps we could have deflected some of the turf issues by referring to other sources. By asking, "Have you read this book?" or saying, "I had a phone conversation with X, and she suggested this." We might have done this to bring in some of the broader issues we engaged in in the final report. Our agenda was to be thoughtful, and we could have been even more thoughtful if we had been able to do more of this all along.

Fitzpatrick's commentary

Jennifer Greene's approach to evaluating NRLP illustrates many of the principles of her writing and introduces some new elements as well. In many ways, the evaluation demonstrates a use of the traditional definition of evaluation, to judge the merit or worth of a product or program. Note how she defines the primary purpose of the evaluation as "to develop a good understanding of, and to make some judgments about, the quality and effectiveness of the leadership institute." Unlike many evaluators, she does not delineate specific questions that are paramount to program managers or other stakeholders during the initial planning stage. Instead, the focus of her evaluation team is more holistic. While they are interested primarily in outcomes, the evaluation touches on the content and process of the program as well. However, while the core of the evaluation may be to judge merit and worth, Greene also emphasizes understanding and program improvement. Her purpose is formative, rather than summative, and her primary audience for this formative information is the program staff. Rather than answering particular questions that they have, she attempts to bring about change, not simply use, by establishing an "ongoing evaluation conversation about value-based issues important to the program." If achieved, this change would certainly be more substantive change than mere use. Like Deming with total quality management or proponents of the learning organization, Greene wants to create a questioning program team. She is rather modest in her success, but evidence for that success is seen in the fact that she had worked with the program people on other evaluations. They know what she does and find it valuable.

As one would expect, Greene makes use of a variety of methods in the evaluation, but relies more heavily on qualitative approaches. The purposive sampling of practicum projects, the content analyses of these documents, and the interviews with participants and others to learn more about these applications illustrate the use of qualitative methods to successfully portray the outcomes of the institute among the most promising participants. Though not demonstrated through this interview, the evaluation report uses quotations from interviews and examples from the practicum projects to provide the reader with a real sense of the best outcomes of the workshop. Her reliance on self-report measures of knowledge and skill, rather than more quantitative measures, reflects a choice that is appropriate to the context and nature of the program and the evaluation. The fact that participants readily reported gaps in skills and applications suggests that the self-reports were successful in tapping critical issues.

In attempting to instill an ongoing evaluative conversation, Greene and her fellow team members must, as she illustrates, become part of the team. This goal may be more easily achieved by an internal evaluator who is present to learn the nuances of personalities, context, and decision making; nevertheless, becoming a part of the team is a necessary step to establish the ongoing evaluative dialogue. The extensive observations during the pilot phase were undoubtedly helpful in achieving that goal in addition to helping the team gain a real understanding of the workshop participants, conflict resolution, and the environmental issues faced by those three states. Communication with different stakeholders in a three-state program when the evaluators are some distance away can be problematic, but extensive exchanges of information, conversations, and meetings can alleviate that problem.

Among the most intriguing aspects of Greene's evaluation are her discussions of the role her values played in the evaluation. She does not take a hands-off posture, nor does she conceal her values regarding environmental issues, conflict resolution, and the means for best achieving not only the goals of the workshop but what she sees as the public good. This is a controversial area. As a team member interested in inclusion, she attempts to hear and reflect in her reports many different voices, but her own is apparent as well, though she balances those values with her role as an evaluator. She comments,

> Because this program dealt with contentious environmental issues, the personal stances of the evaluation team members on these issues were ever present. Our job, however, was not to engage in the substance of the environmental disputes but rather to understand how this program was advancing a different process for resolving them.

Thus, while aware of her values and comfortable with voicing them, she sees her main role as learning of the program's success in teaching those working on environmental problems to resolve them in new ways.

As evaluators, we all recognize that our values influence the choices we make and the conclusions and interpretations that we reach in an evaluation.

In each interview that I have conducted, certain values regarding both evaluation and the program itself are evident. The evaluators interviewed differ in the manner and extent to which these values play a role in the evaluation and, of course, in the values themselves. In this evaluation, the team's voice and values are an integral part of the evaluation process. The evaluators' willingness to voice these concerns and values was probably successful in stimulating dialogue, if not change, since the audience was open to reflection. It is interesting to note how Greene expresses these values during the evaluation (wondering about certain issues), then in the final report, and in her final reflections on what she would do differently. Her honest and frank reflections on these issues should stimulate us as all to contemplate our own choices and stances in each evaluation we conduct.

DISCUSSION QUESTIONS

1. Professor Greene's approach, as she states at the beginning of the interview, is to be responsive to the issues and concerns of the people and the context of the evaluation; to be inclusive of multiple, diverse perspectives; and to be reflective. How does she demonstrate these qualities in conducting this evaluation?

2. What outcomes does Greene see as most important for judging the merit and worth of this program? How does she evaluate these outcomes? Do you agree with her choice of outcomes? Her choice of methods?

3. Greene refers to the "outcome mania" of today. What is she referring to? Do you see an "outcome mania" in your workplace? In public sector organizations in your area?

4. This interview introduces many interesting issues concerning an evaluator's role. What elements of Greene's role do you find interesting? Consider her role in providing feedback to staff on program change, in learning what it was like to be a participant in the program, in writing and disseminating the final report, or in other areas you see as relevant to understanding the complex role she takes in an evaluation.

5. How do Greene and her team communicate and share findings with stakeholders? What seem to be their main methods of communication?

REFERENCES

Greene, J. C. (2005a). A value-engaged approach for evaluating the Bunche-Da Vinci Learning Academy. In M. C. Alkin & C. A. Christie (Eds.), *Theorists' models in action: Vol. 106* (New Directions for Evaluation, pp. 27–45). San Francisco: Jossey-Bass.

Greene, J. C. (2005b). Evaluators as stewards of the public good. In S. Hood, R. K. Hopson, & H. T. Frierson (Eds.), *The role of culture and cultural context: A mandate for inclusion, truth, and understanding in evaluation theory and practice* (Evaluation and Society Series, pp. 7–20). Greenwich, CT: Information Age.

Greene, J. C. (2006). Toward a methodology of mixed methods social inquiry. Research in the schools [Special issue]. *New Directions in Mixed Methods Research, 13*(1), 93–99.

Greene, J. C. (2007). *Mixed methods in social inquiry.* San Francisco: Jossey-Bass.

Greene, J. C., DeStefano, L., Burgon, H., & Hall, J. (2006). An educative, values-engaged approach to evaluating STEM educational programs. In D. Huffman & F. Lawrenz (Eds.), *Critical issues in STEM evaluation* (New Directions for Evaluation, No. 109, pp. 53–71). San Francisco: Jossey-Bass.

FOUR

THE EVALUATION OF THE FT. BRAGG AND STARK COUNTY SYSTEMS OF CARE FOR CHILDREN AND ADOLESCENTS

An Interview With Len Bickman

———❖———

*I*ntroduction: Leonard Bickman is Professor of Psychology, Psychiatry, and Public Policy at Peabody College of Vanderbilt University, where he directs The Center for Evaluation and Program Improvement and serves as Associate Dean for Research. He is a coeditor of the *Applied Social Research Methods Series*, the *Handbook of Applied Research Methods*, and the *Handbook of Social Research* and the editor of the journal *Administration and Policy in Mental Health and Mental Health Services Research*. He has published more than 15 books and monographs and more than 190 articles and chapters. Dr. Bickman has received several awards, including the Secretary's Award for Distinguished Service while he was a senior policy advisor at the U.S. Substance Abuse and Mental Health Services Administration and the Sutherland Prize for Research from Vanderbilt University. He is a past president of the American Evaluation Association (AEA) and the Society for the Psychological Study of Social Issues. He is currently Principal Investigator on several grants from the National Institutes of Health and the Institute of Education Sciences. His research interests include child and adolescent mental health services, Web-based outcomes measurement systems, and the organizational and psychological factors that influence professionals' practice behavior.

Len Bickman's evaluation studies of systems of care for children at Ft. Bragg and in Stark County have received many awards, including the American Evaluation Association's award for the Outstanding Evaluation of 2000 and the American Psychological Association's Award for Distinguished Contributions to Research in Public Policy. Tom Cook has cited the studies as "among the ten or twenty best evaluation studies ever done in any field by anyone." Carol Weiss called the evaluation "one of the landmark studies of the decade," noting not only its excellent research design but also the integrity of the process and the courage in reporting unpopular results. Michael Patton has noted the success of these evaluators in disseminating the findings; engaging their critics in constructive discussion; and ultimately achieving great import, influence, and utilization for the results. We think readers will learn much from Bickman's comments on the factors that influenced this study.

Summary of the Ft. Bragg and Stark County Evaluations

Len Bickman

Vanderbilt University

———•◦•———

The Ft. Bragg evaluation describes the implementation, quality, costs, and outcomes of a $94 million demonstration project designed to improve mental health outcomes for children and adolescents who were referred for mental health treatment. The demonstration, designed to test the systems of care continuum as a means for delivering mental health treatment to children and adolescents, provided a full continuum of mental health services, including outpatient therapy, day treatment, in-home counseling, therapeutic foster homes, specialized group homes, 24-hour crisis management services, and acute hospitalization. Services were provided in civilian facilities.

The evaluation was a quasi-experiment with close to 1,000 families. Extensive mental health data were collected on children and their families over seven waves to evaluate the relative effectiveness of the demonstration. A random-effects regression model for longitudinal data was used to analyze ten key outcome variables that were measured seven times. The results revealed that the outcomes in children treated under the systems of care continuum were no better than the outcomes for children in the comparison group. The systems of care demonstration was also more expensive than the comparison, and there was no medical cost offset of the additional costs.

Given the absence of significant effects for the system of care program implemented at Ft. Bragg, another evaluation of the system of care concept was undertaken to learn if the same absence of effects would be noted in another setting. The Stark County evaluation concerned studying an exemplary, mature system of care designed to provide comprehensive mental health services to children and adolescents. It was believed that the system would lead to greater improvement in the functioning and symptoms of clients compared with those receiving care as usual. The project employed random assignment to conditions, with a five-wave longitudinal design, and included 350 families. While access to care, type of care, and amount of care were better in this system of care than in the Ft. Bragg demonstration, again, there were no differences in outcomes between those receiving the system of care and those receiving care outside the system. In addition, children who did not receive any services, regardless of experimental condition, improved at the same rate as treated children. Consistent with the Fort Bragg results, the effects of the Stark County systems of care were primarily limited to system-level outcomes, but they do not appear to affect mental health outcomes for children and adolescents, such as functioning and symptomatology.

Dialogue With Len Bickman

Jody Fitzpatrick

Fitzpatrick: Your evaluations of the Ft. Bragg and Stark County mental health systems for children and adolescents have received more recognition in the field of evaluation than any study that I can recall in my 25 years of practice. As I note in the introduction, Tom Cook, Carol Weiss, Michael Patton, and others have praised these evaluations. However, I would first like to ask you which elements of the study give you the most pride?

Bickman: I'm most proud of getting the study done. This was the first study in the field and the largest ever done. There were many people who thought we could never get it done because of its size and complexity. Some of my previous grant experiences made me question whether we could successfully complete the project. It is a compliment to the staff who worked with me for us to have received this recognition.

Another thing I am proud of is that we were able to keep the integrity of the design and the measures throughout the study while under considerable political pressure. The studies that had been done in the past had not even looked at clinical outcomes. They had only examined cost and the amount of services. That's what the Department of the Army wanted in the beginning—to just look at the cost to them. The Army people I negotiated the contract with were not used to dealing with research. They wanted the right to approve anything we published, which I refused. They then wanted to be able to comment on anything we published, which I explained was not under their control. Then, they wanted to lower the price because they argued that the publicity surrounding the evaluation would attract better graduate students to the university! It was a battle with the Army throughout the project to maintain the integrity of the design. In the end, however, they were very supportive of us because they now trusted our independence and our integrity. We actually received a rather large contract from them to conduct additional analyses of the data at the termination of the evaluation.

Fitzpatrick: Did you view these studies more as research on psychology and mental health or as public policy studies?

Bickman: I saw it as primarily an evaluation project. It was a policy study, but we embedded several research questions in the evaluation. We have published over 80 articles on this study, many of them in major research journals. We not only had Army funding but a competitive National Institutes of Mental Health (NIMH) grant to extend the project and add additional measures about the families. Every good evaluation has the potential to be good research and to have policy relevance. We thought even if the project [systems of care] doesn't work, we will learn a lot about the mental health of kids. It's a waste not to see the research opportunities as part of an evaluation.

Fitzpatrick: I want to spend some time on the choices you made in designing the studies, but as a political scientist, I'm particularly intrigued with the politics of evaluation and impressed with the attention your study has received by policy makers. Patrick DeLeon, a past President of the American Psychological Association and an administrative assistant to Senator Inouye in Congress, has noted, "Len insisted that all evaluations would represent the most up-to-date level of expertise possible, even when staff within DOD [the Department of Defense] itself strenuously objected. In the end, Len prevailed." Tell us about some of the struggles you endured and what you did that helped you prevail.

Bickman: One important aspect in helping the evaluation prevail was that Lenore Behar, who was the primary contractor, had lobbied heavily for an objective evaluation of the systems of care demonstration. We were a subcontractor, so she shielded us from some of the problems in dealing with the Army directly. But the Army was never supportive of the evaluation until the final report. At first, they thought the system of care project [the demonstration] was not necessary because it was so expensive. So they felt there was no need for the evaluation. The project itself was just too costly. Then, they sent in psychiatrists to visit the demonstration and their reviews were glowing. So now the Army thought the project was good and, thus, no evaluation was needed!

Another problem we faced was developing procedures for identifying and recruiting families. We were new to working with the DOD insurance system and actually new to the whole field of child mental health. We were told that we could use the claims data to locate subjects. However, we were not told that we would not get claims data until 3 to 12 months after the child had the services. We needed to recruit families for the study within 30 days of when they entered services, to collect pre-demonstration data; so obviously, the claims data were useless for this purpose. We had to develop new ways to recruit subjects. At the demonstration site, this was not a problem since we recruited from just one organization. But in the comparison sites, we had to recruit from every practitioner in each area. The recruitment in the comparison sites required us to identify who provided mental health services and ask them to do the initial recruitment. It also meant that we had to make weekly calls or visits to over 50 providers each week. This work with providers to deal with recruitment of comparison groups for the study not only slowed us down but also cost more than we had budgeted.

A major crisis occurred about halfway through the project. The Army told us that we had enough subjects to complete the project and we should terminate the evaluation. At that point, we had only about 300 cases. We said that they had approved a plan for 1,000 subjects. We went to San Antonio to meet with the Army to discuss this. They hired a consultant to look at the [statistical] power issue. [Bickman's concern was with only 300 cases, they would not have a sufficiently large sample size to have adequate statistical power to analyze the data. Recall that a Type II error, failing to find a significant difference when there really is one, can occur when your sample size is too small. Although Bickman did not know the end results at this stage, his final results showed no significant difference between groups. If the sample size had been 300, he could have been criticized at drawing these conclusions because of low statistical power increasing the probability of a Type II error.] We kept trying to find out who this person was because I know most of the people in this area. We finally got the woman's résumé and she had a Ph.D. in electrical engineering! Our first thought was that they confused statistical power with electrical power! However, it turned out that she also had a master's degree in statistics. Then, we had a site visit during which an Army officer gave me a floppy disk and wanted me to give him the data. I told him we couldn't do that! They weren't happy with me over that. We got into a long battle over the statistical power issue. They hired another consultant who produced a report confirming that we had sufficient statistical power. However, the longitudinal design that we had was now reduced to a one-wave, one-tailed *t* test. We did not consider that analysis to be adequate to answer the questions posed by the evaluation. Our detailed report rebutted their argument. What I was told was that in the end it came down to a general calling and saying we should go ahead with the evaluation as planned. I suspect that there was awareness of the Congressional interest in this demonstration, and it did not pay to alienate some powerful people in the House of Representatives over this issue. So I concluded the issue was not really statistical power or electrical power but political power!

We didn't have any other major problems with others concerning the evaluation. We kept our interactions with the treatment facility to a minimum. But with the contract business with the Army, almost every year there was a question of whether we would be funded.

Fitzpatrick: Let's come back to the beginning of the study. What prompted it? I know Dr. Lenore Behar, Director of Children's Services in North Carolina's Department of Human Resources, persuaded Congress to fund a study through the Department of the Army to evaluate the "system of care" concept. But whom did you work with in the federal government? What was their interest in the study?

Bickman: The impetus was that there is a movement that stresses such values in service delivery as "culturally fair," "community-based services," and others such as being "strengths based." The child mental health system was basically nonexistent before this movement started. Reforming that system became a major political movement. The system of care model caught everyone's attention as a way to deal with many, if not all, of the ills of mental health services for children and adolescents. Lenore was the driving force to develop a demonstration to test this system of care. She developed the term *continuum of care*, and she wanted to test it to prove it worked. Lenore used all her political influence with some important North Carolina Congresspersons to persuade the Army to fund the demonstration. The Army was reluctant to be involved in such a demonstration, but they do listen to Congressional requests by powerful Congresspersons.

Fitzpatrick: How did you decide to focus on the concept of continuum of care?

Bickman: I did not make a decision on that focus. That's the disadvantage of program evaluation. You're given a program, a focus. But I did push for examining outcomes. Most studies of mental health treatment in the community (as opposed to university laboratories) do not show that they are effective. I think not looking at clinical outcomes for services that are intended to affect those outcomes is poor evaluation practice. I did not know if the continuum of care would affect child and family outcomes, but I did know that was what the program claimed it would accomplish. If you are claiming to do policy-relevant research, you must look at what happens to people. Most contemporary mental health services do not measure outcomes.

The problem for evaluators is that most programs are not well designed. But they are the ones given to evaluators to evaluate. I can give you example after example of programs that are not carefully thought out. We should be teaching logic modeling to everyone who thinks they can design a social or educational program. Maybe then we would have programs that are evaluable. Often the goals of the program are not realistic. We spend more time and money on doing the evaluation than on planning the project. Evaluators need to spend more time on the planning end in helping program people plan programs that make sense.

There are many places where you can get an education in evaluation, but I do not know of many places where you can receive a systematic education on how to develop a program. I think evaluators are trained to find the assumptions underlying a program. I feel there is almost an unconscious conspiracy between providers and policy makers. The public complains about a problem. The policy makers allocate funds to deal with the problem. The providers develop a program to get the money. And then, we get funds to evaluate and find it fails. There's no real change for the people who have to deal with the problem.

Fitzpatrick: In these evaluations, however, you developed a logic model to describe the theory of the program. Do you think using such models helps evaluators "to get underneath it" and to prompt program people to think through their program, or do you mean evaluators should undertake other activities to help in planning?

Bickman: I have no doubt that logic modeling helps both the program and the evaluation. It is a logical approach to examining a program. While it is not a substitute for empirical evaluations, I do not think an evaluation should be attempted until at least a rudimentary logic model is developed.

Fitzpatrick: Coming back to the Ft. Bragg and Start County models, who was involved in helping you develop these models, and how did you go about the development?

Bickman: An article we published in *Evaluation and Program Planning* provides a lot of detail on this issue. (See Bickman, 1996b.). But, in brief, there was not just one model. There was a progression of models. When Lenore goaded me with "Where's our program model?" I said, "We can't have one until I find out what you're doing." It was a group effort. We observed what program developers and managers were doing and what they had written. From that, we developed the first iteration of the model. Then, we would sit down with Lenore and the program people and play that back to them and revise.

Fitzpatrick: How did the program people react to your model?

Bickman: Positively. They loved having a concrete representation of what they were doing. But what's uncomfortable to them is that it lays bare some of their assumptions that they weren't aware of. I consider it critical for every evaluation to develop a model for the program.

Fitzpatrick: I like your model partly because of the level of detail it provides. I see some logic models that have so many boxes and loops that it is impossible to summarize the "logic" of the program. Some of these models simply describe multiple steps of a program and provide little clue to the underlying theory. Other models are too superficial and, hence, fail to provide the evaluator with a framework for effectively measuring critical elements of program implementation. What choices did you and your team struggle with in developing the model?

Bickman: You hit the nail on the head. The idea is to communicate that you're not testing the program; you're testing the theory underlying the program. This approach puts the model at the right level of detail. Educational models are well known for being too detailed with seemingly endless objectives and subobjectives. The key issue a model should convey is "Why should this program work?"

Fitzpatrick: How would you assess the utility of the model now that you have completed the study and had time to reflect? For example, you write that your study did not examine the effectiveness of services delivered or, for example, whether treatment plans improved as a result of the system. Your evaluation focused on the system level and that was the focus of the model. Would you change that today?

Bickman: I foreswore never to do a systems-level evaluation again. To me, it misses the interface between the clients and services. If I knew then what I know now, I would have tried to evaluate the effectiveness of the services as well as the systems.

In addition, I think that evaluations have to change focus from studying only clients to studying providers as well. The difficulty in changing practitioner behavior in services delivery is the major problem with most human services programs. In 1989, I wrote a chapter that we called "Program Personnel: The Missing Ingredient in Describing the Program Environment." We said that we treat programs as if the personnel who deliver them are unimportant since we rarely collect any information about them. I should have paid more attention to what I wrote, since I collected very little information about the clinicians in this study. I'm doing that now. We are doing a study with pediatricians to see how they deliver services for children with ADHD (attention deficit/hyperactivity disorder). The pediatricians are very ambivalent about the study since they are subjects. I think service providers, especially physicians, may consider themselves above the evaluation. However, since programs are usually designed to change practice, we need to know about the barriers and the incentives to practitioner change, especially the ones that will exist once the program is no longer a demonstration.

Fitzpatrick: The first two steps in the Ft. Bragg study were evaluations of the implementation and quality of the continuum of care. You argued for these intensive evaluations of process, citing Peter Rossi and your own writings on the need to be able to determine if program success or failure is due to a faulty or weak implementation of the theory or to the program theory itself. Tell us a bit more about why you thought examining implementation was important.

Bickman: The worst outcome that an evaluator can obtain is finding that the treatment produced no effect and that the project was not implemented. That means you wasted your time. I wanted to know that the program was delivered with fidelity—to know that if the program failed to produce the desired effects, it was because it was a theory failure. [If you know the program was delivered as the theory indicated and, then, find that the desired outcomes are not achieved, you have a "theory failure." You have proved that the program theory does not work. However, if you do not know whether the program was implemented as planned, and you find that the desired outcomes are not achieved, you do not know whether you have really tested the theory and it does not work *or* whether the theory, in fact, was not tested because the program was not delivered as the theory would require.]

Fitzpatrick: I like your distinction between studying program implementation and program quality. Often, those are combined. Why did you decide to separate the two issues?

Bickman: There is a distinction between measuring quality and measuring implementation. I believe outcomes are easy to measure. Implementation is relatively easy to measure. Quality is the hardest element to measure. That's because measuring quality involves making a judgment about worth. When I use the word *quality*, I mean a process related to the desired outcomes. Most human services don't have measures of quality. Even laboratory studies have difficulty getting reliable measures of the quality of treatment. But my guess is that it is the quality of the services that accounts for the variance in program success. How much quality is enough? We have no idea of the levels necessary to produce effects. Evaluators are missing the whole quality bandwagon. We're in some danger of having evaluation taken over by quality managers. I edited a special issue of *Evaluation Review* on quality and mental health in 1997 with the idea of raising evaluators' awareness of the relationship between quality and program evaluation. (See Bickman & Salzer, 1997.)

Fitzpatrick: How did you measure quality in the Ft. Bragg and Stark County evaluations?

Bickman: We looked at the components that we thought were critical— case management and intake. These components were the "glue" that held the program together. On intake, we asked practitioners in the field, "Was the intake conducted centrally helpful? Did it reduce the number of sessions you needed for assessment?" Ultimately, there is no gold standard on treatment plans. To study case management, we had case managers keep logs of their activities, and we analyzed charts, conducted interviews, and reviewed documents. We used a scale that measured program philosophy. We also interviewed parents and did a network analysis. In addition, we developed a "case management evaluation data checklist" that was our measure of quality, based on concept mapping and document reviews. The checklist included such items as parent involvement in treatment planning, client monitoring and follow-up, and linkage and coordination activities. Our evaluation of the quality of case management involved comparing the checklist to the evidence we had collected from multiple sources. Details about this procedure were published in a special issue in *Evaluation and Program Planning* on evaluation methodology and mental health services.

Fitzpatrick: In spite of years of discussion of the need to examine implementation and describe program operations, many evaluators view implementation studies as less prestigious. Similarly, today many organizations and government entities such as schools, private foundations, and the United Way, are very outcome focused and tend to neglect process. Are implementation studies always important? Why do you think evaluators and funding sources sometimes scorn them?

Bickman: I think the bad reaction to implementation is historical. Implementation or input evaluations were the only evaluations conducted by many community agencies. It was rare to find an outcome evaluation in these settings. In addition, we do not have theories of implementation, so it is difficult to study implementation. If implementation studies are not theory based and are just operationally detailed, describing what is happening, implementation studies are boring. However, in a comprehensive evaluation, we need to know how the program was implemented to learn why it was or was not successful. It is clear we need both in a comprehensive evaluation. But it does add expense to the evaluation.

Fitzpatrick: You note that your implementation study *was* theory driven. Can you tell us more about how theory guided this phase of your study?

Bickman: We developed the implementation plan based on the theory of the program. The program theory guided us not only in measurement issues but also in what aspects of the program it was necessary for us to study. It is impossible to adequately study a whole program, so we had to select those aspects of the program that theory identified as critical to the success of the program.

Fitzpatrick: Ultimately, you concluded that the program did successfully implement the model and that the services were of sufficient quality. Yet, judgments are involved in drawing these conclusions. No program is implemented with 100% fidelity to the model. Similarly, no program is consistently delivered with top-level quality. How did you reach your judgments on fidelity of delivery and level of quality?

Bickman: I think you have identified a significant weakness in this area. Given that program developers usually have no theory related to the quality or amount of services necessary to produce an effect, it becomes the evaluator's judgment of when implementation is sufficient. Moreover, our judgment could be biased since it is in our self-interest to declare implementation a success. There is not much to be gained by evaluating a program that was not implemented. I was always aware of this problem, but I was never challenged on this aspect of the evaluation. You try to describe the evidence as best as you can, and then you make a judgment. Is it half-empty or half-full? It is a value judgment. The fact was that the clients had all these extra services—case management, intermediate services, and so on. This is what the program developers planned.

There were some challenges to the results we reported. Some said that the Ft. Bragg program was not sufficiently mature. But the program had almost a year and a half of start-up time before we started to collect baseline data. Also, if maturity was an issue, we should have seen improvement in the program outcomes over the three years we collected data. Instead, we did not see any improvement in effectiveness over time.

Fitzpatrick: But did the clients get quality case management? Did they get the services case management recommended?

Bickman: The case managers felt they were doing their job, but the amount of contact with clients was amazingly low. I think this is true of most case management. However, we had claims data to show they got the services that one was supposed to get in a continuum of care. What we could not tell, and I do not believe that it is even possible now, is whether the clinical services were of sufficient quality.

Fitzpatrick: Let me address one specific issue on fidelity and quality. Your studies were evaluations of the system of a continuum of care. But one element of that care is therapy, and since the thrust of the continuum is mental health— your outcome measures focus on changes in psychopathology—one would assume therapy would play an important role. But, in fact, relatively few children in the Stark County study received therapy. By parent report, only 14% of children in the Stark County system of care group received individual counseling during the first six months, and the proportion shrunk to half that in the second six months. Is that amount of therapy sufficiently intense to match the model?

Bickman: The label *counseling* is only one category of therapy. The services they delivered included clinical case management and intensive home-based services. That is where most of the therapy was supposed to be delivered.

Fitzpatrick: Do you find that some audiences misinterpret the results to mean that therapy is not effective?

Bickman: You cannot determine the effectiveness of therapy directly from this study. However, one of my explanations for why the system was not more effective was that the treatment wasn't effective. However, in order to support this explanation, we analyzed other aspects of the data. If the treatments were effective, we would expect there to be a dose-response relationship. That is, the more treatment received, the better the client should be. We examined the dose response in both the Ft. Bragg and Stark County study in several ways, and the conclusion was always the same. The amount of treatment did not matter. Clients who received more treatment did not have more positive outcomes.

Moreover, the reviews of other community-based treatments (i.e., not laboratory studies of therapy) concluded that these treatments show no effect. From these studies, I concluded there was not evidence that treatment in the real world was effective for children and adolescents. Notice that I did not say that therapy was ineffective, just that we did not have evidence to support its effectiveness. But the issue of effectiveness begs the question "What is treatment?" It is whatever clinicians do. Let me tell you how we describe most of these services. They are in-home services, day treatment, hospitalization, private office visits, and so on. Would you buy a car if I just told you where it was located? We're describing services by location. We're assuming that they are different because they occur in different settings, but that is an assumption.

But I do worry that what I am saying demoralizes clinicians. Is there anything beneficial about me saying all this? Clinicians are working in a very difficult, emotional area. They do not work in this area for the big money. We also suspect that to be a good clinician, you have to believe in your efficacy. I don't know whether my criticism is constructive for these people. But I strongly believe in what I am doing and that our first concern is to help identify effective services for these children. If the services are not effective, then it is the evaluator's responsibility to say so.

Fitzpatrick: Your outcome studies, of course, have probably received the most attention. In both the Ft. Bragg evaluation and the Stark County evaluation, you found that receiving a continuum of care made no difference in children's symptoms or functioning. Of course, when no difference is found, critics attempt to identify problems in data collection or the design that may have resulted in a failure to identify real changes, a Type II error. A major strength of your design and methods was its resilience in dealing with such criticisms. You collected extensive data on many different constructs from many different sources. You conducted power analyses and subgroup analyses to test various hypotheses and explore extensively for possible effects. For example, you examine whether the continuum of care was more effective for children with different demographics and different diagnoses. You also explore whether differences exist between children who actually received treatment. Tell us a bit about how you planned your design and analyses. Did you identify all possible analyses in the design phase? Do you think it is better to explore the data thoroughly after they are collected to consider subgroup tests and the like? Did you seek input from others on exploratory analyses?

Bickman: There are certain main analyses that we had planned. We also had to learn how to deal with the thousands of variables. We identified 10 key outcome variables; two of them were individualized and represented that child's progress in his or her specific problem area. We did some subgroup analyses, but we didn't have a theory about who should benefit most from the continuum, so we didn't go on fishing expeditions. I am concerned that such analyses creep into our literature and result in the inconsistent results we often see. I think it is important for investigators to report on all the analyses they conducted and explain when they have a large amount of data collected but only a few results reported. I assume they did a lot of other tests that were not significant and that they are primarily reporting only the significant ones. I consider that kind of publishing as biased. Not only does it exploit chance, but it also is not driven by any theory or concept of the program.

Fitzpatrick: While your study is too extensive for me to ask every question I would like, let us explore a few issues. As I mentioned above, you tested for differences in children not simply based on which group they were in but on whether, in fact, they actually received treatment or not. What treatment variables did you examine when comparing outcomes for children receiving treatment with those who did not? For those who did receive treatment, what were the typical treatments, and how much did they receive?

Bickman: We analyzed treatment by amount, such as sessions or days or dollar amount, and what we called negligible treatment, such as only one or two outpatient visits. But all the treatment measures are correlated. A session is a session is a session. We have published several studies on patterns of treatment and improvement as well as dose response based on these studies. A major weakness of our approach was that we had no measure of the *quality* of the treatment and how it varied. In a recent study, we had children tell what they did during treatment. We had nothing like that in these earlier studies. I was not aware that quality was such an important issue until Ft. Bragg.

Fitzpatrick: Your study at both sites used many different measures. Sources included the children themselves and primary caregivers, generally parents. The Ft. Bragg study also collected data from the mental health provider and teachers. Baseline interviews were conducted in the home, but other data collection methods included computer-assisted telephone interviews and mailed questionnaires. Your measures generally focused on the constructs of psychopathology and family functioning and were standardized measures used in mental health research. Your large sample sizes at both sites gave you sufficient power to preclude a Type II error but would have made the cost of collecting qualitative data from all families prohibitive. What issues did you struggle with in making choices about constructs, sources, and methods in data collection?

Bickman: Well, we had no choice in the design. That was given to us. We did have a lot of choices in instrument collection. This was a whole new area for me. We did a lot of research on existing measures. We selected what we thought were the best in the field. We found out that some of the best really were not too good.

Fitzpatrick: Why do you lean more toward existing measures?

Bickman: Because I know what it takes to develop new measures. However, we did have to develop a measure of functioning because none existed at that time. Since then we have developed a whole new system of measurement that better fits the real-world environment than some of the research instruments we used.

Fitzpatrick: Another major strength of these evaluations was your selection of a second site, Stark County, to see if the results would be replicated with a different population and system of care. Researchers and evaluators rarely replicate their own work so systematically, nor do they take such care to select a site whose characteristics strengthen the external validity of the findings. Stark County's clients were nonmilitary, lower-income, publicly funded youth. The system of care was a full, mature system more typical of systems of reform in many communities than the demonstration in Ft. Bragg. So the Stark County results, which did replicate those of Ft. Bragg, added greatly to the external validity of your results. However, replicating a study brings the opportunity for some change as well, though, of course, too much change can threaten the replication. What changes did you consider in planning the design and data collection in Stark County?

Bickman: Basically, we changed what we had been criticized for not doing in Ft. Bragg. The Stark County study was all NIMH funding. They had turned me down twice for this study. The first study included seven cities that were in the Robert Wood Johnson Foundation study of systems of care demonstration. This evaluation did not plan to collect child outcomes, and I thought it was a natural to try to work with them and build in an outcome design and outcome measures. The reviewers said it was ridiculous to study seven cities. So we resubmitted it with one. Then, that city withdrew a month before the study was to start. I called NIMH and they said, "Go find a site." So I picked one that would meet my need for a random assignment design. I also picked a site that was proud of their program and was nationally recognized as a leader in the field.

Fitzpatrick: While your external validity is greater than most evaluations because of your use of two contrasting sites, what limitations do you see in generalizing the results from these two sites? Would you say you had pretty good external validity?

Bickman: The way the ideologically committed critics dealt with the results and the methodology of the study was to say, "We think you did an excellent evaluation, but we don't do that program anymore." That happened with DARE (Drug Abuse Resistance Education). Evaluations found that DARE did not decrease alcohol and drug abuse, so the DARE people argued that the evaluations of the earlier program were irrelevant because the program had changed.

I am not as concerned about external validity as I am with construct validity. I'm not really testing the Ft. Bragg demonstration. I'm testing the concept of a continuum of care. That is why the implementation analysis is so important. It helps me decide if the program is a good representation of the construct. I did not see the generalizability limited by the population of children served or the region of the country. What I was looking for were excellent examples of the theory represented by these projects. If we could not obtain the hoped for outcomes with these excellent and well-funded sites, then it was unlikely that sites with fewer resources would be successful.

Fitzpatrick: Your ultimate interpretation of your results concerns the quality of care delivered. That is, you suggest that rather than focusing on system-level issues, which may be too removed from patients to impact outcomes, policy makers should focus on improving the training of treatment providers and, ultimately, improving the quality of services delivered. How did you reach that conclusion since your study did not directly address the quality of services provided?

Bickman: There were only a few alternative explanations for the results we obtained. First, was the evaluation critically flawed? No one has been able to demonstrate that we did a flawed evaluation. Second, was the demonstration well implemented? We presented evidence that implementation was fine. If the evaluation was good and the program was well implemented, then what do we have left? The theory underlying the continuum model is wrong. There are several factors within the theory that could be wrong. For example, the theory assumes that clinicians are able to assess children's needs and match them to the appropriate services. We showed in a separate study that this did not seem likely. But the key theoretical assumption was that the services were effective. Our dose-response studies, plus the meta-analyses of children's therapy delivered in the community, convinced me that we had to take a better look at the quality of treatment. This conclusion has led me to three areas for my future work in this area.

First, we need to be able to measure outcomes in the real world. My colleague Ann Doucette and I have developed a new measurement system that we believe will allow community service providers to learn what is effective.

Second, we need to look at the process of care to determine which mediators are important in affecting outcomes. We have seen that therapeutic alliance, the relationships between the provider and the client, can be very important. Third, I have started some studies that examine how to change practitioner behavior, so that when we *do* have something that is effective, it can be adopted in the community.

Fitzpatrick: Have your evaluations brought about the changes you desired? In particular, have they helped to change the focus from system-level variables to the effectiveness of the treatment itself?

Bickman: Yes and no. Critics are now talking differently. They are saying we need to consider treatment and services as well as the system. It is not a brilliant insight, but it is a big change. On the other hand, the Center for Mental Health Services is still funding projects like Ft. Bragg to the tune of $80 million a year. To be a good evaluator, you need to be skeptical. I characterize myself as a skeptical optimist, even when it comes to my own work. My skepticism helps me to be a good evaluator, and my optimism motivates me to stay in this field. However, providers should also maintain some degree of skepticism about what they do. I think the continuous-quality-improvement approach has a lot of appeal, but if the providers are sure that they are already delivering the best services, there is no need for continuous data collection or evaluation.

Fitzpatrick: Your results have implications for so many different organizations and systems: any system using a continuum of care or emphasizing a full system of care; schools, and licensing organizations that educate, train, and oversee therapists of different types; managers and supervisors in practice settings; managed care; researchers; and others. Who do you see as your primary audiences? How do you attempt to reach them?

Bickman: I have a lot of audiences—basic researchers in psychopathology, clinicians, and policy people. I've tried reaching them through writing. I don't know how else to do it. Some people read. Other people hear about these studies from others. My latest contract is with a state that is under court order to provide better mental health services for their children. They have been at it for about seven years and have spent about a billion dollars. They just contacted me because they read in their newspapers about the studies I did, because of a legal problem someone associated with the Ft. Bragg study is having. I offered them an alternative way to deal with their problem. However, being the skeptical evaluator, I didn't promise any quick solution or even lots of confidence that what I am proposing will work. I tell them that whatever they do, they should also do an evaluation.

Fitzpatrick: In speaking to mental health researchers, you note the need for them to do more testing in real-world environments so that the changes made in the field can be more readily research based. You call for their help in developing research-validated practice standards. Do you think your studies and the attention they have received have prompted some change in the norms and practice of these researchers?

Bickman: It has already changed radically in mental health funding. NIMH is promoting building bridges with the clinical world very hard. They are seeing more clearly that their responsibility is to improve the mental health of children and that this was not occurring through just the publication of research. Getting into the real world is now a priority. I would like to think that our work helped push that along.

Fitzpatrick: Finally, I like to close with asking the exemplars I interview what they have learned from the evaluation they have done. What might you do differently if you were beginning on these evaluations today?

Bickman: There are things that I would have done, but I did not have the power to do it then. I would have liked to collect data more frequently, not every six months but at least monthly. I would have liked to have more information on the quality of treatment. I'm doing that now.

I think about why I do evaluations. I used to tell students that it was purely hedonistic. I enjoyed it. But that has changed. I think we *can* help kids get better through our work. Often evaluators don't get that opportunity. I feel grateful that I had the opportunity to continue to work in the same field for over a decade. I am hoping that our work here can improve outcomes for children who have mental health problems.

Fitzpatrick's Commentary

Bickman's evaluations of the Ft. Bragg and Stark County systems of care for children have received many well-deserved accolades in the communities of evaluation and mental health. Bickman and others have written in more detail about the measures, design, and results of these evaluations in other venues. (See References.) For this interview, I focused my questions to help us learn more about the challenges that Bickman and his colleagues faced in planning and implementing these evaluations and his reflections on the evaluations.

As in each interview I have conducted, we learn much about the exemplar's approach to evaluation by the choices they make. Bickman's studies are summative. The audience is broad: policy makers and thinkers in the field of children's mental health. His purpose is not formative; his audience is not program managers or staff. And, as such, he need not involve them intensively as users, though he certainly involves them in the development of the logic model. In such evaluations, the distinction between program evaluation and policy analysis is somewhat blurred, but we needn't quibble over terms. Instead, we should simply note the different focus.

Bickman's methods come from the quantitative tradition, but they match the purposes of the study. To clearly establish outcomes for summative decisions, they needed large samples, experimental and quasi-experimental designs, and multiple measures from different sources. But as I note below, he also takes a useful focus on process, examining implementation and quality to enhance his interpretation of outcomes. He selects measures primarily from the research literature, but having learned the strengths and weaknesses of these, he has now moved on to developing measures for use by community practitioners. Though research based, his goals concern learning about what is actually going on in practice and include a genuine commitment to improving mental health services in the field. These evaluations and his integrity and ability in research and evaluation have permitted him to argue effectively for major changes in the way people study children's mental health. As such, his work and writings make a bridge between research and evaluation.

While probably all audiences saw the purpose as summative, Bickman successfully argued that studies of children's mental health must, of course, examine the outcomes on children and their families rather than the process and cost measures originally considered by the funder. This adjustment of focus, in and of itself, is a commendable outcome of his evaluation. But he does not neglect process. As he advocates in his writing, he makes use of logic models to define program theory and identify critical elements of the process to monitor. He then attempts to measure not just the implementation of critical program elements but the quality of those elements as well. The delineation of implementation and quality is an important element because quality is often neglected in process studies. Yet, as Bickman argues, in all likelihood, quality is the most important element in ensuring successful outcomes.

In addition to the many oft-cited qualities of Bickman's work on these evaluations, one of the elements I admired most was his conscious effort to build and learn from previous evaluations and to, then, take the next step in his subsequent studies in order to learn how to improve mental health outcomes for children. This effort is seen in his selection of Stark County for the replication and in his current work. Having focused on system-level variables in the Ft. Bragg and Stark County evaluations and found no effect, he begins to consider what other elements could or must have an effect to bring about change. In current studies, he is examining providers' behavior and becoming curious about the incentives and barriers to changing their behaviors. Having used primarily existing research measures for the Ft. Bragg and Stark County evaluations, Bickman is now developing new measures that can be used by community service providers to provide more effective, practical, and immediate feedback on outcomes. In other words, he doesn't just find problems, he goes on to explore solutions.

Bickman correctly notes that we evaluators must evaluate the programs we are given. But his frustration with ill-conceived programs compels him to argue for expanding evaluators' roles in planning. Like Reichardt (1994), Patton (1997), Preskill and Torres (1999), and others, Bickman sees that our future may be at the beginning of programs rather than the end.

DISCUSSION QUESTIONS

1. Is Bickman assessing the merit and worth of the system of care? How does he do so? What are the strengths and weaknesses of his methodological choices?

2. Bickman's evaluation randomly assigns children and adolescents to different levels of mental health treatment. The developers of the system of care believe that it will result in better mental health services to children. Is it ethical for him to randomly assign children to a treatment that is not thought to be the best (the old treatment)? Why or why not?

3. Bickman argues with the Army over what to measure, the size of the sample, and other methodological issues. Shouldn't he be respecting stakeholder wishes on these issues rather than arguing for his own preferences? What would you do?

4. Would you characterize Bickman's study as participatory? Why or why not? Do you agree with the choices he made regarding the level and depth of stakeholder participation desired for the study? Why or why not?

5. Bickman argues that many programs are poorly designed. To remedy that problem, he says, program managers and staff and others who develop programs need more skills in developing logic models. He also indicates that evaluators should become more involved in program development because they have those skills and can help uncover the underlying assumptions of a program. Think about a program that you know well. Is it well designed? What is its logic model? Can you think of a program or policy that failed because its logic model was not carefully thought through?

Do you think evaluators should be involved more heavily at the stage of program development? What should be their role? What expertise do they bring to the process? What expertise or other attributes do they lack?

6. How does Bickman disseminate his results? Contrast his dissemination process with Riccio's dissemination. How do they differ? Are there elements about the context of each of their evaluations that make their different choices in dissemination appropriate? Or would you have had one of them use more of the ideas of the other in disseminating results? Why or why not?

7. Bickman believes that it is advantageous for evaluators and program providers to be skeptical. He describes himself as a skeptical optimist. To what extent are you a skeptic? Do you agree that evaluators need to be skeptics? Why or why not? Should program providers be skeptics? Why or why not?

FURTHER READING

An article to read that summarizes the results of the evaluation: Bickman, L. (1996a). A continuum of care: More is not always better. *American Psychologist, 51*, 689–701.

Bickman, L. (1996b). The application of program theory to a managed mental health care evaluation. *Evaluation and Program Planning, 19*(2), 111–119.

Bickman, L. (1997). Resolving issues raised by the Ft. Bragg findings: New directions for mental health services research. *American Psychologist, 52*, 562–565.

Bickman, L. (2000). Improving children's mental health: How no effects can affect policy. *Emotional & Behavioral Disorders in Youth, 3*, 21–23.

Bickman, L., & Salzer, M. S. (1997). Measuring quality in mental health services. *Evaluation Review, 21*(3), 285–291.

REFERENCES

Bickman, L. (2002). The death of treatment as usual: An excellent first step on a long road. *Clinical Psychology: Science and Practice, 9*(2), 195–199.

Bickman, L., Noser, K., & Summerfelt, W. T. (1999). Long-term effects of a system of care on children and adolescents. *Journal of Behavioral Health Services & Research, 26,* 185–202.

Bickman, L., Sumerfelt, W. T., & Noser, K. (1997). Comparative outcomes of emotionally disturbed children and adolescents in a system of services and usual care. *Psychiatric Services, 48,* 1543–1548.

Bryant, D., & Bickman, L. (1996). Methodology for evaluating mental health case management. *Evaluation and Program Planning, 19,* 121–129.

Patton, M. Q. (1997). *Utilization-focused evaluation: The new century text.* Thousand Oaks, CA: Sage.

Preskill, H., & Torres, R. T. (1999). *Evaluative inquiry for learning in organizations.* Thousand Oaks, CA: Sage.

Reichardt, C. S. (1994). Summative evaluation, formative evaluation, and tactical research. *Evaluation Practice, 15,* 275–282.

EVALUATIONS WITH A FOCUS ON DESCRIPTION

—•◆•—

Part of the history of program evaluation emerges not from traditional, causal, social science research methods but from descriptive research in anthropology, sociology, education, and political science. The important questions of many stakeholders are concerned with description. Evaluations may be undertaken to describe potential or current students or clients and their characteristics and needs: What proportion of our students are not native English speakers? How many of the patients coming to our health clinic have health insurance? What are the common health problems they present? How do the young spouses of soldiers sent to war cope with child care, family finances, and the stress of being a single parent? Other evaluations are under-taken to describe program activities or actions of program staff: What proportion of class time is used for reading in Harris Elementary School's second-grade classrooms? How is that time used (silent reading, group reading, discussion of reading)? How do our health care providers communicate with patients? What activities do teens and their mentors pursue? Finally, evaluations can focus on *describing* different levels of program outcomes: Do adults complet-ing our diabetes education program maintain an exercise routine and take the appropriate medication? Do students in our remedial reading program increase their reading ability? Do restrictions on wood fires result in less pollution? All these are important descriptive questions to managers or policy makers in different areas.

In this section, we will examine three evaluations that focus on descrip-tive activities. In contrast to the previous section where evaluations focused on determining the merit or worth of a program, this section does not focus on a particular *purpose* for the evaluation. In fact, each of the evaluations described here contribute to decisions concerning the merit or worth of something. But that is not why they are grouped together. Instead, they are grouped together because they illustrate different approaches and reasons for description in eval-uation. In one case, the evaluation team becomes immersed in the program, experiencing it along with the participants, to understand the program and to judge its quality. In another case, as the program begins, the evaluator recog-nizes that little is known about the clients to be served—homeless families, and the initial activities of the evaluation focus on learning more about these families, their characteristics, their needs, and the services they receive. The final evaluation focuses on developing a report card to describe schools across the state on factors important to student success and learning.

The scope and context in which each of these evaluators works are quite different. As such, the interviews illustrate the important role descriptions can play in evaluation in different settings. But the reader will also see the com-monalities. Each evaluator is adapting his or her evaluation to the context of the program and the needs of the stakeholders whom he or she sees as an important audience for the evaluation.

In the first interview, we find David Fetterman, well-known for empow-erment evaluation, using a different approach. He sees the setting for the evaluation and the needs of the primary stakeholder as inappropriate for empowerment evaluation. Instead, he uses some elements of the empowerment approach to learn about the Stanford Teacher Education Program (STEP) that he is evaluating and to judge its quality, but his emphasis is not on empowering a stakeholder group. His in-depth immersion into the program, grounded in studies of other teacher education programs, provides a rich description of the program and results in an evaluation that, while permitting the primary stakeholder to judge the merit of the program, also leads to recommendations for change and improvement. In addition, his interview highlights some of the risks in the role of an internal evaluator, evaluating a program in one's own work setting.

The second interview, with Debra Rog, concerns a large, multi-year evaluation of a program for homeless families in nine cities across the United States. Description is a key part of this evaluation at many stages. On learning that little is known about homeless families, Rog chooses to focus the initial work in the evaluation on describing these families as she works in a needs assessment role. As the program is implemented, Rog works to collect data both on the characteristics of families as well as program delivery. Finally, Rog collects descriptive data on program outcomes which, due to the nature of the data, are very helpful in judging program successes and failures, in spite of the absence of an experimental or quasi-experimental design. Rog vividly describes some of her work with program staff to gain their credibility *and* to gather more valid data.

The final interview, with Gary Henry, does not concern a traditional evaluation. In fact, one might argue that he is not really evaluating a program. Instead, he is developing a "report card" for schools that will allow citizens and parents, teachers and principals, to judge the performance of their school and compare it with others. (Henry's task is comparable to the work described by Hallie Preskill in Chapter 9. Although Henry and Preskill differ in their approach, each are developing an evaluation system rather than evaluating a program.) Henry describes his work in determining the factors to include on the report cards and in identifying a format to convey the information to others in a way that is easily understood and yet permits appropriate comparisons. His work includes reviews of research on factors affecting learning, surveys of citizens concerning their perceptions and information needs, reviews of available data in schools and from other sources, and work with stakeholder groups to identify factors and develop formats for the report card. As Henry notes, the report cards focus on describing immediate outcomes rather than describing the actions and nature of the program. Henry concludes his interview with a reflection on his own learning and adaptation in this project to understand the importance of description.

As you read these interviews consider the following questions:

- What do these evaluators seek to describe?
- How does their descriptive work fit into their overall evaluation plan? How does it inform their stakeholders?
- What types of methods do they use for description? What other methods might you consider?

Each of these interviews is also informative about other aspects of evaluation. With each, consider the following:

- What is the purpose of their evaluation? To what extent does it concern determining merit and worth? To what extent are they concerned with organizational development and learning and with program improvement?

- Who are their significant stakeholders, and how do they involve them in the evaluation? Do their evaluations prompt them to consider their cultural competence in working with different stakeholders or understanding the program itself?

- How do these evaluators differ in the role(s) they choose in planning, conducting, and disseminating the results of the evaluation?

- How do they differ in their methods of data collection and their approach to dissemination?

- What different types of use do you see emerging in these evaluations?

- What do you see as the strengths and weaknesses of each evaluation? How might you conduct it differently?

FIVE

THE EVALUATION OF THE STANFORD TEACHER EDUCATION PROGRAM (STEP)

An Interview With David Fetterman

———◆———

*I*ntroduction: David Fetterman was a member of the faculty of the School of Education and Director of the MA Policy Analysis and Evaluation Program at Stanford University at the time he conducted this evaluation. He is currently Director of Evaluation in the Division of Evaluation in the School of Medicine at Stanford University. He is the past president of the American Evaluation Association. Fetterman has received the highest honors from the association, including the Lasersfeld Award for evaluation theory and the Myrdal Award for evaluation practice. Fetterman has been a major contributor to ethnographic evaluation and is the founder of empowerment evaluation. He has published 10 books and more than 100 articles, chapters, and reports, including contributions to various encyclopedias. His most recent books include *Empowerment Evaluation Principles in Practice* and *Ethnography: Step by Step*. He is President of Fetterman & Associates, an international consulting firm, conducting work in Australia, Brazil, Finland, Japan, Mexico, Nepal, New Zealand, Spain, the United Kingdom, and the United States.

This interview concerns Fetterman's complex, three-year evaluation of the Stanford Teacher Education Program (STEP). In this evaluation, Fetterman chose to use an approach other than his well-known empowerment approach. He describes the reasons for his choice, which provides guidance as to the conditions necessary to use an empowerment approach. As a member of the Stanford University education faculty, though not a member of STEP, Fetterman served in a partially internal evaluator role and discusses some of the problems he encountered in that role. He describes the methods he used, including intensive immersion, surveys, interviews, reviews of literature, and discussions with experts in other teacher education programs, to judge the quality of delivery of STEP and some of the conclusions he reached.

Summary of the STEP Evaluation

David Fetterman

———··———

The president of Stanford University, Gerhard Casper, requested an evaluation of the Stanford Teacher Education Program (STEP). The first phase of the evaluation was formative, designed to provide information that might be used to refine and improve the program. It concluded at the end of the 1997–1998 academic year. Findings and recommendations from this phase of the evaluation were reported in various forms, including a formal summer school evaluation report (Fetterman, Dunlap, Greenfield, & Yoo, 1997), more than 30 memoranda, and various informal exchanges and discussions.

The second stage of this evaluation was summative in nature, providing an overall assessment of the program (Fetterman, Connors, Dunlap, Brower, Matos, & Paik, 1999). The final report highlights program evaluation findings and recommendations, focusing on the following topics and issues: unity of purpose or mission, curriculum, research, alumni contact, professional development schools/university school partnerships, faculty involvement, excellence in teaching, and length of the program. Specific program components also were highlighted in the year-long program evaluation report, including admissions, placement, supervision, and portfolios. (See the STEP Web site for copies of all evaluation reports: www.stanford.edu/davidf/step.html.)

The Methodology

The evaluation relied on traditional educational evaluation steps and techniques, including a needs assessment; a plan of action; data collection (interviews, observations, and surveys); data analysis; and reporting findings and recommendations. Data collection involved a review of curricular, accreditation, and financial records, as well as interviews with faculty and students, and observations of classroom activity. Informal interviews were conducted with every student in the program. Focus groups were conducted with students each quarter and with alumni from the classes of '95, '96, and '97. More than 20 faculty interviews were conducted. Survey response rates were typically high (90%–100%) for master teachers, current STEP students, and alumni. Data collection also relied on the use of a variety of technological tools, including digital photography of classroom activity, Web surveys, and evaluation team videoconferencing on the Internet. Data analysis was facilitated by weekly evaluation team meetings and frequent database sorts. Formal and informal reports were provided in the spirit of formative evaluation. Responses to preliminary evaluation findings and recommendations were used as additional data concerning program operations. (A detailed description of the methodology is presented in Fetterman, Connors, Dunlap, Brower, & Matos, 1998.)

Brief Description of STEP

STEP is a 12-month teacher education program in the Stanford University School of Education, offering both a master's degree and a secondary school teaching credential. Subject area specializations include English, languages, mathematics, sciences, and social studies. The program also offers a Cross-Cultural, Language, and Academic Development (CLAD) emphasis for students who plan to teach second-language learners. The 1997–1998 class enrollment was 58 students. Tuition and board were approximately $30,000.

The program introduces students to teaching experiences under the guidance of a master teacher during the summer quarter. Students enter the academic year with a nine-month teaching placement, which begins in the fall quarter under the supervision of a cooperating teacher and field supervisor. Students also are required to take the School of Education master's degree and state-required course work throughout the year.

The program administration includes a faculty sponsor, director, placement coordinator, student services coordinator, lead supervisor, field supervisors, and a program assistant. In addition, the program has a summer school coordinator/liaison and part-time undergraduate and doctoral students.

Findings, Recommendations, and Impact

The most significant finding was that the STEP program had some of the ingredients to be a first-rate teacher education program, ranging from a world-renowned faculty to exceptional students. At the time of the evaluation, the program and faculty had a unique opportunity to raise the standard of excellence in the program and the field.

The evaluation identified some noteworthy qualities of STEP. These included high-caliber faculty and students, supportive and critical supervision, the year-long student teaching experience, a culminating portfolio conference, and strong support from alumni. Nevertheless, problem areas were identified. Key among these was the lack of a unifying purpose to shape the program. Related to the absence of a clear vision for the program was the fact that faculty designed their courses in isolation from each other and the central activities of STEP, leading to a fragmented curriculum and a lack of connection between educational theory and practice. Instructional quality was occasionally a problem, particularly as students expect to have faculty they can view as models for exemplary teaching. Students also received no systematic research training to help them develop an inquiry-based approach to teaching. Finally, the program may need to be lengthened to accomplish all that is desired.

Final recommendations included developing a mission statement focusing on reflective practice; instituting faculty meetings and retreats to design, revise, and coordinate curriculum and course content; reducing fragmentation in the curriculum and developing a rationale for course sequencing, including more content on classroom practice to balance educational theory; developing a research training program; forging school-university partnerships; and adopting a commitment to excellence in teaching. The findings and recommendations made in this evaluation went beyond tinkering at the fringes of the program. Many recommendations represented significant and fundamental changes in the program.

The use of the evaluation was gratifying. More than 90% of the recommendations were adopted, ranging from small-scale curricular adaptations to large-scale programmatic redefinitions. The success of this evaluation helped launch the development of an undergraduate teacher education program as well. In addition to the impact the evaluation had at Stanford, the teacher education evaluation set a standard for teacher education programs nationally and internationally. The report was used and referenced almost immediately and served as the catalyst for changes in programs throughout the world.

Dialogue With David Fetterman

Jody Fitzpatrick

Fitzpatrick: David, you're known for your development of the empowerment evaluation approach, yet you chose not to use this model for the evaluation of STEP. Tell us a little bit about *why* you took a different approach here.

Fetterman: Well, there's a rational basis for my decision, but it also was informed by personal judgment and experience. The rational part of my decision was very simple: The president of Stanford requested the evaluation. His request was more like the traditional accountability focus of evaluation. There are multiple purposes for evaluation: development, accountability, knowledge. Empowerment falls more into the development purpose rather than into traditional accountability. If I truly believe that, that means I must abide by those distinctions and use the traditional approach when it is more appropriate. A lot of people think I do only empowerment, but I've done traditional evaluation for 20 years. These different approaches inform each other. The choice depends on the situation you're in. I think most evaluators believe that. You can't just be a purist or dogmatic about your approach.

Then, there's the trickier level beyond all that—the personal judgment part. For empowerment evaluation to work, I have to have a sense that there is both group cohesion and trust. Often, one has to make a guess about these traits at a very early phase in the study before you know as much as you'd like to about the context. But, at the early stage of this study, I didn't sense enough group cohesion and trust to proceed with an empowerment approach.

Now let me say, there were parts of the study where I used the empowerment approach, though 99% of it was traditional. I used a matrix tool and interviewed a lot of students to get their ideas about what was the most important part of the program to help us in planning the evaluation. That's not empowerment, but it is applying some of the concepts and techniques.

But the main reasons for not using empowerment were the chain of command—the president asked for the study—and my judgment of the nature of the place—whether the place has enough trust to do empowerment work.

There is a rational process that plays a clear, dominant part in one's choices, but then there's an important intuitive part. We have to admit it. As we get a little more seasoned in doing evaluations, our choices don't always emerge from a logical flow. Personal judgment is involved as well. The important thing is to make these judgments explicit and to link them to the rational. You triangulate to see if there's enough substance to the intuitive. You're just as critical about the intuitive as the rational.

Fitzpatrick: You describe the model you used as a traditional educational evaluation. Tell us a bit about the approach. Would you consider it theory based, decision oriented, goal-free, . . . ?

Fetterman: We began by trying to understand what the model for STEP was—what insiders said it was *supposed to do.* Then, we wanted to look at what kind of compliance there was with the model, but from a consumer perspective. That is, we came up with the basic program theory and then looked at it to see if the action linked up with the plan. It was a mature program and we wanted to look at what it was doing—how it was operating. If it were a new program, we would have used different criteria, but it had been around a while. We also were decision oriented and objectives oriented.

The directive from the president and provost was absolutely clear: This was a Stanford program. They wanted to know if it met that criterion. Was it up to Stanford standards? The president had been the provost at the University of Chicago when they eliminated the School of Education, so the stakes were perceived as extremely high. Many egos were at stake. That's why it was such an intense evaluation.

Fitzpatrick: It must have been an interesting process for you to use a different approach. I think we always learn from trying something new. What did you learn about evaluation from conducting this study?

Fetterman: The approach wasn't new for me because I've always done traditional evaluations along with participatory and ethnographic, but you always learn something new when you do any evaluation. I learned some things that were kind of scary and interesting methodologically. The complexity of the context was astounding. Even when you've known the organization for years, you learn new things about the context in an evaluation, sometimes things that you don't necessarily want to know! I was interviewing one colleague when suddenly, in the middle of the interview, the guy was almost in tears about being pushed away from teaching in the program. He was so hurt and shaken by that, and it had happened 20 years ago! He had been carrying that around all that time. Many faculty members had been hurt by their association with this program. This was not an isolated incident. These feelings explained the landmines we encountered later. It helped explain why some of the responses to the evaluation were so strong.

One of the interesting methodological surprises we encountered was almost a Lake Wobegon effect on students' course evaluations. When you looked at just the survey results, all the faculty got a 3 or above on a 5-point scale in which 1 is *poor*, 3 is *satisfactory*, and 5 is *excellent*, but when you actually observed the classes and interviewed students, the variability in the assessments of teaching quality went from 0 to absolutely stellar. The surveys didn't capture anything below the satisfactory level and had a ceiling effect on the top performers. That was scary because most evaluations rely so much on surveys. If you don't supplement these, you can have a really false perception of the quality of teaching in the program. When you interviewed and observed classes, you saw the full spectrum of instructional quality. The continuum of high-, medium-, and low-quality teaching was almost a normal, bell-shaped curve, but this didn't come out in the surveys at all.

Fitzpatrick: Let's come back to a discussion of your use of this model for a minute. Then, I'd like to return to some of the issues you just mentioned. You noted that group cohesion and trust are two important prerequisites for successful use of the empowerment model that were not present in this situation. What other things did you learn from this evaluation about when the empowerment model might be appropriate and when it might not?

Fetterman: The bottom line is "What's the purpose of the evaluation?" If it is for developing and improving the program, then empowerment and participatory approaches are most useful. Traditional approaches *can* help, but they are less likely to. In those contexts where the focus is more strictly on accountability, more traditional modes are useful. Where the purpose is primarily for knowledge development, meta-analysis and other methods are useful, though meta-analysis can be problematic because it's so hard to meet the assumptions. But the first question is "What's the purpose?" The answer to that question helps determine which way to go. Another level to consider is "What do the stakeholders want?" Maybe what they want is strict external accountability. I'm conducting a project right now that is primarily an empowerment evaluation; however, the stakeholder also has a second purpose—external accountability. There are some areas where I have used empowerment very effectively when the focus is external accountability. So these distinctions, although quite useful, periodically break down in practice. I do not think contrasting approaches like traditional evaluation and empowerment evaluation are mutually exclusive. I would want my bank to use empowerment methods to ask me what hours they should have, what services they should offer, and the like. On the other hand, I want to know where the money is, too. For that, I want an external audit.

A final, but important, issue is whether the organization is conducive to empowerment. You can do empowerment in places that are extremely receptive to it and understand the spirit of it, and also in places that are not conducive but want to be open and receptive to the approach. I have gotten a lot more done in empowerment evaluations when people are receptive to it than when they're not. When the place is authoritarian and dictatorial, they may need empowerment more, even though they're less receptive. But I don't devote most of my time to those places because life is short, and the process is too slow in that environment. When I first started with empowerment, I spent time in every domain (both highly receptive and moderately receptive environments) to see how it worked, but then after a time, you want to work in the places where it will move, to work with people who will help refine it.

Fitzpatrick: Tell me more about the need for group cohesion and trust. That could be a tough standard for many organizations to meet.

Fetterman: There doesn't have to be perfect or complete group cohesion. I did an empowerment evaluation recently with a group that, by their own self-assessment, hated each other. It ended up being one of the best things I've ever done. They ended up realizing that they had so much more in common than they would have guessed at the onset of the process. The process helped them see what they cared about and what they didn't care about. At the end of the first workshop, they were already telling me how much they had in common. They had not recognized how cohesive their group really was already, but I did. In contrast, with the Stanford TEP, they didn't have a "there" there.

The more subtle thing is trust. Even if they hate each other, it's still worth exploring whether there is enough trust to engage in an empowerment evaluation. In empowerment evaluations, most program staff members and participants are much more critical than I would be, so the trust often comes shining through.

Fitzpatrick: Let's move now to focus more on the STEP evaluation. This evaluation has received some national attention in the teacher education field. What particular characteristics of the evaluation or its results have received the most attention?

Fetterman: The key finding, the need to agree on a unity of purpose in a program, has brought responses from directors of other teacher education programs across the United States. This is probably influenced by the fact that the light is on Stanford, and Stanford, for better or worse, is often considered the model, but the absence of unity of purpose in a program has received a lot of attention in and of itself. People are reassessing whether they have unity of purpose.

And it's interesting that this absence of a unity of purpose in the program was one of the last things we found. We found the manifestations at first, but then we realized that the reason all these problems were identified was because of the lack of a unity of purpose. There was no common vision. It was the gestalt of the project.

The second issue receiving attention was our findings on the curriculum and the lack of connection between theory and practice. They didn't have any classroom management courses in the fall quarter. The time you really, really need this is in that fall quarter when you're first beginning to teach. Why didn't they have it then? It was not a convenient time for faculty. As a consequence, students were extremely critical of other courses that quarter that had very little to do with practice. The faculty who taught those courses really appreciated learning about our findings in this regard, in retrospect. The student critique was harsher than it might have been because they were looking for the practice focus even in courses that were explicitly theoretical—because it was absent when they needed it the most. The larger issue here is the idea of having more of a flow between theory and practice within the curriculum.

Another issue that has captured people's attention is our recommendation to teach teachers how to conduct research about their own teaching and for faculty to engage in research activities directly associated with the teacher education program. This might seem obvious in a research institution; however, issues associated with status come into play when we are talking about conducting research in a teacher education program.

A recommendation that appears to have received considerable attention involves maintaining contact with alumni. A lot more places are doing that now. At the beginning of the evaluation, we decided that we were going to interview a lot of the alumni from the program. Our first step was to go to the program and ask for contact information on alumni. We learned there was no list. Guess what? The evaluation is done! They don't even maintain a list! However, that would have been the easy way of dealing with the issue, but it would not shed any light on alumni perspectives. So we contacted a few alumni we knew and built our own list through snowball sampling. By talking to a lot of alums, we learned that beginning teachers need a lot more support than STEP ever realized. That's when teachers are most vulnerable and the time period in which they are most likely to drop out of teaching. This somewhat circuitous path helped us understand the problems of beginning teachers in a clearer light, and in turn, our findings helped other teacher education program faculty and administrators realize that alumni contact was much more significant than they had realized.

Fitzpatrick: You mentioned the president of Stanford commissioned this study. What prompted his action?

Fetterman: A couple of things: In 1994, significant student dissatisfaction was manifested at the graduation ceremonies. Minority graduates complained about the program, suggesting that it was not responding to minority issues. The new Stanford administration wanted to know what was going on. In addition, this president was interested in education. The president was very clear. He wasn't interested in just making money, although there was some concern about the fiscal administration of the program. His primary concern was with the quality of what we were doing. Although the scope of the evaluation was extensive, he was quite generous with his time and with the funding of the evaluation.

Fitzpatrick: I know the new director of the Teacher Education Program became one of your primary stakeholders, implementing many of your recommendations. Did her arrival prompt the study? Was she involved in the planning?

Fetterman: We had already issued the report on the summer program before she came. However, she was pivotal to the use of the evaluation findings and recommendations. She is considered the most prominent and knowledgeable scholar in the field of teacher education. When she said she loved both the summer interim report and the draft of the final report, defensiveness and critiques of the evaluation disappeared. In addition, she implemented over 50 of our recommendations in the first six months of her tenure. Everything was in alignment. The president was in support of the program and, specifically, program changes that needed to be made. The dean supported the efforts to reform the program. The new director had both the credibility and the force of will to implement the evaluation recommendations, and the evaluation findings were credible and ready to be used. If any one of these things had not been in alignment, use would have been diminished, as is evidenced by past evaluations of this program.

Fitzpatrick: You're a faculty member in the school that delivers STEP. So, in essence, this is an internal evaluation. Evaluators often raise concerns about the objectivity of internal evaluations. On the other hand, internal evaluators' knowledge of the program history, staff, culture, and so forth, can be helpful in insuring that appropriate issues are addressed and information is ultimately used. Let's talk a little bit about these issues. First, how did your prior beliefs and knowledge about this program influence the evaluation?

Fetterman: There was an awful lot I didn't know—for example, about the personal histories of folks. I knew the basic structure of the School of Education—that this was a stepchild. STEP is even jokingly referred to as a stepchild! I always knew there were some problems in terms of status; that is, many faculty viewed it as less prestigious than other assignments or affiliations in the School. So, on the one hand, I was more knowledgeable than someone coming in cold and that was important because at a place like Stanford, if they do not think you have some familiarity with the area you don't have any credibility.

But I didn't know a lot about STEP. If I had known more, it may have been helpful, but then I might not have done the evaluation. Anyone else would have been chewed up. I practically was and I've been here a long time. But there were strengths to my being a little bit of an outsider. If I had been a member of the STEP faculty, I might have been too close to it and thus more likely to just tinker around the edges instead of suggesting bold and fundamental changes in the program. The same way that a fish is the last one to discover water, a faculty member in the program might not be able to see what's in front of him or her without the assistance of the entire group or some outside facilitator or coach. At the same time, I might have been better at seeing some of the detailed findings more clearly.

You're right that there can be a downside to being an internal evaluator and independent judgment can be one of them. However, I didn't have any problem with approximating some form of objectivity or independent judgment. I was certainly perceived by some as too critical. But my colleagues wouldn't accept anything that wasn't a quality evaluation. I am in favor of high-quality teacher education programs. That bias made me even more critical when I saw that the program was not operating as intended. Being in favor of something can make you more critical. If you're in favor of a concept, you take it personally if the program isn't working.

At the same time, a lot of the work is not about describing some objective reality. A lot of what we were doing was telling other people's stories throughout the STEP evaluation because we needed to understand what students were experiencing—what their perception of the program was like as they lived it. We spent every moment in the summer with STEP students—from 7 in the morning until noon at the public school where they practiced teaching and in Stanford classes until 7 at night, and then sorting data at night like students doing their homework. You ended up being more accurate by being immersed in the culture. You're much more sensitive to the nuances and realities when you live the life you are evaluating. When put to the test, you're better prepared to confront fundamental program issues because you have a better insight into what people think and believe.

Fitzpatrick: But this seems potentially conflicting. On the one hand, you note you were able to see some of the big issues because you were *not* part of the STEP faculty and, thus, to build on your analogy, you noticed the water. But, on the other hand, you felt that *being* immersed in the day-to-day culture of STEP with students made you better able to deal with the fundamental issues. What made these circumstances differ?

Fetterman: We are talking about different levels of analysis and immersion. I was not invested in how the place was run because I was not a member of the STEP faculty. This allowed me to think out of the box and question things that most folks took for granted. Similarly, I was not a student, but I needed to understand the students' perspectives in order to understand how the program was working or not working. The best way to get that insight is to immerse oneself in the culture as both a participant and an observer to document the insider's perspective of reality. Daily contact and interaction allow you to collect the kind of detailed data required to describe contextual behavior and interpret it meaningfully.

Fitzpatrick: To what extent were key stakeholders (e.g., faculty) able to perceive you as "objective" in your assessment of the program since you were a part of the education faculty? For example, they might have perceived your recommendation for teaching students more about research as self-serving since you are the director of the School's graduate program in policy analysis and evaluation. What kinds of problems did you encounter in their accepting your findings?

Fetterman: The recommendation about research was broad enough that it was palatable to faculty. We are a research institution and there was little research being conducted in that area so it was hard to argue with that finding. In addition, because research is highly valued in this environment, it was hard to ignore a finding that was that fundamental to the values of the place.

I also recommended that they have more of a link with educational policy. That should have been a problem, but it wasn't. People recognized that STEP was remiss in not linking with policy (my program) and with the principals' program. I think in some ways we stated the obvious, but no one wanted to confront this issue in the past.

I also believe that the issue was not one of objectivity. The issue here is credibility and honesty. I've done a lot of evaluations for the Board of Trustees at Stanford. They know me and view me as a very honest and straightforward professional, so I had a reputation as being straightforward with the aim of trying to help. I think this was more important than objectivity because what they were really looking for was an honest judgment call about the operations.

I did have one criticism of that nature—lack of objectivity. When the draft report was circulated, one faculty member said I had left out a lot and went to the associate dean saying I had an ax to grind. The associate dean then called him on it, and my colleague had to admit that I didn't have an ax to grind. There was no history of animosity or any other problem between us.

In fact, if anything, one colleague could not understand why we did not have an ax to grind given what we had learned. My evaluation team learned that one colleague *had* behaved inappropriately during the evaluation. During the last week of summer school, when we took off from classes to write the report, this faculty member asked the class, "Are any of the evaluators here today?" When he learned there were none, he had the students close the door and told them not to talk to the evaluators. He said if they (the students) said anything negative to the evaluators, it could end the program. Thirty of these students came to tell us about this colleague's behavior that night. We had already written the section about his teaching, and we had no reason to change it—certainly not because of this behavior. We considered it negative but separate from our assessment of his teaching. At the same time, I could have reported this behavior in the evaluation report. However, I thought it was atypical and would have misrepresented the norm that I would characterize as proper behavior in the program. My colleague still wonders why we will not use that against him to this day. He does not understand the evaluation ethic, which is not to misuse what we learn or distort what we know.

I did think there might be some areas where I would have to excuse myself from certain program assessment activities because of a potential conflict of interest. However, STEP was a separate enough entity from the School that there really wasn't any significant conflict—it was like reviewing a completely separate program or entity. For all intents and purposes, it was a separately operating program that just happened to be part of the School. That separateness, in fact, was what was wrong with STEP. If it was operating the way it should have been, then I would have known more about it and probably had a conflict of interest. They're even in a separate building.

Fitzpatrick: That's helpful in clarifying how separate they were from you. But, then, your recommendations are to merge more with your own school. Couldn't the nature of that recommendation be perceived as a conflict? You're recommending that STEP would do better if it were in your program. That might be an easier recommendation to make if you weren't a member of that program.

Fetterman: I did not want it to be in my program, just to make links with relevant programs in the school, including mine and the prospective principal's program. These were natural links based on the literature and the recommendation simply stated the obvious—if we want our prospective teachers to be effective they need to know about current policy issues ranging from vouchers to systemic reform. They could acquire this kind of knowledge by making a direct link with the policy program. The same applies to fostering a more productive relationship between teachers and administrators when we recommended that the teacher education program link up with the prospective principal's program.

Fitzpatrick: Usually, more evaluation questions arise during the planning stage than resources permit us to examine. How did you prioritize the questions you wanted to answer? What issues emerged from the planning stage as most critical and why?

Fetterman: Appendix A of the first report listed all of the STEP components and issues that people had mentioned. With this, we found a master list or common denominators that everyone could buy in to. But it was so comprehensive, it meant we had to turn a summer effort into a three-year project. Fortunately, we were given more money and more time to address all the issues. The problem then wasn't which issues do we address, but more what needed to be done first. Not everyone agreed, but we did it by the schedule of the year. We evaluated the summer program first because that was the first event or activity in the calendar. We evaluated students' portfolios when those conferences occurred. We evaluated each component as it came along in the year.

Fitzpatrick: You and your staff became really immersed in the summer program. Three of the five-member team were on-site every day of the summer program. This was quite intensive. Why did you choose this strategy? What did you learn from it?

Fetterman: The need for a five-member team was primarily an issue of size and scope. We couldn't handle that many classrooms with just one or two people. We needed a lot of observations. We were compulsive. I wanted to make sure we had every single classroom covered. We didn't sample—we did them all! We did rotations so we could get an inter-rater reliability going, and we shared digital photographs of what we saw later that day to build reliability and confirm our perceptions. We spent the night organizing and cataloging. We did this at the end of each week and the end of the quarter. Most of the analysis was iterative. Coverage was our number one goal—and quality control to make sure we were on target

Being there every day also gave us more data points to work with. We were able to see the same patterns of behavior over time—that is a form of reliability. In addition, there was a lot of face validity to our observations over time. That's what I love about being in there every single day—it really was ethnographic in nature. If you stay for short observations people have mugging and company behavior, but if you stay a long time they can't sustain that false sense for that long. They get used to you and let go of the company behavior and go back to their normal way of operating and behaving.

Fitzpatrick: Did you structure this initial involvement in the summer program? Or were your observations more open-ended? Tell us a little about what the evaluation team did during their time on-site.

Fetterman: In some cases, the interviews and observations were open ended. In most cases, we had specific things we were looking for. We reviewed the literature associated with teacher education programs and internal program documents and then attempted to document whether program intentions were being actualized. For example, was the student given a chance to teach the class? Did the mentor teacher stay in the classroom to observe? (Sometimes they didn't even stay in to observe the student teacher, even though they were responsible for evaluating their teaching.) We also were assessing the quality or quantity of student engagement in the classroom. We wanted to know if the student teachers were actually "in there" with the kids, or did they fade into the woodwork at the earliest stage and remain that way. Are they really not suited for teaching?

Of course, things emerged that were fascinating, reflecting the dynamic nature of teaching. We saw some great things such as stellar teachers with a certain chemistry with students, and some absolutely pathetic things as well, including lecturing about being student-centered for three hours. Overall, I would say that we used some normal protocols and some open-ended observation. The idea was to describe, not to test. However, observation in our case was really a series of hypotheses about how things should work, and then we used observation to test those assumptions or statements about program operations.

Fitzpatrick: I've written about the importance of observing programs at early stages, and describing and retaining what you see. Tell us a little bit about your view on description at this stage.

Fetterman: It's very important at the early phase of the evaluation. Of course, we had a description of the site (the physical layout) and a lot of very basic preliminary information. But this information wasn't at all insightful about what was really going on, about what chemistry existed between the teacher and the Stanford student and the middle school student. You wouldn't get that without observation. You also need to understand the political interaction between the principal and the teachers in summer school. So, description was critical to get a baseline understanding of dynamics, to understand the challenges and the nature of interactions, and to figure out which interactions to *select* for testing. We needed to know the process to make recommendations for improvements.

We got quite involved in order to provide a sufficiently in-depth description of the program. We hung out during master teacher and student discussions or assessments of student teaching. Luckily, we were well received by the local principal and the teachers. They were very enthusiastic about having us there and providing them with feedback. It was ironic that the university faculty was more defensive and less receptive to critique than the high school faculty.

The different reactions we observed between the university and high school faculty reflected the different norms in each culture or environment. In public schools, you get evaluated and get feedback. You think it's odd if someone comes in and doesn't comment on your classroom. So that culture made the teachers comfortable with our feedback. But that's not part of the culture of academe. So the classroom teachers liked our observation. They wanted us there. They wanted to talk to us about the students. They gave us a little award at the end of the summer as a way of recognizing how important we were as part of their lives on a daily basis throughout the summer. We were all invested in the program, but we had different roles and responsibilities. Our immersion in the program and their reactions helped us develop a very open, sharing relationship which made the observation much more insightful. We gained a clear understanding about the teacher's role in mentoring students on a day-to-day basis because we were right there with them on a daily basis, we weren't just making cameo appearances.

Fitzpatrick: It sounds like these observations were invaluable in giving you a real feel for the summer program. Let me build on a couple of issues you mentioned. You indicated the teachers wanted to talk with you about the students and that you sometimes considered whether individual students were suited for teaching and chimed in during the debriefing process. Can you tell us a bit about that? Did you see that individual assessment as part of your evaluation?

Fetterman: I did not see it as a formal part of the evaluation. However, it was part of reciprocity in the evaluation, and it was a secondary form of data collection. In other words, our job did not involve the assessment of individual student teachers. It did, however, involve our assessment of the master and coordinating teachers' ability to assess the students. Thus, it was useful to hear their views about individual students as data about their abilities to assess student teachers. On another level, there was an expectation that I would share my opinions as a "fellow teacher" and observer. (I also went through a teacher-training program many years ago, so I am quite familiar with the process and the importance of discussing these matters.) However, most of the time we simply listened without arguing or supporting the teachers' assessments or comments. There were two extreme cases that merited some frank discussion, but this required temporarily stepping out of my evaluation role and into my faculty role to make sure the student received adequate counseling and that the master teacher was apprised of potential problems.

Fitzpatrick: Some evaluators argue that this level of immersion can threaten "objectivity." That is, you may become so involved in the details of program delivery that you begin to identify too much with different audiences, such as deliverers or clients. Did you find maintaining "objectivity" or distance to be a problem in reaching your final judgments or recommendations?

Fetterman: My position is that the problem is completely the opposite. You're going to have superficial or misleading information about a place if you're not immersed. The only way to have a good understanding and an accurate assessment, understanding real-world activity right in front of your eyes, is to be immersed. You have to be part of the culture, to help clean up the lab, to understand the extra work and the pressures of their personal lives. Basically, I don't agree with the assumptions associated with this question. Immersion is the *only* way to get the best-quality data. And, I mean long-term immersion, repeated involvement over time—to begin to see patterns as we discussed earlier. You can't see patterns without long-term immersion. Immersion is actually spending time with folks and getting their view of why they're doing what they're doing instead of assuming it. Our job is to take these insiders' perspectives of reality and apply our social science external focus.

Spradley (1970), an anthropologist who studied tramps in Seattle, showed the importance of immersion. He spent a great deal of time talking to tramps. Judges wanted to throw them in jail so they had a roof over their heads, but Spradley learned the tramps didn't want that. They wanted their freedom. He described the very different world views of judges and tramps, and he was able to do this because he was immersed in their worlds. So immersion doesn't threaten objectivity. It's probably the only thing that will give us real quality data. You can't be immersed in everything, but the more you limit the immersion the less you learn.

There is no real or absolute objectivity. We approximate concepts of this nature. We hold ourselves up as models of it. Science and evaluation have never been neutral. We always bring our own lens. Most people have a very naive idea about what objectivity is. It's a nice concept, but it's not real. If we delude ourselves with it, we're just perpetuating a myth. We are *all* wearing a lens when we observe or judge something. The generic perception of objectivity is useful, but it's nonsense. Triangulation is a useful tool to help us approximate this concept without being a slave to it.

Fitzpatrick: I know you used qualitative and quantitative methods to test working hypotheses and the generalizability of observations. In what areas did the surveys, interviews, and observations converge and validate each other?

Fetterman: The way I was trained, you can't do good qualitative work unless you use qualitative and quantitative methods. You must use a combination of both methods. There isn't a qualitative world and a quantitative world. There is one world. In addition, you can't be a purist or an ideologue; you must use any appropriate tool available. Sometimes, you're mixing these methods to triangulate—to test or rule out rival hypotheses.

We used surveys to get a handle on the generalizability of specific student views about the program. Individual interviews helped us flesh out, or explore, some of the commonly held views. Similarly, classroom observations were invaluable to cross-check individual interviews and survey data.

There are times when we get overly invested in how we represent our data—descriptively or numerically. For example, in our interviews with faculty, we found no convergence on their views of their mission or place. There was no shared conception of a mission. The convergence was the absence of convergence—they shared a lack of unity of purpose. This could be portrayed in a numerical fashion, such as percentages who believed the mission was one thing and percentages of faculty who thought it was something else. The bottom line is that both descriptively and numerically we found the same thing— that the group had very little in common when it came to a vision of the program mission.

As discussed earlier, we also compared survey data with individual interviews and our own classroom observations to obtain a more accurate assessment of classroom teaching. Any single data source alone would have been misleading. There was a lot of quantitative and qualitative mismatching. In some cases, the results converged; in some cases, they didn't. The lack of convergence prompted us to explore more. It forced us to probe further.

Fitzpatrick: When there was a discrepancy, were the qualitative results always better?

Fetterman: Not always, but most of the time. For example, on the issue of minority enrollment, all the verbal feedback suggested things were problematic but under control, but when we looked at the numbers, it was obvious that it was not under control. The way they were reporting the data was misleading. They were lumping Asians into the minority category to look better. The initial quantitative information suggested good minority enrollment. This issue illustrates the constant interplay between qualitative and quantitative results. After observing the students for a bit, our gut instinct told us the numbers didn't match what we saw. That led us to go back and look more carefully at how the numbers were derived. Our intuition combined with observation led us to believe that the figures didn't make sense. A lot of evaluation is instinct.

Fitzpatrick: The STEP evaluation could be characterized as primarily a process study, a type of study that I consider very useful. But in higher education we generally measure process. Did you consider examining the success of the program in achieving desired outcomes, for example, student knowledge and skills or performance on the job?

Fetterman: We looked at things students were expected to do in order to become good teachers, to see if they were doing those things. The superficial indicators—grades and so forth—suggested all was fine. We did survey alumni and their supervisors and got some information on outcomes in that way. That was how we learned that students were weak on technology. They weren't trained in a certain category sufficiently.

Fitzpatrick: I think interviews and input from supervisors can be invaluable, but you were learning people's *reports* of what they were doing. Those reports in themselves are very useful for learning what they're struggling with and what they're comfortable with, but you didn't actually go out and observe alumni in their classrooms, did you?

Fetterman: Sure—partly to collect relevant data and partly to establish a bond with them before we asked them to participate in focus groups. However, this was not the focus of the effort—the focus was on the quality of teacher training as a "treatment."

Fitzpatrick: You made use of a variety of technological tools in conducting this evaluation. Your reports present many interesting digital photographs of classroom activities, giving the reader a real picture of the setting and characters. You used the Web for surveys and conducted evaluation team videoconferencing on the Internet. Tell us about these approaches. What worked? What didn't?

Fetterman: Yes, we learned a lot about high-tech and how it can be used in evaluation in this study. I'm on the road a lot, and we used videoconferencing very effectively to keep in touch with evaluation staff and discuss what we were learning. On another level, digital photography was very helpful to us in documenting what we saw in the classroom. Evaluation team members would take pictures of student teachers in the classroom, and we would share them over lunch. These pictures help illustrate what we thought we saw—student teachers fading into the woodwork or actually being involved in the process of teaching. The photos helped document our observations in ways that no one could dispute. It was very powerful. You are able to share with your evaluation team members and others precisely what the teacher is doing, what the students are doing. Once you get the camera, the only expense is the floppy disk—no film or developing required. The photographs also helped confirm our feelings at this early stage. They were a reliability check; the team could consider whether they drew the same conclusion from the picture as the observer had. Pictures also were useful when we prepared the final reports. What a difference a color photograph makes! We went for color for the president's report because it makes such a big impact.

Technology also allowed us to put report drafts on secure areas on the Web to get feedback from the faculty and others. We posted four drafts of the summer report to receive feedback.

We used Nudist as the software for sorting data for all verbatim quotations and observations. It was invaluable—to be able to sort at a moment's notice! You used to have to think twice as to whether to sort again with cards. Now, you can test things out quickly, and it helps keep things organized. We made copies for everyone on the team. If they had an idea, they could play around with it.

We also surveyed alumni of the program using a Web-based survey. The alumni went to the URL and filled out the form; the moment they filled it out, it was sorted automatically. I could be anywhere in the country and sort the data on the Web site. The students could play around with it too.

Fitzpatrick: Let's turn to your results for a minute. Which of the results was most surprising to you?

Fetterman: The political and personal issues in this evaluation were very surprising. I was surprised at how political and nasty it could become. I was astonished at how badly many of the faculty had been hurt by their involvement with the program over the past 20 years. Personally, what I learned about a few of my colleagues' behavior in response to the evaluation was surprising. I don't know if you're ever prepared for the fact that some colleague you've known for a long period of time is either absolutely stellar and very supportive or the opposite where you feel a sense of betrayal and sabotage. Definitely, on a personal level that was quite surprising. When someone close to you, whom you trusted, betrays you, it disturbs your whole sense of judgment and, of course, it's personally disconcerting. The other side is uplifting, when people you don't know that well get up and give speeches in support of you and your work, that's an equally powerful personal experience.

In regard to the actual findings, the two surprises were (1) the differences in what we learned by observing faculty teaching as compared with what we learned from the surveys about teaching and then (2) the lack of unity on purpose or mission. It was surprising that that could even be possible.

Fitzpatrick: Having worked in several different university settings, I have to say that I don't find lack of unity among faculty in academe surprising. Faculty are often either disengaged and doing their own thing in classes or they have strong disagreements about purpose.

Fetterman: Well, you're right, but it's surprising not to find unity of purpose in teacher education. Our review of other teacher education programs showed that they did have this, but our own school did not have a firm sense of purpose of what students should be like when they got out and what they should be doing in the program to achieve that. Lewis and Clark, Trinity, Bank Street, UCLA, and other schools we looked at all have very specific themes for teacher education. When the school is a professional school, it's important to have agreement on the mission. What is the overarching theme? What do we all agree that our teachers should become? What's our philosophy and value system? And then you need to have that reflected in the curriculum and even alumni contacts. It even affects admission issues.

Fitzpatrick: You did review the programs of other schools quite a bit in your evaluation report. Often, evaluations neglect that area. Tell us about your exploration of other programs.

Fetterman: The comparative part was very helpful to constantly look at other programs that were similar. We're supposed to be the stellar institution. To learn whether we're achieving that, we need to look at what other programs are doing. Folks who are running programs often don't have time for literature reviews; they don't do the research on it. I think it's an error not to look at other programs. To inform others of what's going on in the real world is very helpful. We went to teacher education conferences. Through those we were able to talk to these folks and visit some of their programs. We communicated with them by phone and e-mail too, to get their thoughts and learn more about what they were doing. If we really believe in knowledge, we need to pay attention to what others have done.

Fitzpatrick: When did you do this? Was this part of your planning phase?

Fetterman: Most of it was around the middle of the study. We did some exploration of the literature right off the bat. But, then, halfway through the evaluation, we went to a conference. Then, we got into more depth than in the initial collection of information because we knew more about our program and what we wanted to know. This was very intense information. It helped give us a more normative view, to learn what is reasonable and fair to expect of a teacher education program. The hope is that people will also build on our work.

If you make the review of other programs succinct, clear, and relevant, people will realize there is a value added to learning about other programs. We found it and summarized it. People are always excited to learn what others are doing; they just don't have the time to look into it. You don't want to hit them over the head with it. They can make the decisions with the information we provide. If you use it correctly, you'll get tremendous buy-in for your findings. It places your findings in a larger, more normative context.

Fitzpatrick: I'd like to ask a few questions about your reporting style. Your reports (with the exception of the *Summer School Report*) focus primarily on your recommendations. In this way, you depart from the traditional evaluation format of presenting data to back up your conclusions. Why did you choose this strategy?

Fetterman: I think what you'll find is that in all three reports I'll have the data and recommendations. Of course, the *President's Report* is the shortest; they just wanted a couple of pages, and this has the least data. We wrote about 21 pages, and that is really the maximum for that sort of report. The Executive Summary within that report is two pages long and that is the maximum we thought appropriate for an executive summary.

The STEP report to the faculty and the general community was much more detailed, providing data as needed without cluttering the key points. At the same time, we limited the amount of data in the report for fear of data overload—which happened with our *Summer School Report.* (We still had to have the data and in a format ready to use in case anyone took issue with a specific point in the report.)

The *Summer School Report* was the most detailed because it was the earliest report, the most formative in nature, and the one that required the most feedback to make sure we were starting the evaluation on solid ground. After completing that report, we consciously decided to cut back the length and the amount of data in each subsequent report. I think the detail of the summer report scared the heck out of them. The dean loved it. The teacher education program staff members loved it because it focused on the program detail they had to deal with on a day-to-day basis. But the report was a tremendous amount to digest and in some ways got in the way of the key points or judgments.

My colleagues, the School of Education faculty, focused on the rating of faculty teaching. They would argue with us about our draft memorandum focusing on our observations about their teaching. So we would say, "Here's what we didn't include. Students could barely get in the room because the professor's ego was so big." We thought it appropriate to share our observations of their teaching with them in a draft memorandum format before drafting something about it in the interim report. It gave them a chance to respond to our observations and preliminary findings before it reached the draft report stage. This was ethically sound but personally stressful. We had student comments that were pretty negative, documenting problems with teaching that went beyond what we reported anywhere except to that individual faculty member. Writing the report was labor intensive, but providing all that information made it more accurate and harder to argue with.

We ended up writing the same kind of detail in the final phase, but just for us. We had to have a tremendous amount of documentation because the evaluation was so political. But we definitely made the decision for a less detailed final report based on the reaction to the first one. The president wanted it brief.

Fitzpatrick: Did you think the 20-page report was a little long for the president?

Fetterman: Yes, but given the nature of everything around it, the political nature of it and the amount of power associated with it, it was too risky to do something conventional like a one- or two-page executive summary without the detail we provided. I wanted to make sure the president had the straight scoop from me because of how others were trying to reach him through other pathways. I negotiated a length of a maximum of 25 pages with him. Because of his academic background, he might not have respected a report of the usual one or two pages. At the same time, the executive summary within this report to the president was only two pages as per the normal custom in evaluation.

Fitzpatrick: That's helpful: I have a better understanding of why you made the final report less detailed than the summer report which did provide summary tables of student ratings and a narrative description of observations in high-, medium-, and low-rated classes. As an aside, I notice you didn't name the instructors, but instead used names of historic figures in education, such as Maria Montessori (who did well) and Edward Thorndike and B. F. Skinner (who were rated low). The descriptions seem to correspond to how one might think these individuals would, in fact, teach. Were these real descriptions of classes, and you just used other names for anonymity? If so, was it disconcerting to others that the descriptions matched how these people might have taught? Did people think it was fictional or real?

Fetterman: The descriptions were real but we wanted to protect the identity of the individual instructors. The pseudonyms were useful devices to both protect the identity of colleagues and signal to the reader almost immediately what kind of teacher we observed.

Fitzpatrick: Let's move into another area. You mentioned to me that you learned a lot about the politics of evaluation and courage from conducting this evaluation. Tell us more about that.

Fetterman: Well, the evaluation may be viewed as wonderful now, but 18 months ago, I was in big trouble. I don't know if I ever completely appreciated the concept of courage until things hit the fan in a more personal way. It's hard when it's with people you've known for a long time. I usually don't get too caught up with this concern about courage. Chelimsky and Scriven have spoken about it. However, I have not given it a lot of thought over the years. However, this was just unusually personal and nasty on the negative side. There were real highs and real lows associated with the conduct of this evaluation. It was even discussed at my performance appraisal. It's easy to be retrospectively courageous. The hard thing was to do the right thing at the time.

Fitzpatrick: Could you give us an example?

Fetterman: Just continuing the assessment when you're hit with some defensive and inappropriate kinds of behavior becomes a task—just continuing to report negative findings, rather than minimizing them, is a challenge. We could have written the report in such a manner as to make the program look better than it deserved, and it would have helped my own career. In other words, it would have been easier not to take the flak. However, I am glad we stuck with it and continued to provide an honest account of what we observed, even though it was not always pleasant. It certainly paid off in the long run. One example was giving individual faculty feedback on their teaching in the initial draft report. By being honest and giving feedback early, we allowed defensive and periodically combative faculty behavior to emerge in the short run, but this approach minimized conflict in the long run. In other words, in the short run this open, sharing approach did contribute to game playing; the early feedback gave them a chance to attack. I knew at that point that without question we needed to have absolutely solid data and a clear-cut chain of reasoning. If it were too general, it would sound like loose and sloppy methodology, intuitive impressions without the solid backing required to accompany it. It would have been much easier not to report back, but I wanted to make sure that it was accurate at the individual level. So it took courage to go to my colleagues and say, "This is what we found." It took courage dealing with the dean—your boss— knowing how the troops are reacting to him and the report. There was a concern that the evaluation might present a risk to the entire school if these kinds of results went to the president. Politically, conducting the study was a big risk for me—having to be honest in a critical way with people you will have a continuing relationship with. It took courage to keep advocating for students who will be gone while I remain with colleagues I may have alienated.

Fitzpatrick: Do you think people realized there would be so much focus on their own teaching?

Fetterman: Yes, but I don't think they ever expected the detail. But you can't be general without individual data. I needed the individual data for the evaluation to be persuasive. However, I think some faculty seriously didn't know where they stood. I think those at the very bottom and top knew where they were. The people in the middle area were the most significant problem; they thought they were stellar. They thought the evaluation of their teaching was a personal attack. They were so used to subterfuge and combat that they weren't able to initially understand the data. Because it was direct, simple, and straightforward, it was counter to the culture.

Fitzpatrick: But focusing on their individual teaching is more like performance appraisal or personnel evaluation than program evaluation. Evaluation often focuses more on the program than the individual. How did your focus on individual teaching come about?

Fetterman: The needs assessment for the evaluation highlighted the need to focus on people, on individual faculty teaching. We asked what everyone recommended that we look at in the evaluation. They thought a focus on teaching was important as well. We did a six-month planning phase focusing on what key stakeholders thought were the most important things to look at. We decided, based on the time we had, what we would do realistically. However, after consulting with the president about the scope, he simply gave us more resources to do it all. The faculty had their input; they just didn't expect the evaluation of teaching to be anywhere near as thorough and detailed as it was.

Fitzpatrick: Did you encounter any ethical challenges in this process?

Fetterman: Oh, yes, constantly. There was the ethical dilemma of how to handle the information about the faculty member who told the students not to talk to us. I could have reported this to the president, but decided not to. I did let cognizant individuals within the department know, but reporting this to the president would, I felt, affect the findings of the evaluation. To this day, my colleague doesn't understand why I haven't used this information against him. He considers me odd. To him, it's a political decision. To me, it's an ethical decision not to use the evaluation data against him; it's not ethical to use the evaluation for personal reasons or to demean someone. I think he's thinking I'll use it to get something from him. I don't believe in doing that. To do this, professionally, would demean the field.

Fitzpatrick: But you did report it to someone in the department. Did you see that as using the information against him? What was the impetus for that action? Since his actions didn't seem to inhibit the students from coming to you, they didn't seem to have an impact on the evaluation.

Fetterman: Two things: (1) On a micro level, it was necessary to safeguard the evaluation effort by documenting the event and reporting it on a local level to prevent his behavior from disrupting our efforts or having a chilling effect on communication for any segment of the student population and (2) just because a good segment of the student class came to us does not mean it did not have a chilling effect on those who did not come to us. This kind of behavior does undermine an evaluative effort. However, if taken care of, it does not have to become part of the evaluation report.

Fitzpatrick: Were there people pushing you to make the program look more positive than it was?

Fetterman: Quite frankly, I was so busy getting the job done, if someone hinted at that I didn't listen on that level. The challenges were tremendous. The evaluation experience was not all negative. It was exhilarating! We had something that we all cared about and the study had implications for all of us. We all knew it was important to do. We had a personal connection to the students. We felt an obligation to help them out. It was exhilarating working with such talented faculty and talented students.

Fitzpatrick: We all learn from evaluations. If you were to conduct this evaluation again, what would you do differently?

Fetterman: I would do an empowerment evaluation! I think I would! I'm half serious. I obviously made an assessment that empowerment wasn't the approach for that group at that time. But now they're ready. It's easier to be honest with them now; there's so much that's on the table already. The key point now is not so much what I would do differently in that evaluation, but what I would do now for the next step. They're ready for empowerment evaluation. My role would be as coach and facilitator.

Fitzpatrick: Do you think it would be difficult to step into that role now having had the political turmoil that arose in this evaluation and with your having played a quite different role? Would you be able to establish a trusting relationship with them?

Fetterman: Yes. In fact, I am already beginning a much more participatory or empowerment-oriented evaluation focusing on the feasibility of developing an elementary teacher education program at Stanford. This will probably require an empowerment evaluation of the new program, which may at one point lead to an empowerment evaluation of the older secondary school program. Time and distance make a big difference.

Fitzpatrick: David, thank you for sharing the details of this evaluation with us. As practicing evaluators, we learn from hearing the experiences, difficulties, and choices faced by others. It informs our own practice.

Fitzpatrick's Commentary

This interview helps us learn more about the important choice of models or approaches to use when conducting an evaluation. Although Fetterman is recognized for empowerment evaluation, he rightly acknowledges, even emphasizes, that evaluators should choose a model that is appropriate to the context and purpose of the evaluation. To use the same model in all settings would be unwise and inappropriate. Thus, while Fetterman often uses an empowerment approach, he also has used other approaches. Here, he incorporates elements of empowerment but ultimately takes a decision-making approach focusing on the president of the university as the primary audience. He also makes use of elements of an older model, discrepancy evaluation (Provus, 1971), by studying the process of the program to determine if it conforms to the intended model and to other exemplary models of teacher education. The importance of a trusting environment and culture, which he perceived to be lacking at the time of his study, appears central to a successful empowerment approach. Their absence and the information needs of the key stakeholder prompt him to pursue a different model.

This interview is also enlightening in helping us learn about the strengths and weaknesses of the internal evaluator's role. First, the interview reflects the difficulty in categorizing an evaluator as purely internal or purely external. In Fetterman's case, he would be considered an internal evaluator because he was an employee of the same organization as STEP, Stanford University. Although Fetterman did not teach in STEP, he was a faculty member in the College of Education, and as he indicates, the evaluation required him to judge a program conducted by colleagues with whom he had, and would continue to have, relations for years to come. Conversely, he might be considered an external evaluator because he is not a member of the STEP faculty; that is, he was not employed in the unit to be evaluated. As such, he had some distance and independence from STEP. The head of STEP, for example, was not his direct supervisor. He did, however, report to the same dean. That closeness was illustrated by the fact that a discussion of the evaluation arose at his annual performance appraisal. Another element that is important in characterizing his role in this evaluation is that he did not typically play the role of an evaluator at Stanford. Unlike many internal evaluators, that was not a permanent part of his duties. Instead, he was a tenured faculty member with the responsibilities that that position entails. He was thrust into a different role here, though he indicates he has conducted previous evaluations for Stanford. Fitzpatrick, Sanders, and Worthen (2004) and Mathison (1999) describe the internal-external position as a continuum rather than a discrete distinction, and that continuum is evidenced here.

Fetterman's position illustrates some of the strengths and weaknesses of an internal role. His knowledge of Stanford University and its culture helped him in considering the types of evidence that would be valid to the president and to other stakeholders within the university. His familiarity with the environment of the organization allowed him to be accepted and gave him knowledge of the important actors and the manner in which decisions are made. And his continued presence in the organization permitted him to continue to encourage use of the results. In fact, because his recommendations included closer relationships between his department and STEP, he was one of the people responsible for implementing these recommendations. But this strength also hints at the weaknesses of the internal evaluator. Does an internal evaluator have sufficient independence to judge the program? To provide a new perspective? For others to trust that his conclusions are "unbiased"? Fetterman believes that he was able to bring an objective, independent judgment to the evaluation, but the turmoil surrounding the results suggests that some his colleagues, correctly or incorrectly, disagreed. Their views may have been inflamed by the fact that the evaluation described and judged the teaching performances of individual faculty who, though anonymous, may have been identifiable by description. Similar faculty reactions may have emerged in response to these descriptions of individual's teaching performance whether one was an internal or external evaluator. But the concerns about the independence of an internal evaluator are most evident when findings or recommendations have perceived advantages for the individual evaluator, however valid the findings or recommendations may be. Thus, Fetterman's recommendations regarding work with his own department and the need for prospective teachers to learn more about research fall into this category.

The evaluation of STEP is ultimately a process evaluation providing information for formative purposes. Fetterman indicates that the president might use the evaluation for summative decisions (to decide whether to continue the program), but the results appear to be sufficiently positive to merit continuation and then were used for program improvement. As such, Fetterman's methods—immersion in the summer program; extensive interviews with faculty, students, and alumni; reviews of other programs; surveys of alumni and supervisors for feedback—provided a foundation for a view of how the program was delivered and for the elements that appeared to conform to expectations and those that did not. The use of multiple measures (interviews, surveys, observations) and multiple audiences (students, faculty, teachers in the field) added to the wealth of information provided. Finally, his use of technology—digital photography to confirm and demonstrate observations, surveys on the Web, posting of draft reports for the evaluation staff and faculty—facilitated effective communication among stakeholders in a cost-effective and efficient way.

The evaluation raises a number of issues to consider: the choice of an evaluation model and the focus of an evaluation; the politics faced by internal evaluators; the utility of immersion in gaining an authentic sense of what happens in a program; the overlaps that can occur in evaluation in making assessments of clients (students), staff (faculty), and the program itself; and the choices one faces in depth and style of reporting.

DISCUSSION QUESTIONS

1. What is the purpose of Fetterman's evaluation?

2. Description is a key part of Fetterman's evaluation. What does he describe? What elements is he most concerned with? How does description fit with the purpose of his evaluation?

3. Discuss the methods Fetterman uses to describe STEP. In particular, consider his use of immersion into the summer STEP program. How does immersion help his evaluation?

4. Many evaluators whom we interview make use of observation. Contrast Fetterman's immersion and his role in it with Greene's observation of the leadership program. How are their methods and roles alike? How are they different? In a later interview, Ross Conner's staff observe community meetings. If you have already read that interview, consider how Conner's observation procedures differ from Fetterman's immersion and how they are alike.

5. Would you characterize Fetterman as more of an internal evaluator or an external evaluator? In this particular evaluation, what are the strengths of his

being internal, in the sense of being a member of the education faculty at Stanford University? What are the drawbacks, not only to him but to the evaluation?

6. Fetterman's emphasis is more on description than on outcomes. Do you agree with his choice? What factors may have influenced his choice?

7. What outcomes might you choose to measure if you were evaluating this program? Consider both short-term and long-term outcomes. How might you measure them?

8. How does Fetterman involve other stakeholders in his evaluation? Would you consider this a participatory evaluation?

FURTHER READING

Evaluation reports on the STEP evaluation are available at www.stanford.edu/davidf/step.html.

Fetterman, D. M., Connors, W., Dunlap, K., Brower, G., & Matos, T. (1998). *Stanford Teacher Education Program 1997–98 evaluation report.* Stanford, CA: School of Education, Stanford University.

Fetterman, D. M., Connors, W., Dunlap, K., Brower, G., Matos, T., & Paik, S. (1999). *A report to the President: Stanford Teacher Education Program 1997–98 evaluation.* Stanford, CA: Stanford University.

Fetterman, D. M., Dunlap, K., Greenfield, A., & Yoo, J. (1997). *Stanford Teacher Education Program 1997 summer school evaluation report.* Stanford, CA: Stanford University.

REFERENCES

Fitzpatrick, J. L., Sanders, J. R., & Worthen, B. R. (2004). *Program evaluation: Alternative approaches and practical guidelines* (3rd ed.). Boston: Longman.

Mathison, S. (1999). Rights, responsibilities, and duties: A comparison of ethics for internal and external evaluators. In J. L. Fitzpatrick & M. Morris (Eds.), *Current and emerging ethical challenges in evaluation* (New Directions for Evaluation, No. 82, pp. 25–34). San Francisco: Jossey-Bass.

Provus, M. M. (1971). *Discrepancy evaluation.* Berkeley, CA: McCutchan.

Spradley, J. P. (1970). *You owe yourself a drunk: An ethnography of urban nomads.* Boston: Little, Brown.

SIX

THE EVALUATION OF THE HOMELESS FAMILIES PROGRAM

An Interview With Debra J. Rog

Introduction: At the time of this interview, Debra Rog was a senior research associate with Vanderbilt University's Institute for Public Policy Studies and Director of its Washington office. She is currently an associate director with Westat and Vice President of its nonprofit arm, The Rockville Institute. Dr. Rog has over 25 years of experience in research and evaluation, having conducted several other large-scale multisite evaluations following this Robert Wood Johnson Foundation (RWJ)/U.S. Department of Housing and Urban Development (HUD) multisite effort. One of the multisite studies involved six quasi-experiments examining supported housing for persons with mental illness; a second involved a mix of eight experimental and quasi-experimental studies of interventions for homeless families headed by mothers with psychiatric and/or substance abuse conditions. Dr. Rog will serve as the president of the American Evaluation Association for 2009, is a recognized expert in evaluation and applied research design, and has served as the coeditor of the *Applied Social Research Methods Series* (50 textbooks to date) and the *Handbook of Applied Social Research Methods.*

The evaluation of the Homeless Families Program (HFP), which she directed, has received much attention nationally because of its early focus on homeless families, housing targeted to their needs, and systems integration. During this five-year, multisite study, Rog changed roles many times. As she realized that not much was known about homeless families at the time, she began the project with a focus on describing these families and their circumstances. Her focus then shifted to helping sites in planning services and testing some of the assumptions of the program theory concerning homeless families. The evaluation later moved to focus on describing change in the families and changes in the systems that were working with the families, which had been the impetus for the funding. The information was initially used for formative purposes to communicate what was happening across different sites and within sites and, thus, to help sites think about how they might bring about systems change. Ultimately, the evaluation began to examine final outcomes and judge the success of the program in achieving its two aims— improving the stability of families who receive services-enriched housing and creating systems change. The evaluation required much work with stakeholders across different sites to obtain their cooperation and buy-in in order to get valid results and obtain information that would be useful to others. The results of the study influenced programs and policies for homeless families at the local and national levels. As one of the few multisite studies of homeless families and interventions targeted to their needs, this evaluation has been cited widely in the literature on the homeless. It has been one of the main studies to date providing multisite descriptions of homeless families' needs as well as strong support, echoed by other studies, of the role of subsidies in helping families gain and maintain housing stability.

A Summary of the Evaluation of the Homeless Families Program

Debra J. Rog

———•◦•———

The Homeless Families Program (HFP), a joint demonstration effort of the Robert Wood Johnson Foundation (RWJ) and the U.S. Department of Housing and Urban Development (HUD), was initiated in 1990 as the first large-scale response to the problem of family homelessness. The HFP was implemented in nine cities across the nation with two complementary goals:

1. To create systems change by developing or restructuring the systems of health and support services and housing for families

2. To develop and test a model of services-enriched housing for homeless families who have multiple problems

The ultimate goals of the Program were to improve families' residential stability, roster greater use of services, and increase steps toward self-sufficiency.

Each of the nine program sites received approximately $600,000 in grant money and a special allotment of approximately 150 Section 8 certificates (housing subsidies) over five years. The projects were led by a city or county public agency, a coalition or task force for the homeless, or some other non-profit provider. Each project developed a memorandum of understanding with the local public housing authority, which in turn awarded the Section 8 housing certificates (subsidies for housing) to families with multiple problems. For each family receiving a certificate, the HFP lead agency was to provide or obtain services through case management. RWJ's support of the program totaled $4.7 million, while HUD's contribution was $30 million in rental subsidies.

The Evaluation Design

In addition to funding the nine sites and a national program office to guide the sites' implementation, the program also supported a major cross-site evaluation. The evaluation was designed to learn more about several key issues: the needs of families who struggle with homelessness and other problems; how services and systems might be better organized and delivered to meet those needs; and ways in which housing might be delivered to foster stability, service use, and progress toward self-sufficiency.

To gather this information, the study had two major components: (1) case studies of the project sites and three comparison sites where the project was not in place and (2) the collection of extensive family-level data. The case studies were designed to understand the systems within each site and how these systems changed over time. They included a review of key documents; a series of on-site interviews, including individual interviews and family and staff focus groups; and observations and tours of project and system services and other activities.

Data on nearly 1,300 families participating in the services-enriched housing programs were collected through a uniform data collection system designed by the evaluation team in concert with the projects. Data were collected by each family's case manager, who completed the intake, monthly, quarterly, and exit forms. The data system provided an opportunity to learn more about the needs and characteristics of the families served by the program, as well as to assess the implementation of the project.

In addition, a comprehensive assessment was conducted by trained interviewers with mothers in the HFP families who remained in services-enriched housing four months or longer. Finally, information was routinely collected from the public housing authorities on the residential status of all families.

The Results

The study found that families often presented a web of interrelated and deep-seated challenges. Families had experienced a great deal of instability, having moved approximately every 3½ months in the previous 18 months. On average, families experienced their first homeless episode about five years before entering the program. Families had multiple needs, including mental health and physical health services, substance abuse treatment, education and training, and others. Mental health and domestic violence needs were the most pronounced areas of needs and appeared to be present for much of the women's lives. Even after being in housing approximately 9 months, more than half (59%) were considered psychologically distressed and in need of further evaluation for depression. Nearly all (81%) reported some type of abuse by a former partner, and 65% reported one or more severe acts of violence by a partner.

Following participation in the program, several family outcomes were tracked through the evaluation. Despite years of instability, families achieved substantial residential stability after entering the program. In the six sites where data were available, more than 85% remained stably housed at least 18 months, more than doubling the amount of time families spent in permanent housing for the same period prior to the program. Rates of stability dropped in some sites at 30 months but continued to be relatively high. Following participation in the program, families did increase their access to, and use of, an array of services, with the biggest increases experienced in mental health services and alcohol and drug services. Families made little and erratic progress toward self-sufficiency, however, and remain largely dependent on federal and state support. After leaving the program, having received a year or so of case management, 20% of the mothers were known to be working, compared with 13% who reported working at the time they entered the program. The increase is slight and not uniform. Similarly, participation in education also fluctuated throughout the program, with few mothers attaining degrees.

Looking across the nine sites, there was considerable similarity in how the Section 8 programs were administered but more diversity in the implementation of case management. In particular, sites differed greatly in the intensity of the case management offered. Four levels of case management were identified, ranging from one site providing an average of an hour a week of case management, to sites where families met with their case managers for less than one hour a month.

With respect to the homeless families' service system, the evaluation found it to be ill defined and fragmented. In fact, the term *homeless system* is a misnomer as there are often multiple systems that provide services, each with its own level of fragmentation and gaps in services. They also proved difficult to change. By and large, the systems activities of the HFP projects did not result in broad-based changes but rather in some temporary or small-scale fix to improve service delivery. The most common system activities were "project fixes"—that is, filling service gaps for the families served through the project's services-enriched housing. Other activities created "system fixes" in which the services were increased or improved for homeless families outside those in the program, but the changes were usually circumscribed either in scope or time. "System changes," involving more enduring, widespread changes, were rare. The most common system changes involved changes in the role of the public housing authorities. Through the program, the public housing authorities increased their awareness of, and sensitivity to, the needs of homeless families and almost without exception became more active participants in providing housing options for this segment of families.

The study provided critical guidance to others interested in developing initiatives for impoverished families as well as those interested in building and changing service systems in general. With respect to families, the data clearly show that the cycle of homelessness can be broken with the receipt of housing subsidies. The role services play in achieving this stability is less clear from this study's results. The gains in residential stability are encouraging, especially in view of the life struggles these families have endured. However, their continued reliance on federal support and the lack of educational progress and steady employment raise questions regarding the long-term nature of their stability, as well as concerns for their continued vulnerability. In light of major welfare reforms under way, the need to learn how to make more enduring changes to the systems to improve their access and effectiveness is heightened.

Dialogue With Debra J. Rog

Jody Fitzpatrick

Fitzpatrick: Debra, this evaluation has many excellent qualities. That's why I selected it for the focus of this interview. But, I'd like to start with asking you what you thought was the most innovative or exciting part of this evaluation.

Rog: Well, it was both innovative and exciting. We used a mix of methodologies and addressed many different content areas. The whole topic of homelessness among families was a new, emerging issue at that time. Homelessness was ill defined; there still was not a lot known about it. There was especially little known about homeless families—who they were, how many there were, what their needs were, how they became homeless. But providers and others did not believe they could wait for the information before they tried to deal with the problem. Therefore, in our evaluation, it was critical that we try to obtain some of this information, focusing more on describing the participants in the program than we might otherwise, to help increase our understanding of these families. Our evaluation was the first cross-city look at homeless families, though it was not a representative sample. And it is still one of the few substantial evaluations of a homeless family intervention. So the evaluation served many purposes. It was exciting doing high-quality evaluation to meet so many different information needs.

Fitzpatrick: Could you tell us a little bit about how this evaluation was initiated? What made the Robert Wood Johnson Foundation (RWJ) decide to fund the evaluation component?

Rog: The RWJ always has evaluation as part of its demonstration initiatives. So that wasn't particularly new for them. The more interesting issue is why they funded this particular demonstration. It grew out of two earlier initiatives. One was designed to provide and evaluate health care services for the general homeless population. This initiative predated the Stewart B. McKinney Act, the federal government's response to homelessness. In the Foundation's efforts to serve what they thought was a predominately adult male population, they discovered the growing problem of homeless families.

In the second initiative, occurring at the same time as the first, RWJ partnered with HUD to provide and evaluate services and housing for persons with chronic mental illness.

HUD was interested in joining RWJ again, this time to focus on homeless families. RWJ believed that a systems approach was the most appropriate intervention to mount. They felt that families constituted one of the most entitled populations in the country. Their belief was that the services the homeless families needed were already there but weren't necessarily designed to be accessible to the homeless. The Foundation's theory was that money was needed primarily to improve coordination of services for homeless families. The one missing link in the system, housing, was provided through a new allotment of Section 8 certificates (i.e., housing subsidies) for a subset of the population in each community.

The Foundation wanted an evaluation to understand the variation across the sites and to examine how the funding affected systems change as well as outcomes for the families. Initially, the evaluation was pretty modest, but it got bigger over time. The program was first planned for two years, but pre-award site visits helped the Foundation and HUD realize that there would be little systems change in that time. So the time frame was lengthened to five years. As they refined the program, we were able to strengthen the evaluation, including more data collection on the families and their needs and a longer time period for data collection.

Fitzpatrick: Who were your audiences for the evaluation, and how did they become involved in the initial planning?

Rog: There were a lot of audiences. RWJ was obviously an audience. HUD was an audience. We wanted to have great policy impact—at the federal, state, and particularly local levels. So we saw practitioners and program people—both those involved in this initiative and those working in this area—as audiences.

We, the Vanderbilt Institute for Public Policy Studies, were selected based on a concept paper we had written for the project before the program sites were awarded. So we were involved with the program very early on.

We were able to develop the evaluation design closely with RWJ and HUD. Individuals from both organizations provided extensive input on our design and methods. We had several meetings with key staff, and they reviewed all our design papers and instruments.

I also worked really closely with the national office, located in Boston, that RWJ funded to really run the program. These folks reviewed all our proposals, designs, instruments, and so on. We went on site visits together, working as a team. In other RWJ initiatives, the national office typically has responsibility for the data collection that the project providers conduct, typically some form of management information system (MIS). Both because they did not feel they had the skills to design this and because the information the projects would collect would be so critical to our evaluation, the national office agreed to put us in charge of all data collection. We then worked as a team, with the national office stressing the importance and worth of the data to the sites, and with us responsible for developing as rigorous and systematic a data collection effort as possible. Working with each other from the early stages to the end, we were able to have reciprocal influence. The data collection processes, as well as the data themselves, served as key tools for the national office to learn about the sites and to troubleshoot areas of concern. Often problems in data collection revealed other problems in the site. Likewise, working so closely with the national office allowed us to make our inquiries more sensitive to their needs and also incorporate what they knew about the sites.

So the Foundation gave the evaluation a lot of support, and so did the national office; that doesn't always happen. I think, as do others, that this was a key strength of this initiative and why our evaluation was able to be completed so successfully.

Fitzpatrick: How were the sites involved in the planning of the evaluation?

Rog: They were heavily involved in the design of our data collection measures. With the national office, we held early meetings with the sites, explaining the evaluation and enlisting their participation. Much of the data collection we were planning required that line staff complete forms (intake forms, monthly forms, quarterly forms, and exit forms). Many of the sites said they were already collecting a lot of information for other funders and that we should take what they had. They were not particularly pleased with incorporating any new efforts. So we collected and reviewed all their existing data collection efforts. Unfortunately, most were very subjective, and there was little uniformity across the sites. By explaining the diversity and stressing the need for "one voice" among the sites in order to have any policy impact, we— together with the national office—were able to convince them to use a new set of uniform data collection tools. The Foundation was especially supportive in encouraging the sites to work with us.

Fitzpatrick: It can sometimes be difficult to obtain sites' cooperation in data collection, even with the support of the funding agency. Can you tell us a little bit more about how you worked with them?

Rog: We developed draft instruments and went out to sites so the case managers could provide input. In one instance, we totally changed the form. One case manager hadn't liked the way the form was set up and came up with a different format, designing it in a way she felt would be easier to account for the various activities she did in a day. With the new format, we got more data than we had originally planned! The next time I came to visit, the case managers said, "You *did* change it." They were pleased that they had been heard. We bought a lot of credibility with that. The form became one of our most important tools. We got them to buy in, and thus, we got better data.

For the same form, another case manager said, "You're not capturing what I do" with the listing of activities that we had. So I said, "Help me figure out how to understand what you do. What types of work do you do with families?" She and I spoke for quite a while and determined that in addition to formal skill building with families and counseling, much of her time was spent in informal problem solving (e.g., if you don't have a car and need to pick up your child from the day care, how do you do this?). When we added this category, many case managers noted, "That's more of what I do." There was really nice give-and-take.

Fitzpatrick: You must have had times when it was difficult to get site agreement or consensus. Can you tell us about some of those experiences?

Rog: Our data collection wasn't perfect. We still had sites that didn't like what we were doing. There was a lot of concern with political correctness. The intake form, for example, asked for "spouse." San Francisco said, "You can't say that, say 'significant other.'" Then, Nashville said, "You can't do that. We require a marriage certificate for Section 8 housing." So at these times, we made changes that pleased some of the sites but clearly not all.

Sometimes other conflicts would occur. We originally wanted to collect more data on kids—on child abuse—but the national office felt this was much too sensitive to have our trained interviewers collect, even with certificates of confidentiality. We dropped child abuse, but we still wanted to know about violence directed toward the homeless mom. However, as we traveled across the country to different sites we continually encountered roadblocks to this data collection from the sites. So we decided to make it optional—sites could choose to allow our interviewers to collect this information in our assessment interview. Then, we got to our Portland site, and when they looked at the core assessment interview they asked what had happened to the domestic violence questions! When we told them they were optional, they thought that that was a mistake. They wanted them! And they wanted all sites to use them in order to have one national voice on the problem. We brought the different sites together to discuss the issue in a special session at the regular annual meeting. With all the project directors together, the Portland project director was persuasive. The sites finally reached consensus, having all the domestic violence questions included in the family assessment interview. As it turned out, the domestic violence findings were quite staggering—extremely high rates of violence overall and even severe violence in the lives of the mothers. These data, confirming findings from the few other studies that were being conducted at the time, helped to emphasize the mental health service needs of these families.

Fitzpatrick: You mentioned you became involved in the program very early. Tell us about that. Did that early involvement give you an advantage in understanding the program? In planning the evaluation?

Rog: We were selected after the demonstration program had been announced and the call to grantees was out but before the grants were awarded. Therefore, I was able to watch the review of the grantees. Seeing the selection process was invaluable. I gained a much better sense of what the Foundation wanted from the program. We also got to see the early stages of establishing the national program office.

Fitzpatrick: Did that help you establish good relationships with the Foundation and the national office?

Rog: Yes, that and good chemistry. As I said earlier, we were able to influence each other and to understand each other's priorities. We found ways to meld them together. For example, I needed the national office to help me with sites that were not very cooperative in helping our interviewers find families. In turn, as they tried to devise a strategy with a site to facilitate our interview process, the national office inevitably would uncover other issues in which they could intervene and help the site.

Fitzpatrick: You chose to focus on three issues: describing the population served, describing the actions taken by the sites, and examining two sets of outcomes—impact on community systems and on the families themselves. Could you tell us a little bit about why you chose those questions?

Rog: As it was primarily a descriptive evaluation, we didn't think we would ever have definitive causal answers. Further, given the emergent nature of the issue, it probably made sense to be more descriptive and somewhat exploratory. We did err on the side of collecting more detail than one might do in a more controlled study. I have always thought that if you are "design poor, you should be data rich!" Collecting more detailed information on the families and collecting service and outcome information at routine intervals across the study time frame, we felt, should provide greater explanatory power.

We focused on the two sets of outcomes, community systems and the families, because they corresponded to the two major program goals. The initial focus by RWJ was on systems change, but the involvement of HUD with Section 8 housing brought a focus on the individual family. This was a little bit of the tail wagging the dog. Section 8 housing was added to allow sites to work with HUD. But, as a result of having Section 8, the program became more focused on the Section 8 intervention than on the systems intervention. Over time, the project directors were able to put some attention on the systems change component, but in the first three years, their time was consumed with trying to implement "services-enriched housing" with a subset of families, most of whom had multiple challenges and needs.

Fitzpatrick: Were there any other evaluation questions you considered but ultimately rejected? If so, why did you reject these?

Rog: There were other outcomes we would have liked to look at, but we didn't really have the resources to include a lot more than what we had. Because our standardized assessment interview with the families could only be conducted once, we had to measure change exclusively through measures collected by the providers and the housing authority. So we measured service use, employment and education, and residential stability—outcomes the providers could track fairly reliably and that corresponded to the primary program goals. Measures of how families were functioning—with respect to health, mental health, family stability—would have been good but would also have required more interviews with families and, thus, were beyond what we could support.

Fitzpatrick: Let me move back a little. The sites seemed quite involved in decisions on data collection, but did they have input on the evaluation questions you addressed? Or were these primarily to meet the needs of HUD and RWJ?

Rog: The overall research questions were pretty much set by the Foundation, really to track the major goals of the program. The sites' input came in the development of subquestions: What types of needs were we examining? What aspects of stability? And so on. So they had a lot of input on what was looked at. But they did not have input on the overall design.

Fitzpatrick: One element of the study that might be interesting to our readers is the juggling of data collection across nine different cities. How did you manage that?

Rog: Our team really tried to manage all the data collection, including the pieces we collected directly through our interviewers and the pieces the sites collected. The sites collected most of the data, through the efforts of their case managers. We created a data collection process that tracked a client's participation throughout the program—intake, monthly, quarterly, exit. All those forms were completed by each individual's case manager. We also collected data on housing stability from the public housing authorities, and we had our own interviewers conduct one-time family assessment interviews with families in the program.

We did a lot of training with the sites for their data collection. To ease the burden of collection, we tried to integrate it within the programmatic activities. For example, they were encouraged to adopt our intake form as their sole intake form. All sites did adopt it and used it for decision making. This was key to our obtaining intakes on nearly 100% of all participants in the program. We also tried to incorporate some of the monthly forms into their regular data collection and to design them so that they could be useful to the individual providers and to the managers. For instance, we gave periodic reports back to the project directors so that they could use them for management purposes, and we designed the reports in ways that responded to their concerns. They demonstrated its use by their requests. For example, on case management encounter information, they asked to see the data broken out by individual case managers.

All our forms worked pretty well, with the exception of the quarterly data collection forms. These forms were an attempt to track changes in each family (e.g., started school; completed school). Rather than tell us the status, they were to indicate if a change in status had occurred and what it was. However, we had a really poor return rate on the quarterly forms and found out through some investigation that case managers were not returning them because no changes were taking place. Partly they felt it was a waste to send back blank forms (killing trees!), and partly they did not want to tell us that change was not happening. Once we learned this, we had to give them more prompts.

The monthly case manager and service use forms worked better but also had a few problems. The case manager forms were generally completed and seemed to work well. Sometimes we wouldn't get case management forms back because the case worker hadn't seen the client; then we had to build in a process for distinguishing between not seeing the client (i.e., zero encounters) and missing data.

The service forms proved to be more burdensome to complete on a monthly basis and at the degree of detail we wanted. The case managers felt they knew whether a family had been referred to a service and whether they had accessed it at least once. They felt they had less valid information on how much service someone received or how often they received it. So if we had to do it over again, we would definitely streamline that type of data collection.

Each site had a data coordinator. We didn't pay them for that task, but they were designated by the program with the task of getting the data to us. The data collection was done a little more on a shoestring than we had thought it would be. It would have been more desirable to pay someone to be the on-site data collector.

Fitzpatrick: How cooperative were the different sites? I noticed that occasionally you don't receive data from all sites. Were sites free to adapt the evaluation to site-specific needs?

Rog: Cooperation varied across the sites and also by the type of data being collected. About a third of the sites presented the most problems. Early on, though, we realized the strain that the data collection would place on the sites and tried to build in monetary incentives to the case managers for data collection. The Foundation was really keen on this, but a problem emerged. If the program was run by a public agency, we couldn't give incentives because public employees can't accept incentives. The sites could use the funds for training and other supports but not for individual incentives. Some places also did not agree to the incentives because they were adamant that data collection should be part of the case manager's job. In only a couple of sites did the agencies support the notion of direct financial incentives. For the most part, however, sites used the money programmatically, and the "incentive" notion of the funds was lost.

Fitzpatrick: Were there other differences between the sites that were more actively involved in the study? What characterized the sites that participated less? Did they have less commitment or expertise in the area?

Rog: With perhaps one or two exceptions, it was those sites that seemed to implement the program best that also provided the data most consistently and completely. This was a problem as it always made it more difficult to draw conclusions about those sites that did not seem to be fully implementing the program. For example, we believed we had more missing data from sites that had difficulty keeping up with their clients. But it was difficult to know what was missing and what was truly nonencounter data. Similarly, we received less cooperation from some of these sites in tracking down families for our family assessment. Sometimes the absence of tracking may have meant that they lost touch; some of it was due to other reasons. The Foundation tried to support us by informing the sites early on that the Foundation would be considering sites' cooperation in data collection when making decisions about continuation funding. We also involved the national office to try to get sites to contribute data.

Another complication was that most data were collected by case managers, and case managers were defined quite differently across the sites. In the design of the program, RWJ believed that sites could "leverage" case management from other agencies and programs (e.g., case managers from shelters, other service programs). However, this was not always possible, and thus some sites had to use their grant money to hire new case managers specifically for this program. In these cases, the data collection generally went smoothly because the case managers were accountable directly to the program. In other sites, where leveraging did occur—sometimes involving as many as 30 to 50 different agencies—data collection was much more haphazard. The sites had difficulty tracking case managers, let alone the families.

The data collection problems highlighted the problems with such a diffuse network of case managers in a few sites. Many of the case managers in these networks did not see the program as a primary responsibility and thus were lax on data collection. In many cases as well, the case manager had minimal time to work with the family. In addition, case management in a shelter setting proved to be very different from case management in a home setting. Once families are in their own homes, a host of issues and problems reportedly seemed to emerge. Case managers commented on the number of crises that families experienced. Sites with diffuse systems began to feel out of control and gradually moved to fewer case managers. The data collection demands pressed this change. So in this instance, through the data collection process, we all learned a lesson about the way in which case management was being delivered, and this in turn led to a restructuring of the program. Although this change may have occurred in time, it was felt that the evaluation provided a vehicle for learning about it sooner and in a more specific way than we may have otherwise.

Fitzpatrick: That sounds like quite a move away from the traditional research approach, where it would be considered a major error, at a minimum harming external validity, to have the research methods influence the treatment itself. Your approach sounds more like Patton's developmental evaluation, where the evaluator is working with the client to consciously improve program delivery while the evaluation takes place. Did you consciously see yourself in this developmental role? What about the sacrifice to rigor?

Rog: Yes, I think there were some trade-offs in the decisions we made. However, we were already running the risk of jeopardizing external validity by having missing data from a large segment of the people being seen in some programs. Also, I did feel that we were in a developmental, formative role. As I stated earlier, we were all learning about the phenomena of homelessness as the program was unfurling. It did not begin with an extremely explicit theory or with a very elaborate understanding of the needs and problems of families. Therefore, part of our role was to help develop these bases of knowledge and then, in turn, use this knowledge to help guide program efforts. We tracked what we did and how it affected sites, and that became part of the story. It could have diminished some of the generalizability of the findings; however, I think the major finding of the study—that families remain in housing once they receive a subsidy and some level of services—was unblemished by our interventions and could be replicated whether an evaluation was ongoing or not.

Fitzpatrick: You used interviews with families as a major means of data collection. Tell us a little bit about how you made that choice.

Rog: The families were the key beneficiaries. Thus, they were a major source. The case managers provided hard data from the records, employment data, and the like. But the family data were very rich. It was important to have their individual voices, to learn of their experiences. We hired interviewers who were independent of the agencies to do the interviews and trained them ourselves. As we used mostly standardized instruments, we felt that it would be best to have trained interviewers.

Fitzpatrick: Why didn't you use the case managers to do the interviews? Some evaluations have used staff for data collection with good results in making the evaluation more credible to them and in empowering the staff.

Rog: We had initially proposed that strategy, but the case managers were stretched beyond the maximum with the program. So the Foundation gave us a supplement to hire and train outside interviewers. The sites saw the need for the family interviews, too, but staff time was a barrier to getting the interviews completed.

Fitzpatrick: How do you weigh the strengths and weaknesses of staff versus persons independent of the program for collecting data?

Rog: Using program people to do interviews can sometimes be helpful in getting high participation rates. The case manager also knows the interviewee and can sometimes prompt more effectively. It is a yin-yang issue. In some instances, the respondent may be able to be more forthcoming with the case manager, but on some issues the respondent might be reluctant to divulge information they don't want their case manager to know. For that reason, we wanted the interviewers to be relatively "faceless" to the respondents.

Another problem for us was that, as I have mentioned, the case managers' role varied across sites. So using the case managers as interviewers would have introduced unknown variation. We wanted to give each person the opportunity to have her voice, but we also wanted some standardization so that we could have more reliable information. We were concerned that case managers would have difficulty following a standardized process. (They had actually indicated that this would be difficult for them to do.)

For programmatic reasons, we did ask the family if they wanted to release the information gained in the interview to case workers. In some cases, that information became very important for service delivery to the family. Things came up in the interview that case managers never knew because they don't ask these questions—things about rape, suicide, sexual involvement. If the client gave a release, the interview information would be sent to the case managers and red-flagged.

Fitzpatrick: You note that approximately 65% of the eligible families were interviewed. How did you arrive at this sample? Did the others refuse?

Rog: There were varying rates of completion across sites. Four sites had completion rates of 70% or above. Seven sites were above 60%. There were very few outright refusals. The difficulties were in tracking down the families and, in some cases, having no shows. Changing addresses, disconnected phones, and our limited budget made tracking difficult, especially in sites with infrequent contact. We could only pay for two return visits to a family's home. If families were geographically clustered, we could go by more frequently. I visited several sites to see how they tracked families. Again, if sites had a lot of contact with families through the program, it was much easier to find them and schedule interviews. If sites had more erratic contact, we had lower rates of completion. In more than half the sites, we had decent rates of response, and in three sites we had very high completion rates. We did compare respondents and nonrespondents on intake data that we had available and found few differences.

Fitzpatrick: You made use of a mix of qualitative and quantitative measures, as do many evaluations today. Could you discuss how you made those choices? On what issues did you see quantitative measures as most appropriate? And what issues were best addressed by qualitative measures?

Rog: At the systems level, almost everything was qualitative. We had multiple sources—site interviews, focus groups, document reviews. It was a multiple case study design. We chose qualitative methods because we were interested in several key descriptive questions: What does the system of service delivery look like at each site? How does the system deliver services? How does the program view the system? What changes have occurred in the system as a result of program actions? There were no databases existing on the system, and most of the information was only known by key players in the system. Therefore, I think that the qualitative focus was the appropriate choice.

We used a mostly quantitative approach in assessing family characteristics and needs and in examining family outcomes. Why? Because of the large number of families in the study and because the people making the policy decisions needed hard numbers. We tried to collect more qualitative data on the goals families had, but it didn't work well. We had a difficult time training case managers in how to collect this information and struggled with how to compile it in a meaningful manner. We also asked some open-ended questions on families' experience with homelessness and obtained some qualitative data from the case managers each quarter on how each family was progressing. These data added "color" and depth to our quantitative findings and I think increased our credibility to consumer and provider audiences. But we knew that the policy audiences, such as federal officials and state legislators, would attach more credibility to quantitative data. We were persuaded by the experiences Jim Wright had had in his evaluation of the RWJ Health Care for the Homeless Program. Although his study had many of the flaws that we had, he had dramatic results that were not diminished by the methodological shortcomings. He found, for example, that the rate of TB among the homeless was 100 times the rate in the general population. Having those kinds of numbers was dramatic and was one of the sparks for the Stewart B. McKinney Homeless Assistance Act, passed by Congress in 1987.

We also incorporated other qualitative information to help us further understand the quantitative information. In addition to interviews with staff and others in each site, we conducted focus groups with families to gain a greater understanding of their situations and experiences in the program.

Fitzpatrick: While you found some positive results, in particular the finding that families gained much residential stability, many of the goals of this program were not achieved. I was impressed with how directly, and yet constructively, you dealt with these failures in your report. It's sometimes sensitive to convey such information to funders or site managers. How did you convey those results?

Rog: We had been conveying the findings to the Foundation and the national office all along. For example, we learned early on that the case management being provided was not "intensive case management," as they had intended, but a less intense form of the service. This characterization was important to be honest about what was going on and what could be realistically achieved. We also clarified the different levels of case management across the projects and how they may have resulted in different models of intervention.

One area where the program did not achieve its goals was in the systems. As we began to assess the program, we realized that the goals were more ambitious than the program realistically could achieve. Moreover, the sites were enmeshed in developing their services-enriched housing interventions and weren't giving attention to systems in the first few years of the program. Even when they were able to devote more of their efforts to systems issues, major changes were not happening. I always feel a responsibility to understand what's going on and to explain why something may not be occurring. Was it because they are not implementing the activities to achieve the outcomes, or are they doing something else? Is there something blocking the change from occurring? If we had just examined whether they had an impact on the system—yes or no—it would have been a pretty short report and we wouldn't have learned much.

So we took a slightly backward approach and cataloged what they were doing under the rubric of systems change activities. We then outlined each activity and with whom it was conducted, examining how it fit within the framework of what you would want an ideal system to achieve. We then assessed each activity for its potential in creating systems change. We found some sites were making fixes to the system through their projects—these fixes changed the system, but only for the subset of families with whom they were working. Other sites were fixing the system for a greater number of families, but these fixes still either did not affect all potential families or were temporary. In only a few instances were activities put in place that had the potential for system-wide effects. Most of these involved working with the Housing Authority to create changes in their regulations and in practices that had the ability to affect all families who entered the housing system.

We presented this systems fix/change framework and results at the annual meeting with the sites. We were very nervous because it showed only minimal movement by most sites along the path of systems change. But instead they embraced both our framework and results. They said, "That's exactly what's going on! And not only that, but you've given us a tool to bring about more change!" The framework gave the sites a "conceptual road map" for pursuing additional activities or strengthening their current activities.

Using the framework, we were able to categorize the sites along the nature of the system change activities they were doing. We presented it to the most insular site without labeling it, and the staff themselves realized they hadn't made any progress in affecting the system. The framework and our categories presented the facts without any qualification. As long as sites agreed with the data, the facts spoke for themselves.

Fitzpatrick: Summative and *formative* are old terms in evaluation, but I think they're quite useful in helping us consider the purposes of an evaluation. Nevertheless, it's often difficult to characterize a study as purely formative or summative. In addition, as Scriven has noted, the thrust of a study can sometimes change. Would you characterize this study as primarily summative or formative?

Rog: I think it was evolving, but probably more formative than summative. However, it had features of both. We tried to present data on a routine basis back to the sites. We worked more directly with the national program office, and I know they made changes based on data. Our purposes didn't change so much as they evolved.

Fitzpatrick: You conclude that the absence of a theory or model for system change and, more specifically, the strategies site directors should use to bring about change, was a cause of the failure to change systems in the community. That is, when there is an absence of clarity about the model, projects focus more on concrete activities—in this case, working with families—and less on more ambiguous issues. At the American Evaluation Association meeting last fall, there were quite a few sessions on logic models for programs. You seem to be saying that the program lacked a clearly delineated logic model. Do you agree?

Rog: Yes, I agree—there was a general sense of the program and a beginning model that we actually sketched out for the evaluation. However, I rather think they couldn't have developed a more articulated one at that point. The agencies needed to work with families first to learn about potential models. It would have been premature to develop one prior to this work. Though the people at the sites knew a lot about what families needed, they learned more from actually working with families. For example, there was an assumption on the part of RWJ that services did exist but simply weren't oriented toward homeless families. Then, the sites found that some services didn't exist—for example, dental care. So the initial work with the families helped to refine and articulate a more detailed model.

Fitzpatrick: What role do you think evaluators should play in developing a logic model?

Rog: I think evaluators can have a key role in developing logic models. As I noted earlier, we developed an initial program model based on conversations with RWJ. This model guided our evaluation and data collection. When we initially met with each site, we shared a model we developed of their specific project from their grant proposal and other materials. This model was then refined based on what we learned. The model helped to focus on key elements of each project in a more systematic way than might otherwise occur.

Fitzpatrick: Could you tell us a little bit about your dissemination of the results. How did you communicate results to the different stakeholders? What methods did you find worked most effectively?

Rog: We communicated results in a variety of different ways. We presented results at the annual program meetings to key stakeholders from RWJ, HUD, and the sites throughout the process. We also tried to communicate information to the sites every three months. In the fourth year of the evaluation, we actually made a formal presentation in each of five sites on their own site-specific interim results using a community forum.

We also made a couple of presentations at HUD and a number of academic, professional, service provider, and homelessness meetings. The Foundation also arranged a Capitol Hill briefing some time after HFP ended, in which we presented the evaluation findings, the national office described its role, and a few sites described their projects. The meeting was a chance to bring the results to federal policy makers, folks in other interested national associations and agencies, and other providers.

We have also published several articles and chapters, some more academically oriented and one or two for more general audiences. The study findings continue to figure prominently in reviews of homeless families and in reviews of housing interventions. I have written a couple of those reviews, and others in the field have as well.

Fitzpatrick: Tell us a bit about the community forums. Who was invited? Did the sites have a chance to review the results prior to the presentation? What was your goal with the forum?

Rog: The forum for presenting the results was arranged by the site project director and ranged from having just individuals affiliated with the site in attendance to having a broad set of stakeholders, including state and local policy and program officials. Typically, the sites reviewed our presentation materials prior to our visit and also sometimes presented with us. The forums were generally designed for the purposes of information sharing, with some sites strategically inviting some more political guests in the hope of sparking interest for continued funding. In most sites, having descriptive data, even if not definitive on outcomes, was a step above what officials usually have on service programs.

Fitzpatrick: What aspect of the results did you find most surprising? Why?

Rog: What I found most surprising (but probably shouldn't have) was how what was important to the policy audience changed over time. At the outset of the program, in 1990, many people thought that these families were "dysfunctional" and could not make it in housing on their own. Our residential stability results contest that (more than 85% of the families were still in their Section 8 housing after 18 months). It showed people can and will stay housed if they have a subsidy and some level of services. Some people say it's really their personal problems that keep people homeless, but this study presented another part of the picture. We didn't have a control group, but we didn't need one because the findings were so dramatic. Families had moved every 3 months in the 18 months prior to the program; now they remained in stable housing almost the entire 18-month period. However, when we conducted our Hill briefing in 1997, the interest was not in whether these families were stable but in whether they were working. Our employment results were disappointing—the percentage of families working at exit from the services was not significantly larger than the percentage working when they entered the program. Employment was not a central focus of the HFP. At the time it was initiated, welfare reform hadn't come. But by the time of our briefing, the bar was rising.

What other findings were surprising? In some ways it wasn't totally surprising, but the consistency of the high levels of domestic violence and suicide attempts was astonishing, given that sites recruited families differently. No matter which way the site recruited families (e.g., through homeless shelters, substance abuse programs, domestic violence programs, or other ways), the violence levels were similar, and the depression levels within the families were sobering.

Our findings show that the HFP has families treading water, and they're not that much closer to the shore. How vulnerable they remained was striking—some of the more poignant stories came through our analysis of the qualitative data. Nearly all of the mothers had worked at some point in their lives, so they had some level of human capital. Most left work due to pregnancy or lack of child care. But they were still incredibly vulnerable. Their personal struggles with depression, substance abuse, domestic violence, and other issues, all while trying to raise children and stay stable, seemed to have cumulative effects. Although many of the mothers had goals to get and keep jobs or to obtain further education, these goals often shifted quickly. Keeping on one track was not a typical path for the women in the study. Moreover, when faced with a major life event, such as a family member's death, case managers spoke of the women falling off the track entirely, if only for a temporary period.

Fitzpatrick: Finally, even in the most exemplary studies, we recognize, in retrospect, things that we wish we had done differently. If you were to do this evaluation again, what would you change?

Rog: I think we did a really good job, given what we knew about homeless families at the time and given the resources. And we stretched those. The study did make me appreciate experimental control, however. As much as variability is good, we had variability in both the nature of case management and in the needs of families. And what happened is that more troubled families received higher doses of case management, so we could not tease out the independent effects of case management dose. There was keen interest in understanding whether services mattered, but because the variation in services received was confounded with the needs of the population served, we couldn't answer that. It would have been nice to have some planned variation in the service programs, with individuals with similar needs getting different levels of service. But we did not have that kind of control. Even more control on who gets into the program would have been useful. Naturalistic studies are great for some issues but not for others. If I were to do this study again, I would want to build in some level of control, especially given that the interest in understanding the role of services is so keen.

I wish we had done some, but less, data collection across all sites and had focused more intensely on a few sites where we were getting more complete data. With this, we might have been able to put more resources into obtaining more sensitive data on the services families were getting and the outcomes they were experiencing.

Overall, I think we provided key insight into the needs of homeless families and showed the stability in housing that can be achieved. Families did indeed break their cycle of homelessness for an extended period of time. We stood by this outcome, even without a tight outcome design, because it was so dramatic and because it was implausible for something else to account for the change. But this comes from a real rival-thinking posture. We could have taken a conservative approach and said we don't know if the stability was due to the program because we only had a pre-post comparison, but nothing else could have caused this change. We were going outside the textbook to argue that, but the multisite nature of the study strengthened our ability to feel confident that the change was not due to selection factors, history, and so forth.

Fitzpatrick's Commentary

Rog's evaluation of the HFP has many exemplary components. These include active involvement and consideration of various stakeholders' needs, use of a mix of qualitative and quantitative methods consistent with the purposes of the study and the resources available, and dissemination of results to different audiences in interesting, innovative ways. Rog and her staff had the opportunity to be involved in the program at a very early planning stage. They took advantage of that opportunity to learn more about the funder's intents and the sites themselves. They adapted their role and the evaluation during these early stages to better address the state of knowledge concerning homeless families and the information needs of the audiences. During the course of the evaluation, continued adaptation can be noted in Rog's efforts to refine the logic model by developing models from the descriptions of site efforts at system integration.

The focus and adaptation of the evaluation to the state of knowledge in the field—that is, the lack of information on homeless families—is interesting. Policy makers and program managers typically must move ahead without complete information. Some authors have criticized evaluators for their difficulty in understanding and coping with decision making in this state of uncertainty (Swanson, 1989). Rog reveals none of these difficulties. She acknowledges the lack of information, recognizes the need to learn more through programs working with homeless people, and designs the evaluation to fill some of the knowledge gaps. She identifies that describing the homeless family population and the means by which they obtain services was a primary purpose, not so much to evaluate the program as to inform program and policy people for future work. In some ways, the study is a needs assessment that takes place in the context of an early program. Outreach efforts could not await a comprehensive needs assessment, but the evaluation does not, then, neglect the issue but makes use of the program as a tool to learn more.

Similarly, Rog is comfortable with allowing the logic model to evolve. Although I am a proponent of logic models, the current emphasis on detailed logic models may miss opportunities for experimentation as illustrated in the sites and models developed in this study. The initial HFP model surely would have met neither the criteria for linkages between goals and activities specified by Wholey (1987) in his early work on evaluability assessment nor the strictures of United Way guidelines or the federal Government Performance and Results Act (GPRA) at the time (Radin, 1998). Rog recognizes the utility of logic models. Initial models are developed with the recognition that they will become more detailed as they learn of the sites' work. She uses logic models to describe sites' work. But she does not insist on fine-tooled precision when information is scarce.

Finally, this study illustrates comfort with finding and discussing program failure. Families' lives were improved through residential stability, but employment and education gains were not achieved. She discusses the failures to achieve the system integration and change goals that were the impetus for the original funding. Rog is forthright in acknowledging these problem areas, though she helpfully discusses reasons for these failures. Nevertheless, as evaluators, we must be comfortable with recognizing, acknowledging, and discussing program failures. Evaluation is fundamentally about judging the value of something. As formative evaluators, when we identify problems or failures, we have the obligation to go on and provide information for program improvement (which may include eliminating program segments that failed), but we should not shy away from such judgments. Evaluators may serve as advocates for evaluation or for stakeholders (see Datta, 1999), but they lose credibility when they serve as advocates for a program or organization.

DISCUSSION QUESTIONS

1. This section of the book is concerned with evaluations that focus on description. Rog describes several things within the context of a traditional evaluation. What are they? Why does she choose to describe these things?

2. How would you characterize Rog's interactions with stakeholders, in particular with program staff at the sites? Describe her role. Consider the consequences of the role she assumes. Does it help or hinder her evaluation? In what way?

3. Mel Mark has written concerning the consequences of evaluation. One consequence is that the process of an evaluation, the actual activities of the evaluation, can change the nature of program delivery. That consequence occurs several times in Rog's evaluation. Is it appropriate for her evaluation to affect and change the program in the course of the evaluation? Contrast Rog's role in these changes with the roles of Fetterman and Riccio in their evaluations. Would they have wanted their evaluations to result in program changes during the evaluation? Why is Rog comfortable with these consequences when others may not be?

4. Rog uses a case study approach, using interviews with many stake-holders, to describe systems change in the different cities. She uses a more quantitative methodology to describe homeless families and their residential stability. Discuss why she used these different methodological approaches. Do you agree with her choices? Why or why not?

5. At the conclusion of her evaluation, Rog draws some conclusions about the success of the HFP. Although Rog's training is in experimental design, she argues that, unlike Riccio and Bickman, she did not need an experimental design to prove that the Section 8 housing made a difference in homeless families' residential stability. Should she have used an experimental design rather than comparing pre and post levels of residential stability? Why is she so certain that the changes are a result of the program? Do you agree?

FURTHER READING

A summary of the evaluation findings: Rog, D. J., & Gutman, M. A. (1997). The Homeless Families Program: A summary of key findings. In S. Isaacs & J. Knickman (Eds.), *To improve health and healthcare: The Robert Wood Johnson Foundation Anthology 1997* (pp. 209–231). San Francisco: Jossey-Bass.

Hambrick, R., & Rog, D. J. (2000). The pursuit of coordination: The organizational dimension in the response to homelessness. *Policy Studies Journal, 28*(2), 353–364.

Rog, D. J. (1994). *The Homeless Families Program: Interim benchmarks.* Washington, DC: Vanderbilt Institute for Public Policy Studies.

Rog, D. J. (1999). The evaluation of the Homeless Families Program. *American Journal of Evaluation, 20,* 557–561.

Rog, D. J., & Buckner, J. (2007). *Homeless families and children.* Paper presented at the 2007 National Symposium on Homelessness Research. Washington, DC: U.S. Department of Housing and Urban Development and U.S. Department of Health and Human Services.

Rog, D. J., & Holupka, C. S. (1999). Reconnecting homeless individuals and families to the community. In L. Fosburg & D. Dennis (Eds.), *Practical lessons: The 1998 National Symposium on Homelessness Research.* Washington, DC: U.S. Department of Housing and Urban Development and U.S. Department of Health and Human Services.

Rog, D. J., Holupka, C. S., & McCombs-Thornton, K. L. (1995). Implementation of the Homeless Families Program. *American Journal of Orthopsychiatry, 63,* 502–513.

Rog, D. J., Holupka, C. S., McCombs-Thornton, K., Brito, M. C., & Hambrick, R. (1997). Case management in practice: Lessons from the evaluation of RWJ/HUD Homeless Families Program. *Journal of Prevention and Intervention in the Community, 15,* 67–82.

Rog, D. J., McCombs-Thornton, K. L., Gilbert-Mongelli, A. M., Brito, M. C., & Holupka, C. S. (1995). Implementation of the Homeless Families Program: Characteristics, strengths, and needs of participant families. *American Journal of Orthopsychiatry, 65,* 514–528.

REFERENCES

Datta, L. (1999). The ethics of evaluation neutrality and advocacy. In J. L. Fitzpatrick & M. Morris (Eds.), *Current and emerging ethical challenges in evaluation* (New Directions for Evaluation, No. 82, pp. 77–88). San Francisco: Jossey-Bass.

Radin, B. A. (1998). The Government Performance and Results Act (GPRA): Hydra-headed monster or flexible management tool? *Public Administration Review, 58,* 307–315.

Swanson, R. A. (1989). Everything important in business and industry is evaluated. In R. O. Brinkerhoff (Ed.), *Evaluating training programs in business and industry* (New Directions for Program Evaluation, No. 44, pp. 71–82). San Francisco: Jossey-Bass.

Wholey, J. S. (1987). *Evaluability assessment: Developing program theory.* In L. Bickman (Ed.), *Using program theory in evaluation* (New Directions for Program Evaluation, No. 33, pp. 77–92). San Francisco: Jossey-Bass.

SEVEN

THE COUNCIL FOR SCHOOL PERFORMANCE: PERFORMANCE REPORTS FOR GEORGIA SCHOOLS

An Interview With Gary T. Henry

*I**ntroduction:* At the time of the interview, Gary Henry was a professor in the Andrew Young School of Public Policy and Department of Political Science at Georgia State University (GSU). He also served as director of the Council for School Performance, which was housed at GSU. Currently, he is the MacRae Distinguished Professor of Public Policy in the Department of Public Policy and directs the Carolina Institute for Public Policy at the University of North Carolina (UNC) at Chapel Hill. Also, he holds the appointment of Senior Statistician in Frank Porter Graham Institute for Child Development at UNC–Chapel Hill. Henry has evaluated a variety of policies and programs, including North Carolina's Disadvantaged Student Supplemental Fund, Georgia's Universal Pre-Kindergarten (Pre-K) program, public information campaigns, and the Helping Outstanding Pupils Educationally (HOPE). Scholarship, as well as school reforms and accountability systems. He has written extensively in policy research, evaluation, and social science journals, including the *Journal of Policy Analysis and Management; American Journal of Evaluation; Evaluation; Educational Evaluation and Policy*

Analysis; Child Development; and *Public Opinion Quarterly.* He is the author of *Practical Sampling* (Sage, 1990) and *Graphing Data* (Sage, 1995) and coauthor of *Evaluation: An Integrated Framework for Understanding, Guiding, and Improving Policies and Programs* (2000).

Gary Henry and his staff at the Council for School Performance won the American Evaluation Association Award for Outstanding Evaluation in 1998 for his work on developing a performance measurement system for education in the state of Georgia. Today, performance monitoring is commonly used to assess performance in many public and nonprofit organizations. In education, many states and school districts across the country developed standards and performance measures to inform the public, parents, teachers, and school administrators about the performance of schools. These efforts vary greatly in quality and approach. Since the time of the original interview, the No Child Left Behind Act has required all states to report and sanction schools and school districts based on performance standards.

The system developed by Henry and his staff remains exemplary in illustrating a system that makes use of multiple measures linked to learning to assess school performance and presents the information in a way that is readily understood by its intended audiences. Its use of two types of comparisons, all schools and similar schools, permitted stakeholders to judge student outcomes and school performance. This interview will focus on how Dr. Henry and his staff developed this performance measurement system and facilitated its use.

A Summary of the Performance Reports for Georgia Schools

Gary T. Henry and Margaret H. Brackett

———•◦•———

The Council for School Performance was an independent organization created by the Governor and General Assembly of Georgia and housed within the Andrew Young School of Policy Studies' Applied Research Center at Georgia State University. The Council performed two important functions: (1) providing information about the performance of Georgia's public schools and school systems and (2) conducting evaluations of educational programs in Georgia.[1]

The indicators included in the reports and their format were developed through a variety of methods: an examination of existing data collected on schools, a review of literature on the factors influencing student learning and student performance, and a series of work group meetings with teachers, school administrators, citizens, journalists, and school board members from around the state. Working with these groups, we decided to develop a report specific to each school level: elementary, middle, and high school. Although some indicators appear for all school levels, others appear only at the level for which that indicator is relevant to school learning. For example, the percentage of overage students was reported for elementary and middle schools and the dropout rate for high schools. Furthermore, we determined that each report would be limited to one page, front and back, and would be easily understood by parents and the public.

The final reports included both school indicators, which measure student performance (e.g., test scores, dropout rates, chronic absenteeism), and community indicators, which measure how well the community supports its children and their education. Results for a school on each indicator were reported using two comparisons, shown in columns on the card: (1) how the school performs on that indicator compared with all schools in Georgia; and (2) how the school performs on that indicator compared with schools similar to that school in size and demographic characteristics. The Council developed a system to group schools in clusters based on demographic characteristics, such as school size and percentage of students eligible for free or reduced-price lunch. This system enables parents, policy makers, and school officials to compare performance between schools and systems that face similar challenges in educating their students.

To facilitate comparisons, the Council analyzed data on each indicator to sort schools into quintiles, both within the state overall and within the school's or school system's individual cluster (i.e., the group of schools/systems with similar students). The performance reports used a graphical format to illustrate the quintile to which each school or system belongs on an indicator. For example, for the same indicator, one school might be in the first quintile compared with all schools in the state, illustrated with one check mark out of a possible five, and it might fall in the top quintile among schools within its cluster and would receive five stars in that column. This school might be serving low-income neighborhoods and be performing quite well with its students compared with similar schools but not so well when compared with schools serving different student populations. Conversely, a school might be on the fifth quintile compared with all schools in Georgia on an indicator but fall into the first quintile when compared with a like cluster of schools. Such a school might be performing well compared with schools across the state because it is serving a high-income neighborhood and receives plenty of resources; however, its comparison within its cluster shows that the school itself is not performing too well with the types of students it receives.

Once the format was developed and approved, the Council began to produce the report cards for the next year 1994–1995. This was a labor-intensive effort. It involved collecting data from a variety of sources, compiling this information into databases, and updating these databases annually. The researchers identified each school in operation and matched student information for that school with information from the previous year. Changes in student characteristics as well as school openings and closings and changes in attendance zones were closely monitored to ensure data comparability from year to year. The researchers then surveyed over 1,800 schools and Georgia's 180 school systems to collect additional information.

In addition to surveying the schools and school systems, Council staff members also obtained information from information systems maintained by government agencies and public entities, such as the University System of Georgia, the U.S. Department of Health and Human Services, and the Georgia Department of Education. Data collected from these sources and from the schools and school systems were verified, corrected, aggregated, and analyzed over a period of several months to produce the Council's information system. This verification process included in-house checking as well as verification by the school systems themselves to resolve any problems or misunderstandings.

After producing the school and system performance reports, Council staff members distributed the reports not only to the schools and school systems but also to government leaders, news media, boards of education, parent-teacher associations (PTAs), public libraries, and chambers of commerce. The Council worked with professional associations and PTAs in Georgia to expand the distribution to educators and parents. The Council also offered its data on a Web site that supported several analyses that schools and the public might wish to conduct to assess relationships between indicators.

The independence of the Council for School Performance enhanced its ability to provide an objective analysis of educational performance data while promoting quality and progress in education through relevant research.

Dialogue With Gary T. Henry[2]

Jody Fitzpatrick

————•◦•————

Fitzpatrick: Gary, your work in developing a performance measurement system for the Georgia public schools has received much recognition from the American Evaluation Association and from other states that adopted many of its practices. Tell us what you see as the most exciting or innovative part of this system.

Henry: The most exciting part to me was to put data in a format that school district administrators, principals, teachers, parents, and journalists could read and understand. They indicated through phone calls and other conversations that the reports provided a quick and easy way to get information. It took a lot of work with different groups to come up with a reporting system that was detailed enough for teachers but sufficiently accessible to parents. The exciting and fun part was working with all these different groups and finding an interactive, creative way to involve them. People were just chiming in with their ideas, and we were busy trying to find a way to incorporate them into the product!

Fitzpatrick: I know the Governor of Georgia, Zell Miller, established the Council for School Performance, which you directed, in 1993. What was the impetus for establishing the Council?

Henry: Even before Miller recommended a Council, in the early '90s, key legislators in Georgia had attended a Southern Regional Education Board meeting and learned that Georgia was the only state among the 15 represented without a school performance accountability system. They came back and decided something needed to be done. But the elected state superintendent for education did not want his department reporting on school performance. So the legislature decided that they needed some organization outside of the state Department of Education to undertake the effort. At the time, Governor Miller was also initiating the Georgia Pre-Kindergarten (Pre-K) program and the Helping Outstanding Pupils Educationally (HOPE) Scholarship program, which provides free college tuition for students who have performed well in high school. The legislation that established the Council combined responsibility for the production of school performance reports and the evaluation of these new educational programs that were being funded by the Georgia Lottery. The Governor's Office of Planning and Budget issued a request for proposals to the universities in the state to establish a school accountability system and evaluate the HOPE and Pre-K programs. The proposal from Georgia State University received the contract, and we provided the services until a major education reform was passed creating an independent state agency to compile the accountability reports in 2000.

Fitzpatrick: How did you go about defining what the Council would do?

Henry: I had been part of developing a performance-monitoring system for education in Virginia, so I had some idea about what I was getting myself into when I worked on the proposal. I knew some things that worked and some that didn't. We borrowed a lot of ideas from other states and the federal Goals 2000 program. We reviewed their work, and it enabled us to start two steps ahead. We didn't have to reinvent the wheel. But there were surprises. In Virginia, the rural school districts had been one of the biggest supporters of the system. The performance reports were a resource they could not afford to produce themselves. In Georgia, however, the rural districts were initially reluctant to embrace the idea of performance reports because their test scores were low. Rural districts viewed themselves as having greater challenges due to high poverty and the legacy of segregation. They were concerned that the system would make them look bad without acknowledging their challenges. They were not against accountability, but they wanted a level playing field.

Fitzpatrick: What about the urban districts?

Henry: In urban districts, the media jumped on the reports and wrote about them since they were independent, or at least not produced by the same people who run the schools. The educators in these districts already produced a great deal of information on how they were doing, but often the information was closely held and not accessible to the public. So we found ways to make it accessible—to give performance data a new cast, a novel appeal. And because we viewed the press as important allies in getting this information to the public, we took care to work with them. We knew the press wanted to get their facts right, but they work under fixed deadlines in a competitive industry. Therefore, we made the information as easily understandable for them as possible.

Fitzpatrick: In addition to journalists, who were the primary stakeholders involved in this process, and how did you involve them?

Henry: We knew that it would be important to engage superintendents, school board members, teachers, and principals. Our work was overseen by six

Council members who were appointed by the Governor; the Lieutenant Governor; the Speaker of the Georgia House of Representatives; and an ex-officio member, the State Superintendent of Schools. Members of the Council were very emphatic about extending stakeholder status to members of the community in a highly inclusive way—including parents and others in the community. It took almost a year working with these groups to create the architecture of the accountability system. We made it clear from the beginning that our mandate was to develop a performance measurement system and they were being asked to make the system as good as it could possibly be. Once we all got on the same page, there was a great deal of creativity and excitement. The process focused on identifying what indicators we would use. We met in four separate groups— principals, superintendents, teachers, and community members—to reduce the influence of preexisting power relationships on the deliberations. At three points during the process and twice after the system was being implemented, we brought all four groups together. Turnout for the meetings was high throughout; the members all seemed to want to have their say about the reports.

Fitzpatrick: People in the education community can be quite concerned, often rightly so, about the use of gross, aggregate data, particularly outcome data, to measure their performance. How did you deal with these concerns?

Henry: First of all, we acknowledged that their concerns were legitimate. There might be schools doing the best job they could, and yet their performance still doesn't look good because they had difficult-to-educate students. So we designed the system to compare "like" types of schools. That was a great relief to them. Second, we moved away from focusing only on test scores. We have indicators on such issues as staff development, violence and safety, dropouts, and chronic absenteeism. We tried to broaden the base so the performance monitoring didn't just involve test scores and included a variety of important educational outcomes. We also had to develop a relationship built on trust. The stakeholders were wary that we were just another group out to bash schools. We had to demonstrate that what they said was making a difference in the design of the system and that no one group of stakeholders was calling the shots. Every meeting began with an update on where we should be based on the input of all four groups, and, following every meeting, minutes of all four group discussions were sent out to all the groups.

Fitzpatrick: As you note, you combined student performance measures and community indicators in your performance reports. How did you decide what to include as measures or indicators of performance?

Henry: We started from a list that included all the data currently being collected. Then we looked at new and novel ways to develop these as indicators. For example, one indicator we developed was chronic absenteeism. Absenteeism, which had been measured as the percentage of days that enrolled students attended school, had been reported for years but doesn't vary much from one school to the next. Chronic absenteeism, on the other hand, was the percentage of students who missed 10 or more days of school per year. This measure began to identify a significant problem according to some of the literature on dropouts and retention in grade. In some high schools, well over 50% of the students were chronic absentees, while others had quite low rates. So the formulation of chronic absenteeism was a way of taking existing data and making it a more effective indicator of school performance. It worked better than the average number of days attended because it had a positive and negative valence and some variability to it.

We were trying to be comprehensive and still make use of the best available information. As another example, rather than reporting only mean test scores or the percentage of students rated as mastering a subject, we also reported on the percentage of students in the school who score in the top or bottom quartiles of the state. This provides more information about how students are doing—whether there are too few students at the top end or too many at the bottom. They get more information to diagnose any problems and discuss possible solutions that fit the problem.

We did our best to take the data resources and existing research on student performance and develop indicators that could be tracked reliably from one year to the next.

Fitzpatrick: Which measures do you think best predict school performance? What evidence do you have for that?

Henry: There *is* no one best measure. If you only focus on one, this works to the detriment of kids in that school. Test scores are meaningful. Dropout rates are meaningful. The percentage of children who are two or more years older than their classmates (overage) is meaningful. When I got calls from parents, I did not point them to any single indicator to assess the quality of the school. I talked them through the report for the school attended by their child looking at both strengths and weaknesses.

Fitzpatrick: So parents called you?

Henry: Yes. Although I was not always as patient as I should have been when the calls got heavy, it showed that the information was getting out there.

Fitzpatrick: Which measures generated the most controversy?

Henry: I thought that the most controversial indicator would be the reporting of test scores by race/ethnicity. Test scores are one of the few indicators where we have the ability to provide the information broken down by race. And it showed gaps between white and black students. I thought we would get tons of calls and controversy. We didn't receive one. I'm not sure what to attribute that to. Predominately African-American groups like the Urban League and the NAACP expressed a strong desire for the scores to be reported by race because the efforts toward desegregation, especially busing, were being removed around the state. They wanted a way to see if schools were performing up to reasonable standards for all children.

Some indicators did change. We started out with an indicator on the number of incidents involving "weapons." It was a commonly used term and fairly standard category label at the time. But we found when we went out and did qualitative work that definitions of *weapon* varied drastically. It ranged from one school that included nail files to another school that didn't include knives with blades less than 4 inches long. So we revised this indicator. Based on some advice from experts on injury control at Emory University, we began to include one category of weapons: firearms. This definition leads to better consistency across schools in that the definition is not subject to wide variations in interpretation. In the 1990s, before the shootings at Columbine, people didn't give as much attention to this indicator as they do today. Given the shootings that have taken place in schools across the country and the media attention these tragedies have drawn, the public and educators are increasingly interested in these statistics.

Fitzpatrick: Which indicators do you think were used the most by policy makers? By building-level administrators?

Henry: Which were most used? As I've said, we really discouraged anyone from using single indicators. We conducted a lot of workshops with educators and local school boards and briefed legislative committees. Any single indicator can be misleading in a given year. We tried to train users to look at trends and multiple indicators. Each year when the performance reports were released, we tried to identify trends or particularly high or low indicators. The first year, we focused on chronic absenteeism, and that indicator was a focus of schools, legislators, and the press. Parents expressed concern that they had no way to know if their child was skipping school until the behavior escalated into a real problem. Many schools began to join with parents to attack the problem. Some schools, for example, began using an automated system to phone parents when their child was absent. In more affluent schools, the common practice of removing a child for an extended vacation received focus. The chronic absenteeism has been reduced.

Fitzpatrick: One of the things I like best about your reports are that they give two ratings: One is the usual rating—how the school performs compared to other schools in the state. But the second is new and perhaps fairer in assessing how well the *school* is doing. It rates how well the school does compared to schools "like yours." Your performance measurement system was the first one to take student body demographics into consideration in reporting. You mentioned a little about developing this method of comparison to gain stakeholders' trust in the planning stage. Could you tell us more about why you developed this rating method?

Henry: It's fundamental that we separate performance and privilege when we measure school performance. As I noted before, we came up with the idea of comparing "like" schools to persuade the educators that we would be fair, that we would recognize that they don't start with identical students. But I believe in the concept. To judge the quality of a school, we must somehow factor out the unevenness of starting with students with different degrees of preparedness and with different resources and expectations. With our two comparisons, certain schools can *and do* have very high scores in comparison with the rest of the state but still fall at the lower end of their comparison group. We think it's important that schools look at both comparisons to find areas where they can improve.

Fitzpatrick: What do you mean when you say "schools like yours"? How did you develop the groups?

Henry: We used a weighted formula that has a number of demographic variables—school size, school district size, percentage of students qualifying for free and reduced-price lunch, and others. We used regression analysis to identify the variables and cluster analyses to group the schools. The result was a group of reasonably homogeneous schools. We did go back originally and look at census indicators for the community. We tried to see if they would correlate with the variables we used to define the groups, and they did. However, since using them did not change the groups significantly, we did not continue to use census information.

Each year, we repeated the cluster analysis with variables weighted by their standardized regression coefficients. Free and reduced-price lunch was the dominant variable in the regression analysis that identified the factors that relate to the performance variables such as test scores and dropout rates. We only used variables for the adjusted comparisons that were beyond the control of the school, such as the number of students from families which fall below the poverty level. We added school size as an adjustment variable because educators looking for high-performing, similar schools told us the size of the comparison schools was very important for credibility.

Fitzpatrick: The comparison of schools to "schools like yours" seems so appropriate to judge school performance, why retain the other comparison (comparison to all schools in Georgia) at all?

Henry: There are two ways to view a performance measurement system: One perspective is to judge whether the school is performing well. For this to be a fair comparison, we must compare schools with similar challenges. The second way of viewing an accountability system is to determine whether the students in that school are doing well. Schools might be doing well given their limitations, but the students are not doing well in some of those schools. In 1999, we identified 100 schools that were not serving their students very well. We emphasized the need for more focused technical assistance and resources because even though some of these schools were doing well compared to schools like them, their students' scores were low, chronic absenteeism was high, and dropout rates were high. We need to be very fair about school comparisons when judging schools, but we shouldn't delude ourselves into thinking that high *relative* scores are indicators that those schools are serving their students well. As some of the legislators are fond of saying, these students will not receive an "adjusted rating" when applying to college or for a job. The complicated issue has been to keep in mind that while educators could be doing well given the current levels of performance in other schools, this still is not good enough for the students who, after all, will depend on their education for the kind of job they will hold and what they can achieve economically.

Fitzpatrick: Another remarkable factor in your reporting is that all this information is condensed into a two-page report, actually one page front-and-back. Slightly different forms exist for elementary, middle, and high schools. How did you decide on that format? Did you make changes in it?

Henry: We wanted to avoid the traditional thick report that only two or three of the really motivated principals across the state would look at. We worked real hard to get the information into a format where parents would look at all the indicators. We felt we had to limit school reports to one page.

Graphical systems are very efficient in terms of people retrieving data from them, so we used stars to represent the comparisons with similar schools, checks to represent the comparisons with all schools in the state, and up or down arrows to indicate the trend for each school. We packed about 300 bits of information onto each page using these efficient graphical displays. For each school system, we had 125 indicators displayed on four pages.

The most complicated thing was to boil down the indicator labels to just a few words. We took a lot of flack from educators, especially testing experts, about the labels, but everyone else seemed to know what they meant. In many instances, a technically correct label confused most of the audience. It was an effort to put our technocratic predispositions aside and try to design a system that parents and teachers, who might find many of these reports unfamiliar territory, could access and understand.

Fitzpatrick: Schools could receive from one to five checks for each criterion. It's almost like the star system for rating movies or restaurants. Some might argue these checks simplify complex criteria and scores. What is your response to that concern?

Henry: Some folks may find the checks simplistic. But what's really simplistic is trying to boil everything down into *one* overall rating for each school. Our reports with the checks for each criterion promote the notion of looking at multiple indicators. At a glance, anyone can see the measures where performance is high and those where it is low. They can scan for trends as well as for the comparison information on any indicator. We think this type of system encourages a more complex analysis than the overall rating system that Kentucky and several other states presented, where they give just one number for each school.

There is one technical aspect of this that is interesting. We used five rather than four stars because of the significance of being "above average." In our five-star system, three stars indicate a 40th to 60th percentile grouping. This includes those just above or below average. A school that fell just below the 49th to 50th percentile cutoff could be not statistically different from the school just above the cutoff. But in a four-star system, one would be above average (three stars) and the other, below average (two stars). In our system, both received three stars and are considered average. The five-star system saved much gnashing of teeth that may have been unnecessary and would have been caused by an inaccurate representation of some schools as "above average" or "below average."

Fitzpatrick: In order to get the report on one page, front and back, you must have had to cut some criteria you thought might be useful. What did you cut and why?

Henry: One of the things I always wanted to have in the report is a list of the programs, activities, and so on that the school thought was most important. I thought this would be helpful to add a little bit of descriptive information about their programs, but were only able to put in the statistical information. I think the criteria we were missing were criterion-referenced test scores, and they're missing not because of space but because the state stopped assessing student performance on tests that are tied to the curriculum and standards. However, the state tests based on the learning objectives for students in grades 3 to 8 and specific high school courses were required in the education reform of 2000 that I mentioned and are currently in place.

Fitzpatrick: Who received the reports? Were you involved in developing a dissemination plan?

Henry: We sent copies to the principal, the president of every school's PTA, school board members, the local superintendents, the public library, and the chamber of commerce in each locality. All legislators got reports on schools in their own district; education committee chairs got reports on all the schools. Our main dissemination of the reports to others was through the Web. The reports went up every year on the Web and were accessible to everyone.

The key to making this dissemination strategy work was that we placed a great deal of effort in notifying the press that these reports were out there. So every year we did some analysis to emphasize a theme for the press when we released the school reports. The first year, before reports were released, I went to meet with editorial boards and reporters in all eight metropolitan areas of Georgia. Those discussions paid off in the amount of attention paid to these reports outside of Atlanta. I responded to reporters very quickly and encouraged them to use the reports when they're reporting other education-related stories. If they were doing a story on schools in Valdosta, I encouraged them to look at the reports on schools in that area, and I often helped them interpret the results for salient indicators. For example, in a particularly heinous murder case, a reporter discovered the alleged murderer, who was later convicted, was a truant. Based on that, he did a follow-up article with the education reporter on chronic absenteeism in Atlanta-area high schools.

Fitzpatrick: What was the reaction of different audiences to the system? Who were your supporters? Detractors?

Henry: The detractors were usually those who are concerned with ineffi-ciency. After we began producing our report, the state Department of Education began putting a more limited report together, the *Atlanta Journal-Constitution* began to produce a school rating book, and a very conservative group began publishing a ranking of schools. So the biggest criticism came from newspaper editors and other elites who questioned why we need more than one of these reports. Until the Council was created, we had no reports. We had a huge number of supporters. Legislators were key supporters, along with those who do analytical work—the state budget office and school system staff used our data and analyses.

Fitzpatrick: What did you do to deal with the concerns of your users?

Henry: The biggest concern was about training on the proper use of the information, so we offered workshops. They were given by request and could be requested by regional groups, by principals, and by local boards of education. We gave workshops for all different kinds of groups. The thrust of our workshops was to get the participants to analyze how a couple of the schools were actually doing. We would walk them through a report and get them to think about their hypotheses, about why a particular score was high or low, about the strengths and weaknesses they think of, and then to see if their ideas were borne out by other data from the report. So we tried to teach them to use the reports analytically and to look at the options that they have to pursue for improvement. We received a lot of positive feedback from edu-cators and school boards across the state, both urban and rural. We did work-shops for the Atlanta Public Schools, for the Cabinet and the School Board, and for the largest suburban districts, such as Gwinnett County and Cobb County. We did a lot of workshops in regional groups for rural educators and their boards.

Fitzpatrick: Can you give us an example of a school or school district that changed because of your information?

Henry: One of the things that we hear a lot goes back to the breakdown of the test scores into the percentages of students who are in the top 25% and the lowest 25% statewide. Some schools think they are doing a good job when they look at their average, say, by having 60% of their students score above average. But they often find they have a large group at the lower end who are *really* low, say 20% in the lowest quartile. People called back and said, "This was just an eye-opener for us—seeing that we had a large group of kids in that lower quartile." In schools where something had happened as a result of the workshops, there was a collective "a-ha" when they thought their problems were in one area but discovered a different one.

Fitzpatrick: What about an example where someone objected strenuously to the report?

Henry: The most difficult conversation I had was with a superintendent who called and said, "You rated one of my mediocre middle schools with four or five stars and my 'best' middle school with one or two stars. You completely undermined your credibility with me and the parents in my system because you rated my 'best' middle school lower than a worse one." But his "best" middle school was serving a very upper middle-class part of the community. When compared to other similar schools across the state, the middle-class school didn't get as many stars as the one serving a much less advantaged population. The superintendent's answer was political. He knew the parents from the first school would be up in arms. He would get a huge backlash, especially when he had another poorer school doing better.

Fitzpatrick: Did the system have the impact on decision making that you hoped?

Henry: When a new governor was elected in 1998, he established an education-reform commission that made substantial reforms that I mentioned earlier. We kept education performance on the front burner. We didn't influence statewide policy directly, but we were able to show that the state has a large group of very low-performing schools that no one is doing anything about. So I think we had an impact on policy if John Kingdon (2003) is right that policy reform is a reaction to a recognized social problem. It took a while to get to the point where the elected officials were ready and able to deal with the problem. We kept the issue of school performance alive in the media—and education has stayed at the top of the list of the most important issues facing the state, according to public polls taken during the mid- to late 1990s.

Fitzpatrick: Even in the most exemplary studies, we recognize things that we wish we had done differently or would like to change. What would you do differently if you began this again?

Henry: The major drawback was in getting *under* the aggregate data—to look at the patterns for individual students and to analyze student performance rather than school performance. I wished we had a better student information system like the one in Texas so we could better understand, for example, the effects of teacher credentials or peers in the classroom on student achievement. We looked only at school-level data. There was very little that we could do to understand the dynamics below that. But now, I am involved with evaluating the North Carolina Disadvantaged Student Supplemental Fund, and we have the individual student data that we have matched with their teachers to learn more about the relationships between teacher characteristics, school resources and composition, and student performance.

Fitzpatrick: I think we learn something from every evaluation we do, whether it be exemplary or less. That's one of the reasons why I began these interviews—to encourage people to reflect more on their own work after reading about other's choices. What do you think you learned about evaluation from this project?

Henry: One of the things that I think I developed was a broader view of evaluation and the activities that constitute an evaluation. My understanding of evaluation expanded from working on a performance measurement project. Essentially, we were trying to describe the immediate outcomes of schooling. In this project, we were less concerned with causal attribution than with getting an accurate description to large numbers of people. We wanted to inform people about how the students were doing and whether schools were getting better or worse. These were very different priorities than I had brought to earlier evaluation work. For the school performance-reporting project, I was not focused on teasing out whether this policy worked or not. I was not attempting to make causal inferences. We were trying to give accurate and sound information to people concerned with schools so they could make judgments about whether the schools were achieving the results that they feel are important. If I provided a sound description of a school based on outcome information, which could be digested in very little time with very little effort by parents, I succeeded. I didn't have that as clearly in my mind when I started. I didn't understand the importance of giving as comprehensive a picture of the school's results as possible, to give the audiences the tools they need to make an informed judgment about that school—whether to improve the school, whether to move there, whether to send their child there. It was only through the process that I realized that my highest-order goal was a clear, low-cost description. In other evaluations that the Council undertook and has been recognized for, such as the evaluation of the effects of the Pre-K program, we were interested in estimating the program's effects, as I am in my current evaluation work. But in this evaluation, I learned that evaluators can fill a very important role when they provide accurate information that allows parents, the public, and elected officials to answer the question about whether public objectives for improving social conditions have been achieved.

Fitzpatrick's Commentary

At a time when many states were implementing or considering performance measurement systems for schools, the work of the Council for School Performance was particularly noteworthy. Not only was it an exemplary model for other states to consider, but it also provides a useful model for those of us outside of education as many public and nonprofit organizations move toward performance measurement systems. Today, in 2008, performance measures in many fields are far more prominent (Newcomer, 2001; Wholey, 2001). While we may applaud or bemoan these directions in evaluation, they nevertheless reflect the reality of the interests of policy makers, the media, and the public in learning more about what is happening with tax dollars. The good news for us, as evaluators, is that these stakeholders want data. They—parents, citizens, legislators, school board members—want information to help them make value judgments and choices, in this case about their own children's education or about policies affecting many schools.[3]

Henry's system for Georgia was exemplary because it served the needs of these stakeholders by providing good, descriptive information on schools in a readily accessible format. Furthermore, it was exemplary because he respected their intelligence and refused to condense the information down to one easy number, too frequently a score on a test. As a good evaluator, he and his Council found many indicators that not only accurately depicted the performance of schools and the students they serve but also gave a fuller picture of each school's environment and community—which helped reflect its strengths and weaknesses and provide much more useful information for choices and improvement. The Council made creative use of existing information to develop indicators, such as chronic absenteeism, which better informed stakeholders of differences between schools and, hence, areas of need. Equally important, the "people part" of the evaluation was not neglected. Stakeholders, especially parents, teachers, and building-level administrators, were involved in the development process. The Council listened to their concerns and information needs. Once the report cards were developed, many avenues were used for dissemination—the media, the Web, workshops for schools, meetings with legislators—to maximize dissemination and appropriate use of the information.

Partly as a result of listening to stakeholders' concerns, the Council developed one of the most exemplary aspects of the system: comparing schools with schools "like theirs." While we certainly want all students to learn, as evaluators, we can help others differentiate and articulate their purposes and information needs. As Wholey (1997) has noted, "'Performance' is not an objective reality." He sees one of the central roles of evaluators in performance measurement as helping users "achieve some level of agreement on what performance means" (p. 132). In the performance measurement of schools, one of the purposes is to assess students' performance. Another is to assess schools' performance. To judge a school's performance, much less compare that school's success with others, one must acknowledge differences in "input." As a researcher, Henry recognized the need to control for community differences to better judge the performance of each school's faculty and staff. As an educator, citizen, and parent, he also recognized the need to report how well students perform in each school. His use of the two rating methods educated stakeholders about these different objects of evaluation and allowed them to make better judgments.

It is interesting that performance measurement systems might be criticized from both a qualitative and a quantitative perspective. These systems hardly provide as rich and full a picture of a school as ethnographers would desire. Even Henry notes that he wishes the report card could have provided more narrative on the programs and activities thought to be important by each school. From the quantitative perspective, Henry comments on the focus on causality as the sine qua non. Just as performance measurement fails to provide a full, rich picture of a school, it also fails to tell you why certain outcomes are being achieved or, more important, not being achieved. That said, I agree wholeheartedly with Henry that performance measurement, and this system in particular, served evaluation's most important functions well. It provides accurate information to stakeholders to inform their judgments. Description is important. Providing information so that it will be used is important. The qualitative-quantitative debate in the field of evaluation served to broaden our perspectives about what we do and about our methods of data collection. Performance measurement is another important method with its own nuances and challenges. Henry's discussion, and the system he and his Council developed, helps us learn much more about how to use such systems in meaningful ways.

Notes

1. The Council for School Performance performed these evaluation activities for the state of Georgia from 1994 until June of 2002. The Governor's Office of Student Achievement now conducts these functions.

2. Since this interview was conducted, the federal legislation concerning No Child Left Behind Act (NCLB) has mandated certain reporting requirements that differ from the reporting discussed in this interview. Because our focus is on the choices made during an evaluation, the interview has not been updated to reflect the NCLB but, rather, focuses on how Henry made choices in developing this Georgia report card on school performance.

3. It is worth noting, and disappointing, that both James Riccio's early work on welfare reform programs in California and Gary Henry's work on performance monitoring of schools in Georgia were ignored in national legislation for more simplified solutions. Work at state levels can often inform federal initiatives, but other political issues more heavily influenced decisions in these two high-profile arenas.

DISCUSSION QUESTIONS

1. Henry's system is a performance-monitoring system. Is this an evaluation? How is it like a typical evaluation? How does it differ?

2. Discuss the stakeholders Henry uses and how he uses them. What role do they play in the evaluation? Contrast his use of stakeholders with that of other evaluators you have read.

3. Henry argues for the use of multiple indicators to judge schools, but today federal legislation through NCLB has prompted U.S. states to focus on one measure, scores on state standards tests. Advocates of NCLB argue that this focus on test scores makes schools more accountable and helps parents and other stakeholders better understand school performance. Do you agree or do you think multiple measures are more valid? More useful?

4. If you had to select one single indicator to express the success of your organization, what would it be? If you were able to select three to five indicators of success, what would they be? What is your rationale for each indicator? Are they reflective of input, process, outputs, or outcomes?

5. Henry and his staff work to devise a system that parents, teachers, and other stakeholders can readily understand and use. What is the proper balance between making something accessible and understandable to stakeholders and yet providing sufficient information? For example, does the use of stars and check marks lead to better understanding of ratings by more people, or would you use a narrative or some other system?

6. At the end of his interview, Henry indicates that this process helped him appreciate the value of description. How important is it to understand what causes something? How often do we establish causality? To better answer these general questions, identify three important evaluation questions for your organization or an organization you are familiar with. How many of the questions are causal? How many are descriptive? How important is each issue to this organization?

FURTHER READING

There is not one report that summarizes the development and use of this system. However, the reader can access information on the reports on these Web sites:

http://aysps.gsu.edu/publications/arc/csp/default.htm#reportcards: This Web site provides links to many reports and report cards developed by the Council for School Performance.

http://aysps.gsu.edu/publications/arc/csp/csp_interpretations.htm: This is a Web site developed for school personnel in Georgia describing how the reports were developed and how they can be interpreted and used.

http://aysps.gsu.edu/publications/arc/csp/download99/CSP_HS99.xls: This file presents the Web-based report cards for all Georgia high schools in 1999. (Scroll down to see data on the high schools. Scroll across to see the indicators. Middle school reports can be found by substituting MS for the HS at the end of the address.)

REFERENCES

Kingdon, J. W. (2003). *Agendas, alternatives, and public policies* (2nd ed.). New York: Longman.

Newcomer, K. E. (2001). Tracking and probing program performance: Fruitful path or blind alley for evaluation professionals? *American Journal of Evaluation, 22,* 337–341.

Wholey, J. S. (1997). Trends in performance measurement: Challenges for evaluators. In E. Chelimsky & W. R. Shadish (Eds.), *Evaluation for the 21st century* (pp. 124–133). Thousand Oaks, CA: Sage.

Wholey, J. S. (2001). Managing for results: Roles for evaluators in a new management era. *American Journal of Evaluation, 22,* 343–348.

PART III

EVALUATIONS WITH AN EMPHASIS ON PROGRAM PLANNING AND ORGANIZATIONAL DEVELOPMENT

I n the 1960s and 1970s, in a period of major growth, program evaluations were mandated by funding agencies, typically government agencies, for purposes of accountability as well as learning what worked. But early in these formative years of evaluation theory and practice, evaluators realized that their work could serve other purposes, specifically helping program managers and staff in improving programs. Thus, Michael Scriven (1967) coined the term *formative evaluation* to refer to evaluations in which the results would be used for program improvement.

Many formative evaluations occur as a program is being developed. Evaluators who came into a project in the early planning stages often became involved in program planning, through helping program people develop goals and objectives, program theory, or logic models or through conducting needs assessment studies of people the program would be designed to serve. Charles Reichardt (1994) argued that evaluators' efforts at the program-planning stage, not later stages, represent a much more major contribution, writing, "When kudos for solving social problems are handed out, they will go more to those who think of themselves as program creators than to those who think of themselves only as program evaluators" (p. 280). Publications for evaluators on conducting needs assessments also made evaluators more aware of the con- tributions they could make in front-end planning (Altschuld & Witkin, 2000; Roth, 1990; Witkin & Altschuld, 1995).

In the 1990s, new approaches to evaluation emerged with a focus on organizational development, organizational learning, and capacity building (Cousins & Earl, 1995; Fetterman, Kaftarian, & Wandersman, 1996; Preskill & Torres, 1999). Evaluation could be a tool to help organizations improve decision making and their culture for thinking about programs and future directions. But to do so, organizations needed employees with knowledge of evaluation and its way of approaching problems and solutions. James Sanders chose capacity building as the theme for his term as president of the American Evaluation Association in 2001 to 2002. Capacity building refers to increasing the skills of program staff and managers not only in conducting evaluations but also in thinking in an evaluation, or inquiry, mode. These approaches saw the solution to increasing evaluation use in guiding others to use evaluation inquiry as a method to learn more about their programs and their organization.

The interviews presented here build on this new direction for evaluation. Two of these interviews, those with Stewart Donaldson and Ross Conner, are, in many ways, traditional, large-scale, multiyear evaluations. But Donaldson and Conner use evaluation techniques to increase organizational learning, through building program theory to guide programs or through involving stakeholders in data analysis and interpretation, in the process of conducting traditional evaluations to determine the merit and worth of a program. The interviews with Hallie Preskill and Jean King are focused primarily on organizational learning and capacity building. Preskill describes how she uses appreciative inquiry to help an organization develop an evaluation system to improve organizational learning. King describes her work in an evaluation of a school district's special education program to build evaluation capacity in the school district. Her large group of administrators, teachers, and parents guide the evaluation at each stage so that they learn the tools of evaluation. King's goal is not so much evaluating the special education program as giving these users tools that they can use in the future to analyze problems in the district.

As you read these interviews, consider the following questions:

• How are these evaluators encouraging organizational development? Organizational learning? Capacity building? (*Note*: Each evaluator does not work on all these issues. Consider which of these goals is a focus in a given interview and how the evaluator works to achieve his or her goal.)

• Which stakeholder groups are the focus of the evaluator's efforts on the above tasks? How do they work with these groups? Can you think of other ways that you might work with stakeholders to achieve the intended goal?

• What are other purposes of the evaluation?

• How are the evaluators alike, and how do they differ in their approach to organizational change? In their approach to the evaluation?

• How do they differ in their dissemination of results? Do you see differences in the use of the results that may be related to the dissemination?

REFERENCES

Altschuld, J. W., & Witkin, B. R. (2000). *From needs assessment to action: Transforming needs into solution strategies.* Thousand Oaks, CA: Sage.

Cousins, J. B., & Earl, L. E. (1995). *Participatory evaluation in education.* London: Falmer Press.

Fetterman, D. M., Kaftarian, S., & Wandersman, A. (Eds.). (1996). *Empowerment evaluation: Knowledge and tools for self-assessment and accountability.* Thousand Oaks, CA: Sage.

Preskill, H., & Torres, R. T. (1999). *Evaluative inquiry for learning in organizations.* Thousand Oaks, CA: Sage.

Reichardt, C. S. (1994). Summative evaluation, formative evaluation, and tactical research. *Evaluation Practice, 15,* 275–282.

Roth, J. (1990). Needs and the needs assessment process. *Evaluation Practice, 11,* 39–44.

Scriven, M. (1967). The methodology of evaluation. In R. E. Stake (Ed.), *Curriculum evaluation* (American Educational Research Association Monograph Series on Evaluation, No. 1, pp. 39–83). Chicago: Rand McNally.

Witkin, B. R., & Altschuld, J. W. (1995). *Planning and conducting needs assessments: A practical guide.* Thousand Oaks, CA: Sage.

EIGHT

EVALUATION OF THE SPECIAL EDUCATION PROGRAM AT THE ANOKA-HENNEPIN SCHOOL DISTRICT

An Interview With Jean A. King

*I*ntroduction: Jean A. King is a professor in the Department of Educational Policy and Administration at the University of Minnesota, where she teaches in the Evaluation Studies Program. For almost 30 years, she has conducted program evaluations in a variety of educational and social service settings. Given her commitment to evaluation as an educative activity, she is perhaps best known for her work on participatory evaluation. King is the author of numerous articles, chapters, and reviews and, with Laurie Stevahn, is completing a book on interpersonal skills for evaluators. She has received two awards from the American Evaluation Association: the Myrdal Award for Evaluation Practice and the Ingle Award for Extraordinary Service. In 1999, she took a 2-year leave from the university to work as Coordinator of Research and Evaluation for a large school district to learn firsthand about the work of an internal evaluator.

This interview focuses on an internal evaluation of the district's special education program. King describes the process she used in working with a large self-study team of administrators, teachers, classroom aids (paras), and

parents to build evaluation capacity in the school district. King and her colleagues acted as facilitators to guide and serve the self-study team in directing
the evaluation of the special education program. The team determined the
focus of the study and data collection methods, developed surveys and interviews, interpreted results, drew conclusions, and made a report to the School
Board. King and her colleagues worked to facilitate the process by establishing the format of the meetings, guiding groups, analyzing and preparing data
to present to the groups, and ensuring that groups based their conclusions on
data. In her interview, she describes the role and actions she took to help the
district build capacity while simultaneously evaluating the special education
program. King's experiences in capacity building in this evaluation dramatically changed her views of program evaluation and her subsequent writing
concerning capacity building.

Summary of the Evaluation of the Special Education Program at the Anoka-Hennepin School District #11

Jean A. King

University of Minnesota

—•◦•—

The evaluation of the Special Education Program at the Anoka-Hennepin School District was both participatory and developmental, a self-study framed within the six-year cycle of a state-mandated curriculum review process and a political setting in which parent advocates wanted a process that would force the Special Education Department to respond to their concerns. The inclusive evaluation, involving more than 100 people at one time or another on the Self-Study Team, had a dual intent: to provide a broad array of perceptual data collected from numerous stakeholders using diverse methods and, simultaneously, to create a process for continued evaluation activities.

Anoka-Hennepin is one of the largest districts in Minnesota, serving at the time of the study roughly 40,500 students, 11% of whom received special education services, and employing more than 2,000 full-time teachers and 450 classroom aides. The district's *Citizen Involvement Handbook (1999–2000)* gave the following demographic summary: "young community, hard working, [many who] work out of the community, poor, high school-educated, rising number of immigrants, and increasing minorities." Because of a relatively low tax base in the district, funding remains an ongoing challenge, addressed in part by a small central administration and a flat administrative hierarchy. Despite this, the district is known for innovation and its commitment to the use of standardized data for accountability and improvement. Years before the state adopted graduation testing, Anoka-Hennepin routinely required students to pass such a test, and in the 1990s, district personnel were active in the development of performance assessments and state graduation standards. I was serving at that time as the district's Coordinator of Research and Evaluation, their internal evaluator.

The infrastructure for the self-study included three components: (1) a team of three evaluators, which met several times a month and often late into the night (the Evaluation Consulting Team); (2) a team of the three evaluators and the district special education administrators, which met twice a month (the Data Collection Team); and (3) a large self-study team with representation from as many stakeholders as we could identify, which also met once a month (the Self-Study Team). In addition, my staff supported the effort by preparing data and materials for meetings, a continuing challenge given the volume of data collected. I had worked previously with the two other evaluators—Vanessa McKendall-Stephens, a local evaluator specializing in inclusive evaluation practice, and Laurie Stevahn, a social psychologist with expertise in cooperative learning and conflict resolution—and chose them because of their technical expertise and interpersonal and facilitation skills. The study was originally designed to last a year but ended up taking over a year and a half to complete.

The self-study process included the following activities: (1) process planning by the Data Collection Team; (2) data collection from multiple sources (e.g., teachers, administrators, paraprofessionals, parents, parent advocates, interagency service providers) using multiple methods (surveys, stakeholder dialogues, telephone interviews, focus groups, e-mail questionnaires, community forums, and observation); (3) data preparation and review by the Evaluation Consulting Team; (4) review and analysis by the Self-Study Team; and (5) development of commendations and recommendations by the Self-Study Team. Members of the Evaluation Consulting Team facilitated the monthly Self-Study Team meetings, which were structured as working sessions held over the dinner hour (5:00 p.m. to 7:30 p.m.). Each month, participants completed a simple evaluation form at the end of the session that asked three things: plusses and wishes (on a form) and questions (on index cards). Collectively, over the 18 months, the Self-Study Team framed issues and concerns for the study, reviewed instrumentation, analyzed and interpreted data, and developed commendations and recommendations.

We began Self-Study Team meetings with a brief review of the previous month's work, the answers to any questions people had raised, and an introduction to what was planned that evening. Then, we would have dinner. People sat in teams at tables and would either work on the tasks at hand while they ate or wait until after their meal. The evaluators took turns joining table teams, responding to questions, and monitoring the time. The group's camaraderie grew as the months rolled on, and by the end, people reported satisfaction with their involvement and a sense of accomplishment with the results.

The evaluation's extensive findings identified a lengthy list of concerns, the most important of which included the following: (1) special education referral and due process procedures, which parents and some staff found confusing; (2) the need for professional development in adapting and modifying curriculum and instruction for special-needs students; (3) issues around inclusion of these students in their schools; and (4) parental involvement and communication. The 17-page report, developed collaboratively, included a description of the process, commendations, recommendations prioritized in 15 issue areas and the self-study data analysis and interpretations as an appendix. Members of the Self-Study Team gave a formal presentation at the School Board meeting, including one minority report from a parent who had actively participated in the process but chose to express his thoughts separately from the Team's. District administrators used the process and findings of this evaluation to establish a continuous improvement model that now provides ongoing feedback into the district's special educational program.

Dialogue With Jean A. King

Jody Fitzpatrick

———•◦•———

Fitzpatrick: Jean, I know you selected this study because it has served as the foundation for much of your work on using participatory methods to build evaluation capacity. Perhaps we could begin with your telling us a bit about how this study changed and informed your evaluation practice. How was it different from what you had done in the past?

King: It was surely the biggest participatory study I had ever engaged in— the study team had over 100 people on it—and the size of it made all the participation activities a challenge. Second, it was the most overtly political environment I have ever worked in. I tend to avoid those kinds of situations, but in this case, the internal self-study was monitored by an external force. In Minnesota, parents are allowed to raise concerns directly with the State Department of Education. In this case, the Department of Education staff had called our Special Education Department, saying they had received complaints and needed a response. One of our Associate Superintendents said, "It's time for Special Education to conduct its six-year curriculum self-study. What if we make it a highly visible, public project and add these concerns?" The State Department agreed, and for that reason, we had a State Department representative [a "monitoring supervisor"] sitting in on every single meeting—sitting with a piece of paper and taking notes—so that was different, not a typical participatory process. Because of the political nature, we were purposeful about what people would do.

Fitzpatrick: What prompted you to change your practice in this setting?

King: The politics and all that involved. When I was the internal evaluator [at Anoka-Hennepin], I worked very hard to "pass." I tried to make evaluation a friendly process, was usually called "Jean," smiled a lot, brought cookies, and so on. This was the only situation where I was always called "Dr. King from the University of Minnesota" to distance me from district staff. To ensure that people didn't think the evaluation was being controlled internally, we also hired two external evaluators who were truly "objective outsiders" with no role in the district.

We were very consistent about that "objectivity." We had to be because of the public eye on the evaluation. But at the same time, we were very inclusive, having everyone participate. It was an interesting tension.

Fitzpatrick: Tell me more about that tension.

King: There was one father with two extremely handicapped children, and he was truly angry at the district. He came loaded for bear. At the first meeting, he raised his hand, stood up, and launched into a diatribe on the special education programs. An important feature of the self-study was that the Associate Superintendent came to every meeting and would answer any questions that people had related to special education or the evaluation. She explained the inclusive, public process for the evaluation—that we would include everyone. Fine. When the second meeting came, this father again stood up and raised his hand to complain. We thought we'd never get anything done since he did this at every meeting. So we talked with him by phone, met with him before each meeting and after if necessary, met with him at the district office—throughout the whole process. Then, guess who gives a minority report [at the final presentation to the School Board] *and* brings one of his children in her automated wheelchair? It wouldn't have mattered what we did. The politics of the situation were such that no matter how objective we were, he was having none of it. I learned you can't always win through inclusion. He had not changed his opinion based on our objective data. It did not matter to him.

Was his truth real? Perceptions are reality to people. The real question he raised was to what extent a school district can serve every individual child regardless of the cost. The district is well-known for having a small tax base and is always strapped for cash. Special education is not well funded, so funding special education is especially challenging. It's a dilemma. Of course, you want to serve every child, but can you realistically provide a full-time aide for every special-needs child? Who gets the limited resources? It's a difficult situation.

Fitzpatrick: So different views of the program remained at the conclusion of the evaluation. Did you hope your participatory process would change his views? Is achieving such a consensus part of the goal of your participatory process?

King: With such a sizable number of people and a controversial topic, we didn't expect consensus. We were after statements that could be supported with more than one piece of data. Our hope was to get people to support their deeply held opinions with solid evidence. As we say on campus, "What is the warrant for that claim?"

Fitzpatrick: I know you had come to work with the school district because they had had an unsuccessful search to replace their previous internal evaluator. So you were taking a leave from your university position to act as an internal evaluator there for two years. Before we move further into the specifics of the study, can you tell us a bit about what it was like beginning there as an internal evaluator? What did you do to begin in this position?

King: It was an easy beginning—there was a list of evaluation projects waiting for me. What was the reason to take this leave? I was worried. I had been teaching evaluation, and I had been an external evaluator, but I wanted to walk the walk of an evaluator inside a big organization. So it was a convergence of good things. I am a school person at heart. I love schools. The Associate Superintendent is an intuitive evaluator. The district had done great work in the 1990s on outcomes evaluation. The culture focused on collaboration and data. So it was a perfect place to be dropped, and I was lucky to work in a university that would let me do this.

Fitzpatrick: Was this the first study you did for the district serving in this new position as an internal evaluator?

King: No, this study started at the end of my first year and was my first big participatory study. I had been doing other studies, but they were more with me as the evaluator working with people, showing them the evaluation process.

Fitzpatrick: What was the focus of those evaluations?

King: There were several studies. The state high school graduation requirements had changed to standards based. I was the leader of that study. It was definitely less participatory. Also, the district had set up the Blueprint for Literacy plan, and part of my work was to help evaluate the Blueprint Implementation Committee's efforts. I also served as the research/evaluation person on a number of committees working on school improvement.

Fitzpatrick: You mentioned that the evaluation of the special education program was prompted somewhat by a complaint to the State Department of Education whose staff then contacted the district. Can you tell us a bit more about the context for starting the evaluation?

King: This was part of a routine, state-mandated curriculum review process. It was special ed's turn. And although the State Department of Education pushed the district, at the same time the culture in the district was such that administrators wanted to integrate evaluation into the special education program. Part of my charge as an internal evaluator was to foster evaluation across the district, so my involvement made sense. The special education program was large, and they wanted a continuous improvement process.

Fitzpatrick: Who were the significant stakeholders for the study?

King: The easier question is "Who wasn't?" I'll never forget this. We sat in the Associate Superintendent's office. We actually did a chart of who the stakeholders were—a 13 × 4 chart since there were 13 categories of disabilities and four levels (pre-, elementary, middle, and high school), and we wanted to be sure that we had representation in all 52 cells. On it were parents, regular education teachers, regular education paras, and special ed paras. Then, we added community stakeholders, the State Department, and the politicians. We wrote this all down on a huge piece of paper. Clearly, the State Department was more important. They had the power to do things to the district. [But] if we think of primary intended users, to use Patton's language, we were very interested in having the special education administrators and teachers as key users. We wanted administrators because they could use the information. And then the members of the School Board were important stakeholders because, while they didn't actively participate, they were paying very close attention.

Fitzpatrick: In an article describing this evaluation, you indicate the district hired you and the other evaluators to be "objective technicians and skilled facilitators." Tell us a bit about their expectations.

King: The "objective technician" part was representing the profession of evaluation, making sure people weren't leaping to conclusions, were applying the standards of good evaluation practice, and so on. The facilitator piece was helping to guide the self-study meetings. It was clear the district couldn't do that. The perception was that the special education staff would influence and control the self-study too much. That's why I became Dr. King, a university-based professional evaluator collaborating with two completely external colleagues.

In theory, the process didn't allow for letting people's past perceptions influence their conclusions. The process we used comes right out of social psychology. At every meeting, we set up table teams, mixtures of folks—parents, aides, teachers, community members, and staff. Each table team would receive a notebook. When people came in, they could read the results of the last meeting. The new pages in the notebook would be the new data or analyses for the night. We structured activities where people would work at the table and study the information and each table would submit its analysis. Between meetings, we would type that up across tables [type up each table's analysis so people could compare] and distribute the comparison at the next

meeting, where it would be discussed. The groups were responsible for interpreting and synthesizing from month to month and ultimately for generating
and rank-ordering recommendations.

Our job was to correct any incorrect statements and keep the process on
course. For example, two different times the data were bimodal—there were
strong feelings both for and against a particular item. Looking at the mean,
people at a couple of tables noted, "People are neutral on this issue," which
was wrong. And part of our job was to correct that misstatement. Respondents
did have strong feelings on that item—they just had different strong feelings.
We were very clear that our task was keeping the claims accurate, and table
teams understood that. People knew we were in charge of the correctness of
the data and claims.

We collected an absurd amount of data. We could not convince the study
committee that a sample would be sufficient. I had a small staff, and we could
just barely get the data analyzed and out in time. Sometimes we would pass
out data, and someone would say, "These numbers don't add up." So we would
take it back, correct it, and distribute it with next month's analyses. Sometimes
I just turned it around and said, "There are probably errors in this data, and it's
your job to find them."

When we got near the end of the process, after well over a year, we got
frustrated because teams would write a claim but not be clear about what data
they thought supported it. The table teams had the data in front of them, and
the rule was you couldn't make a claim unless you had data to support it.
A team would say, "We are making the claims based on these five points,"
but what five points? They wouldn't write them down accurately since it was
boring to do that. We couldn't figure it out, but they didn't want to copy all the
data over on their sheets.

One of the secretaries said, "Let's print the data on labels, then table teams
will easily put clearly labeled data with their claims." It also showed them, if
they're not using half their labels, they're probably missing something. We
made the decision that it was more important to have an accurate link between
the data and the claims than to save the money it cost to print all those labels.
Teams had to "prove" their conclusions with the data. Sometimes we had 8,
maybe 10, table teams working simultaneously. If they all came up with the
same conclusions, and we could check where those conclusions came from,
we felt confident that the claims were supported. This is a technique that I use
all the time now—having many different groups look at the same data. It's like

replicating by having separate teams all looking at the data, and at the same time, people enjoy the discussions they have about the data.

Fitzpatrick: I know you moved to a participatory method, but can you tell us a bit about the planning phase that preceded your choices? Who did you involve in shaping the focus of the study? What did you do?

King: In point of fact, it was the Associate Superintendent, a gifted woman, who shaped the focus of the study. She created the Evaluation Consulting Team, which consisted of the three evaluators (me plus the two outside consultants), and then a Data Collection Team, which consisted of the Evaluation Consulting Team plus six special education staff, including the Director of Special Education. We were the groups that met in between the big self-study team meetings. We were the ones who shaped the focus of the study over time. The State Department of Education person, who had a helpful attitude, sat in on this as well. She took a positive attitude of "Let's make this work." She made it as good as it could be. She was more of a check—if we missed something she thought was important for the State, she would mention it. Otherwise she just smiled.

Fitzpatrick: Why did you decide to put the focus in this study on building evaluation capacity? One of your articles indicates that the program had been "almost continually controversial," so there must have been many different questions or issues that the evaluation could have addressed.

King: I hope I can articulate this because building capacity was the obvious choice. The father I mentioned earlier was the perfect example. There was no way an evaluation, no matter how rigorous, could have pleased him. In Minnesota, an individual can go directly to the State Department of Education and report a concern, and the State Department is required to track that concern. In this politically charged environment, we couldn't do a traditional formal evaluation and have it be of great value. It might address the concerns of the moment, but not future ones. So we thought, let's do a really good job of involving people and create an ongoing, inclusive evaluation process so that from that point forward, evaluation issues can always be addressed collectively. Not only are you getting the results of the study, but you are putting in place a structure for continuing the work.

I was not the one who made this decision, but the idea was by making the evaluation process public and participatory, we would build an awareness about the issues confronting the special education program and let stakeholders see that the district had a mechanism to handle concerns about the program from that time on. That was the desired goal. The sense was to work with people to change their awareness of the challenges the program faced from the very beginning, rather than bringing them in later. It's rather amazing to me that the district took this focus. The Associate Superintendent's view was we're in it together—we have nothing to hide.

That's why the commendations are in the report. People in the special education programs in the schools were working really hard, and the data showed that. For every bad thing, the Self-Study Team found many good things. We really needed to congratulate people for the good work they do.

Fitzpatrick: I understand that the initial contact from the State Department of Education concerning complaints created a politicized environment for the self-study, but I think in many states a parent can bring a complaint to the State Department. What had been controversial about the special education program?

King: As I recall—and I never did get to see or learn about the specific complaints—it was the number of the complaints. There were too many, in the State Department's opinion.

Fitzpatrick: You mentioned that the impetus for making the evaluation process public was to build an awareness of the issues confronting the special education program and the challenges they faced. What issues or challenges did administrators want to make others aware of?

King: Basically, that the special education department was doing a good job with extremely limited resources. I mentioned that the School Board took great pride in its fiscal efficiency, which meant that every department struggled to do their job within budget. A number of unfunded special ed mandates coupled with a growing number of special-needs students made it really hard for special education.

Fitzpatrick: Since you did not complete a traditional report on this evaluation, I'm not really sure of the evaluation questions your study was trying to answer, and your data collection and results addressed many different issues. Were there specific evaluation questions you were trying to answer that guided you?

King: Our focus was broad. There were two overarching questions: (1) What was going right? (2) What was going wrong? It was the first function of the Self-Study Team that met monthly to generate specific issues. It was participatory from the beginning. We really wanted people to raise the concerns they had.

It was not primarily an outcome study because the concerns were more with process. Those were the political issues that had been raised. We had people get together and identify the issues. The Evaluation Consulting Team had the two overarching huge questions. The large Self-Study Team shaped them into specific issues. The types of questions they raised were process. What sort of experiences are the students having in their classes? Are the paras overstepping their bounds? Are parents getting good communication on a regular basis? We developed the survey and interview items with them. It was highly interactive all along.

The Evaluation Consulting Team did raise the question of outcomes. We wanted to look at the Individual Education Plans (IEPs) to see if kids were progressing, but the notion of outcomes in special education is very difficult, and given what we were looking at, the process questions were central. Another consultant (separate from our team of three) was hired to collect quantitative process observation data. I think it's important to mention that this person collected additional formal data for us, and we fed that information into the table teams' analyses.

Fitzpatrick: So tell us a bit about how you decided how to get people involved. How did you come up with the process for involvement? What kinds of things did you do to encourage involvement?

King: We met starting at 5:00 p.m. once a month with the Self-Study Team. We provided a lovely meal, really good food (fabulous desserts), and child care. We met in a new building at a nearby community college with a gorgeous view of the river. You could see the sun setting. We truly respected the people there. The setting was right. Creature comforts were attended to. One of the external evaluators is a social psychologist, and the other has an amazing ability to connect with people, and we used everything they knew about having people work together. We really needed to make it an inviting, wonderful process. Participants didn't get release time or payment for this.

The table team had one set of materials that they shared at their table. We thought that we would switch the teams so everyone would get to know each other, but when people came back after the first meeting, they didn't want to switch. They met their table team members in the line for supper the first evening and wanted to stay together.

Fitzpatrick: About how many people came each time, and who were they? About what proportion were teachers and paras and parents?

King: Of the 100 invited, we had about 50 people regularly attend each month, or about eight tables. I'd say roughly two thirds were school employees. As I said before, there were special ed and regular ed teachers and paras, building principals, special ed administrators and other central office folks, then parents, people from advocacy groups, and community members. Each table team was a mixture of different types of roles. Many people attended consistently, which was helpful because explaining the process to newcomers was difficult. Not surprisingly, the parents were the toughest group attendance-wise—only a few parents attended consistently, and we always hoped for more.

Fitzpatrick: You mention that you were especially concerned with "bringing many people to the table during the study, especially those whose voices often went unheard in the district." Whose voices were those? How did you try to involve them?

King: The parents were our first concern, and there were a sizable number of parents, several of whom came representing other groups. The group we never successfully involved were the parents of color—at that time they comprised about 8% of the parents in the district. The proportion of special-needs parents who were minorities was higher, about 15%. We did everything we knew to get them involved—food, child care, meeting off campus. We would even drive to pick people up. Even doing all of that, we could get people to come for a month or two, but getting that sustained commitment was difficult.

Fitzpatrick: What about the comfort level of parents on the Self-Study Team? House and Howe (1999) in their book on deliberative democracy write about the role of the evaluator in helping those who are less frequently heard to be heard. Often, the problem is the unequal status of participants. Your teams consisted of a mix of teachers, administrators, paraprofessionals, and parents. How did you attempt to deal with the unequal status of these participants?

King: In the table teams, democracy lived. People got to know each other as people. People got to know each other and feel comfortable. We didn't measure it; we didn't study it. But there is a concept in social psychology called "leaning in," meaning that groups engaged in meaningful conversation physically lean toward each other. Watching the table teams month after month, I can report that our groups leaned in.

In social psychology, one way of dealing with power is group norms. We had group norms—everyone has a right to speak, process these data, conflicting ideas are welcome, speak your truth, and so on. We developed these at the first meeting and had them available in the team notebooks. You never know if you succeed perfectly. People came back, or we looked at who didn't come back and invited others to replace them. We were aware of who was coming to dinner. This was held off site rather than at a school site. Maybe we should have held it at a church somewhere.

Fitzpatrick: Do you feel that House and Howe's concern about unequal status is overdone?

King: No, it's a critical concern. But the first real issue that comes before that is how to get folks to show up. Once they come, you can structure a satisfactory experience so that people *can* participate successfully.

Fitzpatrick: Administrators and teachers were in the table teams?

King: Teachers were, for sure, and principals. The Associate Superintendent was there and would answer questions and represent central administration. This kind of discussion is culturally difficult. It's clearly a challenge. You want people to participate. But the people you really want to participate are extremely difficult to recruit and retain. You do the best you can to manage the situation. Although there were very few immigrants at that time, we had African American students with special needs, and getting their parents to participate was a primary concern. One of the evaluators was a person of color, and her sense was that we had not gotten enough input from parents of color. So at the end of the study, we did phone interviews with parents of color to validate the data we collected. But did people's unequal status limit their participation? These were special-needs parents. They were very committed. They weren't shy. They were advocating for their children and working to make the system better for all kids.

Fitzpatrick: You used many different types of data collection. In fact, the many different types of data collection you completed over one year were quite impressive: surveys, telephone interviews, focus groups, and dialogues with teachers, administrators, paraprofessionals, and parents as well as observations of meetings. This was a tremendous undertaking. How did you decide on these methods?

King: There was a sense that we wanted a lot of data—that to ensure coverage we really needed everyone's opinion. So we felt we should collect qualitative and quantitative data from everyone we could think of. It was only possible because I had an amazing staff, who would drop everything to process the data for the monthly meeting. For the qualitative data, they would do the typing.

Fitzpatrick: How did you manage carrying all this out?

King: Having three evaluators was essential. We could check each other. I can't imagine what it would have been like without the Evaluation Consulting Team.

Fitzpatrick: I noticed that you developed a new form of focus group, the data dialogue, partly because of your shortage of resources. In the data dialogue, a few participants talked to each other, but without a focus group leader, and then they recorded the qualitative data. Can you tell us more about that? How did it work? What structure or guidance did you provide?

King: We called it the poor person's focus group. The Data Collection Team was meeting, and we were well into the study, and someone said, "You know, we'd really better get some qualitative data." And we said, "There's no money. There's no way. We can't do it. It's too complicated." So one of the external evaluators, the social psychologist, said, "Well, what if we adapt this technique, the three-step interview? We'll have people come and invite them to a public meeting, but rather than have one large group discussion, we'll divide them into groups of three people. We'll have them sign in and give their consent to use the data—we can have a demographics sheet—then send people off with the questions." The questions were on different colored paper, so we could tell which groups were discussing which questions. They had the conversations. People would hand in the sheet when they were done. They could go, then, but they usually wanted to hear what other groups said. So we would have refreshments and, after that, do a debriefing with the large group. Not only did they have wonderful conversations, but they would meet people and find out what other people thought and go home happy.

Fitzpatrick: How were the groups composed? Were they a mix of people or were they grouped by similar roles?

King: That depended on the purpose of the data dialogue. Sometimes teachers would talk to teachers and paras to other paras to get role-alike discussion. Other times we'd mix people up to get cross-role conversation. It really depended on the questions we were trying to answer.

Fitzpatrick: Was there a group leader?

King: Not an assigned one. Typically, someone would take a leadership role in the group, but we did not control that. Three people is the perfect group size. It's small enough that people really can talk but large enough that there is an audience of two. We would invite one person to be the recorder. The obvious limitation is you get what they write down, but we wanted to let people chat.

Fitzpatrick: Do people vary in how much they write down?

King: Some write a lot. Others feel they should come to consensus and then write that down. Either way is fine. We review the directions as people come into the meeting room and have them sign in.

Fitzpatrick: Tell me about some of the data you got from this.

King: We did the process with the teachers and paras at one meeting. They had completed surveys, but we hadn't given them a chance to talk. We had the teachers and paras come at the same time. The dialogue data documented how they felt about teaching special-needs kids, provided stories and examples. With the parents, surveys had been sent to a stratified random sample, but we knew that some wanted to speak, so we had a session for people who wanted to talk. They came. Those who showed up really wanted to be there, and sometimes they told us how well their child had been served. Other times they expressed specific frustrations. Again, the stories added to the more formal survey data.

I should tell you how we analyzed the qualitative data from these dialogues. The surveys had open-ended questions, too. So we couldn't easily summarize these for work groups. We had parents and teachers come in and do two days of qualitative analysis. It was a group of 8 to 10 parents and teachers, and they worked for two full days to analyze the qualitative data. We used the same process of small groups doing the analysis and cross-checking each others' analysis. There was a huge amount of paper. This was in the summer, and everyone was a volunteer. We just provided lunch. It gave the parents a chance to speak. This process created a place for them to speak.

Fitzpatrick: What forms of data collection were most informative for you and your Evaluation Consulting Team? What about for the larger Self-Study Team? Did groups differ in what forms of data they found most useful? What was your role in facilitating that?

King: There was no one type of data that was more valuable. All the forms of data collection were valuable. Some people liked the survey data means, others liked the survey frequency data, some wanted the qualitative stories— different people liked different data, but it all had to be looked at. It was the Self-Study Team that did the analysis. Our role was facilitating. We also had that technical role of making sure that any claims made were proper. That was a critical role.

Fitzpatrick: Since the report I read did not include analyses or data, I don't know much about your actual results, although I do have information on your commendations and recommendations in your written materials. Can you tell me about what you learned about the program from the data collection?

King: That some students were served incredibly well and others less well and some not very well at all. But, by and large, special-needs students in the district were attended to. Communication was a problem—changing regulations, getting anything out to anyone clearly was a problem. There were problems with communication internally and with parents. Not all parents understood their options. Another problem was that regular classroom teachers needed to work more on adapting and modifying the curriculum for special-needs students. This will always be true. There are actual skills in doing that, and many teachers hadn't learned those skills in their training.

Fitzpatrick: Now, I know a major role of the Self-Study Team and the smaller table teams was to review the results and develop recommendations. You indicate that 53 recommendations were developed around issues presented in more than one data source. The self-study group was divided into 10 smaller groups to identify their top recommendations from these. How did that process work?

King: We had grouped the recommendations into general topics like parental involvement, staff development, and so on but needed a way to prioritize what should be worked on first. We were out of time—the whole process had taken several months more than we had planned—so we gave table teams the list of recommendations and had them individually rate each recommendation on a scale of 1 to 3, where 1 meant *do it right now* and 3 meant *put it on the back burner.* We added up the individual ratings, calculated a mean, and that's how we got the list of recommendations for immediate action.

Fitzpatrick: Did the top issues or concerns that these work groups identified from the results differ from what you and the Evaluation Consulting Team saw as the central issues? What if they had? Whose issues should be given priorities?

King: That's a false dichotomy. We supported the table teams. We took their work and used it, but the only correction was when there were technical errors. The lesson I learned is when you have huge amounts of data, some of which contradict each other, it is so important for people to have to say what data went with their claim. People had to have data from more than one source to make a claim. We worked hard to teach people that you can't make a claim from just one data source. But it's still very difficult when data contradict each other. We wanted everyone to understand that you're going to have challenges about making general statements, but it was such a community process.

Fitzpatrick: There must have been some judgment involved for you, the facilitators, in determining whether the claims or recommendations that the work teams made were based on the data. Can you describe how you facilitated when that was a problem? Tell us a little bit about how you carried out your role then.

King: Remember that we had multiple tables working with the same data each month. Also, each table had professional educators, community members, some of whom were highly educated, other staff—in other words, people who were able to make sense of the data in front of them. They really learned over the course of the study. They got better at data analysis, so our role was more comparing and contrasting the results across tables. People at the tables would write the claims and identify the data that they thought supported them. If different tables produced similar claims using similar data, that was great. We would look at the different versions of the claim and pick the best one, editing it if need be. If there were different claims supported by the data, we brought those back to the group for discussion the following month. Remember, our role was to ensure the accuracy of the claims.

Fitzpatrick: Were you ever surprised at some of the conclusions or recommendations that a team or teams ultimately developed?

King: No. By the time the groups had processed all of the data, the claims were so clearly linked to specific data that the results were not a surprise. Transparency was part and parcel of the analysis process.

Fitzpatrick: One of the really interesting things that you did was to survey participants about the process to learn what they thought about it and their involvement. You're actually using evaluation to evaluate your own process! That's great—practicing what we preach. What did you learn from this? Was there anything you learned that prompted you to change your process for capacity building in the future?

King: I should explain why we did that. You will recall that the district wanted very much to involve people in this self-study process, so part of what we were charged with was to understand what people learned from participating. They really did learn about survey construction, data analysis, and the tentative nature of evaluative conclusions—that several positions could be supported with data. That was really important from the district's perspective because they wanted a community, professionals and parents, who understood the challenges of evaluation.

So what I learned was the value of having people think about what they're learning. It's being more purposeful about the instructional value of evaluation. We assume people will learn things, but people aren't aware, and if they're not aware of what they're learning, they may not learn as much. So the key was helping them to be purposeful about the learning process. Part of that is demystifying evaluation for people.

We made a link between their participation in the evaluation and how they felt about it. We fed these results back to them as well. In retrospect, it was a good idea. It validated for them the positive effects of all the time they had committed to the self-study. We sensed that. The group was very close. There were about 50 people who came to the monthly meetings regularly and participated. Actually, reflection helps me as well. It was this study that altered my research agenda—shifted it from participatory evaluation to evaluation capacity building.

Fitzpatrick: Why did it do that?

King: Because I saw the potential in building these skills. I came to the district with that in mind, working with community people and parents to make sense of evaluation. They learned also.

Fitzpatrick: Was there anything that was surprising?

King: No. It was pleasing. The Evaluation Consulting Team would look and say, "Yes, this is what we had hoped."

Fitzpatrick: Bringing our focus back to the self-study of the special education program, you developed 6 commendations and identified 15 issues areas where you developed specific recommendations or suggestions for improvement. Let's talk about the commendations first. What prompted you to consider developing commendations?

King: That came at the very end as we rushed to finish the recommendations. There was a sense that the special education teachers were working as hard as they could be expected to work. And there was a sense in the group that it was important to give people credit for the hard work, for the many successes that the data showed. How can you have 53 recommendations and say nothing positive at all? The commendations are sometimes very broad. You can drive a truck through them. But so much of the process had been set up with a negative frame. The commendations were to acknowledge that there were some positive things—some strong commendations that could be made about the program.

Fitzpatrick: One of your commendations was pretty broad: "All staff, throughout the district, are caring, dedicated, compassionate, and diligent when working with students to help them reach their maximum potential." The others are more focused. For example, "Parents have expressed that their children are well served and supported by District 11 staff." Tell us about your role in developing these commendations and your thoughts on them.

King: They were supposed to come out of the data, but just hearing that first one makes me cringe. You couldn't have data that supported that claim. But, at the time, that's what we put forward, probably late one evening. I don't know. I would edit these commendations now. We did use the same process for commendations and recommendations, but with far less time available. The table teams worked with the data and supposedly had to support all of these. I know the teachers felt very strongly that they were doing the best they could. My experience in studies like this documents what I call the "yes, but" syndrome. People quickly skim through the positives, going "Yeah, yeah, yeah," and move right to the negatives. So these were the "yes" part before page after page of recommendations.

Fitzpatrick: The issue areas and recommendations, of course, address many different aspects of the program. Which areas did you feel were most in need of change based on your evaluation results and your discussions with the evaluation team and self-study team?

King: The Evaluation Consulting Team purposely did not make separate analyses and have separate reports. Laurie Stevahn and I use an evaluation practice continuum: At one end is evaluator-directed evaluation, and the other end is client directed. We were operating in the middle or perhaps a bit toward the client-centered end of that continuum. The evaluator and the participants were working collaboratively. We were the technicians; we were preparing the data. But as far as analyzing the data and interpreting it, we didn't do that. This, of course, would make many of my colleagues wince.

But it's not a question of good or bad. Along the continuum, there are choices about what one's role is. In this case, we really were in this collaborative mode. I came to understand much better what it meant to be a coach, to be a support. Being a coach, being a support, means supplying the data, not commenting, except to make sure that any claims made were technically correct—making sure people don't misuse by accident. It's important to emphasize how much data there were. There was so much information people were crunching. Because we, the Evaluation Consulting Team, were purposely outside, we were relying on the participants' knowledge of the settings and context to determine which recommendations should be implemented first.

Having said that, I remember a meeting where the Data Collection Team said, "Whoa! Are there some of these we can do right now? We can change our newsletter. That will address one of the recommendations." Again, the emphasis was on the so-called low-hanging fruit, what they could do right now.

Fitzpatrick: Parent involvement, especially with the IEPs, seemed to be an area of concern. What had your results shown on this?

King: That the majority of parents were quite well served by the system, but a few were not. A sad one is the example of the father I discussed earlier. In a large system, that's probably always going to be the case. You work to make the system better over time. Having process data makes a difference.

Fitzpatrick: You remained with the district, in some capacity, for a couple of more years. One strength of an internal evaluator is being able to encourage use of results. Which recommendations or what types of recommendations were most frequently implemented? Were you able to make use of your role there to encourage use?

King: That's a hard question to answer. All of the people who reported to this Associate Superintendent met regularly. There was this structure of top administrators, and I was part of that structure. We called ourselves the COSOBs, for Central Office SOBs—we even had T-shirts—and we were absolutely integrally involved with seeing that the recommendations were implemented. So we would pull out the evaluation reports on different issues (special ed, middle school) we were considering. We literally would go to the recommendations and make sure we were working on them. To help with this, the Associate Superintendent instituted a policy of our collectively developing "key messages." We would say, "What were the key messages coming from this study?" And they would be sent out to the principals and staff. One administrator would work on it, and the COSOB group would talk about how to get recommendations to happen. We weren't always successful, of course, but that was the idea.

Here's an example. Probably, 10 years earlier, the district had done a huge study on middle school education. Ten years later, the COSOBs came back to do a similar study. The process we used was very similar to the special education study. It had the same concept of involving a diverse and inclusive self-study committee. The district was aware, 10 years later, that some recommendations had been well implemented but others were not and we really needed to get some new data. They still had the information from the evaluation a decade later.

Fitzpatrick: Do you think your work on involving so many stakeholders and building evaluation capacity encouraged use of the results? Or what is the purpose of involving others in this way?

King: The purpose was partly use, but remember our ultimate intended users were the Board members, and they did not participate. So the other reason for having people participate was for them to learn and understand.

This was equally important. We have evidence that people learned from it. People became close because they worked together on the data for over a year. It was like summer camp.

We had to do this self-study because of the state. The School Board received it and accepted it. But the process of teaching and learning was the outcome.

Fitzpatrick: The process itself was the outcome?

King: And the learning as well.

Fitzpatrick: How do they use that learning? What is it that they're learning?

King: Well, certainly the professional educators in the crowd learned about evaluation, and it helped them to make sense of evaluation. This is a fairly minor point, but they learned how we used the table teams. Many said, "This is great! I can use this with my teams back at school with parents." At the first meeting, we had the team line up by the length of time they'd been involved with the district, and people said that's a great idea. Parents said we could use the data dialogue idea with other parents. So people took the processes and used them in other places.

Fitzpatrick: Of course, a primary reason for building evaluation capacity is to have spillover effects to future issues. The superintendent had expressed the desire to become a "data-driven" district in making decisions. Did you see this occurring?

King: Absolutely. The district remains committed to using data of many types. The point I would want to make is this would not have been possible 10 years ago before personal computers. Think how technology has changed what we can do with small groups. How lucky we are that anyone can go manipulate data! We could not have done that before. Look at *USA Today* putting numbers on the front page. People are used to looking at numbers, and these evaluation processes help them to do that.

Fitzpatrick: You chose not to complete a summary report on the findings but rather to describe the process, the data collection, and then the commendations and recommendations. We evaluators often live by the written word but that's sometimes not so true in real-world practice. Why did you decide not to write a report presenting results?

King: We did not write the formal traditional report that people often write. But we did compile all the information we collected, and members of the Self-Study Team made a presentation to the School Board. But the reporting was really designed to be what was needed for the situation.

Why didn't we choose to present findings in a formal report? I don't remember making that conscious decision. We wanted a report that was not too long. We wanted to include all the recommendations. This was going to be the historical document. The materials related to the self-study were already long—they went on and on. In retrospect, I believe we were putting in the key information.

It was the time pressure, too. The study went on much longer than we wanted it to. When you meet only once a month, you are constrained. There were also resource pressures. Who would write a more elaborate report? It would have to be us. And I think it's important to realize the three members of the Evaluation Consulting Team were always available to anyone who wanted information or had questions.

Fitzpatrick: I always like to close with asking what you learned from this study. As you have indicated, you now use this capacity-building process in many other settings. What might you change today if you had to do this again?

King: I would not have had such a large study committee. One hundred, even 50 people, is too large and really has implications for participatory work.

Fitzpatrick: What's a good number?

King: Eighteen to twenty. There's always the few who don't attend. You can do this process with a larger group—we demonstrated that—but the facilitation role becomes more challenging. There were three of us, so this was well staffed, but even so you were *managing* it. With the smaller group, you're actually thinking. It has implications for participatory work when you're in a large organization.

Fitzpatrick: Do you have to go with 50 or 100 in a large organization?

King: It depends. In this study, we needed to. People needed to be present.

In the middle school study that followed this one, we had a smaller group, and it worked well. This couldn't be that way because of the political climate. We simply had to have representatives from the various stakeholder groups.

The other thing that I learned was the techniques. Laurie Stevahn, one of the external evaluators, was a key actor in this because of her knowledge of social psychology. These techniques that she helped put in the process revolutionized my work.

Fitzpatrick: Tell me more. What do you mean?

King: The table teams, the three-step interview, the structuring activities—they're the key. I've taught school for a long time. These strategies are surefire. They're winners because they're absolutely based on psychological principles.

Fitzpatrick: Thank you, Jean, for a great discussion of this project.

Fitzpatrick's comments

King's focus in this evaluation is capacity building, and she gives us a picture of what that can involve. To help those on the Self-Study Team learn about evaluation, King and her colleagues serve only two roles: as "objective technicians" and as facilitators. As "objective technicians" their role is to make sure groups can support their conclusions with at least two pieces of data. Of course, as King notes, she and her colleagues also consider how to structure table teams to facilitate discussion, they prepare data for review by the teams, and they serve as liaisons between the self-study team and other administrators at the central office. They also develop some methods of data collection such as the data dialogues. But her point is this: For capacity building to occur, she and her colleagues strictly limit their roles so others can gain competency in evaluation.

The Self-Study Team makes decisions concerning the focus of the study; data collection, including the sources and methods of collecting data and sampling strategies; analysis and interpretation of the data provided to them; and the development of conclusions. The Evaluation Consulting Team refrains from sharing their expertise to advise the Self-Study Team on the types of things evaluation can do or the methods they use. Instead, their interventions with the Self-Study Team concern making sure they do not make "errors" with the data—that is, forming conclusions that are not supported with data. As such, the Self-Study Team learns several things. They learn to support their conclusions with data, and they learn that different groups may draw different conclusions even if required to support conclusions with data. Through a discovery process, they also learn some things about how data are collected and the types of information different kinds of data can provide.

The evaluation takes place in a school district that supports collaboration and using data, thus King's choices are consistent with the culture. The district wants to build competency in evaluation in the special education program. As such, King's approach seems to serve that purpose. Although the concerns of the State Department and the School Board made the evaluation more political and resulted in the presence of the State Department representative at meetings, the capacity-building emphasis was most consistent with the needs of the organization. It involved a risk that the Self-Study team might not address issues of concern to the Board or the State Department of Education, but the involvement of the State Department representative met their concerns.

As King indicates, the focus of this evaluation is on process and perceptions, which responded to parents' and State Department concerns. In an apparently rare move out of their usual role in this study, King reports that the Evaluation Consulting Team considered evaluating outcomes and "wanted to look at the Individual Education Plans (IEPs) to see if kids were progressing," but the concerns that had been raised with the State Department were with process. The section on descriptive evaluations demonstrates that description can play an important role in evaluations. As King notes, the focus of the evaluation was broad: "What was going right? What was going wrong?" As such, the Self-Study Team, just beginning to learn about evaluation, could choose to describe many things. Their choice was to focus on describing perceptions of key stakeholders—that is, teachers, paras, and parents. King reports, "There was a sense that we wanted a lot of data—that to ensure coverage we really needed everyone's opinion." Was the team's choice made with awareness of all the things evaluation can do or because surveys and perceptions are what people new to evaluation often consider? That is unclear. Nevertheless, with comprehensive data on opinions, the Self-Study Team was able to identify some successes and some problem areas.

As King reports the results, she does not seem to find them particularly surprising, nor do I. Some students and parents, the majority, are served well, and some are not. Communication, teachers to parents and special education teachers to regular classroom teachers, is a problem area. But, King notes, that will always be true. The results are important, but less important than building competency to address evaluation issues in the future.

The interview also provides us with a second perspective, in addition to the interview with David Fetterman, on serving as an internal evaluator. King knows the district well and, in terms of her own values, remarks, "I am a school person at heart. I love schools." She has been a teacher and recognizes the demands, particularly in light of the scarce resources of the district. So she identifies with the teachers who are working hard. Her focus, however, is on competency building. King wants to make sure that the people on the Self-Study Team learn, and that, she believes, will be the enduring contribution. Unlike Fetterman and others who have focused on description, King and the Self-Study Team do not have a specific model or theory to test. The district wanted the evaluation to "build an awareness about the issues confronting the special education program." By involving many in the evaluation, the district believed that they could accomplish that task. More like a traditional internal evaluator than Fetterman, at least partly because this is her full-time position with the district, King does not see her role in the evaluation in highlighting the lack of resources that make it difficult to meet more students' needs, as an external evaluator might. Instead, it is to help the organization build internal capacity. Given her limited role in the evaluation, the Self-Study Team truly becomes the internal evaluator, as its permanent members are largely teachers and principals. Nevertheless, they find areas of special education in need of improvement, and as an internal evaluator, King will be around for a time to encourage use of the recommendations.

King, like Stewart Donaldson, recognizes that program people can be more receptive to evaluation results if we begin with the positive. (See Chapter 9 for the interview with Stewart Donaldson.) She begins with commendations to acknowledge the work of teachers. Her role is always positive and facilitative. That role is undoubtedly a great influence in helping the team function effectively and carry out the evaluation.

King's interview helps us learn more about capacity building and the roles and choices evaluators can take in pursuing that goal.

DISCUSSION QUESTIONS

1. What are the purposes of King's evaluation? Discuss the choices she makes in choosing between capacity building and meeting the needs of the School Board and the State Department of Education.

2. King's evaluation, as she notes, has a broad scope. As with Fetterman's evaluation, she and the self-study team decide to learn about what works and what does not. Other evaluations are guided by evaluation questions that indicate a specific focus. What do you see as the strengths and weaknesses of each approach?

3. Stakeholder involvement can be characterized by its breadth (how many different groups are consulted) and its depth (to what extent each group is involved). Consider the breadth and depth of stakeholder involvement in this study. Who are the key stakeholders for the capacity-building part of the study? For the evaluation of the special education department? How does King choose to involve each? Discuss the strengths and weaknesses of her approach to stakeholder involvement for the different purposes of this evaluation.

4. What are the strengths of King's approach to capacity building? What are the disadvantages?

5. Do you think an external evaluator would have approached the evaluation of the special education department differently? If so, how?

6. As noted in the introduction to this section, many evaluators are concerned with capacity building, with helping organizations to better conduct, understand, and use evaluations. Think about your own organization or a place where you have worked. Would building evaluation capacity be helpful to that organization? What evaluation competencies would you hope to improve in the organization? How might you go about it?

FURTHER READING

This paper describes the evaluation: King, J. A., Stevahn, L., & McKendall, V. J. (2002, April). *A case study of a special education evaluation for building evaluation capacity.* Paper presented at the annual meeting of the American Educational Research Association, New Orleans, LA.

Compton, D., Baizerman, M., & Stockdill, S. (2002). *The art, craft, and science of evaluation capacity building* (New Directions for Evaluation, Vol. 93). San Francisco: Jossey-Bass.

Johnson, D. (2000). Laying the foundation: Capacity building for participatory monitoring and evaluation. In M. Estrella, J. Blauert, D. Campilan, J. Gaventa, J. Gonsalves, I. Guijt, et al. (Eds.), *Learning from change: Issues and experiences in participatory monitoring and evaluation* (pp. 217–228). London: Intermediate Technology Publications/Ottawa, Ontario, Canada: International Development Research Centre.

King, J. A. (2007). Developing evaluation capacity through process use. In J. B. Cousins (Ed.), *Process use in theory, research and practice* (New Directions for Evaluation, No. 116, pp. 45–59). San Francisco: Jossey-Bass.

King, J. A., & Volkov, B. (2005). A framework for building evaluation capacity based on the experiences of three organizations. *CURA Reporter, 35*(3), 10–16.

McDonald, B., Rogers, P., & Kefford, B. (2003). Teaching people to fish? Building the evaluation capability of public sector organizations. *Evaluation, 9*(1), 9–29.

Mott, A. (2003). Hand in hand: Evaluation and organizational development. *The Evaluation Exchange, 9*(3), 8.

REFERENCE

House, E. R., & Howe, K. R. (1999). *Values in evaluation and social research.* Thousand Oaks, CA: Sage.

NINE

EVALUATION OF THE WORK AND HEALTH INITIATIVE WITH A FOCUS ON WINNING NEW JOBS

An Interview With Stewart I. Donaldson

———————

*I*ntroduction. Stewart Donaldson is Professor and Chair of the Psychology Department, Director of the Institute of Organizational and Program Evaluation Research, and Dean of the School of Behavioral and Organizational Sciences at Claremont Graduate University (CGU). He has conducted numerous evaluations, developed one of the largest university-based evaluation training programs, and published numerous evaluation articles, chapters, and books. His recent books include *Program Theory-Driven Evaluation Science: Strategies and Applications* (2007), *Applied Psychology: New Frontiers and Rewarding Careers* (2006, with D. Berger & K. Pezdek), *Evaluating Social Programs and Problems: Visions for the New Millennium* (2003, with M. Scriven), *Social Psychology and Policy/Program Evaluation* (in press, with M. Mark & B. Campbell), and *What Counts as Credible Evidence in Evaluation and Evidence-Based Practice?* (in press, with C. Christie & M. Mark). He is a cofounder of the Southern California Evaluation Association and is on the editorial boards of the *American Journal of Evaluation, New Directions for Evaluation,* and the *Journal of Multidisciplinary Evaluation.* Dr. Donaldson received early career achievement awards from the American Evaluation Association and the Western Psychological Association.

In this interview, we learn more about Donaldson's approach in practice through focusing on his evaluation of The California Wellness Foundation's Work and Health Initiative. For the purposes of this interview, and to illustrate his approach with a specific evaluation, our discussion will focus on the program Winning New Jobs (WNJ). However, since this program was only one small part of the Initiative, we will occasionally refer to other programs that were part of the whole evaluation. In the interview, Donaldson discusses his methods for working with stakeholders to develop program theory and his use of a 360-degree feedback process to turn the tables and give users the opportunity to give the evaluation team feedback on their performance. Donaldson's evaluation of WNJ moves from a focus on continuous program improvement to a summative phase. He describes how he develops his role and how that role changes. During this six-year evaluation, he and his evaluation team collect data on the population served, program implementation, short-term and long-term outcomes, and sustainability, making use of a mix of qualitative and quantitative approaches.

Summary of the Evaluation of the Work and Health Initiative

Stewart I. Donaldson

Laura E. Gooler

Claremont Graduate University

————————

The mission of the Work and Health Initiative, funded by The California Wellness Foundation, was to improve the health of Californians by funding employment-related interventions. Fundamental to this Initiative was the perspective that important relationships between work and health are shaped by an evolving California economy. The goals of the Initiative were to (1) understand the rapidly changing nature of work and its effects on the health of Californians, (2) increase access to high-quality employment for all Californians, (3) improve conditions of work for employed Californians, and (4) expand the availability of work site health programs and benefits.

To accomplish these goals, The California Wellness Foundation funded four programs involving more than 40 partner organizations working together to improve the well-being of Californians through approaches related to employment (see Donaldson, Gooler, & Weiss, 1998; Donaldson & Weiss, 1998). The Future of Work and Health (FWH) and the Health Insurance Policy Programs (HIPP) were expansive and comprehensive research programs designed to generate and disseminate knowledge of how the nature of work is being transformed and how that change will affect the health and well-being of Californians. In the HIPP, current statewide trends related to health and health insurance within California were examined through extensive survey research on an annual basis. In the FWH program, researchers throughout California examined the changing nature of work and health and identified some implications for improving working conditions and lowering employment risks.

The Initiative also included two fully operational demonstration programs in 17 sites throughout the state to assist both youth and adults in building job skills and finding employment. The WNJ program aimed to help workers regain employment lost due to downsizing, reengineering, and other factors driving rather dramatic changes in the California workplace, and thereby put an end to the adverse health consequences that most workers experience as a result of unemployment. Finally, the Computers in Our Future program aimed to enable youth and young adults from low-income communities to learn computer skills to improve their education and employment opportunities— thereby improving their own future health as well as the health and well-being of their families and communities.

Evaluation Approach

Systematic program evaluation was used to guide the strategic management of each program in the Initiative, as well as to inform the entire Initiative. Our evaluation team, Claremont Graduate University (CGU), was awarded the contract to evaluate the Initiative. Our role was to serve as an integrating, synthesizing force in evaluating the goals, objectives, strategies, outcomes, and impact of the Initiative. We identified cross-cutting goals and synergies, worked to enhance these goals, and evaluated in an effort to maximize the overall impact of the Initiative. In addition, CGU developed evaluation systems that provided responsive evaluation data for each program. These data were used to continually improve the program's effectiveness as well as to evaluate its impact.

To ensure that the perspectives and problem-solving needs of those with a vested interest in the Initiative programs (e.g., The California Wellness Foundation, grantees, program administrators, staff, and program recipients), collectively known as stakeholders, were understood and addressed, the evaluation team adopted a participatory theory-driven evaluation approach (Donaldson, 2001, 2002). Key objectives of this approach were to empower stakeholders to be successful, facilitate continuous program learning, assist with ongoing problem-solving efforts, and facilitate improvement at as many levels as possible throughout the life of the Initiative (see Donaldson, 2002). Decisions about evaluation design, goal setting, data collection, program monitoring, data analysis, report development, and dissemination were highly collaborative.

The participatory theory-driven approach rested on developing program theories for each program and using evaluation data to guide program development and implementation. Program theory was defined as a sensible and plausible model of how a program is presumed to reach its desired outcomes (see Donaldson, 2001). Each program theory was developed collaboratively and was based on the stakeholders' views and experiences, prior evaluation and research findings, and more general theoretical and empirical work related to the phenomena under investigation. Such frameworks provided a guiding model around which evaluation designs were developed to specifically answer key evaluation questions as rigorously as possible given the practical constraints of the evaluation context.

Data Collection

Data collection efforts were based on the premise that no single data source is likely to be bias-free or a completely accurate representation of reality. In general, we followed the tenets of critical multiplism (Cook, 1985; Donaldson, 1995; Shadish, 1993). Evaluation plans were designed to specifically encourage each grantee to use multiple data collection strategies with different strengths and weaknesses. A special effort was made to understand cultural and language concerns so that the methodologies employed yielded accurate data. In addition to evaluating program outcomes, impact, and potential side effects, evaluative efforts were both formative (i.e., aimed at developing and improving programs from an early stage) and process oriented (i.e., geared toward understanding how a program achieves what it does over time).

Formative Evaluation Tools

To support continuous program improvement throughout the life of the Initiative, the CGU evaluation team

- provided midyear evaluation reports,
- facilitated midyear conference calls to discuss program evaluation findings and recommendations with grantees and The California Wellness Foundation's program officers,
- provided year-end evaluation reports,
- facilitated year-end conference calls to discuss program evaluation findings and recommendations with grantees and The California Wellness Foundation's program officers, and
- provided grantees an opportunity to evaluate The California Wellness Foundation's program officers and CGU evaluators on an annual basis.

In addition, these efforts were supplemented with several interim evaluation reports and frequent communications with grantees and The California
Wellness Foundation's program officers to provide timely feedback based on
evaluation data collected throughout the year.

Summative Evaluation

The CGU evaluation team collected and analyzed extensive quantitative
and qualitative data pertaining to the impact of the Work and Health Initiative.
Approximately 200 evaluation reports were written and provided to grantees
and/or The California Wellness Foundation throughout the life of the Initiative.
In an effort to determine the most useful format and content for the final summative evaluation report, CGU initiated several discussions with the
Foundation. As a result of those discussions, CGU wrote the final report to
conform to the following guidelines:

- The main purpose of the report was to provide a summary of evalua-
  tion findings and conclusions in a relatively brief manner.
- Qualitative as well as quantitative findings were presented.
- The report reflects CGU's candid evaluation of the Work and Health
  Initiative from an external evaluation perspective and does not neces-
  sarily reflect the views of the grantees or The California Wellness
  Foundation staff involved with the project.
- The summative evaluation report was a confidential internal document
  presented to the Board of Directors of the Foundation.

At the request of the Foundation, CGU offered to provide copies of supporting documents, previous evaluation reports, and data tables or conducted
additional data analyses to justify or expand on findings and conclusions
presented in the summative report. CGU also provided summative evaluation
reports for each program to the appropriate grantees and continues to produce
and disseminate public documents describing key findings and lessons learned
from the Work and Health Initiative (e.g., Donaldson & Gooler, 2003).

Winning New Jobs

The evaluation designs and findings for each of the four programs and for the
entire Work and Health Initiative are too complex and extensive to adequately

describe in this summary. Therefore, we decided to briefly summarize the design for one of the Work and Health Initiative programs, Winning New Jobs (WNJ), as a way to illustrate theory-driven evaluation in practice.

Program Description

The original mission of WNJ was to provide job search training to 10,000 unemployed and underemployed Californians over a four-year funding period. This project was based on a theory-based intervention, JOBS, which was developed and initially tested via a randomized trial in Michigan by the Michigan Prevention Research Center (Vinokur, Price, Caplan, van Ryn, & Curran, 1995; Vinokur, van Ryn, Gramlich, & Price, 1991). Organizational readiness assessments were used to select three unique organizations in different California communities to implement WNJ (see Donaldson, Gooler, & Weiss, 1998).

The core program theory used to guide the evaluation of WNJ is shown in Figure 9.1. As the figure illustrates, the WNJ program, a one-week, half-day workshop, was designed to increase participants' job search self-confidence, job search skills, and problem-solving strategies, including inoculation against setbacks (i.e., expectations of setbacks). These skills and psychological factors would then lead to greater reemployment and improve mental health. Furthermore, the WNJ program was hypothesized to have impacts at multiple levels: participant (e.g., increased job search self-efficacy and reemployment), organization (e.g., staff skill development, reputation enhancement), community (e.g., increased access to job search services), and the policy environment (e.g., financial support for the continuation of the program).

WNJ Evaluation Questions

A rather extensive process consisting of several meetings, phone and electronic discussions, and document submission and revisions with program stakeholders was used to develop and prioritize evaluation questions using the core program theory shown in Figure 9.1. The same type of collaborative process was used to decide how to allocate resources for data collection. In summary, given resource and other practical constraints, compromises were required to decide which evaluation questions to answer and how to answer them. It is important to note that the final evaluation design did not focus on some of the hypothesized relationships (e.g., links to mental health outcomes).

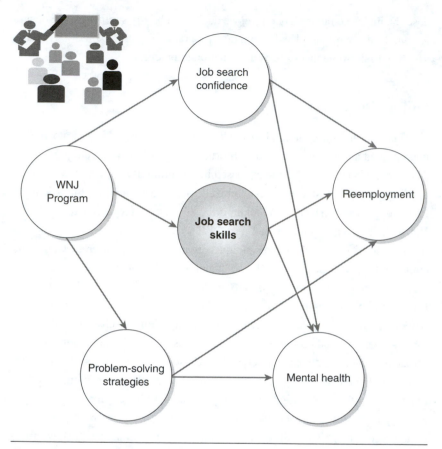

Figure 9.1   Winning New Jobs Program Theory

The core evaluation questions included the following:

1. *Program implementation:* Can the Michigan JOBS program be implemented in different types of service organizations in California? What does implementation look like? What are the key challenges and success factors of implementation?

2. *Program service:* Whom are the sites serving (e.g., population characteristics of service recipients)? How many people are served at each site?

3. *Short-term outcomes:* Does WNJ increase people's confidence in their ability to use their newly acquired/enhanced job-seeking skills?

4. *Reemployment outcomes:* Do people find employment? And what does their employment situation look like?

5. *Program sustainability and replication:* Does WNJ generate resources for program sustainability beyond the life of the grant? Do other California organizations learn about and adopt the WNJ model?

Data Collected to Answer
WNJ Evaluation Questions

To address these questions, extensive standardized eligibility, demographic, pre-test, post-test, and employment follow-up data were collected at each site. Overall, data were collected for more than 5,100 individuals, including eligibility, demographic, and pre-test data for 4,960 individuals, post-test data for 3,684 individuals, and employment follow-up forms for 3,476 individuals who completed the workshop. These response rates were considered adequate for the nature of the program and types of analyses conducted. In addition to these data, various types of qualitative implementation and outcome data were collected. Furthermore, databases tracking participants in other parts of the country and the world were available for comparison purposes. This collection of databases was used for both formative and summative evaluation of the WNJ program.

Evaluation Conclusions and Use

Summative evaluation findings demonstrated that the three WNJ organizations trained 5,290 unemployed or underemployed Californians over a four-year period. The preponderance of the evaluation evidence indicated significant improvements in both short-term skill and psychological outcomes. In addition, evaluation evidence showed that 65% of the participants who completed the WNJ program reported becoming reemployed within 180 days of completing the program.

The California Wellness Foundation reported using this evaluation to guide future investments in their Work and Health Priority area, as well as future investments in the evaluation of foundation programs and initiatives. They also commissioned follow up evaluation work to look at the impact of the Initiative programs over time. A number of key publications were derived from this evaluation that helped further understanding about work and health programming, as well as contemporary evaluation practice (see the References).

Dialogue With Stewart Donaldson

Jody Fitzpatrick

———•◦•———

Fitzpatrick: You've selected your evaluation of The California Wellness Foundation's Work and Health Initiative as representative of your approach to theory-driven program evaluation. Why do you think this particular evaluation is most illustrative of your approach?

Donaldson: I've been conducting theory-driven evaluations for close to a couple of decades now, and one of the things that I've noticed is that some people think this approach is very academic—an ivory tower approach almost like laboratory research. I would say that probably most published evaluations are what I would call efficacy evaluations, and I've done these types of evaluations. This is when the investigator sets the conditions for the study and has complete control. If theory-driven evaluation is good only for that purpose, it's pretty limited. That's not a robust way to practice evaluation.

I chose this application for our interview because it illustrates how the theory-driven approach is much more robust than the efficacy trial. It can be used to examine how an intervention works out in real organizations, in the real world where there's not a lot of control over who gets into the program and who doesn't. This is evaluating in a real-world context that is similar to what most evaluators face. So I wanted to focus on this evaluation because I wanted to show that theory-driven evaluation can be applied in the circumstances most evaluators work in.

Fitzpatrick: So you wanted to show that evaluation should not be what you call an efficacy trial but should be grounded in the real world and, conversely, show that theory-driven evaluation works better in the real world than the efficacy trial. It's not an ivory tower approach but is adaptable to the setting. What aspect of the World Health Initiative evaluation did you feel was most exemplary in demonstrating the ability of participative theory-based evaluation to work effectively in the real world?

Donaldson: Given the large number of people who were involved and the differences across sites, I think our ability to build the continuous improvement function into the evaluation was the most exemplary part. By continuous improvement, I mean what many traditionally consider formative evaluation. In doing evaluation for continuous improvement, there's a lot of detailed work. It was gratifying, toward the end of the project, to see how the evaluation had been used to improve the programs along the way and to find out that many of the stakeholders believed that the evaluation process created a community of learners and "learning organizations."

When we first began working with these same stakeholders (e.g., program designers, managers, trainers, Foundation staff, etc.), they seemed to have had a very different view of evaluation. Some saw it as something they would be punished with and believed it wouldn't have any value to them. At most of the sites and programs we were able to make the evaluation timely and useful. We tried to help them mount programs that had a chance to be implemented. At the same time, we let them know we were going to do a summative evaluation at the end.

Fitzpatrick: The four programs that emerged from the Work and Health Initiative were quite different. What similarities were there in developing the program theory?

Donaldson: The similarities are in the process and role of the evaluator. Even though you're trying to engage stakeholders in this process, the evaluator really has to be a strong leader. Related to that, you don't use evaluation language when you develop program theory. Most grantees or stakeholders don't understand it. *Theory* has kind of an academic, negative connotation. Instead we say something like, "Before we do any evaluation, we really want to understand your program. For us to design a good evaluation, we really need to be sensitive to what you're trying to do." As they're talking about it, we're trying to conceptualize it.

One thing I've learned over time is that it's really important not to treat this as a one-directional process. It's important to move right to left *and* left to right, really probing the assumptions in somebody's program theory. I now instruct my students to start at the right (with desired outcomes), to ask, "Where are you going with all this?" Once they are clear about where they believe they want to go, we explore how they plan to get there. Sometimes it's really helpful to take just one participant. How will this participant be different or change after completing this program? How does this change or transformation occur? In other words, start with what the client will be like at the end and move backwards. Most people do exactly the opposite. Most people want to start on the left side of the model, with the details of the program.

If you start with "What are the components of the program?" you can quickly get lost in details that aren't central to the program theory. So, instead, start with defining what the program is trying to achieve, what the client will ideally be like in the end.

For example, in one of the programs, Computers in Our Future, stakeholders were concerned with describing all of the ways they were going to have participants interact with computers. Instead of starting with that level of detail, we started by asking them to define the purpose of the program. They collectively viewed the purpose to be improving the health of the participants. On the surface, most people would not find it reasonable to believe that learning computer programs is a major determinant of health. However, after we worked for a considerable amount of time helping the stakeholders conceptualize their program, we were able to articulate a concise program theory and help them design a program that made this link more plausible.

This bidirectional approach to making implicit program theory explicit has several other important advantages. It is very common to discover the program under investigation is poorly conceptualized. For example, when you take a presumed outcome and examine it carefully, it is common to find that the program as designed has very little chance, based on what we know from prior research and evaluation, to account for a significant portion of the variance in the presumed outcome. It is also common to discover that the relationship between a program and its presumed outcomes may be conditional or better explained by taking moderating factors into account. All of this can be useful for improving the design of the program in advance of implementation and evaluation, which can lead to substantial savings in time and resources. In addition, once the presumed program theory has been formulated, it is important to conceptualize alternative program theories and potential unintended consequences. This step can be used to identify plausible competing program theories and potential side effects that should be examined and/or minimized.

Fitzpatrick: What differences occurred in developing program theory across the project?

Donaldson: Throughout this project, some groups were much more anxious and hostile about the evaluation than others. Their feelings, of course, make frequent interactions somewhat stressful and unpredictable. Some groups were happy to be part of the process, while others were very nervous about trying to articulate a program theory because they were skeptical about the evaluation itself. It's easier to develop program theory when you have a motivated group that has a well-formulated program. WNJ was the easiest because this was a program that had been well developed and tested at the University of Michigan through randomized designs and under a number of conditions, though it was initially developed for auto workers who were downsized in Detroit. So, the real question with WNJ was "Can you take that program and implement it in California with a very different population?" The Michigan group was very clear about what they were trying to accomplish and were open to the evaluation.

For two other projects in the Initiative, defining *program theory* was much more difficult. As I mentioned, Computers in Our Future, unlike WNJ, which began with a previously formulated and tested model, began with a generally defined problem—kids and young adults in the inner cities were being left out of the computer and information revolution and in order for them to have good employment situations something needed to be done about that. So the grant was to develop programs, however, that made sense and seemed culturally appropriate to the local communities to meet this issue. There was no curriculum in place. Many of the people we dealt with really had not thought much as to how they were going to get from Point A to Point B. So, really the exercise of developing program theory itself had a huge impact on program development.

The other difficult project was the Future of Work and Health (FWH) program. It was difficult to get the first grantee to articulate program theory and to work with the evaluation team. There was a lot of resistance and no real buy-in. For a number of reasons, the grantee decided not to continue with the grant. Then, the Foundation decided to take it inside, to do the program themselves. The Foundation had always been the client we were evaluating *for.* Now, they began to have a dual role. They then seemed to become less enthusiastic about the evaluation of the FWH program. They felt the same level of evaluation that was going on in the other programs wasn't necessary.

In the end, we could only get to a really basic kind of model arguing, "You have to at least try to tell us what you're trying to accomplish with this program." That program theory really didn't emerge until close to the end of the project.

Fitzpatrick: Those examples are very helpful in showing an array of different circumstances. With Computers in Our Future, you indicate developing a program theory which didn't exist yet had a huge impact on the program. Can you tell us more about that?

Donaldson: In the Computers in Our Future program, there were 11 diverse grantees responsible for developing 14 community computing centers.

The process of developing program theory eventually led to a group vision of acceptable, desired short-term outcomes (e.g., technology skills, career development knowledge, job search skills, basic life skills), desired long-term outcomes (e.g., increased participation in future education, internship, and employment opportunities), and identified curricula that needed to be developed and implemented in order to achieve these goals. Without a common program theory, it is very likely grantees would have carried out very different activities that would have been ill-defined, unmeasurable, and not tightly linked to desired outcomes and the goals of the Initiative.

Fitzpatrick: The resistance of the initial grantee with the Future of Work and Health project is also interesting and a not uncommon problem. Can you tell us a bit about how you attempted to work with that grantee? What do you think went wrong?

Donaldson: In my view, the primary problem was the grantee was not comfortable working with Foundation staff and the evaluation team to clearly define the program. It seemed like the grantee did not want to be held accountable for a set of predefined activities. Instead, the preference was to do things and see how they turned out (a trial-and-error approach). The tension around disagreements about how to manage this program between Foundation staff and grantee staff eventually led to the termination of the grant. The pressure that was imposed by initiating discussions of program theory forced the problem to be addressed sooner rather than later and saved the Foundation from additional costs in terms of time and valuable resources.

Fitzpatrick: You've talked about the differences between working with these groups. What else makes developing program theory difficult or relatively straightforward?

Donaldson: Three things are important. The stage of the program is a key issue. If a program has been well tested and been running and is clearly defined, it's easier to develop program theory as opposed to when they have the money and sort of know what they want to do but aren't that sure. Then you're helping them develop it. A second issue is some programs are more complex than others. Some are pretty molar, monolithic, and have clear direct effects. Most human service programs in this Initiative were complex and multifaceted. The effects are subtle. They are diffuse. There is a lot more complexity. So, to get a good conceptualization is more time-consuming and difficult. The third issue is the group dynamics. If the two groups, the evaluation team and the program team, can set up a good relationship with clearly defined roles, the program people understand why we are defining program theory at this time. That makes it go pretty fast and it's pretty enjoyable. On the other hand, if they don't like the evaluation team, if they don't like being evaluated, or there is dissention within the group itself, it's much more difficult. There was one group that I think really assigned roles. One person from the program was always attacking the evaluation team, so the program leader would remain in good standing.

Fitzpatrick: Did you consider developing an overall program theory for the Work Health Initiative to show how choices were made about directions in funding and options?

Donaldson: One of the things we signed up for in our original proposal was evaluating the four components and then evaluating the entire Initiative. One thing that was nice was we were one of the earliest grantees. Usually evaluators come in downstream. So, in the first year, when many sites weren't even selected yet, we were spending a lot of time trying to develop an overall framework for the Initiative and to develop, I don't know if I would call it a program theory, but at least a conceptual framework, because from an outside perspective these are really four very different programs. We started to make some progress. We had a couple of big meetings, but once we started defining the work, it became really clear that people did not have anything in their budget to work on cross-cutting issues. We began reporting this to the Foundation— that the program people are drowning in the detail of their own programs and that we would need additional resources to get at the whole macro level. The Foundation wasn't willing to put more resources in it. The Foundation felt if they pushed people into cross-cutting issues, it would hinder the development of their own programs.

Fitzpatrick: So you had to drop that initiative to focus on individual programs. Perhaps we could focus on WNJ for a minute. The theoretical model for WNJ is essentially this: WNJ builds job search confidence, job search skills, and problem-solving strategies. Each of these immediate outcomes then contributes to both reemployment and better mental health, the ultimate outcomes. Can you tell us a bit about how you developed the program theory for the WNJ program? What controversies or questions emerged?

Donaldson: Fortunately, there was an extensive theoretical research and evaluation literature to draw upon. We also traveled to Michigan with those who were going to implement the program, and we were able to observe the program in action and interact with some of the participants. This helped us to develop a grounded understanding of what the participants would experience. We had discussions with program managers and trainers at each of the implementation sites in California and had extensive discussions with the Manpower Research Demonstration group, who were primarily responsible for making sure the program was implemented according to plan in the California organizations. Through observing the program in action and from all of these discussions, from talking with trainers (from the California sites) and the trainers of the trainers (from Michigan), it became pretty clear what the core model was.

A central issue that came up was whether they should adapt for California residents or try to remain true to the original model. There were some different views on that, to the point that the decision was made to do it only in English, which, in California, cuts out a significant portion of the population. For the most part, the Foundation supported the Michigan team's view that sites should strive to remain true to the model. A question for the evaluation became "If you deliver the program as it's supposed to be delivered, do you get the immediate outcomes?" The curriculum was adapted somewhat so that it was relevant to diverse California workers, but they stayed with the same conceptual model: If you can get those immediate outcomes—improved confidence, job search skills, better problem-solving strategies, the participants should have better employment and mental health outcomes. So the real issue was "Would this work with an ethnically, educationally, and occupationally diverse population?" These were the questions that emerged. The developers saw this as a relatively robust program that should work across the world. Journals had published much on the success of this model. But some of the people in California felt they needed to give it a California flavor.

The Michigan team seemed very interested in issues of local adaptation but was concerned that too much deviation from the model could lead to no effects. At the end, we saw there were clearly some things they could have done to make WNJ more effective in California. For example, language and cultural adaptations would have enabled them to serve much more of the population in need, and additional services to remove nonpsychological employment obstacles that many Californians faced would have helped improve reemployment outcomes. The issue of maintaining program fidelity versus making significant local adaptations was a balancing act and seemed to produce creative tension throughout the project. In the end, after hearing all of the arguments, the Foundation staff made the decisions on this issue because they controlled the resources.

Fitzpatrick: Did you test to see if the program theory's assumptions concerning unemployment and its causes were the case with the California population?

Donaldson: The Michigan group presumably had done a needs assessment in Detroit. They believed that psychological factors were limiting reemployment efforts. That was the basic assumption. There are people in California who fit that profile. They really do need to be motivated, and this program would work well for them. But, if the clients have needs beyond that, as we found that many of the program participants did, more service is needed. As we went around watching the program being implemented, we saw these other needs. We went into Fresno, and there's an exercise dealing with why employers don't hire you. One of the first answers from a participant is "My criminal record hinders my being hired." The next participant says, "It's all my tattoos and body piercing." The next one says, "I don't have a driver's license." Then, we went to the Silicon Valley site, and the answer is "They just want to hire young people. They want people right out of college." These were higher-level professionals dealing with age issues. The characteristics of the workers, occupations, and economy seem to make a big difference in why people were unemployed.

Fitzpatrick: I can see how these sites differ from each other, but how do they differ from the model?

Donaldson: Well, if you give them job search skills, the program works as intended in achieving its immediate goals. They get job search skills, but they don't have driver's licenses or child care. It's not going to work in achieving the ultimate goal—getting them employed—because these other needs aren't met. We had a lot of discussions with the Foundation and program staff about whether psychological factors are a major barrier to employment for the California worker we were serving, and it always came back to the empirical question— can we use this model with different populations? No matter what your issues are, this should have some effect. Again, in these real-world situations, program people don't have much control over who comes into the program.

They also struggled with whom they should try to reach. Do they go after the Latino population? Do we limit it to the "ideal" participant? The thing that the project team did agree on, based on the research base from other work, was that depression was an appropriate factor to use as a screen. If a person is showing signs of depression, they can ruin the group dynamics that occur during the program and are necessary to gain job search confidence and problem-solving skills.

Fitzpatrick: It sounds like these discussions were mainly among Foundation people. Were the people running the programs very involved in these discussions?

Donaldson: Not early on because the sites were just being selected then. The discussion continued when we brought the program people on board later. But the program theory was already well in place at that point.

For the most part, we did see the immediate changes they were expecting. Most participants seemed to gain confidence, job search skills, problem-solving strategies, and 65% of the participants reported being employed 180 days after the program. Of course, another external factor relevant to reemployment is whether there are available jobs in their community that match their skills.

The model for WNJ represented a mid-level of complexity among the four Initiative programs. The model for another program (HIPP) was a little more detailed, and for the Future of Work and Health, where we had difficulty getting the model articulated, the final model consisted of only one step.

Fitzpatrick: How complex should a model be to adequately convey the theory of a program?

Donaldson: In trying to critically understand a program, to develop program theory, you can think and think and think until you get this massively complex model because many things are very complex. That tends to be a real hindrance in an evaluation. I strive for a fairly parsimonious model. If a group of stakeholders wants to do some logic modeling of key links, that's OK, but that's different than developing the program theory. Program theory clearly represents the presumed active ingredients of the program and how they lead to desired outcomes. You're trying to consider whether the paths leading into this outcome have any chance at all for accounting for a significant portion of the variance in the desired outcome. Often when you do that, you see there's not a chance that these actions could lead to a significant change in the variance of that outcome. I take each path and really think carefully about the timing, when it should occur, and whether there are key moderators of that path. But to put that all in the model is really counterproductive; however, as evaluators, we really think carefully about these paths. I try to address complexity in the evaluation war room. If we think there's a real key moderator, we really want to measure and test that.

Fitzpatrick: In your writing on program theory, you discuss four sources of information for program theory: prior theory and research, implicit theories of those close to the program, observations of the program, and exploratory research to test critical assumptions. To what extent did you rely on each of these in your development of theory for WNJ?

Donaldson: The extent to which you can do all of these in any one program theory is limited. In practice, the program dictates which method you're more able to use. With WNJ, we relied very heavily on looking at prior theory and research around this whole model. With most programs I come across in the effectiveness area, there's very little prior research, but with WNJ there was. We went to Michigan. We could see that this prior research really influenced their model. We didn't do exploratory research in this case, though we did observe the program being implemented and the trainers from Michigan training the trainers who would implement the program in California. I can't emphasize how important it is to pull away from the conceptual jargon and go see what's happening. I'm a strong believer in trying to observe the program in action and doing it in a way that you're not changing the way the program is delivered. You want to get a realistic view of what's happening.

Fitzpatrick: Let's move away from program theory to the development of the evaluation questions. You note in your report that the evaluation was participatory. Typically, evaluation questions were developed through discussions with staff and managers from the sites as well as program managers from the Foundation. Can you tell us a bit about how you worked with these stakeholders to develop the questions?

Donaldson: When we initially set up the contract for the evaluation, the Foundation was very interested in being involved in the process and having all the key grantees involved. So in developing the program theory and the evaluation questions, we identified all the people we thought would benefit from being included at this stage. And then, we used a number of ways to communicate, the most personal being face-to-face meetings, which we would have fairly regularly, not at Claremont but at the Foundation or at their site so we could also do observations. We had a lot, probably in the hundreds, of conference calls because people were geographically dispersed. So it would be common to have 8 to 10 people involved in a conference call across the state. We also used a lot of e-mail.

Every year the Foundation pulled all the grantees together to review the Initiative. So at least once a year, usually more often, we had face-to-face contact. We had to have everybody's buy-in before we moved forward. Grantees ranged from the management team at the Foundation to people at all the sites, and sometimes sites had subcontracts, so there were representatives at all levels.

Fitzpatrick: Did you involve clients in your planning?

Donaldson: The clients were represented through the actual trainers. Also, from time to time, we would observe and get to interact in a meeting format with selected clients. It wasn't feasible to engage the clients at the same level as the other stakeholders though.

Fitzpatrick: How did you decide on the final focus? For example, with WNJ, you focus on five core areas—implementation, service (population served), short-term outcomes, reemployment outcomes (longer-term outcomes), and sustainability and replication. These five core areas are pretty comprehensive. Were there areas you considered and rejected?

Donaldson: Once we had agreement on the conceptual theory, we moved to Step 2, formulating and prioritizing the evaluation questions. The evaluation team is really the facilitator and leader. We're not saying, "What do you want to do?" but "Here's what we could do. These are the things that are most feasible." Then, sometimes, others would say, "No, no, what about this?" The Foundation played a real hands-on role here; they were very involved. Others, because of the funding relationship, would want to follow the lead of the Foundation. As the Foundation people were involved, we decided on these core areas. WNJ was moving faster than the Computers in Our Future program. When we got to the point of developing the program theory for Computers in Our Future, the Foundation staff often wanted to look at WNJ as a model. The major group decisions—and this is not always ideal—were largely influenced by the Foundation representatives, but with a lot of input from everyone else. In a sense, they were paying for all of this, so being a key client, they would come down on certain sides of issues and influence the process.

What did we consider and reject? There were a number of things we could have done and didn't. One of the big tensions in the project was at the method level, and another tension involved measuring mental health outcomes. This is a health foundation; we're working on employment to improve health. We strongly encouraged looking at some outcome measures of health and had a fair amount of support from the group for this. But about half of the program team and many of the sites felt very uncomfortable asking mental health questions of participants. They felt it would send the wrong message. We had to compromise and just focus on the reemployment outcomes. Others argued the ultimate purpose is health. But both the sites and the Foundation said we had to really know what happens with reemployment. Looking at health outcomes is something that would have been nice to do, but we didn't.

The big issue was the evaluation team, and the Michigan people who had developed the model really felt we should pursue conducting a randomized trial or at least a quasi-experiment. But there was intense resistance to this approach from program people who would have to implement this type of design. The counter position was that this was a demonstration project, and we already had the experimental data from earlier studies.

Fitzpatrick: I noticed across both WNJ and Computers in Our Future you have similar types of evaluation questions—for example, some implementation (describing program delivery), service (describing recipients), and, then, assessing various outcomes. Is this a common pattern that emerges in theory-driven evaluation?

Donaldson: This is a common pattern. It's a simple framework. Each program has an action theory. It will achieve something, an immediate outcome. And the program has to be delivered well to achieve that outcome. So, each of these, the critical program actions and the immediate outcomes, needs to be examined. Then, we can move to the conceptual level. If we achieve the immediate outcomes (e.g., job search confidence and skills), do they, in fact, lead to the desired long-term outcomes (e.g., reemployment)? You usually have at least three levels being addressed—actions, immediate outcomes, and long-term outcomes.

Fitzpatrick: You note your evaluation was both formative and summative. Who were your primary audiences for this study? How did these audiences (and others) use the information?

Donaldson: We started with the formative piece. Remember, this was a six-year process. Many of these programs had a lot of implementation and design issues. For four to five years we were in this heavy formative evaluation phase but still building databases for the summative piece. We produced over 200 evaluation reports, and we tried to give rapid-cycle feedback to the relevant grantees. People at the Foundation, the program management team, and the sites were reading the reports and trying to make decisions with respect to how to implement the programs. For the formative phase, the audiences were the Foundation, the program management team, and the trainers—all up and down the organizations involved.

People were getting reports and sometimes reacting with concerns. Few like to be evaluated, but they were getting regular evaluation feedback from us from the start. Most of the grantees would agree that this feedback influenced how far they were able to get with the program. That is, regular evaluation feedback and discussion about program accomplishments and challenges dramatically enhanced the quality of program implementation.

For the summative report, the first set of users was the Foundation Board and staff. They have invested somewhere around $22 million on this Initiative. Now that we've been evaluating the programs for about six years, we need to lay it all out. They want to know whether this was worth their money. So they were the first stop—the President, the staff, the Board. Then, we arranged with them, once that process is completed, to disseminate the findings as broadly as possible so others can learn about the Initiative, and we distributed summative evaluation reports to the grantees. So, we involved everyone in the summative evaluation as well.

Because sustainability is a big issue, the sites can now use these numbers to try to get more funding and learn how to move forward. We have pretty massive databases. We get e-mails and calls asking us to look at certain things for them, so we're still answering questions for them.

Fitzpatrick: Often formative evaluations are most directed to program managers and staff because they're the closest to the program, the people most able to make changes. What would the Foundation do with the formative evaluation?

Donaldson: There was a large range of stakeholders and grantees. In addition to a formal report, we did have a relationship with the sites where we would give feedback in between the formal reports. We also allowed them to have input into our formative report, not to change major findings, but they could make factual corrections or append a challenge to our findings. The Foundation had a senior program officer who ran each of these programs. They would receive copies and be involved in discussions of the reports. They would sit back and listen to discussion by the sites, program management, and evaluation teams about issues contained in the reports.

Someone from outside might say, "Boy, this foundation was micromanaging," but the general feel was they wanted to be hands-on and be a part of it. The Foundation would say to everyone publicly that the evaluation was just one form of input. The evaluators don't always see the things that the Foundation staff see. There are other forms of input. All of the sites sent reports to the Foundation. If some issue came up, the players could build a case against it in their reports. The Foundation also told the sites, "You're funded now. The evaluation won't influence that funding." At first, no one believed it, but as we modeled it over time, people became quite comfortable. Oftentimes, the Foundation would side with the grantees.

There is one thing that I thought was critical to this whole relationship with these various audiences, and this was our use of 360-degree feedback. When you step back and look at some of the literature on stakeholder-evaluator relationships and the psychology of evaluation, when you get into this frequent interaction, you can quickly get into the view that the evaluators are always the ones criticizing. The program people can think the evaluators aren't doing anything, just critiquing others doing the "real" work. It became clear to us that we needed to let all the players evaluate us and the Foundation. So we set up a process where they could give us formative feedback on how the evaluation was going.

Fitzpatrick: The 360-degree feedback sounds like an interesting way to change the environment. How did that work? How did the grantees give feedback? Do you think they felt safe in what they could say?

Donaldson: Each year, the grantees were asked to provide feedback about the strengths and limitations of the management of the Initiative by the Foundation and the evaluation of the Initiative by CGU. We experimented with methods for doing this. For example, one year, the evaluation team received the feedback and reported about it; another year, the Foundation team received the feedback. In the end, we decided an ideal procedure would be to have someone outside of the Initiative run the 360-degree process and make it as confidential as possible. Of course, it seems impossible to create a situation where the grantees would feel completely comfortable writing a negative evaluation of the foundation that is funding them. As some of the Foundation staff would joke, "You have many 'friends' and there are few barking dogs when your job is to give away money." Nevertheless, many of the grantees reported liking the opportunity to evaluate instead of always being evaluated.

Fitzpatrick: What was the most useful feedback the evaluation team received?

Donaldson: The most useful feedback about the evaluation itself was the observation that, early on, the evaluation reports were primarily focused on program challenges. I think most evaluators assume that is where they add value and forget about the psychology of evaluation. Grantees are looking to see if you have seen and reported all their program accomplishments. Based on this feedback, our reports began by detailing program accomplishments before we noted the challenges. It was amazing the positive effect this had on the process. Grantees were much more open to addressing challenges if they believed we were aware, and made others aware, of their accomplishments. A little sugar helps the bitter pill go down.

The Foundation staff reported liking and learning from this process as well. Evaluation of the Foundation program officers by grantees during the first three years of the Initiative revealed several factors that contributed toward successful management of the overall Initiative. These included Foundation staff's sensitivity and responsiveness to the concerns and needs of grantees and demonstrated interest and involvement of program officers in grant programs. In addition, grantees viewed The California Wellness Foundation's program officers as very accessible, approachable, and hands-on. Program officers were also commended for being solution focused, rather than problem focused. Grantees suggested several areas for improvement which the Foundation attempted to address, including (1) clarifying roles and responsibilities of Foundation staff, program management teams, and sites; (2) providing more education on how Foundations operate; (3) communicating clearly about changes in Foundation policies or program expectations; and (4) hiring a professional facilitator for the convenings of grantees.

Fitzpatrick: You note you used a process of continuous program improvement. What were some changes that occurred as a result of that process?

Donaldson: As noted above, approximately 200 evaluation reports were written and discussed with the grantees throughout the project. I believe there were numerous changes that occurred as a result of these reports and discussions. For example, eligibility criteria, recruiting strategies, and target numbers were modified in WNJ; report content, report format, and dissemination strategies were changed in HIPP; and the content of the core curriculum in Computers in Our Future was developed and changed in response to this continuous improvement process using formative evaluation. However, when you are involved in this dynamic process with over 40 organizations, it is risky to claim you can establish cause and effect here. That is, the Foundation and grantees often internalize and use the evaluation feedback (which is a good thing) and see this as part of the program management and development process, as opposed to attributing these changes solely to the evaluation. That is, it was common for the evaluation team members to feel like others were taking credit for their findings, ideas, and insights.

Fitzpatrick: Do you always have a focus on continuous program improvement?

Donaldson: No, because sometimes the evaluation budget won't cover the expense. I do evaluations where that is just not in the budget. But when you have complex human service programs, I feel that's where the big payoffs are. It's very rare that I find a program that is so sound that we just do the summative piece. I'm sure such programs exist, but they're few and far between.

What I focus on in continuous improvement is the speed of the feedback. We look for early warning signs that occur between formal reports. If you look at the literature and writings on utilization, many people argue there is more use for enlightenment than direct utilization. But when you get into this continuous improvement model, that couldn't be further from the truth. I guess you could get into a position where people aren't using what you're given, but on this project we had a big influence. I would love to do a project where half receive continuous improvement feedback and the other half do not and examine the differences. But, in this project, when we weren't evaluating something, we could see a year where no progress was going on. If no one's looking, nothing may be going on.

Fitzpatrick: In quite a few cases things didn't work out as planned. For example, with WNJ, the target number to be served is ultimately reduced to half the original goal due to recruitment problems, and the eligibility criteria are broadened. Also, you suggest skill development was a greater need for participants than building self-confidence and job search skills, which had been the focus of the WNJ model. How did the different stakeholders react to these findings?

Donaldson: I'll make a general statement first. When you get into these feedback cycles and continuous improvement, as you deliver what we might think of as negative feedback on areas that need improvement, the stakeholders are in a position where they can go one of two routes. One route is "What we've been doing so far hasn't worked. How do we improve on that? What different strategies can we use?" The other main route is "Maybe that's not a realistic goal." Instead of changing activities, they change their goals. Oftentimes, they feel that if they have the opportunities and support to change goals, they would much rather do that. With WNJ, the original vision was 10,000 participants. As we began going through the process and selecting sites and looking at sites' capacity and population, there was discussion by the sites, the program management team, and the Foundation that led to the feeling that they couldn't achieve 10,000 participants. So the Foundation cut it down further to be about 6,500. Then, as we were in the continuous improvement cycle, some sites were really struggling and were off track in reaching those goals. So rather than fail and have a big gap in the end, there was a decision made by the Foundation, which we weren't necessarily supportive of, to bring the target more in line with where we would end up. The revised goal was 5,000, so the sites have met their numbers.

Now, the Foundation, in retrospect, really questioned whether they should have changed the goal. There's nothing wrong with having 6,500, and so you're a little short. We don't expect perfection, but keeping the number at 6,500 might have motivated the sites to close that gap.

We handled it in this way. When you're writing a summative report, sometimes those responsible for delivering the program want you to leave out the history, but we didn't. We said, "Here's where we started. Here are the changes along the way." We reported the changes in numbers so we were not leaving things out. That may not present as rosy a picture as the Foundation and program people would have liked. Some questioned whether we really need all that in there. We said, "Your input is important, but at the end of the day when we have all the evidence, it's important for us to own the report," and the President of the Foundation was strongly behind that. We were able to retain our objective, independent view of things, and we believe that benefits everyone. These Board members are very smart and pretty tough. If they think we are just doing public relations (PR) for the program officers, it won't be credible.

Fitzpatrick: I'm also interested in your conclusion that more of the focus for job training needed to be on skill building. More than half of the population you served had education beyond high school. Did this group still need skill building, or were you referring to other potential audiences? How did you reach the conclusion that they needed skill building?

Donaldson: When you go out and look at how the program is being implemented, there are three very distinct communities. It is almost hard to see it's the same program because of the populations involved. I referred to how different the participants were in Silicon Valley from those in Fresno. The way the exercises went was very different. If we were looking in Silicon Valley, for example, where many participants had been let go from a tech company, part of what we would hear was they hired young people right out of college with up-to-date technology skills, so someone who had been working for a while and was not on the cutting edge would be replaced by a younger person with more current skills and also at a cheaper salary. They would put these people through a motivational workshop (WNJ), and they would get through and be really geared up to go, but they still wouldn't have the high-tech skills that companies want. So the motivation wasn't enough. And that same process was going on in Fresno, though it looked a lot different. If someone doesn't have a driver's license and didn't have the skills for the job they want to go for, the motivation and what was in the curriculum was not enough. This concern was something that we raised from the start with the program. Is there a way to do more tailoring and needs analysis? But it's really difficult once a Foundation decides what they're going to do, for us to say, "Let's go back and consider if this is the right program." Michael Scriven was on the Board of Advisors for the evaluation, and when he first came on, he did a needs assessment for Computers in Our Future, but it had no impact on the project. It was just too late for this type of input to influence program design. The train had left the station.

A big goal for the Foundation was that, once they pulled their money out, these programs would still be part of the agency. This didn't happen, with the exception of one organization. That organization in Fresno has participants first deal with basic things (having transportation, child care, skills), then they put them through WNJ to gain the confidence and job search skills. That makes a lot of sense to me.

Fitzpatrick: But how did you arrive at the decision that skills were what was needed? Did that emerge from data you collected?

Donaldson: Job-relevant skills were one of the additional needs that some of the participants identified, and we noted this in our observations of the program in action. This finding was confirmed by data collected during interviews of the WNJ trainers and program managers and was consistent with other research on employment issues in California.

Fitzpatrick: Your data collection makes use of both quantitative and qualitative methods, though with the large numbers of people in the two service delivery programs, your emphasis there is primarily quantitative. With WNJ, you measure implementation through structured observation forms and participant reaction forms. You collect data on participants' demographics and employment history and pre-post paper-and-pencil measures of some of the immediate program goals—for example, self-efficacy, self-mastery. Then you conduct telephone interviews for four periods following the workshop to learn about employment outcomes. How did program theory contribute to your selection of measures? How do you decide what measures to use?

Donaldson: As I look across all the evaluations I have worked on using this approach, the best payoff for spending all that time up-front really trying to understand the process you're trying to evaluate and articulating the program theory is that it helps you to design a much better evaluation. It's so easy to miss things if you don't understand the program in a grounded way. It's easy to miss things about how the program is supposed to lead to certain outcomes. That up-front work helps you identify the key concepts that you should measure and the timing of those measures.

If you don't collect data at the right time, you're going to miss it. There's a large literature suggesting that most evaluations are very insensitive. I'm referring to meta-analyses and some of Mark Lipsey's work. By using program theory to help you consider the timing of your measures, you are in a position to collect information on the right things at the right time. This is where the interplay of going back and looking at other research on the topic is very useful. You may find another program looked at changes in participants at three months and found nothing but at six months found a whopping effect, so that really helps you in timing your measures. The program theory of WNJ helped us decide when to measure reemployment as well as the intermediate outcomes.

The other issue is that when you really get down to it, what this Initiative was about was improving something way down the road, health. A lot of people who don't go through the exercise of developing program theory say, "This program is about health and that's 20 years down the road, so it's not worth evaluating." But program theory shows you the intermediate steps to measure.

Fitzpatrick: Which measures that you used on WNJ did you find to be the most meaningful or informative?

Donaldson: What I have found very informative, although not completely conclusive, was comparing our numbers to those found with the efficacy trials in Michigan and other places around the world. They had roughly the same programs and had pure control groups and experimental groups. We modeled our measures after those used in the efficacy trials. When we compared our group to their experimental group and control group, considering how much more disadvantaged our population was, our numbers still looked pretty good. I thought that was very informative. In the other trials, they were dealing with someone who had been recently unemployed, auto plant workers in Michigan. Those people were devastated, and the program was trying to keep them from going downhill. The control group received written materials on job information—real standard information. It does not seem surprising to me that this program is better than a booklet. But in our evaluation, the reemployment numbers looked pretty good, especially considering participants, on average, had been unemployed for 12 months. However, it is important to note reemployment programs are constrained by the available jobs in the local community. For the most part, this program was implemented during good economic times.

The implementation data—both qualitative and quantitative—were very useful. There are so many things that don't happen the way they are planned in the program design. Data bring that to the surface, and you can deal with it.

On reemployment outcomes—all the sites really see the game as reemployment—we tried to compare our numbers to critical competitors in the communities, other programs for the unemployed, and that worked against us. Few other programs kept data, and those that did collected it for PR or promotional uses. We had pretty rigorous data, so we're always going to look worse than PR data. So the reemployment data finally gave a benchmark to how it was working. On the other hand, when people were trying to get it adopted in their organizations, others would say, "This looks much worse than our other programs." The key to the goals of replication and institutionalization is you have to be able to demonstrate they are better than existing services. We weren't able to do that because we weren't able to study existing services. We strongly encouraged the Foundation to consider requiring that the control group be the best existing program on future evaluations.

Fitzpatrick: Which types of data collection were most persuasive to your different stakeholders?

Donaldson: The trainers and program managers really liked qualitative data. They liked anecdotes and stories of success, in particular, for obvious reasons. People with a stake in the success of the program often assume that if you do qualitative measurement, you will get a more accurate and positive picture. That's interesting to think about. Is there some artifact to the qualitative approach? Or is it that the quantitative is insensitive to changes?

Fitzpatrick: Were your qualitative results more positive than the quantitative?

Donaldson: No, we're aware of these issues. So we made sure we weren't using weak qualitative measures. A lot of the qualitative measures were extremely informative. People with an obvious stake in outcomes like qualitative success stories. Outsiders, such as Board members and representative of the Foundation, want the numbers. That's really clear to me. For me personally, I get a lot out of the mixed-design approach. Numbers give me one piece of the picture, but I get a lot out of interviewing people. It's the interplay between the qualitative and quantitative that is really informative. In increasing our depth of understanding, it's the qualitative things that push us forward. But the quantitative is necessary and does give an important piece.

You can really get bogged down in methods issues. A huge advantage of the theory-driven approach is we avoid getting bogged down in any of these issues until we have a really developed program theory. There is a tendency to want to start thinking about methods before the program theory or conceptual framework is developed.

Fitzpatrick: Can you give an example from WNJ of some findings based on qualitative data that were really useful for you?

Donaldson: I discussed some of the qualitative findings about participant needs and the value of observing the program in operation earlier. We also gathered a wealth of qualitative data about program implementation by interviewing the trainers and program staff. This was very useful for understanding program implementation challenges, as well as how similar the WNJ program implementation was to the original JOBS model. At the end of WNJ (and all the Work and Health Initiative programs), we interviewed most of the key people involved in the project to understand their views on program success and challenges. These data were also quite informative for identifying key the lessons learned and for generating ideas for how to improve this kind of effort in the future.

Fitzpatrick: This was really a massive evaluation that continued for four to six years depending on the program. How did things change as time passed?

Donaldson: Obviously the initiative in each program went through phases. Initially, we were just trying to develop an evaluation framework that everyone would buy into. With some programs, for example with Computers in Our Future, there was a lot of discussion about just what a program would look like, so the kinds of things the evaluator does at that stage are very different from working with a program that is more well-defined and developed. For example, the discussion is much more focused on testing program theory, as opposed to program development, when a program is clearly defined.

For a long time, we really didn't have anything that might be considered recommendations for improvement because we weren't collecting data, but we were giving feedback. As soon as there was data, the whole dynamic changed dramatically. Now, they could, with some degree of confidence, reject evaluation findings. The key is how you model this process. If they react and you react or get defensive, you're not modeling what you want this to become. You're trying to model that everyone is trying to learn. Then, as they see their funding is not being affected, they become more comfortable with hearing and accepting evaluation findings and conclusions. It takes some cycles for people to believe you're doing what you say you will do.

Then, the other major transition is at the summative stage. With the continuous improvement model, at some point you have to notify everyone that you're no longer involved in just improving but need to move to summative evaluation. As you can imagine, it has taken a while to get them to buy into the continuous improvement, learning organization model, so that then when you move to a summative phase the anxiety and tension rises again. Now, we're saying we are going to judge the merit, worth, and significance of the work. They think, "You're doing what we thought you would do in the beginning!" Some of them get very nervous. It changes the nature of relationships.

Fitzpatrick: If you were to do the evaluation again, what would you do differently?

Donaldson: I like this question, not just for the purposes of this interview, but I love to step back and think about this. The dark side of this project is we sure used a lot of staff hours and killed a forest with our reports. So a number one concern is writing so many reports. If I were to do it again, I would argue the key is how effectively you communicate evaluation findings with grantees, not how many documents you produce. The Foundation really pressed us to produce many reports. I see a lot of RFP's with unnecessary reporting requirements. Too many written reports slow down the communication process. What I would do differently is really look at how to streamline how we communicate, discuss, and act on evaluation findings. In most situations, it seemed like conference calling (rather than written reports, face-to-face meetings, e-mail, or Web communications) was most effective in this project. People seemed to prefer to talk for an hour on the phone to the other methods we used.

The other issue that really played out in this project is that the stability of the workforce has dramatically changed. Throughout all of these projects, there was significant staff turnover. You spend all this time building a relationship, developing program theories, and getting everyone on board, and then a couple of years later it's entirely a new staff. This can undercut the entire process unless you find a way to plan for it and prevent disruptions. The new people don't know about the development of the theory. You have to start over. In your design you have to plan for turnover by putting extra time into educating and orienting new staff and getting their buy-in.

Finally, we feel really fortunate that we were able to get into the project when we did, but I guess you always want more. If we had been there one step earlier, when the committee designed the Initiative, we might have been able to make the Initiative more effective by conducting rigorous needs assessment. The needs were already determined by someone else when we were hired. The passions and commitment were so strong to those programs that, as I've said, the Foundation didn't want to reconsider these issues.

Fitzpatrick: How do you think a new needs assessment might have helped?

Donaldson: I can really only speculate at this point. I would like to believe that systematic needs assessment might have expanded the content of some of the programs and possibly led to the creation of different and more programs. If so, the Work and Health Initiative might have been able to produce even stronger and more long-lasting effects. Of course, evaluators always seem to want more involvement (and budget). In the end, I feel very fortunate that The California Wellness Foundation had the foresight to involve us early, invest in evaluation focused on continuous improvement, and create an environment where we could remain objective and present negative findings in a timely manner.

Fitzpatrick's Commentary

In this evaluation, Donaldson's focus on continuous improvement builds on the learning organization models that are prominent today. This evaluation, and those we have learned about in other interviews, have clearly shown the changes from the early stages of evaluation, when the definition was purely judging merit and worth and the focus was seen as primarily summative, to today, when most evaluations have a formative emphasis and Mark, Henry, and Julnes (2000) view questions of judging merit and worth as only one of the four purposes of evaluation. In fact, Donaldson's evaluation addresses each of these four purposes: (1) judging merit and worth (the board's summative assessment of the Initiative), (2) program and organizational improvement (the continuous improvement component), (3) oversight and compliance (formative evaluation information provided to Foundation staff), and (4) knowledge development (testing of the Michigan model for external validity). As such, Donaldson's evaluation becomes comprehensive both in the scope of questions addressed and in the purposes it served.

Through this interview, we learn more about Donaldson's approach to theory-driven evaluation, an approach he has written about widely in other settings. We see how he uses program theory to gain a greater understanding of the program and the link between program actions and outcomes. Developing program theory with those connected to the program and the evaluation helps him begin a vital process of communication with the stakeholders and gain a greater understanding of the assumptions behind the program. Of equal importance, the theory helps him in determining what to measure in the course of the evaluation. That is, rather than developing evaluation questions targeted to information needs of a specific group or groups or to the stage of the program, Donaldson conducts a comprehensive evaluation of the program theory. He explains that most theory-driven evaluations take this comprehensive approach, examining key elements of process and outcomes. Thus, in this example, theory-driven evaluation helps Donaldson understand the program, communicate with stakeholders, and select appropriate types and times for data collection. It differs from many theory-driven evaluations in that it does not use multivariate techniques to assess the extent to which the identified mediators in the theory affect the outcome but instead uses the theory as a tool for planning and communication.

Donaldson describes the program theories he develops as parsimonious, and indeed, they are. In my work, I've come across some program theories that have so many boxes and links that the theory is lost. I agree with Donaldson that models that are *too* intricate can fail to communicate the theory for *why* the program activities are supposed to achieve their outcomes. For program models to be useful for planning and evaluation, they must be more than flowcharts of the progress of clients through a program. They must convey the assumptions upon which the program is based. I prefer models that are more detailed than Donaldson's written models, linking program activities to immediate outcomes to convey those assumptions, but Donaldson is using the models to stimulate discussion, questioning, and understanding with his stakeholder groups. As such, these written models may serve well as heuristic devices among the stakeholder to identify key elements of process and outcome.

Like Bickman (see Chapter 4), who was an early advocate for using program theory as a tool to improve evaluation, Donaldson observes that developing program theory, helping program staff and administrators articulate their assumptions concerning the program and how it works, can reveal problems in conceptualization. We see such problems emerge in the WNJ model with the focus on self-esteem and self-confidence; it is successful with the unemployed in Michigan but is insufficient for the California populations because these populations confront different barriers to employment. While the groups in Fresno and Silicon Valley differed in their educational and employment histories, they both needed other work skills besides the self-esteem that was the focus of WNJ to help them find jobs. (*Note:* The effect of theory-driven evaluators in helping program people recognize problems in the conceptualization of programs is reminiscent of an earlier evaluation approach, evaluability assessment. Joseph Wholey developed this approach to determine if programs were ready for evaluation, but practitioners found that the evaluability assessment approach itself was useful for program personnel in identifying problematic links between program actions and outcomes. (See Smith, 1989.)

Donaldson's interview also illustrates the struggle evaluators sometimes face between testing an existing model well, primarily for purposes of external validity, versus making adaptations for differing characteristics of a new population (Latinos and high-tech employees laid off in California). While Computers in our Future required the development of a new theory because it was a new idea, WNJ had an existing, tested theory. Donaldson and his evaluation team raised questions about how the theory would work in California and would have preferred more needs assessment of California populations to examine whether the Michigan model's assumptions were appropriate for the new audiences. We can envision here the pressures from different stakeholder groups. The people who developed the model in Michigan were very interested in the model being implemented in the same way. The Foundation ultimately decided that was the way to go as well. Program people were not involved as early in the process, but one would expect that stakeholders closer to the clients, and the clients themselves, would have argued for adaptations. Donaldson notes that some California people pushed for "a California flavor." In the end, the evaluation helps document that some adaptations are necessary for the program to succeed in this new setting, one very different from Detroit. As such, the results add to knowledge about the model itself but knowledge the Detroit researchers may not have welcomed. That is, the model doesn't generalize to settings as different as this one, and as Donaldson notes in his comments concerning what he would do differently, local needs assessments can be critical in determining whether a program theory will work in a new setting.

This evaluation was extensive—six years and more than 200 reports. Like Debra Rog's evaluation of homeless families, Donaldson's evaluation is both formative and summative. Donaldson's comments illustrate the different strategies he takes in these approaches. Communication with program staff at the sites is extensive during the formative phase. In fact, Donaldson makes some excellent suggestions for creating a good environment for communication: Acknowledge accomplishments as well as challenges (don't feel your job is just finding things to change); let them critique you and your evaluation; when they do criticize you, *model* the learning behavior you hope they will show when you give feedback on their program. In the end, Donaldson observes that they may have overdone written reports, to meet Foundation requirements, and urges evaluators and funders to make more extensive use of oral communication through conference calls and face-to-face meetings. This type of communication encourages the give and take that is necessary to stimulate use. (I'm reminded of Michael Patton's introducing himself and his approach to users by saying he will do an evaluation, but not a written report. His emphasis prompts the user to recognize that what they are paying for is the advice, not the report.) Yet, when Donaldson moves to the summative phase, his focus is on the Foundation and its board, who want to judge the ultimate worth of the Initiative. Other sources receive the reports, but at much later stages.

While Donaldson sees the evaluation as participative, as he frequently notes, the Foundation is the major player, and he believes that other stakeholders frequently deferred to them. The Foundation staff note, "There are few barking dogs when your job is to give away money." The Foundation wanted to be a key player and was. Its role may have been very collaborative, working closely in a partnership fashion with grantees so that all could learn and the gains of the programs would be maximized, as with many foundations today. Nevertheless, it is difficult for an evaluation to achieve a truly participative environment when the stakeholders have such uneven status, as House and Howe (1999) have noted in their model of deliberative democracy. But, clearly, many different stakeholders are involved in the evaluation and benefit from its results.

Donaldson begins this interview with his desire to show that theory-driven evaluation is not "an ivory tower approach almost like laboratory research" but how it can work in the real world. We see his use of theory working to improve programs and his observations in the field, giving him a real sense for what is happening and how programs have to adapt and change. We see his extensive communications with stakeholders and his suggestions for how to improve their receptivity to evaluation results. I think he succeeds in his goal of showing how his approach works in the real world. Where Donaldson and I differ is in whether most evaluations are efficacy evaluations. I think our different perceptions of the evaluation literature may come from reading different literature. At least in my reading, most evaluations are not efficacy evaluations but are evaluations of programs developed by administrators, policy experts, or elected officials who hire the evaluator to address their concerns. These evaluations do occur in the rough and tumble world of real clients, real providers, and the unpredictable changes that occur in program delivery and, subsequently, in evaluations. Each of the interviews in this book describes evaluations in such settings. Their approaches to adapting to this real world differ, but all are struggling with making choices to conduct informative evaluations in real-world settings. Donaldson succeeds in illustrating how his approach to theory-driven evaluation makes that transition and how he uses research and theory development to enhance the evaluation.

DISCUSSION QUESTIONS

1. How do Donaldson's efforts lead to organizational development and learning? Do you think his efforts build evaluation capacity among staff in the organizations he works with or in the Foundation? Which of his efforts do you find most effective?

2. What do you see as the strengths of the WNJ program theory? The weaknesses? How does it help the evaluation?

3. Donaldson indicates that he, as many evaluators, saw informing stakeholders of their "challenges," or problem areas, as the value added that the evaluator brings. Without an outside voice, an evaluator examining the program, he believes little progress is made. But he finds that they want their accomplishments acknowledged as well and adapts his report to do so first. What is the value added of evaluators? What do they bring to the program? Should we acknowledge accomplishments? Why or why not?

4. Donaldson indicates that he thinks oral means of communicating evaluation findings, whether in person or through telephone calls, are a better way to communicate results than by a written report. Do you agree or disagree? What is the advantage of the oral report? What is the advantage of the written report?

5. Who "owns" an evaluation report? Donaldson relates an interesting incident in which their evaluation report documented changes in goals concerning the number of clients who would be served. Goals had been lowered to make it more feasible for organizations to achieve the goals, and Donaldson reported that. Others objected to the report containing that information, but Donaldson responded, "Your input is important, but at the end of the day when we have all the evidence, it's important for us to own the report." Do you agree? Why or why not?

6. The 360-degree feedback process that Donaldson uses in this evaluation originated in human resources and management to permit lower-level employees to give feedback on supervisors' and managers' performance. Donaldson's adaptation of it in evaluation is an interesting one. What do you see as the advantages and disadvantages of this process?

FURTHER READING

A summary of the evaluation can be found at www.cgu.edu/include/SBOS/CalWellnessSummary.pdf: Summary of the Evaluation of The California Wellness Foundation's Work and Health Initiative.

REFERENCES

Cook, T. D. (1985). Post-positivist critical multiplism. In R. L. Shotland & M. M. Mark (Eds.), *Social science and social policy* (pp. 21–62). Beverly Hills, CA: Sage.

Donaldson, S. I. (1995). Worksite health promotion: A theory-driven, empirically based perspective. In L. R. Murphy, J. J. Hurrel, S. L. Sauter, & G. P. Keita (Eds.), *Job stress interventions* (pp. 73–90). Washington, DC: American Psychological Association.

Donaldson, S. I. (2001). Mediator and moderator analysis in program development. In S. Sussman (Ed.), *Handbook of program development for health behavior research* (pp. 470–496). Thousand Oaks, CA: Sage.

Donaldson, S. I. (2002). Theory-driven program evaluation in the new millennium. In S. I. Donaldson & M. Scriven (Eds.), *Evaluating social programs and problems: Visions for the new millennium.* Hillsdale, NJ: Lawrence Erlbaum.

Donaldson, S. I. (2007). *Program theory-driven evaluation science: Strategies and applications.* New York: Lawrence Erlbaum. (Greater detail on the evaluation can be found in this book.)

Donaldson, S. I., Berger, D. E., & Pezdek, K. (2006). *Applied psychology: New frontiers and rewarding careers.* Mahwah, NJ: Lawrence Erlbaum.

Donaldson, S. I., Christie, C. A., & Mark, M. M. (in press). *What counts as credible evidence in applied research and contemporary evaluation practice?* Thousand Oaks, CA: Sage.

Donaldson, S. I., & Gooler, L. E. (2003). Theory-driven evaluation in action: Lessons from a $20 million statewide work and health initiative. *Evaluation and Program Planning, 26,* 355–366.

Donaldson, S. I., Gooler, L. E., & Weiss, R. (1998). Promoting health and well-being through work: Science and practice. In X. B. Arriaga & S. Oskamp (Eds.), *Addressing community problems: Psychological research and intervention* (pp. 160–194). Thousand Oaks, CA: Sage.

Donaldson, S. I., & Scriven, M. (2003). *Evaluating social programs and problems: Visions for the new millennium.* Mahwah, NJ: Lawrence Erlbaum.

Donaldson, S. I., & Weiss, R. (1998). Health, well-being, and organizational effectiveness in the virtual workplace. In M. Igbaria & M. Tan (Eds.), *The virtual workplace* (pp. 24–44). Harrisburg, PA: Idea Group.

House, E. R., & Howe, K. R. (1999). *Values in evaluation and social research.* Thousand Oaks, CA: Sage.

Mark, M. M., Donaldson, S. I., & Campbell, B. (in press). *Social psychology and policy/program evaluation.* New York: Guilford Press.

Mark, M. M., Henry, G. T., & Julnes, G. (2000). *Evaluation: An integrated framework for understanding, guiding, and improving policies and programs.* San Francisco: Jossey-Bass.

Shadish, W. R. (1993). Critical multiplism: A research strategy and its attendant tactics. In L. Sechrest (Ed.), *Program evaluation: A pluralistic enterprise* (New Directions for Program Evaluation, No. 60, pp. 13–57). San Francisco: Jossey-Bass.

Smith, M. F. (1989). *Evaluability assessment: A practical approach.* Boston: Kluwer Academic.

Vinokur, A. D., Price, R. H., Caplan, R. D., van Ryn, M., & Curran, J. (1995). The JOBS I preventive intervention for unemployed individuals: Short- and long-term effects on reemployment and mental health. In L. R. Murphy, J. J. Hurrel, S. L. Sauter, & G. P. Keita (Eds.), *Job stress interventions* (pp. 125–138). Washington, DC: American Psychological Association.

Vinokur, A. D., van Ryn, M., Gramlich, E. M., & Price, R. H. (1991). Long-term follow-up and benefit-cost analysis of the JOBS Program: A preventive intervention for the unemployed. *Journal of Applied Psychology, 76,* 213–219.

TEN

DEVELOPING AN EVALUATION SYSTEM FOR THE CORPORATE EDUCATION DEVELOPMENT AND TRAINING (CEDT) DEPARTMENT AT SANDIA NATIONAL LABORATORIES

An Interview With Hallie Preskill

*I*ntroduction: Hallie Preskill is a professor in the School of Behavioral and Organizational Sciences at Claremont Graduate University, where she teaches courses in program evaluation, organizational learning, appreciative inquiry (AI), consulting, and training design and delivery. She conducted this evaluation while she was on the faculty of the University of New Mexico, Albuquerque. Some of the books she has coauthored are *Reframing Evaluation Through Appreciative Inquiry* (2006, with T. T. Catsambas), *Building Evaluation Capacity: 72 Activities for Teaching and Training* (2005, with D. Russ-Eft), *Evaluation in Organizations: A Systematic Approach to Enhancing Learning, Performance and Change* (2001, with D. Russ-Eft), *Evaluative Inquiry for Learning in Organizations* (1999, with R. T. Torres), and *Evaluation Strategies for Communication and Reporting* (2nd ed., 2005, with R. T. Torres and M. E. Piontek). She received the American Evaluation Association's Alva and

Gunnar Myrdal Award for Outstanding Professional Practice in 2002 and the University of Illinois Distinguished Alumni Award in 2004. For over 20 years, she has provided consulting services and training workshops for schools, health care, nonprofit organizations, the government, and corporate organizations. In 2007, Dr. Preskill served as the president of the American Evaluation Association.

In this interview, Preskill introduces the reader to the principles and practices of AI and describes how she used it to help a department of training and development to build an evaluation system for their activities. In particular, she discusses why she saw AI as appropriate for this task, in this organization, and the steps she took to help them identify and consider valuable components for an evaluation system. AI focuses on recognizing what has succeeded, rather than on problem areas, and, from those successes, identifying how other successes can be achieved. She makes use of a one-day meeting with most employees in the unit to have them identify and discuss occasions when evaluation was working well in their organization and the circumstances surrounding those occasions. They then make use of that discussion to envision what a successful evaluation system might look like in the future and to make recommendations for achieving such a system.

Summary of the Development of an Evaluation System for the Corporate Education Development and Training (CEDT) Department at Sandia National Laboratories

Hallie Preskill

Claremont Graduate University

The mission of the Corporate Education Development and Training (CEDT) department at Sandia National Laboratories (SNL) is to create and implement a wide range of results-oriented development and training solutions that contribute to Sandia's mission. As such, CEDT offers an extensive array of learning opportunities delivered through instructor-led classroom training, Web-based and computer courses, self-study, coaching, mentoring, and consulting on a wide variety of topics.

During the past few years, there have been many cultural and organizational changes at SNL. As with many organizations today, departments within SNL are increasingly being asked to provide metrics, indicators, and evidence of high performance. CEDT employees understand this requirement and want to ensure that they are providing useful information that demonstrates the positive effects they are having while also improving their programs and services.

At the time that we were called to work with the organization, CEDT's programs and services were evaluated primarily through pre- and post-class assessments and post-course reaction surveys. With the large number of courses offered, CEDT employees found it difficult to identify exactly how data were being collected throughout the organization and how to systematically interpret and share the findings of these evaluations. In other words, there was no "system" for planning, organizing, implementing, or using the evaluation data that were being collected. Choices for when and how to collect evaluation data were fairly idiosyncratic, and up to this time, there were few templates or mechanisms for designing and sharing data collection instruments, findings, or reports. For these reasons, the instructional designer, the

senior training consultant, and the manager of technical and compliance training of the CEDT organization at SNL contracted with me and one of my associates (Barbra Zuckerman Portzline) to help achieve the following goals:

- Identify how CEDT is currently evaluating both CEDT and non-CEDT
  courses
- Deliver a report that includes information on
  - what is working and not working in the current system and recom-
    mendations regarding ways to collect and report evaluation data:
  - how the various evaluation components may be integrated into a
    more comprehensive system;
  - possible software tools and techniques that may be used to collect
    evaluation data.

To accomplish these goals, we

1. reviewed and analyzed existing surveys, interview guides, and other
evaluation-related documents;

2. developed a matrix that described how each of CEDT's programs and
services were being evaluated; and

3. held a six-hour Needs Analysis Meeting with CEDT employees, which
was designed to provide insights into what an effective evaluation system
would do. The purpose of this meeting was to understand

what evaluation activities currently exist,

what evaluation activities are working,

what type of evaluation data are being collected and not used,

who uses evaluation information and for what purposes,

how evaluation findings are communicated,

what methods appear to work well, and

what methods do not appear to be working.

The data collected from these three methods (material review, development of a matrix, and the Needs Analysis Meeting) provided the basis for a
written final report. In the style of a traditional needs analysis, the report first
described *what was* happening with regard to CEDT's current evaluation

methods. It then explained *what should be* in an organization's evaluation system. The last section of the report included recommendations for bridging the gap between *what is* and *what should be* with respect to CEDT's evaluation methods, processes, and systems.

Dialogue With Hallie Preskill

Christina A. Christie

———•◦•———

Christie: In my experience, when I've had people ask me, "So what is an appreciative inquiry?" it's always been a bit of a challenge for me to offer them a reasonable answer. I've only read about appreciative inquiry (AI) as an organizational change method, so there were many things that struck me about the AI evaluation report you've provided for my review in preparation for this interview. I've never read about what it's like to actually conduct an AI, particularly as part of an evaluation. Could you describe for me what your experience has been with AI?

Preskill: I came across AI in the organizational learning and development literature about eight or nine years ago and became excited about the possibilities it offered evaluators, particularly those who use participatory, collaborative, democratic, and learning approaches to evaluation. And the more I learned, the more I became convinced that the approach could not only enhance the use of evaluation findings but that it could contribute to process use and building evaluation capacity. So I started reading everything I could on the topic; took a five-day workshop from David Cooperrider and Diana Whitney, the founders of AI; began conducting workshops on the applications of AI to evaluation; and eventually began writing about its uses in evaluation.

Christie: Before we get into the details of the CEDT evaluation project and how you used AI, can you give me a brief explanation of what AI is?

Preskill: Sure. AI has been used as an approach to organizational change and development since the mid-1980s. In a nutshell, AI is a process that builds on past successes (and peak experiences) in an effort to design and implement future actions. The philosophy underlying AI is that deficit-based approaches to organizational change are not necessarily the most effective and efficient. In other words, when we look for problems, we find more problems, and when we use deficit-based language, we often end up feeling hopeless, powerless, and generally more exhausted. To the contrary, proponents of AI have found that by reflecting on what has worked well, by remembering the times we were excited and energized about the topic of study, and when we use affirmative and strengths-based language, participants' creativity, passion, and excitement about the future is increased (see Cooperrider, Sorensen, Whitney, & Yager, 2000; Whitney & Trosten-Bloom, 2003).

Christie: Okay, let's talk a bit about how you applied AI to the development of the CEDT evaluation system.

Preskill: CEDT is the internal training function of Sandia National Laboratories, which is one of the United States National Laboratories for Defense. They do a lot of research and testing on antiterrorism technologies, and most of their work is classified. They are located on the Kirtland Air Force Base in Albuquerque, New Mexico.

The CEDT department offers an extensive array of learning opportunities delivered through instructor-led classroom training, Web-based and computer courses, self-study, coaching, mentoring, and consulting on a wide variety of topics. While some evaluation of the department's services and offerings had been occurring, there was no system or coordination of these evaluations.

Christie: How did CEDT come to hire you to do an evaluation-focused AI?

Preskill: One of the instructional designers had been in my evaluation course a few years back. One day, I received an e-mail from him saying, "Our evaluation team met today, and it was decided we would like to meet with you to discuss the Sandia Corporate training and development evaluation process."

Christie: The CEDT "evaluation team" wanted to meet with you, suggesting that they had an evaluation team?

Preskill: They had recently put together a team of three. As with many organizations, they were increasingly being asked to prove their department's effectiveness. They knew that CEDT employees were collecting evaluation data, but few knew what others were doing, and there was little sharing of data collection instruments and/or evaluation findings. The organization had no system for gathering data, aggregating it, making sense of it, and then acting on it. They just didn't think their process was very effective. I think that's why they put together the "evaluation team" and then called us in.

Christie: How did you come to use AI with this group?

Preskill: For a while, I had been thinking about what an "evaluation system" would look like in an organization. I have always been surprised at how ad hoc many evaluations in organizations seem to be. Without a coordinated or strategic system for evaluation, it is difficult to compare evaluations from year to year and to share what is learned from evaluation practice. Without an evaluation system, you also struggle with identifying programs that are being under- or over-evaluated and with deciding how to effectively allocate evaluation resources. Perhaps most important, the lack of an evaluation system significantly limits the impact evaluation may have at a strategic level and, thus, its ability to provide information on critical organizational issues. As we talked with the evaluation team and learned what their needs were, it became clear that we would need to not only understand what kinds of data they were collecting and how, but that we would need to be very clear as to what would work in their particular context. Conceivably, that meant talking with a large number of employees. Given that our time and resources for this project were limited, my business partner and I decided that in order to design the "ideal system," AI would be an appropriate strategy for the six-hour Needs Analysis Meeting. We chose this approach because it would offer participants a way to raise issues and concerns about current evaluation practices while also helping them envision an evaluation system that could work based on previous positive evaluation experiences.

Christie: How did you get this CEDT group to agree that AI was the appropriate method to use in this case?

Preskill: The evaluation team knew of another AI project taking place elsewhere in the organization, for another purpose, so AI wasn't completely countercultural. They also purported to be a learning organization. Thus, they wanted to model open-mindedness and were willing to try new things. Given the presumed organizational acceptance of AI and the desire to be a learning organization, I think they felt it was worth a try. When we talked about using AI, they seemed very receptive. We gave them an introduction to AI and why it might be a good fit with this project.

Christie: Your former student, the instructional designer, had a position of authority such that he could actually say, "Yes, this is something we want to do."

Preskill: Yes, however he reported to one of the people on the evaluation team.

Christie: So you had buy-in from the top?

Preskill: Yes. The vice president of the department was consistently kept in the loop as to what was happening. She was the one who initially authorized the funding to bring us in. And she authorized the final proposal. On the day of the AI meeting, she and her colleagues—two VPs—were full participants.

Involvement of the leadership was critical at two levels. First, there had to be support for any changes the system would require in the organization's infrastructure. Second, if the new evaluation system was going to require new resources, the organization's leadership was going to have to develop a business case for securing these. Another advantage of having the leadership in the room is that it symbolically communicates that what we are doing is important, that we're going to see this through, that you're going to have what it needs and what it takes to make it happen, and that the results, whatever those are, are going to be used.

Christie: How did you determine the topics of primary interest for the inquiry?

Preskill: Our scope of work was referred to as a needs analysis—to determine the evaluation need, or system, and then to come up with a framework from which they could develop that system. My colleague and I developed a scope of work—what we saw as the requirements of the project. The scope of work was to review and analyze the materials of the existing evaluation system and to obtain input from the department's employees regarding what elements were critical in an evaluation system for their organization. Our proposal included planning for and facilitating the AI meeting, debriefing the meeting with our evaluation team and a few others, analyzing the data generated from the meeting, and developing what they called "a user-friendly report" that described current evaluation methods and the ideal evaluation system.

Christie: In short, CEDT presented you with an opportunity to use AI to conduct a needs analysis for a comprehensive evaluation system.

Preskill: Exactly. And we were very excited. It was an opportunity to do two things: one, to develop an evaluation system for an organization and, two, to use AI for this purpose. I knew it would be a learning experience for all of us but that it would also test what I believed about the potential for AI in evaluation. I had a lot of faith that it would work.

Christie: As a methodology?

Preskill: Right. AI has been used very successfully in organizational change contexts around the world, in a wide variety of settings. People have used it for large-scale organization change, for changing organizational and community culture, and for getting movement where there was stagnation in organizations and communities. At the time we started this project, we were not aware of anyone who had used AI for evaluation purposes. Since that time, however, we have found several evaluators who are using AI processes, which is very encouraging. We have tried to highlight some of these in a book that Tessie Catsambas and I wrote, *Reframing Evaluation through Appreciative Inquiry* (Preskill & Catsambas, 2006). We have included 16 cases from around the world in which AI principles and practices have been used in evaluation.

Christie: You mentioned that you wanted to involve as many people as possible in developing the evaluation system. An all-day meeting can be quite a commitment for people. What was recruitment like for the AI meeting?

Preskill: An e-mail invitation, co-signed by the department's director and the evaluation team, was sent to all of the department's 52 employees. The e-mail said that evaluation has been an issue and we've hired a local consultant to come in and help. By communicating beforehand why this was important and why employees should show up, that it was going to be a different kind of day, 43 (83%) of the employees attended the meeting. Part of me wants to say that participation was a reflection of the organization's commitment to evaluation. I think these people are generally committed to what they're doing. But I didn't get the sense that they were all as crazy about the evaluation as I wanted them to be. I think they were curious, maybe. I think it was communicated that it would be worth their time to participate. And I think they felt they needed to be responsive to proving their value and worth in the organization. In fact, one of the department's goals focused on demonstrating effectiveness.

Christie: Was the meeting framed as a professional development experience, or was it framed as an activity that the organization was engaging in?

Preskill: Good question. No, it wasn't billed as a professional development day. It was referred to as a workshop. However, we ended up calling it the "Big Day Meeting" because everyone was invited to participate.

Christie: It seems obvious that it's critical that active, engaged participation is needed for this type of process to be successful. To me, the setup is incredibly important because that will impact whether people want to participate and the level at which they choose to engage in the process. Aside from the e-mail invitation that you described, what was done or what factors contributed to the successful setup of the Big Day Meeting?

Preskill: It was a time in the organization when they liked the notion of being a learning organization. They had just reorganized, so I think they felt energized to a certain extent but also frustrated with some of the limitations of their technology (particularly with regard to evaluation). I think they respected their leaders. I also got the sense that they felt they were in this together. I believe they saw this as worthwhile in the larger picture of what they needed to do to contribute to the organization. There was a lot of internal pressure to show results. I think they were frustrated that they couldn't either gather the necessary data or aggregate it or report it in a way that was meaningful and useful.

The commitment to our meeting came from knowing they had to figure out a way to more effectively collect information and use that information to advance as an organization. Overall, people were saying, "We don't have the technology" or "We don't have access to our data" or "The forms we're using are poor, and I don't know how to make them better." Some might have been motivated by personal need, irritation with the current system, and knowing that they had to change, so the AI we were going to embark upon was as good as anything.

Christie: Did you describe the AI model to participants before the Big Day Meeting?

Preskill: Not in this case. I don't think you always have to teach participants what AI is. If you start by describing the underlying theories, it often serves as a barrier—some participants will want to debate its principles instead of experiencing it. Rather, I just say, "This process may be a little bit different than what you might have experienced in the past. If you want to know more about it, at the end of the day, I'll be happy discuss it with you, and I can refer you to some great resources."

For clients who have no knowledge of AI, I like to give them a taste of the AI process before I tell them about AI's underlying theories and principles. I think it is one of those processes that either requires a leap of faith and trust that it will work or it needs to be experienced. We are so used to being negative and finding faults that when we talk about focusing on what has worked, what has been successful, many people just assume it is one of those "Pollyanna and rose-colored glasses approaches" and that it won't address the pressing issues and problems. However, our experience has shown that problems do get addressed, but in a very different way. After engaging in AI, this becomes clear to most participants.

Christie: What do you do if you have resistant participants?

Preskill: I'll have my client go through an exercise where they experience the first phase of AI—they conduct appreciative interviews. For the CEDT evaluation team, we put together a couple of handouts, described the process, and then answered their questions. They got it right away; for some people, it intuitively makes sense. And it's in line with the culture they are trying to create—a collaborative culture, one that is focused on success versus problems. You're usually willing to believe that you can solve problems by describing and discussing success. But some do have a harder time with it.

Christie: I found it interesting that, in fact, it's only in the very beginning of the evaluation report that you claim this to be an AI project. It struck me that it doesn't matter what you call it. The focus is the process, beginning with stories about what has worked—the positive pieces. But in my experience, people do like to talk about what is "wrong." How do you keep AI participants focused on the positive?

Preskill: First, it's critically important to remember that the first phase of an AI is Inquire (or Discovery, depending on which labels you use), where participants conduct paired interviews using a specifically designed interview guide. There are three sets of core questions that are tailored to the inquiry. The first question is the Peak or Best Experiences question that asks interviewees to tell a story about a time when they felt excited, energized, hopeful, and successful relative to the topic of the inquiry (e.g., conducting an evaluation). They are asked to describe what was happening, who was there, their role, and the core factor that contributed to this successful experience. The next two questions are the Values questions. Here, interviewees are asked to describe what they value most about the topic of the inquiry as well as what value they bring or add to the topic of the inquiry. The third question is called The Three Wishes question. Reflecting on the story they just told, interviewees are asked, "If you had three wishes for having more exceptional experiences like the one you just described, what would you wish for?"

So while some people might think they are going to have the opportunity to explain what is wrong, whose fault it is, and what the problems are, the questions asked in these interviews steer them in a very different direction. I will admit, there are times when a person has difficulty talking about successful experiences. We are so conditioned to dissect a problem and to come up with quick solutions that it may take some time to shift our mental gears. However, when someone starts talking about what didn't work and can't seem to focus on the appreciative questions, the rule of thumb is to let the person say what he/she wants to say and then to try again. It then usually works. I think people see really quickly that they're not going to get where they want to go if they start talking about what didn't work. It's not going to be creative. It's not going to be innovative. It's not going to give them excitement, joy, or hope for something to be different. At the same time, there are people who have to tell you the negative things first. No matter how you try to redirect, they have to tell you. So you let them, and then you say, "Okay, now let's talk about something that did work."

Christie: Okay, let's get back to the CEDT Big Day Meeting. Can you explain exactly what you did and what happened?

Preskill: After some preliminary introductions by the vice president and the evaluation team, we began the meeting by asking each person to pair up with one other person and to interview each other for 10 minutes each. They were asked to consider the following:

> Think of a time when you knew that a CEDT evaluation process was working well. You were confident and excited that important and useful data were being collected, and you felt energized about the evaluation process. What was happening? Who did it involve? What made this evaluation process (or outcome) so successful? Why was it successful? What was your role? What value did you add to this evaluation process?

After 20 minutes, the pairs were asked to join two other pairs to form a group of six. In this group, they were to tell the highlights of their partner's story (2 minutes each) and then to look for themes across the group's stories. As the themes emerged, they wrote them on flipchart paper. (An easel with paper was placed at each table.) Each group was then asked to share their themes with the larger group.

After a brief discussion about the similarities and differences between the groups (there were many commonalities among the lists), the Imagine phase of the AI process was initiated. Participants were asked to work with their groups of six and to discuss the following question for 30 minutes, writing the themes of their group's visions on flipchart paper:

> Imagine that you have been asleep for five years, and when you awake, you look around and see that the CEDT Department has developed a comprehensive, effective, and efficient evaluation system. This system provides timely and useful information for decision making and action, relative to the programs and services the department provides in the areas of education, development, and training. The evaluation system has been so successful that the United States Secretary of Energy has announced that the CEDT Department will be receiving an award for outstanding evaluation practice. As a result, the *Albuquerque Journal* is writing a story about your evaluation system. You agree to be interviewed by one of the newspaper's reporters. In your interview, you describe what this evaluation system does, how it works, the kinds of information it collects, who uses the information, and how the information is used. Discuss what you would tell the reporter.

The groups spent about 20 minutes sharing their themes and discussing the ideas generated from this phase. As we broke for lunch, people were laughing and talking—there seemed to be a pretty high energy level at a time when people's energy is usually waning. I remember the department manager saying she thought this process was a great way to get everyone involved and engaged. I also heard participants saying, "This process is energizing," "It's refreshing to be looking at all the things we do well," and "Thank you for including me in this meeting, I feel like I'm contributing."

After lunch, we began the Innovate phase. This is often the most challenging part of the process. We had just spent half the day talking about what an evaluation system looks like when it works and what we want the system to look like. Now it was time to design it. Participants were asked to develop provocative propositions (design or possibility statements) that describe the organization's social architecture (e.g., structure, culture, policies, leadership, management practices, systems, strategies, staff, and resources) when it had an evaluation system that was supporting effective evaluation practice. These statements were written in the affirmative, present tense and described what the system would be like if it were highly effective and functioning at its best. In essence, these statements reflected the concrete components and characteristics of their desired evaluation system.

Christie: So you facilitated this process, and the groups generated the themes?

Preskill: The themes were derived by the participants' statements, and we collaboratively organized and labeled each of the categories. We then placed the pages of flipchart paper around the room and asked everyone to go to the page(s) that represented statements they were most interested in and passionate about.

Christie: So here are two provocative propositions I read in your report: "Evaluation findings are commonly used for decision-making purposes" and "All evaluation data are managed by our technical system that provides easily accessible reports."

Preskill: Right. They're stated in the affirmative present tense, and they reflect what participants want from their evaluation system.

Because we were contracted to actually design the evaluation system, we modified this fourth and last phase—Implement—and only asked participants to make recommendations regarding what they wanted to make sure was represented in the system. However, in most AIs, this is when participants sign up for what they want to work on. So if they had not hired us to develop the evaluation system, participants would have worked toward making these visions a reality. Specifically, participants were asked to do the following in their original pairs:

> Review the provocative propositions, and develop three to five recommendations for what would need to happen to make any of these provocative propositions come true. Join the other two pairs you have been working with and share your recommendations. Summarize your group's recommendations on a piece of flipchart paper.

Christie: In this case, the CEDT AI, you put the pieces together. Do you think that this group could have put the pieces together and come up with what you came up with?

Preskill: No, not a comprehensive evaluation system. I think they could have gone through the phases, and they would have figured out how to make evaluation better in their organization, but because there was limited evaluation capacity, I don't think they could have conceptualized the entire system.

Christie: As an evaluation professional, you were then hired to use the AI data to create an evaluation system—a system tailored to the specific needs of this organization. What distinguishes your work for CEDT from what other consultants do who use AI as a method for organizational change, and what specifically makes this AI an evaluation method?

Preskill: Yes, that's correct. Most people use AI as a method for organizational change. And I've done that too. My primary interest, though, is using AI for evaluation. When my coauthor and I came together to do the AI book, we had to figure out how and when AI is appropriate and useful for evaluation. We've come up with four applications and purposes: (1) to focus an evaluation (to develop an evaluation's key questions, list of stakeholders, logic model, design and data collection methods, as part of an evaluation plan), (2) to design or redesign surveys and interview guides, (3) to develop an evaluation system like we did for the CEDT department, and (4) to build evaluation capacity.

Christie: AI, then, is a tool or an additional methodology for evaluators rather than a theoretical perspective or model for how evaluations should be conducted from Point A to Point D. Basically, you are using the same steps and procedures one would if using AI for organizational change, but in an evaluation situation.

Preskill: Clearly, it's another tool. And, yes, the steps are the same, just used in an evaluation context. But I also believe that you could try to practice most of your evaluation with an appreciative philosophy in addition to using its process as a method. In other words, it can frame how we think about inquiry—how we engage people, the language we use, what we choose to focus on.

Christie: Are all organizations ready to use AI? Does the organization need to be willing, ready, and stable for an AI to be conducted? Reflecting on AI as an evaluation method, would you say the needs analysis phase is an ideal phase to use AI?

Preskill: Yes, but no more so than doing a typical evaluation. AI being an approach to inquiry, there is always going to be an organizational readiness factor. One of the great benefits of AI is its infinite flexibility. For example, an evaluator might use only the Inquire phase in an evaluation (the paired interviews) or may add only one appreciative question to a survey or interview guide.

When my colleague and I conducted an evaluation of a program funded by the Coalition for Sexual Assault Programs in New Mexico, we used AI only to focus the evaluation. We had a five-hour focusing meeting that included a group of eight women from all over the state—a very diverse group. We started the meeting by asking them to conduct paired appreciative interviews. They had no common experience with the program (each was involved with the program in different ways and at different levels), so we couldn't just start with "What would you like to know about the program's effectiveness?" Rather, we asked them to describe a time when they felt the program was making a difference in their communities, that they were proud and excited to be a part of this organization. It was really phenomenal to see how the process brought the group together very quickly. We collected a lot of data about what the program was doing and what it was like when it was working well. From there, the group developed 30 evaluation questions, which they then prioritized and agreed on where to focus the evaluation's limited resources. In that brief period of time, we were able to not only design the evaluation but using AI also helped contribute to the participants' greater understanding of the program and evaluation. I was particularly touched by the two Native American women who thanked us for allowing them to share their stories and to feel honored. One said, "We would not have spoken out in a large group."

Christie: Overall, I think you are arguing for using AI as a method for gathering important information that can be used to inform an evaluation and as a way for encouraging people to share their story, in whatever context that may be. I agree with you, I think most people want to be given the space to tell their story. Thank you for sharing some of your AI experiences with our readers.

Preskill: Thank you for asking me to do so.

Christie's Commentary

Dr. Preskill, with a few of her colleagues, has recently been writing about and using AI techniques in her work as an evaluation consultant. For many readers, this interview will serve as an introduction to AI as an evaluation method. With this in mind, I focused the interview with Dr. Preskill on AI as a process and the role it can play in evaluation, in addition to the specific outcomes of the CEDT AI. And in some places, the interview moves beyond the CEDT example, which serves as the foundation for the interview, to discuss AI more generally as a tool for evaluation.

Preskill takes the philosophy and principles put forth by organizational change AI theorists and applies them to the evaluation context. She suggests that AI principles translate well to an evaluation context, although it is not clear from this interview how AI differs as a process when used as a tool to facilitate organizational learning when compared with its use as an evaluation tool. Perhaps it does not differ significantly, though in our interview, Preskill maintains that AI can be used more flexibly within the evaluation context. That is, an evaluation can simply be guided by an AI philosophy or instruments can be designed from an AI perspective.

AI, Preskill maintains, is a method for evaluation that increases the use of the evaluation processes and findings, an area of evaluation that she has been thinking and writing about throughout her career (Preskill, 2004). Specifically, she has been concerned with how evaluation can be used to promote organizational learning, development, and change and highlighting the role of process use in these areas (Alkin & Christie, 2004). From our interview, it is clear that she sees AI as a natural extension of this work.

Skeptics may argue, as Preskill acknowledges, that AI can be viewed as being "Pollyanna" or seeing the world through "rose-colored glasses" and as such is not an appropriate tool for evaluation, a science concerned with generating, systemically, rigorous information about programs designed to improve the human condition. And Preskill is sensitive to this argument. Consequently, she asks that participants—and I assume she would ask the same of evaluators unfamiliar with AI—to refrain from judgment until after experiencing or using AI in an evaluation context. Indeed, she mentions that she often prefers not to tell stakeholders that what she is doing is called AI; that is, she avoids labeling the process until they are engaged in it. Nevertheless, it is important to acknowledge that Preskill suggests using AI in organizations that are open and have a desire to develop a vision for how a program should be. Her CEDT evaluation offers an example of what can be considered an ideal context in which to use AI, an organization that was already familiar with and engaged in AI, one that is motivated to be characterized as an open, learning organization.

Dr. Preskill suggests that AI can be used as a framework for approaching specific evaluation activities, such as data collection instrument development or focusing the evaluation—framing questions in the affirmative rather than from a deficit perspective. She maintains that AI yields the same information as "traditional" evaluation methods, yet participants feel much better about the process. In fact, Preskill suggests that data are often more contextual, rich, and meaningful, and so she believes that at times, the data are better. Although this sounds convincing, there are contexts and situations where one could argue that this may not hold true beyond the purposes for and contexts in which Preskill has used AI—mainly organizations desiring to enhance organizational functioning. For example, when assessing the impact of a program on psychological functioning, it may be that a measure that detects both strengths and deficits in functioning is necessary to understand true program impact.

To her credit, Preskill does not argue that AI is a method that is appropriate for all evaluation contexts or problems. Rather, she believes that there are contextual conditions that are more suitable for its use. If systematically studied as an evaluation process, we may have not only an empirical measure of the impact of AI on the use of evaluation processes and findings but also a better understanding of the contexts and conditions that make its use in evaluation appropriate. This evidence would certainly help counter critics who may argue, just as they do with other less traditional evaluation approaches (e.g., empowerment evaluation; Scriven, 2005), that AI is not a method for use in evaluation. This is so, as Preskill describes in our interview, because the evaluator serves as a facilitator of the AI process rather than a critical external bystander. On the other hand, I would think that there are many in the evaluation community who will enthusiastically embrace AI as an innovative addition to our evaluation toolkit.

Preskill's book (Preskill & Catsambas, 2006) and the *New Directions for Evaluation* (Preskill & Coghlan, 2003) issue on using AI in evaluation serve as the first major texts on AI in evaluation, laying out why, when, and how AI can be used as an evaluation tool and offering numerous case examples illustrating its use.

DISCUSSION QUESTIONS

1. Preskill is helping an organization develop an evaluation system here, rather than actually evaluating a program. She remarks that most evaluations are "haphazard," at least partly because of the absence of a system. Do you agree? In what circumstances or what types of an organization might an evaluation system be helpful? In what ways can an evaluation system be helpful? Are there any circumstances where an evaluation system might be a hindrance?

2. Who are the stakeholders in this development phase? Who are the stakeholders of the proposed evaluation system? How does Preskill involve each group?

3. Try to use the first step of AI, the Inquire phase, to consider the strengths of an evaluation (either an individual evaluation or a system) that you know. Identify an evaluation in your organization or one you know where the process for the evaluation worked well. You might consider the processes of identifying the evaluation questions and focus, collecting the data, disseminating the results, and/or using the information. Describe what worked well. Describe and discuss the circumstances that prompted it to work well. Who was involved in the evaluation? What was the role of the evaluator? The other stakeholders? What do you learn from this exercise about improving future evaluations?

4. One of Preskill's concerns is that evaluation tends to be problem, or deficit, focused. Do you agree? Do you view problem focus as a problem for evaluation? Should evaluation be focused on strengths and successes or problems? (Consider the purpose(s) of evaluation. When evaluation is about determining merit and worth, making a judgment, should we focus on strengths or problems? When evaluation is for formative purposes, should we focus on strengths or problem areas?)

5. What is the purpose of the evaluation system that Preskill is helping CEDT design? How might an evaluation system be used to evaluate training and development activities?

6. What do you think AI has to offer evaluation? What are the strengths and weaknesses of it as an evaluation tool?

FURTHER READING

A summary of the evaluation: Preskill, H., Dudeck, W., & Zuckerman-Portzline, B. (2005, February). Using appreciative inquiry to develop a training evaluation system in Sandia National Laboratories. In L. Webb, H. Preskill, & A. Coghlan (Eds.), Bridging two disciplines: Applying appreciative inquiry to evaluation practice [Special issue]. *AI Practitioner*. Available at www.aipractioner.com/newshop/0502popcont.pdf

REFERENCES

Alkin, M. C., & Christie, C. A. (2004). An evaluation theory tree. In M. C. Alkin (Ed.), *Evaluation roots* (pp. 12–65). Thousand Oaks, CA: Sage.

Cooperrider, D., Sorenson, P., Jr., Whitney, D., & Yager, T. (2000). *Appreciative inquiry: Rethinking human organization toward a positive theory of change.* Champaign, IL: Stripes.

Preskill, H. (2004). The transformational power of evaluation: Passion, purpose and practice. In M. Alkin (Ed.), *Evaluation roots* (pp. 343–355). Thousand Oaks, CA: Sage.

Preskill, H., & Catsambas, T. T. (2006). *Reframing evaluation through appreciative inquiry.* Thousand Oaks, CA: Sage.

Preskill, H., & Coghlan, A. T. (Eds.) (2003). *Evaluation and appreciative inquiry* (New Directions for Evaluation, No. 100). San Francisco: Jossey-Bass.

Preskill, H., & Russ-Eft, D. (2005). *Building evaluation capacity: 72 activities for teaching and training.* Thousand Oaks, CA: Sage.

Preskill, H., & Torres, R. T. (1999). *Evaluative inquiry for learning in organizations.* Thousand Oaks, CA: Sage.

Russ-Eft, D., & Preskill, H. (2001). *Evaluation in organizations: A systematic approach to enhancing learning, performance and change.* Boston: Perseus Books.

Scriven, M. (2005). Empowerment evaluation principles in practice. *American Journal of Evaluation, 26,* 415–417.

Torres, R. T., Preskill, H., & Piontek, M. E. (2005). *Evaluation strategies for communicating and reporting: Enhancing learning in organizations* (2nd ed.). Thousand Oaks, CA: Sage.

Whitney, A., & Trosten-Bloom, A. (2003). *The power of appreciative inquiry.* San Francisco: Berrett-Koehler.

ELEVEN

EVALUATION OF THE COLORADO HEALTHY COMMUNITIES INITIATIVE

An Interview With Ross Conner

Introduction: Ross Conner is now Professor Emeritus in the School of Social Ecology, Department of Planning, Policy, and Design, at the University of California at Irvine (UCI). Prior to his retirement, he was the founder and director of the Center for Community Health Research at UCI. He is currently President of the Board of Trustees of the International Organization for Cooperation in Evaluation (IOCE), involving national and regional evaluation organizations throughout the world. He continues to pursue his interests in community health and evaluation. His most recent work has focused on cancer control, working with Chinese and Korean communities in Southern California. In addition, he recently completed an assessment and strategic review of The California Endowment's Communities First grant program, which has supported more than 1,000 communities in selecting and acting on health improvements. He is the author or coauthor of nine books and numerous articles in various areas, including health, education, criminal justice, and leadership development. His writings also include papers on evaluation utilization in program improvement and policy formation, experimental and quasi-experimental designs in evaluation, international and cross-cultural evaluation issues, and evaluation training.

Conner's evaluation of the Colorado Healthy Communities Initiative (CHCI), which involved 28 different community-based health promotion planning and implementation projects, received the American Evaluation Association's 2002 Outstanding Evaluation Award. CHCI was intended to improve the health of communities in Colorado by helping communities find their own solutions using local, broad participation; consensus decision making; a broad definition of health; and capacity building. One of the challenges of the evaluation was determining how to evaluate an initiative that differed in each community. Healthy cities and communities programs around the world had struggled with this problem. Conner's evaluation focusing on telling the story of each community, describing the communities and the processes used and the immediate outcomes achieved, provided the first model for such evaluation efforts. Conner discusses how he defined his role in the evaluation and conducted the evaluation in a way that was congruent with the principles and goals of CHCI.

Summary of the Evaluation of the Colorado Healthy Communities Initiative

Ross F. Conner, Sora Park Tanjasiri, Marc Davidson,
Catherine Dempsey, and Gabriela Robles

Around the world, cities, towns, and regions are involved in "healthy communities" and "healthy cities" projects. Rather than relying on "expert" assessments of a community's health needs and "expert" models of health care and health promotion, these projects typically involve citizens defining the important dimensions of health for themselves, then working together to achieve their visions of a healthy community. The stakeholders involved in these efforts are central actors in establishing goals and objectives and in implementing action projects.

Using this model, The Colorado Trust established the Colorado Healthy Communities Initiative (CHCI) to empower citizens to make their communities healthier. Community members, representing all aspects and sectors, defined what a "healthy community" meant for their particular community, then worked together to make their vision a reality. Begun in 1992, the CHCI involved 29 different communities in Colorado in a three- to five-year process that, within each community, involved strategic planning followed by action project implementation.

The CHCI program was unique in several ways. First, it used a broad, community-based definition of "health." Second, it emphasized participation from and collaboration among many different individuals, sectors, and interests in a community, not only in the definition of health but also in actions to affect and change community health. Third, it fostered capacity building on an individual and group level to facilitate more effective involvement of citizens. Fourth, it involved a variety of "communities," ranging from small inner-city neighborhoods to large multicounty areas, and from ethnically similar to ethnically diverse populations. Fifth, it engaged many of the communities in a community indicator project designed to help them measure and track the health of their communities. Finally, it included a comprehensive cross-community evaluation of the processes and effects of CHCI activities to capture the diverse CHCI experiences, to document the effects of the program, and to foster learning within the CHCI programs and in other communities undertaking similar efforts. There is a listing of the four major project reports at the end of this chapter, along with instructions on how to obtain copies.

The CHCI Description

Program Background

The Colorado Healthy Communities Initiative (CHCI) began as a result of work conducted by The Colorado Trust on possible choices for Colorado's future. The study, which examined existing demographic, social, and economic trends and results from focus groups with citizens and leaders around the state, found that Coloradans were not participating in decisions that affect their communities and their future, although they had a desire for a sense of community and a measure of control over their destiny. They favored prevention efforts, involvement of individuals, and local action to solve local problems. The Colorado Trust created CHCI in response to these findings. The CHCI began as a $4.45-million, five-year initiative and eventually grew to an $8.8-million, eight-year effort based on several "healthy cities" models then in operation around the world.

The CHCI was based on four principals: participants should be representative of the diversity of their community, participants should follow a consensus decision-making approach, a healthy community is defined broadly based on what it means to participants, and participation should result in the development of skills in participants and capacity building for the community.

Program Model

The CHCI model, adapted from the National Civic League's approach to healthy-community work, involved two main phases. The first phase, which occurred over 15 to 18 months, involved strategic planning. The second phase involved action-focused implementation activities and lasted from two to three years. In addition, a community indicators project was introduced midway through the Initiative in the majority of communities. A total of 28 communities were brought into the CHCI in one of three cycles, with the cycles starting one year apart.

The planning phase had a set of seven steps that typically occurred during 12 to 15 meetings, each about three hours long and led by outside facilitators. During this phase, stakeholders undertook a series of activities and discussions to analyze and define "community health." These discussions led to the development of a community vision that guided the final steps of the stakeholders' work, which was the identification of key issues and the development of action plans to address these issues.

Following the completion of the planning phase, communities were eligible to apply for implementation grants. Unlike the planning phase, the implementation process did not have prescribed steps and was left to the community to carry out. Communities were advised to build quickly on the momentum of the planning effort and to begin working on their implementation plans as soon as possible.

The Community Indicators Project was an unexpected outcome of the CHCI and became an important component of the Initiative. During the planning phase, communities developed a community health profile, which was a compilation of community-specific data that allowed stakeholders to recognize and understand trends in various health and quality-of-life issues. These profiles typically relied on existing data and, to varying degrees, framed the planning groups' choice of issues to address during the implementation phase.

It became clear midway through the Initiative, through the example of one community, that expanding and updating these profiles would allow communities to measure, on a regular basis, how well they were progressing toward their vision of a healthy community. The Colorado Trust made additional funds available to 15 communities to continue this work, which became known as the Community Indicators Project. Each of the 15 communities received technical assistance during a two-year period to find creative indicators that accurately captured and tracked the key areas and topics that uniquely defined and determined health for them.

The CHCI Evaluation

The CHCI was distinctive in having a comprehensive evaluation that began while the Initiative was being designed. Although many observers have

called for evaluating healthy cities, there have been few studies of these programs and none that have focused on the processes, outcomes, and impacts
that a comprehensive evaluation would require. The evaluation design for the
CHCI blended traditional and nontraditional methods designed to capture the
Initiative's diversity of operations, outcomes, and effects.

The evaluation had three general goals: to track the CHCI program as it
was put into operation in individual communities, to identify short-term outcomes for the participants and for the projects, and to investigate longer-term
outcomes of the projects on the communities.

Several different evaluation activities were employed to accomplish these
goals: (a) In-depth case studies were conducted with sites selected from each
cycle to reflect the diversity among the communities. Comparison case studies
were also undertaken in several Colorado communities. Communities selected
for the comparison case studies each used a different approach to health-
promotion planning, though they shared equivalent health goals. (b) Stakeholder
surveys, developed with input from stakeholders, were sent to all stakeholders
at the end of the planning phase. About 1,000 stakeholders in 28 communities
completed the nine-page survey. (c) Implementation progress reports, regularly
submitted to The Colorado Trust from the communities, were used to assess
project activities along the dimensions of participants, actions, and outcomes.
(d) Interviews with community leaders were conducted in selected case study
communities at the beginning and end of the implementation phase. These
interviews were designed to track changes in how the communities made decisions and to gauge the success of action projects. (e) Community-based indicators were implemented by a subset of 15 communities for long-term assessment of
the impact of the CHCI and other activities on communities' health and well-being.

Initiative Communities

The CHCI involved a total of 29 communities in three different cycles. Of
these, 28 communities completed the planning phase, and 27 completed the
implementation phase.

There was a great deal of diversity among the communities. The CHCI
communities varied greatly in their geographic size. Globeville Community
Connection in metropolitan Denver was the smallest community, with only 2
square miles. In comparison, the largest was Healthy Plains in Northeast
Colorado, which at 9,247 square miles is larger than several states in the United
States. A total of 10 of the 28 CHCI communities were urban, another 10 were

rural, and 8 were frontier (i.e., with population densities of six or fewer people per square mile). The CHCI communities covered a range of population sizes from 2,700 in the Custer 2020 project to 249,000 in the Boulder County Healthy Community Initiative. Although 5 communities had a population of more than 100,000, the majority of communities had populations of less than 30,000 people.

With a few notable exceptions, the CHCI communities, like the state as a whole, were largely white, with nearly half of the communities having more than 90% white populations. Five CHCI communities had Hispanic populations of 30% or more; one community was 60% Hispanic. Only one community had a significant African American population, and only one had a significant Native American population. The CHCI communities tended to be poorer than the state average. Based on the available data for 26 of the communities, more than 50% of the communities had per capita incomes less than $12,000; by comparison, the average per capita income in 1990 for the state of Colorado was $14,821. Only six of the CHCI projects had per capita incomes above the state average.

Major Outcomes

An initiative as long, large, and ambitious as the CHCI has many outcomes. We briefly highlight the major outcomes from the 15- to 18-month-long strategic planning phase, when the communities were defining health and proposing projects, and from the two- to three-year implementation phase, when the communities implemented action steps. We also highlight unanticipated outcomes that cut across these phases.

Planning Phase. Large groups of citizens (about 50 on average) came together and, more important, stayed together for a long period of time as they worked to define health and plan projects to improve their communities. These citizens demonstrated their commitment to work together toward community change. The CHCI planning groups were generally very diverse in terms of community sectors and interests, bringing in those that were traditionally uninvolved in health-focused projects, such as business and education. However, they were not as diverse in terms of individual demographic characteristics, such as age, income, and racial-ethnic background.

The CHCI community stakeholders thought broadly about health. All communities easily moved beyond an illness- or wellness-focused view to an analysis of the underlying factors that determine health, such as housing, education, the environment, and citizen involvement in governance. In moving from ideas to proposed actions, the CHCI groups generally used consensus decision making, but at a price. Sometimes, risk taking was avoided, and consensus was achieved at the expense of diversity of viewpoints. Nonetheless, there generally were benefits for both individuals and groups in terms of increased skills and abilities to accomplish community work. At the individual level in particular, many stakeholders said that they increased their abilities to understand community problems, to collaborate productively with others, and to take a more active leadership role in their community. At the group level, the large majority of stakeholders felt that they had garnered the support of key powerful people in the community and laid a foundation for future work together.

Implementation Phase. In keeping with the CHCI principle to include a broad representation of the community, groups maintained broad and active partnerships with diverse sectors of the communities during the implementation phase. These partnerships varied from formal coalitions and collaborations to informal cooperation and coordination. Although maintaining partnerships is challenging and requires attention and hard work, such partnerships were important to facilitate successful activities. During implementation, the CHCI projects not only undertook the activities that they originally proposed, but they also took on additional activities, in part as a response to new opportunities that arose from new partnerships. On average, each CHCI project undertook six sets of primary activities around different issues. The majority of the primary activities focused on specific topics or issues in the community, such as programs for youth development; other activities focused on community development processes, such as fostering citizen participation or increasing intracommunity communication.

The majority of CHCI projects resulted in important outcomes for the communities. These ranged from issue-focused outcomes, such as the creation of a new family resource center that facilitated family services, to community development-focused outcomes, such as the formation of a civic forum that catalyzed community involvement, to engaging high levels of citizen participation in activities. Issue-focused outcomes were more common than community-development-focused outcomes. A small minority of CHCI projects evidenced signs of change in community decision making and governance. In a few communities, citizens involved with the CHCI were influencing community-wide decision making in different ways, such as participating in important community decision-making bodies or causing significant policy changes. These changes have the potential for creating community-level change.

Unanticipated Outcomes. An active, vital coalition of all the CHCI projects formed during the planning phase. This informal coalition shared valuable experiences, insights, and support and eventually grew into an independent organization, the Colorado Center for Healthy Communities. This group assisted other individuals and new communities in similar efforts as well as provided guidance as the original CHCI communities continued their work. Many CHCI communities put individualized community-based indicators in place. These indicator sets are as varied as the communities, containing measures of many different key issues from housing to transportation to economic development. These sets of measures allow the communities to track the progress they are making toward achieving their vision of a healthy community.

Dialogue With Ross Conner

Christina A. Christie

Christie: Describe the framework you used to guide the overall evaluation design of this program.

Conner: It was definitely a collaborative, community-based approach. It involved a lot of different stakeholders. At the outset, we didn't know what the program was going to be. All we knew was that it was going to be different things in different places. I started working with the program developers from Day 1, so I knew the general focus of the program, but we did not know what the specific purposes would be. We just knew that they would be varied. In fact, we didn't know where or what the communities would look like. All we knew was that they [The Colorado Trust] planned for about 30 communities that would be brought into the project at different times over a couple of years. In addition, the definition of community was also up to the communities. We didn't know whether they would be large or small. Would they be neighborhoods? Would they be counties? They turned out to be areas as small as what most folks would call neighborhoods and up to six county areas that are larger than some U.S. states.

Christie: How would you say your evaluation approach was influenced by the program philosophy and design?

Conner: It meant that the main stakeholders and the evaluation team worked together from the beginning. In the very early stages, these stakeholders primarily involved the program funding staff and the implementation team for the planning phase; as the CHCI progressed, the stakeholder group expanded to include the communities. Working together at the beginning, we decided what the program would involve—the program logic model and the principles were developed from there. Then, a shell of an evaluation plan was created that would be filled as the realities of the program developed and as the community stakeholders began to be involved.

One real benefit for the implementation of the evaluation was the decision by the funder to have three rounds of communities funded rather than funding all communities at the outset. So the program first involved about 10 communities, then a year later about 10 more came on, and finally a last set of about 10. That was fortuitous and really kind of accidental. It wasn't planned but had the great benefit of giving the program implementers a good feel for how things were going and for what needed to be adjusted. It also gave the evaluation team a chance to learn about the programs and to feed our information back formatively, which was very useful to the program. Additionally, it gave us a chance to refine the evaluation plan and then develop it further as we went along. Keep in mind that, except for the general principles that were laid out, there was never *a* program that was instituted. It was a concept, and each community then made it real. I was creating and adjusting an evaluation design that would capture the main processes within each community and also across communities and across time.

Christie: A bit more about the evaluation design, if you don't mind. I have read some of your work that describes evaluations you have conducted. For example, in a recent *New Directions for Evaluation* volume you discuss an evaluation of a program called "Tres Hombres," where you used a randomized design. Would you say The Colorado Trust or Tres Hombres is most illustrative of how you typically conduct evaluations? And to what degree has your training with Campbell influenced your approach?

Conner: The similarities between the two evaluations are in *the way* I work with those involved in the evaluation—the stakeholders, the clients, the funders, whatever the group might be. However, the questions for each were different. In the case of the Tres Hombres program, the migrant workers with whom I worked really wanted to know if the program was making a difference. In this case, we had a control group design where we set up contrasts, because this is how we could best understand whether the program made a difference. The Colorado Trust program, on the other hand, had different evaluation questions. The funders knew that because of the complexity and diversity of the individual community projects, the program at best would be *contributing* to change, not solely causing it. They didn't want or need to spend the relatively large resources necessary for implementing a causal design.

The common thread is that I am responding to the questions that are being asked for the evaluation and then adapting the evaluation design to those questions, the reality of the context, and the conflicts and restrictions presented. This includes giving people the chance to say, "Not these kinds of questions," or "Ah! Yeah, there are different kinds of questions we can ask here, about short term and long term, about impact, outcome, process." That's our jargon, but they can understand it in a different way. Coming in too soon with the evaluation design can cut off that useful process. And if you do it right, it builds the bond with stakeholders. Then later, when you are in the field and you've got to make some adjustments, people are on board with you.

As you mentioned, I trained under Don Campbell and the experimental/quasi-experimental approach. My dissertation looked at the implementation of randomization in a set of about a dozen different programs. Over the years, I haven't abandoned that. I just realized that there are classes of [evaluation] questions that don't need that approach. There are also programs that are at different stages that aren't ready for that approach. It is a costly approach. And it's one that, in order to work well, requires a great deal of control and consistency.

I believe that the questions need to be the anchor. Then, we have a variety of designs which can be used to answer the questions. In The Colorado Trust's case, the questions were about process and about short-term outcomes and some indication of whether this was beginning to move down the path toward impact. The Colorado Trust funded someone to go back to these communities about five years later to track the situation and found, amazingly, that it had continued.

Christie: The Colorado Trust program was based on four general principles: one, broad representation of individuals participating in a community-wide process; two, broad definition of health; three, consensus decision making; four, capacity building. How were these principles reflected in the evaluation?

Conner: We certainly focused questions on each of these principles, as you can see in the survey and the reports. Moreover, we involved some of these principles in planning and implementing as well as reporting the evaluation findings. I looked for diverse research assistants because I wanted the evaluation team to look like the communities. Also, the evaluation process involved consensus decision making—for example, when developing the survey. I think that is one of the reasons why we had such a high response rate. And in my own very modest way, I tried to build capacity in public communities. In general, the principles were the anchors for some of the questions we asked.

Christie: In what ways, if any, did the evaluation influence or inform the development of the community indicators study that was conducted by 15 of the communities?

Conner: I knew at the outset that I would need and want some sort of community-based, community-wide measure of the impact. But because there wasn't a program to design a study around, I put that on hold and trusted it would come up during the process. And sure enough, it emerged from one of the communities that tried something like it on its own. Fortunately, it was early on. The other communities thought this was interesting because it was a way to begin to get a sense of what is happening. I got excited because of what this presented for supplementing the evaluation. And the funder saw the benefit to the communities and added a little extra money so that there could be some partial support to replicate this in 15 of the communities.

This is another example of how the expertise was really shared. The evaluator definitely brings certain kinds of expertise, but the community members do too. And sometimes, they [the community members] lead us in a way that we might not anticipate, but we, the evaluators, have to be open to that. In this specific case, the communities, through a model case, showed the way, as opposed to the evaluation setting the frame.

Upon reflection, I would say that the desire to have something like a community indicators component existed and that the evaluation helped set a context for it to emerge. But it wasn't imposed. What one project was doing really intrigued people, and it gave me an opportunity to say, "Hey this is a great way to have localized community measures." For example, in one community, open space was defined by measures of deer and elk population. That wouldn't work in suburban or metro Denver, but it works in the rural areas. There was a different kind of measure for urban areas. This made it real. It was a way for them [communities] to tell their story.

I think evaluators should see their role as helping people create their story. We can be their scribes, to ensure that the story not only gets told but also told in the best way. The community members were delighted to see the particulars emerge and to know that their story could be heard by others and also that they could reread their story as a way to remember where they had been. We evaluators know that certain ways of focusing on outcomes are better than others. Most people don't have that expertise. That's okay if we as evaluators bring it, working collaboratively.

Christie: How do you respond to people who ask, "Where is the objectivity in your approach?"

Conner: Ah, is anybody really objective? I tend to put objectivity in quotes these days. We, along with those involved in the study, need to set the standards so that they make sense and are real for them [the program stakeholders]. There are certainly outside standards that are recognized and brought in.

Christie: How did you deal with the issue of objectivity in The Colorado Trust evaluation?

Conner: The theories of change and the principles served as benchmarks, again, in a way that would be adaptable to the different communities that were going to be involved in this. It wasn't a recipe but rather a general instruction people would follow. That provided enough objectivity—to know where to look. We continued to look at other things, but it provided the right kinds of anchors.

Of course, there was no way to do a controlled study. That was the challenge. The methods we have are not well suited at all. Our methods are generally coming from psychology, economics, and are more individual focused than community focused.

Christie: That provides us with a nice transition to methods. Could you talk generally about how you decided upon the methods used in the study?

Conner: My initial idea was to do a pre-test at the beginning, with the people involved, to provide a look at the overall project, across all communities. I was quickly informed, really by the people who were developing the program, of the challenges of doing a standard pre-post design due to the concept of the Initiative—that people [communities] would be developing the various parts of the program and so there wasn't really anything to measure from the outset. Therefore, the idea of a post-program measure became very important. A measure where, at the point of data collection, those who were involved in the program, as well as those who have fallen away, could comment on what had happened and provide their assessment of how it went. Thus, it was very important to involve people from each of the communities in the development of the post-measure.

Christie: You mention in one of your evaluation reports that stakeholder advisory groups helped to design your stakeholder survey. How were these advisory groups selected?

Conner: For each community, we made an announcement at one of the early meetings, asking for a volunteer or two to assist with the evaluation planning. We generally had one person from each community—sometimes two— whom we worked with, so a total of about 30 people from around the state. It was a good mix of people representing different sectors of the communities. But, boy, they all wanted everything. And that was a challenge.

Christie: Yes, I know. There are great advantages to stakeholder participation, but there are also challenges. And one of them is you've got people who become really engaged and involved, and they really want the evaluation to yield all of the answers to a litany of questions.

Conner: Yes, they do. But, through discussions with the evaluator in a genuinely collaborative process, stakeholders begin to understand what is involved in answering different kinds of evaluation questions. So, in the CHCI case and the stakeholder survey, together we [the evaluators and the stakeholder advisory group members] worked to determine the most important issues, then to create the specific survey questions to get the best answers.

Christie: How did the stakeholder advisory group contribute to the development of the survey?

Conner: When developing the survey, we had an evolving group of advisors because we included folks from each of the three funding cycles. The community members were excited about the information that could come from the stakeholder survey. Each advisor wanted to add more and more questions, and the potential length of the survey just kept growing and growing. Finally, we compromised at nine pages of questions, which I thought was still way too long. I held my breath wondering whether we'd get many of these surveys back.

Christie: How was your response rate?

Conner: With a little cajoling, we had a very high response rate—80%. I think this was because it was the community members themselves who developed the survey. We had piloted the questions enough, and they really caught people's attention. Many people even took the time to answer the question that often ends the survey—"Feel free to include anything else you'd like." We had obviously struck the right chord. They felt they could talk and share ideas and experiences, and they certainly did.

That then created a new challenge for us: We had so much data to analyze. We did rolling summarizations for each group of funded communities. We didn't want to release any information until data were collected from everybody. We also fed back information to everybody in the "project family" [the 28 communities] before it went out to anyone else. That meant we had to hold off releasing the information until everyone had taken a look and given their opinions. In this way, we obtained interesting, valid, and reliable lessons from the data, and these helped provide a forward-looking focus on recommendations for changes.

Christie: This evaluation was recognized, in part, because of its success in addressing methodological challenges. And so, I wanted to ask you to discuss some of the challenges and what you did to overcome them.

Conner: One challenge is the attempt to track a small number of the communities after they finished their planning stages. We developed a profile of how the community operates. Two years later, once they implemented things, we went back and did another set of interviews with stakeholders representing the various segments of the community. It turned out that people really could characterize how their community went about doing business. We gave the initial profile to a second group of interviewees two years later and asked whether they thought it had changed. These interviewees were not necessarily involved in the program. We told this second group, "Here's what we developed two years ago. Is it the same in this community now? Or are things different, and how are they different?"

Could we really characterize the way communities "do business" via this two-stage method? It worked out better than I thought. We were able to develop a profile that people would agree on and then to use it a few years later, in a comparative way, to identify changes.

Christie: You used case study methods—you did case studies of communities, and then you did cross-comparison case studies. Would you talk a bit about why you selected case study as a method?

Conner: In the case of following the set of communities during the planning process, we knew it was going to play out in as many different ways as there were communities. So we couldn't follow them all but wanted to try to get a sense of it [the planning process] across a variety of settings. We consciously picked a variety of urban, rural, and frontier communities—and on both sides of the Rockies, which is a very important political and sociological divide for people in Colorado. Therefore, I think we had a pretty good set. We got a really good picture of these planning communities.

Christie: What did these case studies entail?

Conner: My research assistants went to the community meetings but would not sit taking notes. They were quiet participants and, after a meeting, would go back and write a report. We had a rough frame of topics and issues to watch for. I was fortunate to have good people as research assistants who were accepted right into the community. It went quite well, and it wasn't intrusive at all.

Christie: Did they interview folks or was it mostly observation? Did they do informal interviews?

Conner: Observation and informal interviews. They might talk to people after meetings. And they had a lot of contact between meetings. Those case studies were used to tell the project's story. It gives you a sense of how it played out and how different it was in each community.

Christie: As the stories were evolving, was information being sent back to folks in the community? Or was it more of an informal communication process?

Conner: Written evaluation reports were created after the process was finished.

Christie: You also did interviews with key community members. Correct?

Conner: We did for a subset of case study communities, to follow the developing longer-term effects.

Christie: How were the leaders selected? Were they the same leaders over time?

Conner: At that point, the research assistants really knew the communities quite well because they had been involved during the planning phase. They really got to know things from the "coffee shop" perspective, as it were. It was pretty easy at that point to develop a diverse list of potential people to interview. We intentionally selected people who weren't directly involved in the program. At the two-year mark, once implementation had run its course, we looked at the list again. We made some adjustments because some people had moved and new faces had arrived, so we shifted things around.

A benefit of the case study method is that you're really in touch with the group, so when there are changes, you often know about them. It's different from participant attrition in a more traditionally designed study. A disadvantage to the case study method, however, was that it was evident to the stakeholders when we were looking for triangulation on a particular component or issue. We obviously wouldn't say, "Tina said that . . . ; what do you think?" We would instead say, "Someone else said . . . What's your view about this?" Or "Several people said . . . , but several others said . . . What do you think?"

Christie: I suppose that is a risk, also—getting to know people too well. You spend a lot of time in these communities, and people from the communities were spending a lot of time together participating in the program. Perhaps that is just the way things go.

Conner: Yes, I think so. But if you handle it well, and I think we did, you can avoid having it make a significant impact on the study.

Christie: I know you made some assessments about the extent to which they [communities] had succeeded in carrying out the program. How was that done?

Conner: My research team back in California went through all the file material—the implementation reports. The communities themselves filed quarterly reports directly to the foundation. The reports used a frame that I had helped develop to make them consistent. We got copies of the quarterly reports, and we analyzed them.

From the outside one might think, "Aren't they just going to present a rosy picture to the foundation?" But in fact, people were amazingly frank and honest. There was no whitewashing going on. Of course, in many of the communities, we were doing the case studies, so we knew what was happening. This provided a mechanism to triangulate what was reported to the foundation. The reports were very accurate, which I think is also a credit to the foundation staff, who approached this in a collegial way, with learning as the main purpose. It was a feeling of all of us together working on this, not the feeling that the foundation had the answers.

Christie: How do you think releasing your evaluation reports *at the end* of the evaluation impacted the utilization of the findings?

Conner: Waiting a little longer gave a more reliable picture of what was going on. This also helped to continue the trust that we built among the communities. From a pure scientific standpoint, perhaps releasing information sooner might have made sense—for example, to add to knowledge and allow policy makers and program developers in other places to use it, but even from that standpoint, the number of communities was so small that it was important for us to have everyone in the study before we drew and disseminated final conclusions.

Christie: This evaluation was noted for its impact. In what ways have you observed the impact?

Conner: I'd say there was great impact on the people who were the primary question askers—The [Colorado] Trust. In addition, there were many requests from other foundations from around the country and around the world that were, at the same time, developing or implementing similar kinds of programs.

On the communities themselves, I'd say the survey provided a way for them to express their opinions. I don't think there were surprises there because people really shared during the planning process, so the communities really had a good sense of where things were. The survey was more of a way for them to tell their story to others.

The fact that we held off to the end to provide the written report doesn't reflect what was happening with respect to learning, particularly within communities. Quite a bit was learned and shared along the way, as part of various evaluation components, like the case study discussions and the survey responses. When the final reports came out, like I said, their content wasn't a surprise to the communities. When the reports were released, they really made an impact at the state level and, of course, with the funder, who started other initiatives like this one.

Christie: Just to summarize, the impact the evaluation had on the communities was really occurring all throughout the evaluation process, and the final reports had their greatest impact on folks external to the communities.

Conner: The evaluation approach and the program itself were interesting to people. It fit in with the World Health Organization's (WHO) "healthy community" projects that were going on around the world. The program staff for the WHO programs had been calling for evaluation for many years, but not much had ever occurred. This, I believe, was the first attempt to do this systematically and comprehensively.

Christie: Which components of the evaluation do you think provided the most meaningful information?

Conner: For the communities, it was being able to give a picture of what occurred in that community. For The Colorado Trust, the board, and the staff, we provided the kind of overarching information that they were interested in. Although they were certainly interested in the communities themselves, they really wanted to know, at an Initiative or statewide level, is this making things better? Is this helping or not? Their mission is to improve the health of Coloradans.

Christie: I'm curious, Ross. How did you get pulled into this evaluation?

Conner: I received a call one day from The Colorado Trust. They had been checking out evaluators for this project. They knew I was involved in this community work, so they asked me for a meeting to talk about possibly getting involved. As it turned out, I was going to be in Denver for some grant review meetings, so we had breakfast, and right after that, they got back in touch and said, "We would love to have you involved in this." In this relationship, we had our courtship before marriage. It was a long relationship, as it was with the communities. You don't just end relationships like that; I'm still in touch with some of the people, some there and some who have moved to other jobs and locations.

Christie: So an important contribution was how you went about conducting this evaluation?

Conner: Yes, that's true.

Christie: You also had a high level of stakeholder participation in this evaluation. In retrospect, what were the challenges of this participation?

Conner: This evaluation stretched over a long period of time, which means inevitably there are changes. People come and go. Reality happens. Life happens. It takes patience, and it takes an evaluation team that really wants to be partners with the communities and to follow the journey with them—through the good times and the challenging ones. Here's an example of a challenging time: I was with my research assistant at one community meeting where the discussion got so heated that the sheriff had to come to calm things down.

Christie: Would you mind describing what happened?

Conner: Well, in this case, there was a religious right segment of the community that was invited to participate. They attended, but they did not come to participate. Instead, they came to collect information to send to their attorney, they said, to sue these people because they were spending "blood money"— money that had come from abortionists.

One of the CHCI program's principles is to bring all segments of the community together to decide on a vision for the future. The idea is that people with different ideas will agree to disagree on some issues but, working collaboratively, they will develop a vision on topics and move forward in areas where they agree. The religious right is one segment that exists in some communities, so they should be one of the groups at the table. In this one particular community, the main stakeholder group was open to inviting this segment of the community in; however, this segment did not come to work collaboratively but instead to object and obstruct, and so the process ran into a rough, rough spot and, for a while, hit a wall.

Christie: How was this resolved?

Conner: It involved the head of the foundation coming down to a meeting, with all factions present, to explain the goal of the foundation. He did an excellent job. Things calmed down. The religious right faction, unfortunately, never really participated.

Christie: What would you say was gained from the standpoint of the evaluation?

Conner: From an evaluation standpoint, it did present an interesting contrast. You have to be ready to grab comparisons when they present themselves, as compared to randomly assigning them and setting up your own comparison. And here was one. It put an interesting test to some of the principles as well. It was a case of just one, but an informative one. You would expect differences in how much people worked together—and how they got along. And sure enough, we found those differences in these communities. So it gave me more confidence in other parts of the data, knowing that where it seemed like things would not go well, people sure enough said, "It didn't go well."

Christie: You show a really nice bar graph of the stakeholder groups that *weren't* present in communities in a report. Could you talk about the particular stakeholder groups that were not involved in the evaluation?

Conner: Youth, in particular, were not represented. When you think about the process—long meetings that went on for months—it's not one that's well adapted to youth, so it's not surprising that they weren't involved. I should caution, though, that what is presented in that graph is the communities' assessments of who was missing. We realized there was no benchmark on who was under- or overrepresented. Census figures were out of date, if data even existed in the categories we were interested in. So the stakeholders' opinions were the benchmark. We said, "Based on your understanding of the representation of different sectors and interests in your communities, who is underrepresented? Who is overrepresented? Who is adequately represented?" That's where those figures came from. Every community felt that youth were underrepresented, even several communities that we thought had made a really good effort in getting youth involved. A lot of communities really tried hard to include folks from low socioeconomic groups but didn't succeed. The reasons for this were some of the lessons learned and the ideas we passed on about what could be done differently elsewhere.

Christie: To remedy this, in one of your reports, you offer the suggestion of inviting people to the table before it feels like an afterthought. You say, "This marks a meaningful change in program design." I was interested in understanding the impact of your recommendation.

Conner: When we did our reports, the program planning was completed, so it was too late for our recommendations to affect the communities' work on this initiative, although our suggestions could be used in future work. But there was a lesson there for other people doing similar initiatives in different communities in different places. Has it been used? I don't know. It's much tougher to *really* involve people early, before you make fundamental decisions about the process. Let me state this another way, using a metaphor: Inviting people to the table isn't enough; you need to have them involved in deciding on the shape of the table, the location of the table—whether there's even a table. Do you want simple representation or genuine involvement? We thought about lessons we could offer to outsiders who may be starting this process, and this was one of them.

Christie: I found the consensus decision making very interesting. You found that some communities were able to do it and others had a tougher time with it. Could you talk about how these communities differed?

Conner: The community I mentioned earlier, where the sheriff had to appear at one meeting to calm things down, serves as an interesting comparison and illustrates why it works and why it doesn't. You need people who can respect differences, so you can move forward. In this one community, you had people who would come to the table, but they were coming to the table really to destroy it as opposed to help build something from it. When we developed the stakeholder survey question about consensus, we spent a lot of time working with our stakeholder advisory group to agree on the definition of what consensus meant for the survey. Each of the words for that definition was very carefully selected. Consensus requires people to look beyond their interests and include other perspectives, then to develop ideas and plans with everyone pretty much willing to go along.

The process of consensus decision making brings people together. If it works properly, the shared vision isn't the *education* vision or the *business* vision, and it isn't *my* vision; it's *ours*, together. The group creates something new, which can then be a foundation for moving forward together and achieving new things. The communities that have succeeded at this are able to go beyond a particular sector's vision and create a new vision, a new framework that is co-created; this allows them to do business differently.

Christie: I can't help but say how struck I am by your role in this evaluation as a facilitator and teacher.

Conner: That's a real compliment because facilitation done well is quite a skill. During the planning phase in each of the communities, there were two professional facilitators, so I really got to see how facilitators work. I have great respect for them and for what they do, and I hope I picked up a little bit of facilitation skill that I'm able to use.

I think as an evaluator in community-based programs, you wear a lot of hats and have to be ready to shift. You have to know where you stand and know the expertise that you bring. Everybody involved brings different kinds of expertise. An evaluator brings skills in asking and answering evaluation questions, in the pros and cons of research methods, and so forth; it's this expertise that starts the interaction and relationship. But what keeps you effective, as part of the relationship, are the sensitivities, the human skills—knowing when to push, when to hold back, when to be a devil's advocate, when to be supportive, when to talk, and when to listen. This is when the facilitator or teacher roles become important.

Christie: Yes, I agree. Before we wrap up, upon reflection, what would you do differently if you were to conduct this evaluation in the future?

Conner: I would probably try to devote more of the resources to the short-term outcomes. By the time we got to that point in the project and evaluation, the resources had been used, so we weren't able to follow up like I would have liked, although it turned out all right. The independent, follow-up study that the funder did a few years later looked into longer-term outcomes and even some impacts in the communities, and they found them.

Christie's Commentary

When Dr. Conner began his work, the program was, by design, undefined. A program unique to each of the 28 funded communities was to be developed by each community. Conner was commissioned by the program funder to provide an overarching initiative-level assessment of the overall program process. The emergent design and inevitable diversity of programs presented a particular evaluation challenge.

Conner used a collaborative, community-based framework to guide his evaluation design and implementation. This evaluation approach allowed him to be responsive to the complexities of the evaluation as a result of the features of the program and provided him with the flexibility necessary for examining program processes at both the community and initiative levels. It is difficult to imagine how a more structured evaluation design could have been implemented, given the goal of the program.

Conner's responsive strategy required an evaluation team that could spend a significant amount of time in the community. He and his research assistants traveled often to Colorado to observe program processes and, in most instances, lived in Colorado or even lived in the communities they were studying, reflecting the influence of ethnographic style. Yet members of the evaluation team kept a critical distance when communities made decisions about a program's direction or shape. However, they were careful not to stand out as planned observers of the process and, consequently, did not take notes during meetings but did assist when setting up community meetings. These actions reflect a delicate balance between participation and persuasion.

Conner's emphasis on collaboration is evidenced throughout the interview. He acknowledges that he, as an evaluator, has a unique set of skills that he brings to the evaluation table but is cautious not to overemphasize the importance of these skills in relationship to the unique skill sets brought forth by other stakeholders. This awareness authenticates his vision of shared expertise. Conner points out that this approach to collaboration helps build rapport with stakeholders, a rapport that is necessary for facilitating both process and instrumental use (e.g., Patton, 1997; Preskill & Torres, 1998; Weiss, 1998).

I was also struck by Conner's sensitivity to the language he uses with stakeholders, which I suspect reinforces the collaborative climate he aims to foster between evaluators and stakeholders. This was illustrated when he described the process of focusing evaluation questions with stakeholders and used the words *impact, outcome,* and *process.* He quickly points out that he uses "our [evaluator] jargon" and acknowledges that nonuse of these terms is not necessarily a reflection of an inability to understand evaluation processes.

At first glance, Conner's mixed method evaluation approach may not bare its complexity. He uses not only quantitative and qualitative data collection and analysis methods (with a reliance on self-reported measures of impact) but also mixed method study designs, as illustrated by his use of comparative case studies. However, he acknowledges that he expended as few resources as possible on this evaluation component. Additionally, throughout our interview, Conner describes the role of the evaluator as one of a "storyteller," which some may argue represents a more constructivist paradigm, seemingly diverging from his postpositivist training under Campbell.

As I noted in the interview, this evaluation was recognized in part because of its impact. Throughout the interview, it was apparent that *use* was fostered at the community level by informal reporting and communication as well as participation in the evaluation (Alkin, Christie, & Rose, 2006). Formal full reporting did not take place until the completion of the evaluation, so that the results from all 28 communities could be used to support conclusions. With respect to generating information for conceptual uses (Weiss, 1998), Conner maintains that the findings from this evaluation, as well as the processes used, were much anticipated by organizations throughout the world, especially those using a health cities concept. These types of projects had appeared difficult to evaluate because of their diverse focuses and different approaches. That is, these projects are designed by cities or communities to plan locally based initiatives to address locally based problems, but the focuses and actions taken by each community differ based on the community's circumstances and characteristics. Conner has developed a model that can be used to evaluate the processes and outcomes of projects of this type. I expect that others have indeed learned from Conner's evaluation of the CHCI and hope that additional insights can be gained from the discussion with Conner presented here.

DISCUSSION QUESTIONS

1. How does Conner's evaluation help with program planning and organizational development? What types of learning are taking place in the communities? What role does Conner and his evaluation team play in this learning?

2. Who are the primary stakeholders for the ongoing work during the evaluation? How does Conner involve each of these groups in the evaluation?

Who are the primary stakeholders for the primary reports, and how will they use them?

3. Conner notes that "as an evaluator in community-based programs you wear a lot of hats and have to be ready to shift." How does Conner's role change over time? With different stakeholders? What different roles have you seen other evaluators take in this book?

4. Contrast Conner's role with King's role in the evaluation of the special education program at the Anoka-Hennepin School District. How do their purposes differ? How do they differ in the roles they take? To what extent are their different roles a result of their different purposes?

5. Conner indicates that it is important for evaluators to "know where they stand and know the expertise they bring," noting that everyone brings different types of expertise to the table. What do you think are the important skills that evaluators bring to a project?

6. Conner cites the critical role one plays as a facilitator, and that role involves both supporting and playing devil's advocate, pushing on issues. How important are these personal skills to his evaluation? To any evaluation? Consider the interviews you have read so far. Do you see each evaluator playing supportive and critical roles? How do they balance these roles? (*Note:* There is considerable variation across those we have interviewed in the extent to which they take a supportive role versus a questioning or critical role. Look back and see if you can identify these differences.)

FURTHER READING

There are four evaluation reports on the Colorado Healthy Communities Initiative:

- *Citizens Making Their Communities Healthier: A Description of the Colorado Healthy Communities Initiative (1998)*
- *The First Steps Toward Healthier Communities: Outcomes From the Planning Phase of the Colorado Healthy Communities Initiative (1999)*
- *Working Toward Healthy Communities: Outcomes From the Implementation Phase of the Colorado Healthy Communities Initiative (1999)*
- *Communities Tracking Their Quality of Life: An Overview of the Community Indicators Project of the Colorado Healthy Communities Initiative (1999)*

This document draws from these reports to present the highlights of the program and its outcomes. For more detailed information, we encourage you to read the source documents; copies can be obtained from The Colorado Trust at www.coloradotrust.org/ under Publications.

Conner, R. F., Easterling, D., Tanjasiri, S. P., & Adams-Berger, J. (2003). Using community indicators to track and improve health and quality of life. In D. V. Easterling, K. M. Gallagher, & D. G. Lodwick (Eds.), *Promoting health at the community level* (pp. 43–76). Thousand Oaks, CA: Sage.

Conner, R. F., Tanjasiri, S. P., Dempsey, C., Robles, G., Davidson, M., & Easterling, D. (2003).The Colorado Healthy Communities Initiative: Communities defining and addressing health. In D. V. Easterling, K. M. Gallagher, & D. G. Lodwick (Eds.), *Promoting health at the community level* (pp. 17–42). Thousand Oaks, CA: Sage.

REFERENCES

Alkin, M. C., Christie, C. A., & Rose, M. (2006). Communicating evaluation. In I. Shaw, J. Greene, & M. Mark (Eds.), *Handbook of evaluation* (pp. 384–403). London: Sage.

Patton, M. Q. (1997). *Utilization-focused evaluation: The new century text*. Thousand Oaks, CA: Sage.

Preskill, H., & Torres, R. (1998). *Evaluative inquiry for organizational learning*. Thousand Oaks, CA: Sage.

Weiss, C. H. (1998). *Evaluation* (2nd ed.). Upper Saddle River, NJ: Prentice Hall.

PART IV

EVALUATIONS CONCERNING CULTURAL COMPETENCE

E valuators have always been concerned with being responsive to the setting of the evaluation, its context, and its stakeholders. But not until the late 1990s did we begin giving attention to the particular issue of cultural competence. Karen Kirkhart's 1994 presidential address at the American Evaluation Association (Kirkhart, 1995) made many evaluators more conscious of the need for them to be knowledgeable about and sensitive to the multiple cultural perspectives they encounter in conducting evaluations. Many have since written about the need for evaluators to be aware of their own values and learn of the values and culture of the stakeholders in conducting an evaluation. Saumitra SenGupta, Rodney Hopson, and Melva Thompson-Robinson

(2004) have written that "culture is an undeniably integral part of the diverse contexts of evaluation, and therefore an integral part of evaluation" (p. 6).

What is cultural competence in evaluation? And how do we achieve it? SenGupta et al. (2004) define it in this way: "Cultural competence in evaluation rests on active awareness, understanding, and appreciation for the context at hand, and it uses responsive and inclusive means to conduct evaluation" (p. 12). Evaluation, as the root of the word indicates, is about values. Whose values do evaluators use in judging the merit or worth of a program or policy? What is their role in understanding and incorporating the values of other stakeholders whose values and goals may differ from those of the majority? As an example, the education of children who are home schooled is often evaluated by their state's standardized tests. Do these measures take into account the values of parents or others who home school their children? Should they? Does the evaluator have an obligation to learn more about the values of home schooling families and to incorporate those values into the examination of children's learning?

Evaluations, by their very nature, are political. Evaluators are dealing with many different stakeholders with different value orientations. Many evaluations concern programs for immigrants or lower-income people, whose values are likely to be different from those of the mainstream and from those of most policy makers and (yes!) of most evaluators. Drawing on the definition presented by SenGupta et al. (2004), a culturally competent evaluator should bring active awareness to the settings and culture that he or she is evaluating; work to further understand that culture and its values; and, as appropriate, in a responsive and inclusive manner, incorporate these culture values into the evaluation. There are no strict guidelines to conducting a culturally competent evaluation. Instead, it requires a careful examination of one's own values, openness to learning about the values and strengths of a new culture, and a willingness to be responsive and flexible in carrying out the evaluation as one learns more about the new culture.

In this section, we present two evaluations in settings that require particular cultural competence. The first evaluation is a parent-child reading program in Trenton, New Jersey. The African American evaluator, new to Trenton, learns much about the neighborhood and its history. In conducting the evaluation, she identifies different perceptions and beliefs about the program among the program administrators, staff, volunteers, and the parents who attend the program. Her sensitivity to cultural differences prompts her to not only learn more about the community and those who live there but also to identify these different views of the program, which generally reflect the cultural context of the group holding those views. These differences become an important outcome in her results and lead to changes in the program.

The second evaluation is in an international setting, a village in rural Tanzania. A team of U.S. and Tanzanian evaluators and social scientists work to conduct an evaluation of a children's center established for orphans in need in this small village. They encounter cultural differences among the team in ways of communicating and managing the evaluation and occasionally struggle with these differences, hoping to learn from each other's experiences. Most important, they encounter a different culture in Idweli, the small Tanzanian village where the study takes place. The director of the evaluation is able to spend some time in Idweli to get to know the village leaders, the power structure, the individual people, and what they value. His immersion into the culture gives him an awareness of the children and their needs, as well as the views and needs of parents and other caregivers. The relationships he develops ultimately help him to be able to carry out the evaluation while at the same time dealing with a funding source that has different priorities and expectations.

In reading these cases, consider the following:

- What cultural differences is the evaluator encountering?
- What does the evaluator or the evaluation team do to learn more about the culture? Do their activities help or hinder the evaluation?
- Is their evaluation design and data collection adapted to or influenced by the culture?
- Are there other adaptations to the culture that you might have made if you were conducting the evaluation?
- What constraints influenced these evaluators' choices and actions?

Finally, as with the other interviews you have read, consider these questions regarding these two evaluations:

- What is the purpose of each evaluation? How did the evaluator determine that purpose? Who influenced that purpose?
- How did the evaluators involve stakeholders in their evaluation?
- What types of methods did the evaluators use? To what extent were these adapted to the culture in which they were conducting the evaluation?

- How did the evaluators disseminate their results? Who were their primary audiences? How did they differ in their dissemination strategies? To what do you attribute these differences?

REFERENCES

Kirkhart, K. (1995). Seeking multicultural validity: A postcard from the road. *Evaluation Practice, 16,* 1–12.

SenGupta, S., Hopson, R., & Thompson-Robinson, M. (2004). Cultural competence in evaluation: An overview. In M. Thompson-Robinson, R. Hopson, & S. SenGupta (Eds.), *In search of cultural competence in evaluation* (New Directions for Evaluation, No. 102, pp. 5–19). San Francisco: Jossey-Bass.

TWELVE

EVALUATION OF THE FUN WITH BOOKS PROGRAM

An Interview With Katrina Bledsoe

Introduction: At the time of this interview, Katrina Bledsoe was a faculty member in the Psychology Department at The College of New Jersey. She is currently Deputy Director of a national Children's Mental Health Services project, funded by the Substance Abuse and Mental Health Services Administration (SAMHSA), at Walter R. McDonald and Associates, Inc. in Rockville, Maryland. Bledsoe was trained at Claremont Graduate University (CGU) and helped design and coordinate CGU's Master's Program in Evaluation. Although she represents a new generation of evaluators, Bledsoe already has 12 years' experience evaluating community-based education programs, including drug and crime prevention efforts for communities of color and health and education programs. Her recent work has concerned cultural influences on health and leadership development programs for African American managers. She is past chair of the Diversity Committee for the American Evaluation Association. Dr. Bledsoe is also the author of articles featured in journals such as the *American Journal of Evaluation*, and author of chapters in the *Handbook of Ethics for Research in the Social Sciences* (in press), the *International Handbook of Urban Education* (2007), and *When Research Studies Go off the Rails: Solutions and Prevention Strategies* (in press).

The evaluation of the Fun With Books program takes place in Trenton, New Jersey, and Bledsoe, who is new to Trenton and the program, takes some time to learn about the city, the area, and the neighborhood, particularly as she senses major cultural differences between those delivering and those attending the program. She works with program staff to develop program theory and then conducts an evaluation, using some standardized and some new qualitative and quantitative measures, including videotapes of parents and children at the program, to examine immediate program outcomes. Bledsoe and her colleagues make quite a few recommendations for changes in the organization and in the program, and she discusses how her recommendations are used.

Summary of the Evaluation of the Fun With Books Program

Katrina Bledsoe

The College of New Jersey

Literacy is the foundation of learning. Fostering a child's reading success is essential not only for the well being of the individual but also for schools. Children who do not learn to read often have ongoing academic problems such as in comprehension and writing and subsequent employment problems later in life. The Children's Home Society of New Jersey (CHS) asked the Evaluation Research Team at The College of New Jersey to conduct an evaluation of the Fun with Books program at CHS. The evaluation explored the extent to which the program encouraged the basics of school success, such as intellectual competence, motivational qualities, and socio-emotional skills.

The Team examined best practices in preliteracy instruction, child outcomes in literacy achievement, and general approaches to preliteracy instruction in community-based literacy programs. The study focused on four areas: Does the Fun with Books program lead to an increase in (1) in-home reading between parent and child? (2) the child's motivation to learn? (3) the child's capacity to learn? (4) the child's opportunity to learn?

Program Description

The Fun with Books program began in 1999. Fun with Books is part of a larger umbrella program called the Family and Children Early Education Services (FACES). The program has four areas of concentration: health/behavioral health, parent education, child care, and family literacy. Fun with Books was designed to address the last area, family literacy.

Fun with Books is an interactive family literacy program that uses children's literature and music to support the development of preliteracy and school readiness skills in young children. The then six-week program was offered to families in Trenton and the surrounding communities that had at least one child in the age group between birth and six years; however, older siblings also participated in the programs. The program further supports parent–child bonding and provides cognitive stimulation to children through reading and interactive activities. Parents are shown how to make reading a fun part of their daily activities at home. Families are also provided dinner and an opportunity to interact with their children in a constructive manner.

Activities consist of parents and staff reviewing the book of the week and exploring the book's theme. There are structured arts, craft, and music activities in which parents engage with their young children. The activity and music are designed to highlight the theme of the book. At the end of each session, parents are encouraged to read the story with their child. With every week's attendance, each family is given the book to add to their home library. Each week the program focuses on various themes that directly relate to an area of literacy development (e.g., colors, food, sounds, shapes, numbers, and animals). The final session serves to connect all the themes discussed during the program's duration.

The primary goals of the program are to encourage parents to read to their children at home throughout the week, enhance parent–child interaction, and provide activities that support cognitive development and preliteracy in young children. The program is concerned not only with literacy but also with providing an outlet for families to socialize with other families. Two instructors, a lead teacher, and an assistant facilitate the program. In addition, one to two volunteers from local business and community organizations in Mercer County assist with program activities.

Methodology of the Evaluation

The original methodological approach of the project was conceptualized as a nonexperimental pre-test/post-test. Data were gathered from approximately 10 staff members and administrators, 17 families, and 31 children on a variety of measures including surveys, videotaped observations, interviews, and focus groups. These measures were designed to obtain attitudinal, behavioral, and contextual data. They included a parent survey, a child social awareness assessment, several observational measures, and interview questions. Participants were assessed within the context of the program. Archival data searches were also conducted to obtain historical and organizational information.

General Program Results

Parent survey data and staff interviews indicated that families engage in reading, playtime, and other related interactive activities outside the program and are motivated to read together. However, the evaluation was unable to determine whether these behaviors changed during the program. Parent surveys, staff interviews, and observational data also indicated that Fun with Books provides children with an opportunity to gain preliteracy skills (e.g., provided access to books, provided time and space to engage in reading) and that children are interested in books. Child observation data indicated that children are attending to the stories being read.

Program and Evaluation Recommendations

Recommendations were provided to the organization at the program and evaluation levels. Results and postevaluation meetings indicated that the program staff and administration should clearly identify the program strategies for staff and participants; that staff should provide information and training to volunteers who work with the clients about the program and its goals; that the program should be longer, perhaps X weeks rather than the current Y weeks; and finally, that the program should use school readiness measures to monitor progress.

Recommendations for program evaluation included formulating an internal/external evaluation team that would be primarily responsible for developing and updating strategies for program improvement as well as evaluation, benchmarking other family literacy programs, and conducting regular process and outcome evaluation on an annual basis.

Project Conclusion

The data collected suggested that Fun with Books is a successful endeavor for CHS, demonstrating that the organization was committed to developing and delivering innovative and responsive programming. Yet the evaluation could not truly determine if in-home reading was being accomplished or was increasing over the long term. The evaluation team felt that there was much room for improvement, if not in the actual program strategies, in the *articulation* of these strategies. That is, much of the continued success was contingent on being able to establish consistency in program delivery across staff members by automating and standardizing program strategies such as types of games played and music used, as well as developing a strategy for evaluation.

Dialogue With Katrina Bledsoe

Jody Fitzpatrick

————◆◆◆————

Fitzpatrick: Katrina, you work with The College of New Jersey evaluation team conducting evaluations in a variety of settings in Trenton and the mid-Atlantic. Is this evaluation typical of the evaluations that your organization conducts?

Bledsoe: It is typical of the evaluations I conduct within the context of my position. Much of my work is community-based, grassroots work with small organizations. Even if the evaluation is multisite, it's grassroots.

Fitzpatrick: I asked you to identify an evaluation in which cultural competence was a factor. So, unlike many of the other interviews in the book, I put some constraints on your choice for the interview. Nevertheless, I'm still curious about your selection of this evaluation. What did you find particularly intriguing about this evaluation?

Bledsoe: The Fun with Books evaluation illustrates the politics of the community itself. The city of Trenton is complex and political, and it's hard to divorce the cultural and contextual aspects of it from the evaluation. The politics and socioeconomic differences of the community were a real draw for me on this evaluation. The project involved working with people who are benevolent and blending that with the reality of the situation of Trenton and the consumers with whom they were working. There is a large disparity between those doing the service planning and those receiving the services.

Trenton is a small city and, in many ways, a much closed one. You really need to know the history of the city to understand the politics of the situation. I believe that in any evaluation, it's good to know the history, but in this case, knowing the history, background, and context was critical.

Fitzpatrick: Well, let's learn a little bit about that context. How did the evaluation first begin? Who contacted you about conducting the evaluation and what were their interests?

Bledsoe: How I became the evaluator is a little odd. It started in 2002. I had just completed graduate school and had accepted an academic position at The College of New Jersey as a community cultural psychologist. People knew I wanted to connect with community-based organizations, because of my interest and because of my position. One of my colleagues was giving me a tour of the host organization's facilities. I was on-site about 10 minutes when the CEO said, "Oh, my gosh, you *do* evaluation! We have this amazing program. It's our flagship program. It's one of the most successful we run. People keep coming. It would be great to have an assessment of it. Would you be interested?" And I was, of course, willing. Although family literacy was not my area of expertise, the program seemed related to my emphasis. Additionally, it seemed like an opportunity for me to get to know the area. So, within 10 minutes after I arrived at the organization, I was handed an evaluation! In that city, there aren't *six* degrees of separation—it's more like two!

Fitzpatrick: So you were already seeing that Trenton was different. What else did you learn about Trenton that was important to the evaluation and made you aware that cultural competence was going to be important?

Bledsoe: I was the least savvy of the evaluation team about Trenton, so in addition to reading historical documents, I also drove around—to places people tell you not to go. I thought, "I'll drive around and look at places where I can get out and walk around and not be too conspicuous."

Fitzpatrick: What did you learn from that?

Bledsoe: Between reading about the history, taking tours of historical establishments, and driving around, I began to understand Trenton's background. Trenton is a community of 92,000 people with a median household income of $32,000. It's the state capital of New Jersey and has a rich history. The battle that turned the Revolutionary War around for the United States, the Battle of Trenton, was fought here. Back in the 1930s until the late 1960s, Trenton was a vibrant area. Because it was a large manufacturing area, it provided a substantial percentage of employment for working-class people. Large companies such as Champale, the champagne company, and Lennox, the china company, were all in Trenton.

Now, all of those businesses have either moved to other areas or have been outsourced to other countries. By the mid-70s Trenton had experienced a tremendous downturn. Essentially, the people and organizations with the jobs and money left the people with no such resources to fend for themselves. Once that break occurred, it was easy to see who owned the resources and who didn't. White flight began. As the years wore on, although it is the state capital and the governing body is there, Trenton became associated with crime, poverty, and gang activity. Now, people don't want to go there because it seems to have little going for it, except for city government and social services. You can conduct your daily activities in the next township over and never see Trenton, although in some cases it is only five minutes away from middle- and upper-middle class neighborhoods. In some parts, there are magnificent homes, but in other parts, there are some of the most dilapidated homes I've ever seen. This just highlights the significant divide between the powerful and the powerless, the rich and the poor, the whites and the communities of color.

I also learned a lot about the residents. Many own their own homes, but not because they personally paid them off. They're the offspring of people who were, at one time, middle class. Years ago, you could be of any background, arrive in Trenton, get a manufacturing job, and be of the middle class. Now, you have the *formerly* middle class's offspring, who don't have the opportunity to get the jobs, thereby leading to a high unemployment rate—about 11%. So to understand why you have a Fun with Books program, you have to understand Trenton's history and cultural and socioeconomic climate.

Fitzpatrick: What particular problems or strengths do these residents who are poor, but were raised in better circumstances, present for a program like Fun with Books?

Bledsoe: On the positive side, I think residents bring a true desire to achieve the same financial, political, educational, and personal successes that exist in more affluent areas. On the challenge side, they bring astute knowledge that they are not being treated fairly by the county and the state, in comparison to how people are treated in other cities with higher median incomes. I think Fun with Books' greatest challenge is in trying to view the participants as equals, with similar values. It's difficult given the socioeconomic disparity. Yet, the participants *are* the same, with the same desires for access to quality resources.

Fitzpatrick: Who were the key audiences for your evaluation and what did they hope to learn from it? Were other stakeholders involved in the evaluation?

Bledsoe: The staff of the program, the Board and the CEO, and the top administrators of the organization were all audiences for the evaluation. Additionally, there were several external consultants who had been consulted about evaluation of the program, and were evaluators by identification but weren't performing the evaluation, who were interested in our findings. The staff wanted validation of what they were doing, of course, since they were the frontline service providers. The administrators also wanted validation. They had altruistic motivations, but they realized they would receive additional funding if they could show success. I think that happens with any evaluation.

Fitzpatrick: That people want to show success?

Bledsoe: Let me clarify that statement. I think people like to show what they want to show with an evaluation. If they want a program to be successful, they want the evaluation to demonstrate findings that justify the existence and continued support of the program. Conversely, if they do not want a program to continue, they want the findings to support that justification. In the case of most of the organizations with which I work, they are looking for validation to continue services and funding.

Fitzpatrick: What actions did you think were important during the planning stage of the evaluation?

Bledsoe: My first focus was on identifying who was invested in the evaluation. I've learned from my experiences in community-based work that you have to get to know people to build trust, especially when you're working with people who don't receive the services to which they are entitled. We spent time at the organization and in the community. We had several meetings, some of them informal. We also attended a few sessions of the program we evaluated, just as observers. During our meetings, we did try to make some decisions about the services they thought they were offering. We explored the program, the historical documents, and some documents that weren't directly related to the program. We wanted a "big picture" understanding of the organization and the context in which it was operating. We balanced that with understanding the theoretical grounding behind their work. But the key was getting to know the invested stakeholders. We wanted them to feel they had our attention, trust, and honest interest.

Fitzpatrick: I noticed you developed a conceptual model of the Fun with Books program. Can you tell us about developing that model?

Bledsoe: We spent some time looking into the literature. My colleague is a developmental psychologist, and since we were looking at kids ages 0 to 6, I relied on him to understand the developmental theory behind that age group. We also spent a lot of time in meetings with staff and administrators working to articulate the program theory. People would say, "We *know* this works! We see that parents are reading with their kids during the program!" And we would counter, "Okay, but what do you want them to walk away with when they leave the program at night? Reading skills? What's the long-term outcome?" We had four or five months of weekly meetings trying to articulate what they wanted parents and kids to leave with after their night at the program and upon what foundations they were resting the objectives. They would often answer the latter part of the question with the statement "We know the literature." I would counter with the question "What literature? There's a lot of literature out there." They would say, for instance, "Well, cognitive stimulation is important in encouraging children to read." And I'd say, "What does cognitive stimulation look like?" I was really adamant about that. I wanted to know exact, measurable definitions.

So that's how we developed the models—talking with administrators and staff in the organization and using the literature to validate their assertions. Their external consultant had a background in educational evaluation and assisted us in trying to put pressure on the organization to articulate a program theory. The process was somewhat complicated because people were caught up in the denotative and connotative meanings of words. In graduate school, it was much easier for me if I could see a visual model because I really resonate with visuals and pictures. So I said, "Would it help you to articulate what you mean if I drew it on a piece of paper?" Our stakeholders seemed to respond to that strategy. We went through about five iterations, and we could have gone through more, but at the time, the model we decided upon seemed to demonstrate what we thought was a realistic program process, considering no model had been articulated prior to this exercise.

Who was involved? The stakeholders—the program director, the CEO of the organization, the external consultant, and some of the staff members. So, between all the parties involved, we were able to decide upon a model. But it was no easy task.

Fitzpatrick: How did you decide on the purpose of your evaluation and, specifically, your eight evaluation questions? Do you always have this many questions?

Bledsoe: What drove the question development were the abstract assertions of the organization. Statements such as "increases cognitive stimulation" and "increases motivation to learn" sounded informed, but when it came to concrete measurement, there was none. So a lot of our questions were derived from these abstract processes and outcomes that were said to be common developmental psychological science, but they had no data to support whether these outcomes were being obtained.

For me, the number of questions to use depends on the organization and what they think they want. People have a thousand questions. But I try to limit those questions to the ones they are really tied to. So I may or may not use a high number of evaluation questions. This organization really wanted to know a great deal of information because they didn't have any information on the program. "People keep coming back," they insisted. But they wanted to know *why*. The other need they had was to have a program that was based upon "scientific" concepts. They wanted to say that "science" drove their findings and, by extension, drives the program. So the questions were developed from the literature as well as from what the client wanted to know.

Fitzpatrick: So they saw evaluation as science and science driving this. I know many clients and funders think that way. Do you find it necessary to deal with that perception?

Bledsoe: Absolutely, especially since "science" seems to be the battle cry of governments and funders, meaning if the program is supported by science, then it must be okay. I haven't been able to do one evaluation of late without having to address the use of science to drive the evaluation. Now, what people understand about science driving an evaluation is quite limited. Many don't understand the data-driven aspect of evaluation, and still others have a limited understanding of what qualifies as results driven by data. That's probably the hardest conversation I have with clients, when I tell them that we have nothing to show unless we have concrete answers from their consumers. Sometimes that talk resembles a therapy session.

Fitzpatrick: Did you become aware that cultural competency was a concern during the planning stage? If so, how did it emerge then?

Bledsoe: We did know that cultural competency was going to be a concern. You can't drive into Trenton and not realize that there's a cultural, socioeconomic issue. Immediately, when we arrived to do the evaluation, the organization said, "We have this program, Fun with Books," and probably the second or third sentence was, "The population is low-income, primarily black and Latino parents, some who work and some who don't." That ethnic culture and socioeconomic divide became clear immediately. California, where I'm from, addresses the issue of race/ethnicity very differently. There, it's covert. On the East Coast, you have a lot of different people in a small space. Race and ethnicity are out there. People sometimes say something wrong, something offensive with little knowledge and, sometimes, with little regret. I'd have staff workers of the program who would start a statement with "This is the way this group lives, interacts, etc." And they would feel comfortable with those statements and stereotypes. Because they had been working with a particular underserved group for some time, the staff felt they were making accurate assessments about a particular ethnic or socioeconomic group.

Fitzpatrick: So you saw the clients were low income and that raised the cultural competency concern?

Bledsoe: Definitely. The minute they began describing their clientele and I noticed that the staff was predominately white, socioeconomically stable, and *not* from Trenton, I thought, "This is going to be a challenge." Additionally, knowing the history of Trenton, including its issues with ethnic culture and socioeconomic status, we knew we were going to have to start thinking about what it meant to be "culturally competent," especially in relation to education and literacy. We know that many of our undereducated populations in the United States are usually, although not always, associated with underserved ethnic groups, since the system usually fails those communities first and foremost. Now, when I say "culturally competent," I mean having the ability to understand what you know about the groups you're working with, having a good understanding of the cultural milieu, and also understanding when you don't get it and being willing to admit that fact and learn.

Fitzpatrick: You've discussed the demographics and differences between Trenton and its suburbs. Those differences involve both economic and racial or ethnic differences. Did you feel you and your staff had the cultural skills and experiences to evaluate and work with this program? What strengths did you bring? What deficits?

Bledsoe: We were, in some ways, very culturally competent and aware, but in other ways we struggled. The co-principal investigator and I are both African American. Our five undergraduate students were white. The counseling graduate student, who also was white, had been working with a fair number of diverse populations. The undergraduate students were from our college, but because of the reputation of Trenton—some of which is not undeserved—hadn't spent time there. My co-principal investigator and I have a lot of understanding of low-income groups, not because we are African American but because we have worked with a lot of low-income groups. We felt we had that competency, and because of our developmental and methodological backgrounds, we felt we had the skills to do the evaluation. What competencies we lacked, and had to overcome, were that we were not from the Trenton community and were not *actually* low income. Our not being native Trentonians, however, was the standout issue.

Another issue was the heterogeneity *within* the ethnic groups. You can look around and say, "Everyone's black, or everyone's Latino, or everyone's

Eastern European." But within those groups, there are notable differences. For instance, Jamaicans have a very, very different culture from Gambians. Your stereotypes don't work in the long run. We sometimes assumed that because we were African Americans, we would have immediate rapport with the black community, if not other communities of color, because we share the receipt of similar stereotypes based on ethnicity and race. Yet that was an erroneous assumption because it did not consider other issues that might interact with race and ethnicity, such as socioeconomic status.

Additionally, we didn't anticipate the economic disparity between the clients and the program staff and the impact of that disparity on the program. Trenton is in the middle of one of the wealthiest counties in the country. The average income in the county is $80,000, and as I mentioned earlier, in Trenton it is $32,000. About 25% of the city's resources are devoted to providing social services such as shelters, social programs, food banks, and so on. There are a lot of people driving in and providing social services and driving out. We weren't prepared for the politics surrounding the "haves and have-nots." We weren't prepared for the psychological influence that knowing that information had on the consumers and the staff. We really had to come to an understanding about that issue.

Fitzpatrick: That economic difference—between those served on the one hand and program staff and evaluators on the other—often exists in programs we evaluate. What can evaluators do to help bridge the gap? How do you, with more education and more resources, become culturally competent in the issues that concern clients?

Bledsoe: I've found the best way to become culturally competent is to go to where people live. Spend time with them, in their daily situations. You can't read a book and assume that you know what to expect or that you will understand the cultural nuances. Likewise, you can't be of a similar background and assume that your experiences are identical. It's important that you make an effort to get involved with your clients, at least on some level.

Finally, I believe it really helps to have a key informant, someone who is part of the community being served and has entrée into its gates. That person serves as a guide, if not your credible reference to gaining access. Additionally, that person can serve as a translator of the culture. I'd like to think that I am always culturally competent, but I'm not. I miss things, and I am sometimes unconsciously and sometimes consciously biased. Admitting that bias and monitoring it helps me to inch closer to accurately representing the situation, and the clients, rather than what I think should be the case.

Fitzpatrick: You chose a mix of quantitative and qualitative approaches—for example, surveys of parents, interviews with staff, videotapes of parent-child interaction, but your approach is primarily quantitative. How did you go about deciding what measures to use?

Bledsoe: Well, I would say we chose a quantitative approach to provide numerical data, but the most interesting explanations of that numerical data came from the qualitative data. That is, although we approached the data collection on specific constructs and questions from a quantitative perspective, our most interesting information came from the interviews and unofficial postevaluative meetings.

When we first began the process of choosing measures, we had a lot of discussion amongst our team about what would be realistic. I relied quite a bit on my colleague in developmental psychology. What are the measures we should use to assess the behaviors and attitudes of kids and their parents? He gave us some background in the area based upon his approaches and his research. We also explored the literature. What seems reasonable or similar to what we're exploring in the current situation? Finally, we talked with the staff and found that they also wanted to be able to share their experiences. We decided that interviews and meetings might be the best methods for getting at those experiences.

Fitzpatrick: You identified some of your measures, the parent survey and the parent-child interactive inventories, from research. Others were developed specifically for this project. Tell us about using that mix. Is that something you do often in evaluations? Why did you choose to use that mix in this particular evaluation?

Bledsoe: I admit that I do "mix and match" previously developed measures with those that the team develops. Since a lot of my work is community based, it makes sense. Communities can differ greatly from one another, and although there are universals that can be assessed with known measures across communities, some aspects cannot and need measures developed specifically for the situation and for the evaluation.

The reason we chose to mix and match previously developed inventories with our own was that for some of the aspects for which we wanted to gather information, such as social awareness of the child, there was no previous information from which to draw. So we assessed the situation and tried to design items that we thought would be representative of the concepts we were after.

Fitzpatrick: You encountered some problems in collecting the data, in particular a much reduced sample size for the post measures. What happened?

Bledsoe: For the record, this is why people don't like doing community-based projects—because they're not perfect, they're messy. We put together a design with which we *thought* people would be able to comply. The only problem, though we were warned, was we occasionally lost people. We would start out with a group and do some pre-test measures, but then, we wouldn't get the same group back to do post-test measures. One, maybe two, weeks you would have a group of parents, and then they wouldn't be there. They wouldn't return for a variety of reasons: transportation issues, young parents, parents who are working. All of these reasons created legitimate problems in attendance. So when we started reviewing the data, we realized we had more surveys on the front end of the evaluation than on the back end.

Fitzpatrick: What types of data, in the end, did you find most informative?

Bledsoe: To be honest, I would say that the interviews that we did were *very* telling. We gathered a lot of different information from the staff about the program, the organization, and the consumers. I also thought that some of the data we collected from the children on the Social Awareness Scale were useful. The Social Awareness Scale gave us the opportunity to assess whether or not kids were "cognitively aware" enough to actively participate in the program. (Remember, the program is for children ages 0–6.)

The observations were also very telling. We videotaped the parents and kids at the program, and being able to assess the interactions between the child and the parent was invaluable. Those observations allowed us to see the smaller picture—how the family interacted while reading, how kids responded to their parents and vice versa, and so forth. From this we could draw some conclusions about parenting skills.

Fitzpatrick: The observation data suggested the parents weren't interacting with their kids at the program as much as I thought they would be.

Bledsoe: No, they weren't. We saw some interaction, but part of the reason behind this lack of interaction was related to how the parents viewed the program. The program sponsored dinner for the participants, and it was also an opportunity to meet other parents. Additionally, there was a facilitator for the kids. Some people, not all, viewed it as "Whew! I don't have to do anything. The facilitator is doing it." Once, we watched a young mom and a young dad, single parents, talking. We joked, "They're 'hooking up' over there." In many ways it was a time for people to relax. They wanted to spend some time with their kids, yes. But, parents didn't interact with their children as much as the staff would have hoped.

This issue highlights the many competing goals of the program. The program serves a variety of purposes—reducing parents' stress, getting parents to read with their children, identifying social services needs for families, meeting new people.

Fitzpatrick: Your summary table of results indicates that with the exception of the major goal, increasing in-home reading, the other goals of the program were achieved. I found the summary table to be a really useful device for summarizing results to stakeholders with the three columns of evaluation question, evaluative conclusion, and explanation. But do you feel the data were sufficient to conclude that each of those goals was achieved?

Bledsoe: We wanted to synthesize data that we thought would help us to reach an evaluative conclusion. There was some bristling by the organization's CEO about our reluctance to draw a positive conclusion about whether the program led to increased in-home reading. Originally our conclusion was "No." But when the CEO voiced concern at making that conclusion, we finally decided that "Inconclusive" would be a nice, palatable word. We had nothing concrete to show that an increase in at-home reading had occurred, so we didn't want to say it did.

Our main instrument, the parent survey, was not as helpful as we had hoped. We felt there was some measurement error, so we found it more revealing to rely on the staff interviews and other measures. Although there are useful data to be to be mined out of the evaluation, there were parts of the parent survey that even when read to the participants, they didn't understand.

Fitzpatrick: Why do you think they didn't get it?

Bledsoe: I think the definitions we were using, although we would state what we thought they meant, didn't resonate with the participants. They weren't coming from that abstract perspective. They rejected our standards. That is, they rejected our operational definitions. For instance, we didn't place a high emphasis on grocery shopping as a family as a way to have quality interaction with a child. But a lot of parents considered that chore family-bonding time. In some cases, it was the only time the whole family was together. So we really had to reconceptualize what *family interaction* meant.

Fitzpatrick: Do you think that's a cultural difference?

Bledsoe: I think it is, in terms of socioeconomic status and social class. There *are* cultural differences. People didn't *rebel* against the "standard." They feel, "That's just not *my* standard." People would say, "This is Trenton, not Princeton."

Fitzpatrick: Is it ever the role of the evaluator to get them to accept that standard?

Bledsoe: It depends on if following the standard is in the best interest of the group. But then, that's a judgment call, and maybe that's not *your* call. Sometimes though, there is a place for advocacy, whether on behalf of the organization or on behalf of the consumers. Sometimes I do become an advocate. In those cases, I become the internal evaluator and hire an external evaluator.

In the case of the Fun with Books program, I was not an advocate. For instance, the staff wanted to discourage spanking, but acceptance of spanking varies from culture to culture. In Trenton, spanking will get you a free trip to Child Protective Services. Sometimes parents said to the staff, "Why are you getting on me about that? That's how I control my child." As evaluators, we would say, "We're not going to make a judgment call, but if you're going to spank here, Child Protective Services is going to be on you." An evaluator can take on that role of advocate of a "standard" on behalf of either the consumer or a high-level stakeholder if there's a grave injustice being committed, but when the evaluator takes on that role, a level of objectivity is compromised. In the case of the Fun with Books evaluation, there was no need for us to take on that role.

Fitzpatrick: Some evaluators make use of criteria to define success. Did you consider that? Or how did you decide what was success?

Bledsoe: Early on, we did develop criteria. But that was later discouraged, not on our part but on the part of the organization. We described criteria, and they said, "We can't do that. We really can't say." So we decided against using criteria. For instance, the organization was really focused on the concept of cognitive stimulation. I asked, "Can we measure that? How would we know that children are being cognitively stimulated? How can you tell a three-month-old is being stimulated when parents read to him/her? What does that look like?" People said, "You're making this way too hard!" So we discarded the idea of criteria for those abstract concepts.

Fitzpatrick: So tell me more about your negotiations with the clients over the findings in the report on at-home reading. You felt you should report that there was no increase, but they bickered with you. What did you do then? What should the role of the evaluator be? Did you feel you were changing your results?

Bledsoe: We politely told them that we'd be willing to consider alternative wording, but we would not be able to say anything that remotely resembled an accomplishment of the overarching goal of in-home reading. I didn't feel as if we were changing the results per se, because the information provided really was inconclusive. So that was a fair and comfortable compromise for me.

I believe the role of the evaluator changes depending on the situation. I think the role is multifaceted. Sometimes you're the judge and jury. Other times you're a facilitator. Still other times, you're an advocate. And still others, you may find yourself involved in program development. It depends on the context, the resources, and the desires of the stakeholders. To limit evaluators to one facet of the position is to disregard the complexity of it.

Fitzpatrick: Your recommendations address problems common to many programs: staff members, participants, and volunteers not knowing what program goals are; changing the program with each delivery for a variety of reasons, including changing goals; serving a broader group, children aged 0 to 6, than may be possible with one strategy. Yet many evaluations miss these problems in their focus on outcome data. One great thing about your evaluation is that you identified these problems. Tell us how you learned about these problem areas.

Bledsoe: We learned people had little idea of what the program goals were. If they did, their goals really differed from board members', administrators', providers', and clients' goals. Goals ranged from giving more love, to feeling love, to reading more, to eliminating stress. People were operating with different mind-sets. As a result, those different goals prompted the staff and others to use varying program strategies.

We learned the most about these differences in interviews and in informal settings. We had postevaluative meetings in which all the high-level stakeholders discussed the results. In those meetings, people confessed, "You know, I thought about it, and we didn't ask XYZ," or "I didn't know what the concept we put forth really meant." So we started to reflect, prior to the final report. We found that we missed a lot in the evaluation; however, if we did the evaluation now, we would still miss a lot. It's just the nature of the program and its context. We would still need those informal and postevaluative meetings.

Fitzpatrick: Did the differing cultural perceptions and backgrounds of staff, volunteers, and parents affect these issues of program goals and implementation?

Bledsoe: I think they did. I think some of the staff viewed the program from a social service perspective because providing social services is what they did for a living. Additionally, they didn't live in Trenton. Some went home to very wealthy homes or to homes that didn't resemble the inner city. For staff, the thought was "Everyone in Trenton is so downtrodden." As a result they saw the program's focus as providing social services. Volunteers also saw it as a social service endeavor because they wanted to be benevolent. They needed a cause. That's not a negative, but when you have a cause, and when you're trying to be benevolent, you sometimes want to help people improve so they can adhere to your standards. Some volunteers voiced a sentiment that was similar to "I really want to help them learn how to adhere to the white standard."

The parents liked the staff and volunteers who worked in the program, but they were acutely aware of the economic and ethnic/culture differences. Most of the staff were white and middle class. Most of the clients were black and Latino, lower class, and, in some cases, at poverty level. The clients knew they were underserved and that they were at a disadvantage. But parents weren't saying, "I'm looking for love from Fun with Books." But the volunteers and some of the staff were thinking, "These clients and their kids need love. I'm going to give it to them." So the parents who came to have dinner with their kids and other parents thought, "Hey, I just came from my minimum wage job. I just want to relax and have fun." And the staff and volunteers thought, "These people need love and help in trying to provide their kids with needed skills to enhance reading." That cultural divide contributed to different views of the purpose of the program.

Fitzpatrick: What did parents think the purpose was?

Bledsoe: They saw it as an opportunity to get together with other families, a chance to de-stress, spend some times with their kids, meet other people, and, occasionally, arrange for help in some way. They saw it as more of a social support, rather than a program to teach their kids to read. They seemed to feel, "If my kids learn how to read earlier, that's great." But they were there for family bonding, cooking, and social support from other parents. If you asked the administrators, the organization wanted to make an impact on literacy. That definitely didn't translate to the parents. It translated somewhat to staff, but that was dependent upon whom you asked.

Fitzpatrick: Do you think that all have to have the same vision of the goal in order for the kids' literacy to increase? Sometimes to get the target audience to participate, you have to make it appealing. I recall reading years ago that the goal of Foster Grandparent programs was really to provide a social outlet and purpose for the seniors.

Bledsoe: I agree that in many cases you want to make the program appealing to clients. They don't always have to know what the underlying goals are to achieve them. In this case, in-home reading leading to literacy was the goal.

Parents needed to be invested in the program goals to carry out the strategies long term, away from the organization, and without prompting. They needed "buy-in" to the goals, and that perceived buy-in wasn't there outside of the program.

Fitzpatrick: You ultimately recommend further training of both staff and volunteers—on the program itself but also sensitivity training on these culture issues to "make them aware of the unique perspectives of the clientele the program serves and help to dispel myths and stereotypes that could alter the quality of service to the families." You also recommend an orientation for parents to make them more aware of the purposes of the program. These types of recommendations, particularly those about staff, can be difficult. What actions did you take to increase the likelihood that these recommendations, and others, would be used?

Bledsoe: We were very fortunate. We knew the organization wanted to make changes to the program. There was already discussion among staff, not so much among parents, that people did not understand other people. The organization knew that the staff had certain ways of viewing the world and that they needed to move past those views. We just amplified that belief, and that made addressing recommendations such as increased cultural competence easier. To increase the likelihood that they would implement the recommendations, we couched them in terms of what they *could* do. To the board members and the administrators we said, "This is doable. It shouldn't be as difficult a transition for you as it might be for other organizations. You're already on the way to doing such and such." All in all, they were a pretty savvy organization. They were primed for utilization. They just needed evidence to corroborate their perceptions.

Fitzpatrick: The eight evaluation questions stated at the beginning are all outcome questions with no hint of a formative focus. Yet the most useful part of the report seems to be the recommendations for change and improvement. Was this a surprise?

Bledsoe: Not really. As we began data collection, we realized that we would be providing recommendations for changes and improvement rather than providing real concrete evidence of the accomplishment of the larger goal. In many ways, the recommendations were perhaps the most important part of the report, especially since the organization felt that they were in a position to execute them.

Fitzpatrick: Have the results of your evaluation, your recommendations and findings, been used?

Bledsoe: Yes, the organization has changed the length of the program in the manner we recommended, making it longer in terms of number of weeks offered. Additionally, they are in the process of developing school readiness measures. They have also divided up the zero-to-six age range. Now, they do a zero-to-three program. We suggested they identify the program strategy, and they have done that by hiring a person to fully *develop* a program strategy. They also spend more time with volunteers to orient them to the purpose of the program and to the clients. They also developed an internal evaluation team, as we suggested. That evaluator has now been there a couple of years. Our main stakeholder, the director of Fun with Books, had been collecting some demographics on the program clients prior to the evaluator's arrival, but now the organization does regular tracking.

Like many programs, Fun with Books thought they were unique. Prior to beginning the evaluation, I went online and found other programs similar to the one they hosted. By the time the report debuted, they were asking, "What are other people doing?"

Fitzpatrick: One of the great things about evaluation is that we always reflect on what we would have done differently. No evaluation ever goes exactly as planned. If you had this evaluation to do again, what would you do differently?

Bledsoe: I would be more flexible. For instance, the major challenge we faced was with data collection. Data collection on the project made me cry, literally. My colleague said, "You're going to have to pull yourself together. We are doing the best we can to gather both pre and post data." I said, "People aren't showing up! They're not coming back! What can we do? Our design is ruined!" At the time, this was my *first* major community-based evaluation. I thought, "We came up with the simplest design *ever*, and we can't even do that!" Over the years though, I've become a *lot* more flexible.

If I were to do the evaluation now, I would still try to pursue the pre-tests and post-tests, but I would explore how to do it outside of the context we were given.

Finally, I would review the evaluation questions more thoroughly and stand my ground on not measuring all of them since I never particularly wanted them all anyway. I still like the major outcome question (increasing in-home reading) and the question concerning parents and children participating in interactive activities together. Additionally, the question concerning children exhibiting an interest in books is still of great interest.

Fitzpatrick: What did you learn about evaluation from doing this study?

Bledsoe: As I mentioned earlier, this was my first evaluation when I arrived in The College of New Jersey and Trenton. I learned that community-based evaluation is not easy. In graduate school, I wasn't the principal investigator. This study really stretched me to understand communities. I often think about the conversation I had with Huey Chen about evaluation being part science and part art. You can't get to the science until you've done the art. The art is important.

I also learned that one evaluation approach does not fit all. We had planned in advance that we would use several approaches, but how those approaches were used was very different than we anticipated. I have been a proponent of the theory-based/theory-driven approach for some time now. I still am, but I find that participatory approaches are particularly useful in the kind of work I do. Truthfully, you go with the flow. Approaches are helpful, yes. But you also realize that in one situation you're going to need one approach, in another, an even different approach.

I also learned that utilization is possible. Organizational learning is possible. But to achieve both, relationships are key. Every evaluator wants to get to the truth, whatever truth that is. But you really have to develop a relationship with people to get them to the point where they can tell you the truth. Even if their truth doesn't match the so-called "objective" truth, they may be willing to tell it to you.

Finally, I learned that cultural competency is necessary in most evaluative situations. Just about every evaluation requires you to consider the cultural standards and the cultural boundaries. For example, if you're doing an evaluation on the effectiveness of an Internet technology program, you have to think about the culture of the organization or community that is hosting that program. If most of your clients are, for example, women, or are immigrants, you have to consider what the Internet means to them (e.g., What cultural value does the Internet have to immigrants? What is it used for in that culture?). It's going to mean something different to every person and every culture.

Fitzpatrick's Commentary

Dr. Bledsoe gives us insight into the evaluation of a program where cultural competency among staff and evaluators was critical. She describes her efforts to learn about Trenton and how its history and culture influence the characteristics of the clients served and to learn about the clients themselves. Furthermore, she talks about her own views of cultural competence. Although she is African American, as are many of the clients, her education and socioeconomic status were different from that of the program participants. She states that cultural competence is "having the ability to understand what you know about the groups you're working with, having a good understanding of the cultural milieu, and also understanding when you don't get it and being willing to admit that fact and learn." She works to understand more but realizes that she doesn't know everything and works to continue learning. As she demonstrates, learning is central to the task of evaluation. Ultimately, she works to help the organization improve cultural competence among their staff in a productive way. But, as she notes, cultural competence arises in almost every evaluation. The people being served by the program can differ from the evaluator and the team. Those differences are important to acknowledge and explore in order to effectively evaluate the program. An evaluator needs to examine his or her own experiences and consider how the experiences and views of those she is working with may differ from her own. Ethical considerations can emerge when program goals conflict with the cultural expectations of either a client or a staff group. The confusion over program goals and, hence, program activities seen here is influenced by the different cultures of the groups.

Dr. Bledsoe is also frank in talking about the goals of the administrators in conducting the evaluation. As in many evaluations, the administrators want the evaluation to show that their program succeeds. They think it is great. Many people attend and others come back for more. It must work! Dealing with these expectations is another important element in the craft of evaluation. Evaluators need to work with clients throughout the process to help them recognize that, in all likelihood, the evaluation will reveal some successes and some failures. Dr. Bledsoe works toward this by helping them develop a logic model to articulate what they are hoping to do. This discussion, and others, helped them recognize their differing views of clients and program goals. Nevertheless, some conflict occurs over the ultimate findings of the evaluation, and Dr. Bledsoe reaches a compromise that she feels comfortable with by reporting that the findings on in-home reading, a critical goal, were "inconclusive" rather than her original conclusion that the goal was not achieved. The Guiding Principles of the American Evaluation Association can often be helpful in working with clients both at the beginning of the project, to acquaint the client with our professional obligations and standards, and at points of disagreement. (See Morris, 2007, for ethical cases and responses by evaluators showing the differing approaches to such conflicts.)

Ultimately, Dr. Bledsoe finds that, although her primary approach was quantitative, her most useful data were the qualitative data, interviews with parents and staff, and observations and videotapes of parent–child interactions. These data helped identify some program successes that were not evident in the survey data. Also, a study that began as one to substantiate outcomes becomes a formative one with recommendations for program improvement.

This evaluation showed great strengths in use. Several specific changes were brought about as a result of the evaluation, from lengthening the program to narrowing the age of children served, to cultural competency training for staff and volunteers, to an orientation for parents. Part of the purpose of both training and orientation efforts was to clarify program goals. Another import impact of the evaluation was that it made program administrators and staff aware of other similar programs, and they began to seek information on them. Such actions led to long-term learning and change. Finally, the value of the evaluation was shown in the organization's hiring of an ongoing, internal evaluator to assist with future efforts.

DISCUSSION QUESTIONS

1. What does Bledsoe do to learn more about the culture of Trenton? How do these activities improve her cultural competence?

2. Think of a program that you are familiar with that might require you to stretch or work to achieve sufficient cultural competence to effectively evaluate that program. What might you do to gain cultural competence? Under what circumstances do you think it would be appropriate for you to realize that you can't gain sufficient cultural competence to conduct an adequate evaluation and you should advise the organization or funder to look for someone else?

3. To what extent does Bledsoe adapt her evaluation design and data collection to the culture of the clients? Of the staff and administrators? What are the strengths of her methodological choices with regard to cultural competence? The weaknesses? What might you do differently?

4. Bledsoe recommends that the strategies used in the program should be more standardized across staff. What is the balance between consistency of approach and taking advantage of an individual staff member's strengths and judgment to achieve program goals?

5. Bledsoe learns a lot from observing Fun with Books in action. She learns more about how parents, staff, and volunteers perceive the program and

what they do in it. Contrast those we have interviewed in their observations of the programs they evaluate. Do they all observe the program in action? In what manner do they observe it? Are they active participants or quiet observers? Note that the nature of the program, what is being delivered, can ease or hinder observation and the manner in which it is conducted. How might you observe this class if it were being evaluated? What would be the strengths and weaknesses of your approach?

6. What do the administrators who initially ask Bledsoe to conduct the evaluation see as the original purpose? Is that purpose achieved? How do they react to the final recommendations? Discuss how Bledsoe's manner of conducting the evaluation influences these changes.

7. The CEO of the program, however, is not pleased with how the final results are presented in the report, which indicate that an important goal, parents increasing the extent to which they read with their child at home, is not achieved. Bledsoe compromises by suggesting she change the results to "inconclusive" on this issue since no significant differences were found, rather than definitely saying that no differences occurred. Do you agree with her choice? What would you do in this situation?

FURTHER READING

Summary of the evaluation: Bledsoe, K. L., & Graham, J. A. (2005). Using multiple evaluation approaches in program evaluation. *American Journal of Evaluation, 26,* 302–319.

Bledsoe, K. L. (2005). Using theory-driven evaluation with underserved communities: Promoting program development and program sustainability. In S. Hood, R. H. Hopson, & H. T. Frierson (Eds.), *The role of culture and cultural context: A mandate for inclusion, the discovery of truth and understanding in evaluative theory and practice* (Evaluation and Society Series, pp. 175–196). Greenwich, CT: Information Age.

REFERENCES

Bledsoe, K. L. (in press). Presto, it's gone! When research ceases to exist right before your eyes. In D. Streiner & S. Sidanie (Eds.), *When research studies go off the rails: Solutions and prevention strategies.* New York: Guilford Press.

Bledsoe, K. L., & Hopson, R. H. (in press). Conducting ethical research in underserved communities. In D. M. Mertens & P. Ginsberg (Eds.), *Handbook of ethics for research in the social sciences.* Thousand Oaks, CA: Sage.

Hopson, R. H., Greene, J. C., Bledsoe, K. L., Villegas, T., & Brown, T. (2007). A vision for evaluation in urban educational settings. In W. T. Pink & G. W. Noblitt (Eds.), *International handbook of urban education.*

Morris, M. (Ed.). (2007). *Evaluation ethics for best practice: Cases and commentaries.* New York: Guilford Press.

Shadish, W. R., Newman, D. L., Scheirer, M. A., & Wye, C. (Eds.). (1995).*Guiding principles for evaluators* (New Directions for Program Evaluation, No. 35). San Francisco: Jossey-Bass.

THIRTEEN

EVALUATION OF GODFREY'S CHILDREN CENTER IN TANZANIA

An Interview With Allan Wallis and Victor Dukay

———◦●◦———

Introduction: In this interview, we discuss the evaluation with two people central to the evaluation: Victor Dukay, who was the director of the evaluation project, and Allan Wallis, the co-principal investigator, who had responsibilities for the overall research design and report. He was most directly involved in analysis of the social and economic sustainability aspects of the evaluation.

Victor Dukay is President of the Lundy Foundation, which was formed in 1991 to support the building of collaborative leadership and the strengthening of the capacity of nonprofit organizations. Before forming the Foundation, Dr. Dukay was CEO of an executive jet leasing company and also consulted in the aviation industry on equity financing, leveraged buyouts, and negotiating corporate acquisitions. He has an M.B.A. as well as an M.A. and Ph.D. in human communications. He was the director of this evaluation, entering initially as a consultant to Africa Bridge, the nonprofit organization that facilitated the village planning process for the Children's Center. He later helped obtain funding for the building of the Center and, eventually, for the evaluation.

Allan Wallis is an associate professor of public policy with the School of Public Affairs at the University of Colorado's Downtown Denver campus. He has conducted research on housing and regional planning in the United States and teaches courses on urban social problems, urban politics, and growth management. He facilitated the development of a comprehensive HIV/AIDS Service Plan for the State of Colorado and the Denver metropolitan area.

This evaluation takes place in a rural village in Tanzania and, as such, encounters many cultural challenges. Dr. Dukay's knowledge of the village and the Children's Center they are to evaluate gives them access to and knowledge of the village and its key actors and leaders. They also establish a team of U.S. and Tanzanian evaluators from many different disciplines to help them deal with the cultural challenges the evaluation presents. The ways in which they lead, manage, and guide the team is one of the key points of discussion in this interview. Although the nature and management of the team are important in an evaluation in a different country, the team management skills they develop would be useful to any evaluation team. The evaluation, then, compares children orphaned by AIDS and other tragedies and living at the Center with orphaned children living with relatives and with children living with their parents on key measures of physical well-being and psychosocial development. They use a mix of quantitative, standardized measures; existing data and new surveys; interviews and focus groups to examine program outcomes. They also collect information to assess village support and involvement in the Center to examine its sustainability.

Summary of the Evaluation of Godfrey's Children Center

Allan Wallis and Victor Dukay

Idweli, a village of approximately 2,500 people in southwestern Tanzania, has been severely affected by HIV/AIDS. Approximately 40% of the children in Idweli are orphans, partly due to HIV/AIDS and partly due to a devastating petrol truck accident in 2001, which resulted in the death of over 40 men, most of them parents of multiple children. The Children's Center, a project designed to serve some of the most needy of these orphans, began with the dreams of Godfrey Msemwa, a medical student in Dar Es Salaam who had been raised in Idweli. Godfrey and his brother Fred, who had also left Idweli to pursue higher education, wanted to do something to help the orphans in Idweli; however, before they could proceed with their plans, Godfrey died in a drowning accident. Friends established Godfrey's Children, a nonprofit organization, to pursue his goals. One of their first steps was to contact a United States-based nonprofit organization, Africa Bridge, to ask for assistance in helping the villagers identify their needs.

In November 2002, Africa Bridge facilitated a planning process involving children and adults in Idweli. That process concluded with a commitment to develop the Godfrey's Children Center, a place where the neediest orphans of Idweli could live, be cared for, and be educated. Villagers were actively involved in building the Center and in its operation and administration. Since research indicated that children in institutionalized settings often do not fare as well as children living with an extended family, plans were made for a hybrid institution: a center where children would live in a dormitory-type setting but would remain in their village of origin, where they would be cared for by people hired from the village, attend the village school, visit with family, and in other ways remain integrated with village life. The Center would also serve other children in the village by offering preschool and after-school programs. Fifty-eight of the neediest orphans were selected to live at the Center.

Purposes and Methodology of the Evaluation

Dr. Dukay, who had consulted with Africa Bridge, recognized that it was important to evaluate this new hybrid institution, not only for its effects on Idweli and its orphaned children but also to develop ways to evaluate other interventions for orphaned and vulnerable children in Africa. Dukay obtained funding from the Rockefeller Foundation for these purposes. Given the numbers of orphaned and vulnerable children in Africa, he believed it was critical to explore new ways to meet the needs of these children and their over-burdened caregivers. Although the research on institutions suggested that children removed from family and relatives fared poorly, the large number of orphans in Africa calls for more research on innovative ways to meet the needs of orphaned and vulnerable children. A literature review revealed that fewer than a dozen such systematic evaluations had been conducted on facilities serving HIV/AIDS orphaned and vulnerable children in Africa.

Dr. Dukay created a team of 13 people, seven from Tanzania and six from the United States, with expertise in children's mental and physical health, sociology, anthropology, community development, and communication to evaluate Godfrey's Children Center. The evaluation focused on three elements: changes in children's physical well-being, changes in their psychosocial development, and the socioeconomic sustainability of the Center.

Ideally, the evaluation of the Center would have involved collection of pre and post measures of the psychosocial well-being of its orphans. However, the Center was already operating for eight months before the data collection could begin. Consequently, the study employed three comparison groups: orphans living in the Children's Center, orphans cared for in the village, and non-orphans in the village. A total of 209 children participated in the evaluation.

The team identified or developed a number of qualitative and quantitative measures to assess children's physical and mental health. Physical health was assessed directly by measuring the body mass index (BMI) of each child and indi-rectly through interviews and focus groups with physicians, parents, and care-givers. Multiple psychosocial measures were employed, including a standardized test for symptoms of depression (the Children's Depression Inventory), a stan-dardized measure of social integration (Social Support Questionnaire), and a stan-dardized measure of coping skills (the Strengths and Difficulties Questionnaire). Existing data were collected on school attendance and performance on school-based tests. In addition, interviews were conducted with all children and with their caregivers regarding physical and psychosocial well-being and sources of support, and with all key parties involved in the development of the Center. Focus groups were also conducted with caregivers and villages elders.

The team was quite concerned about the cultural validity of the evaluation and the choices made regarding measures. Although the standardized instruments selected for use in the study had demonstrated validity and reliability in the United States and Europe, they had not been applied in sub-Saharan Africa and specifically with a population of orphaned and vulnerable children. The Tanzanian members of the team played a vital role in adapting the instruments for the evaluation context. They helped identify question wording and response formats that might be difficult for the children to understand and suggested modifications. They also participated fully with their U.S. counterparts in analyzing evaluation findings. When standardized measures were used, English-based measures were translated into Kiswahili, then translated back, and, finally, pilot tested. Tanzanians were selected and trained to conduct all field work, including an ethnographic analysis.

Results

Results of the evaluation showed that the psychosocial well-being of children living at the Center was either equal to or better than that of the comparison groups. Given that the literature on children in institutional settings generally shows such orphans faring more poorly than children living with extended families, the findings of this evaluation were seen as demonstrating the success of a new type of hybrid facility.

On psychosocial measures, Center children were found to be significantly less depressed than both village orphans and non-orphans. Center orphans did not differ from orphans and non-orphans in the village on other psychosocial measures such as emotional symptoms, hyperactivity, prosocial behavior, peer relationships, or total difficulties. Finally, no differences were found among the three groups of children in either the numbers of people they could rely on for social support or the types of people they would turn to for support. Interestingly, all three groups reported that they are most likely to turn to a friend for support. However, non-orphans reported their biological mother as the second most likely person they would turn to for support, while Center orphans reported turning to their teachers for secondary support, reflecting the close relationship between Center orphans and their teachers. Village orphans reported that older siblings were their second strongest source of support.

No significant differences were reported among the three groups in school attendance or test scores. However, Center children, selected because they were the neediest orphans, had the lowest pre-Center school scores and on postscores, obtained only five months later, had caught up with the village orphan and non-orphan groups. Of the three groups, they showed the greatest gain in test scores. In interviews, children from the Center indicated that they liked school more and had higher educational aspirations than the village orphans or children living with their parents.

On physical health measures, no significant differences were observed between the three groups based on body mass index (BMI). However, physicians and caregivers observed that Center orphans were healthier than the other groups, with fewer diseases and infections and greater weight gain over the period.

Interviews and focus groups were conducted with all 209 children in the study, 181 caregivers, and 70 other adults. These qualitative measures provided much useful and rich information. Caregivers and key informants observed that Center orphans were receiving necessary medical treatment, eating well, having school needs taken care of, and staying out of trouble. Orphans in the village were reported to be treated less well by those who cared for them than birth children, probably because of economic stresses. Children's interviews were analyzed qualitatively and quantitatively. While field workers struggled with some nonresponsive children during the interviews, analyses of those responding indicated that orphans in the Center felt significantly more positive about their current lives (school, living situation, general level of happiness) and their future than either village orphans or non-orphans.

Results on sustainability of the Center and involvement of villagers in the Center once it began were less positive than the results concerning the Center's impact on children. Villagers reported feeling quite involved during the planning and development stage but less involved once the Center began. While a majority of the villagers interviewed (56%) indicated they supported the Center's current activities, 44% felt that the Center was not currently being supported by the community. These villagers felt that people had not been educated about the advantages of the Center, that villagers had forgotten about the Center, or that the Center was controlled by the donors. They believed that it was important to educate the villagers about the Center and their role in controlling and contributing to it.

Dialogue With Victor Dukay and Allan Wallis

Jody Fitzpatrick

Fitzpatrick: Vic, how did you first become involved with this project?

Dukay: I was first asked by Africa Bridge to do some executive coaching on how to set up nonprofits, write grants, and approach funding sources. Toward the end of that work, Africa Bridge asked if I would be interested in traveling to Tanzania with some of their people to examine the problems created by HIV/AIDS in a small village there. I said, "Sure, I'd love to do that." So I ended up there through an invitation. I fell in love with the children. I was completely enamored with the fact that these children, who are in the middle of nowhere and devastated by the loss of family, wanted to start the Center. As someone who had been orphaned at the age of 15, I felt a strong connection to the children.

In the course of one of my visits to the village I found myself on a flight with a senior researcher from the World Health Organization, Brian Williams. He told me that there was virtually no systematic evaluation of support for HIV/AIDS orphans. I was struck by this remark and moved to try to do something to address this lack of knowledge.

Fitzpatrick: Allan, you became involved at the evaluation stage and were part of the evaluation team. How did you become involved with this project?

Wallis: I became involved with the project early on, as the Center was being completed and Victor began considering approaching the Rockefeller Foundation for the evaluation. I wrote a brief concept paper on how the evaluation might be designed and conducted.

Dukay: Allan and I have known each other for 10 to 12 years and have worked together on other evaluations.

Fitzpatrick: One of the issues I would like to discuss is your evaluation team. You pulled together a team of 13 people, including people from Tanzania and from the United States, to plan and coordinate this evaluation. They had expertise in many different areas. Vic, did you put together the team and how did you decide on its composition?

Dukay: Yes, I did put together the team after Allan and I and two others in the United States, who I've also worked with on previous projects, talked about what would be helpful in the evaluation. We discussed what we wanted to evaluate and what types of people could help. It was important that we have some colleagues from Tanzania on the team. I had worked with a psychiatrist from Tanzania who specialized in children's mental health and asked her if she was interested in working on the project. Once she agreed, I asked her if she could recommend others. She identified an additional psychiatrist in her department and one who worked in a hospital in the city of Mbeya near Idweli. I had also developed a relationship with a young man who was from Idweli, where the Center was located. I asked him if he had contacts in Dar es Salaam and, through him, found a social anthropology professor who could be helpful. Then he recommended an ethnographer, who also joined the work. So by the time we met as a team in Tanzania we had three psychiatrists, an anthropologist, and a sociologist, all from Tanzania.

An important reason for assembling a team with such diverse backgrounds was to help insure that we were correctly interpreting the social and cultural context of the village and Center. For example, when trying to understand the hybrid nature of the Children's Center, it was important to know that in Tanzania over a third of all children are raised by extended family, but only about a fifth of these are orphaned. Consequently, we came to understand that the extended family was already a heavily utilized support option, but it was being stretched to the breaking point by the high incidence of HIV/AIDS and the growing number of orphans. We also learned that in their culture, children often lived in different, extra-familial circumstances. For example, until recently, among the Safwa people (the dominant tribe in Idweli), adolescent males were sent by their families to live together in a dormitory-type facility until they reached the age of marriage. Without such understandings of the cultural context we could easily have misinterpreted what we were hearing in interviews and focus groups. So having psychiatrists, anthropologists, and sociologists from Tanzania was essential to the conduct of our study.

Fitzpatrick: Can you tell us a bit about how the team worked together? Were there areas where you all worked on the same issue and other areas where you delegated responsibilities?

Wallis: I think it helped that most of the American team members knew each other from prior work evaluating a leadership training programs. So we had collegial respect, and moreover, we really enjoyed working with one another. We came to the proposal with an enthusiasm for being able to work with each other again and a passion for HIV/AIDS research. So for the American side, that was really a plus. We also had a new person from the United States, Claude Mellins, who is an adolescent psychologist with a program at Columbia University. He has worked with orphans of HIV/AIDS in the United States and added further expertise to the team.

Dukay: The project team had two components. First, the team needed to have the necessary skill set to conduct the evaluation. But a second major factor was the interpersonal piece, wanting to work together and having a passion for AIDS/HIV and giving a voice to people who don't have a voice. We were largely volunteering our time or working for reduced pay, but we wanted to work with colleagues who had a proven track record and who we felt could work together.

But the Tanzanians were mainly new to us. So on the first trip, part of our goal was team building. We took some pains to work on that issue, all of us getting to know each other so we could work well together.

Fitzpatrick: Allan, you were part of the team. How did you find the collaboration?

Wallis: It was very enjoyable to work with a collaborative team of people. Carl Larson, who is a nationally recognized expert on what makes a team excellent, was a real asset in this regard. Carl coached us on how we could function as a high-performing team. I've been involved in many team projects, but this was the first where we were very conscious of needing to develop a team. I think we were especially conscious of that because of our different cultures and the fact that for much of the project we would have to communicate via e-mail and phone. It was very useful for us to all meet in Tanzania and to work face-to-face during the design phase of the project. This allowed us to know each other in a more intimate way, and that's important when you're dealing with very busy people who have a lot on their plate.

Dukay: In the sub-Saharan African cultures, results-driven structures and accountability are not as strong or as clearly defined as in the United States. In the private sector in the United States, there's a lot of energy put into doing projects using team theory to maximize the ability to achieve project goals. We wanted to transfer some skill sets to our Tanzanian team members about how to do projects like this so that they could work more effectively with one another and with us.

In a very practical sense, what this boiled down to was deciding how we would hold each other accountable for our assigned project work. If someone was late in completing something or not doing a really good job, we needed to decide how we could call them to task. We needed to know how to do this in a culturally appropriate way. Communications deemed appropriate in a U.S. context might seem offensive in a Tanzanian context; so we were not only trying to understand the cultural dimensions operating in the village but within the evaluation team itself.

Fitzpatrick: What did you do to learn how to work as a team?

Wallis: We literally had a seminar with all of us sitting around a conference room table in the place where we were staying near the village. Our in-house expert, Carl Larson, went over the elements that make for a high-performance team. This included issues on how we would hold each other accountable for our work. There are different ways of doing that in Africa. There were cultural and gender issues. Can a woman from Africa who is actually much more senior than one of the male team members in Africa hold him responsible? How can you tell someone, "You're not following through on what you're supposed to do"? So, on the rare occasion when we were all together physically, we could talk together about how to keep each other accountable. We made use of that discussion throughout the project.

Dukay: We also had weekly conference calls throughout the 18-month period of the project. In each, we spent some time talking about how we were functioning as a team. What's working well that we should build on?

There were not only gender differences but age differences. A senior female team member from Tanzania acknowledged that it would be difficult for her to call an older male colleague to task if he underperformed, because that is something that a younger person simply does not do in their culture. This created a major challenge from my perspective, but it was one that we had to acknowledge and work with.

Fitzpatrick: What did you do?

Dukay: I spent a lot of time talking to our other teammates, especially to our senior team member in Tanzania, a woman, saying, "I'm a white guy. I'm a man. I'm not from Africa. I need help to understand the issues here." I would ask her for help on how to approach a woman and an older man on the team who were not working well together. In hindsight, the woman had made it very clear that she was not going to discuss performance with the older man. I learned not to invite people like that to join the team when doing a project like this. We need people who are willing to engage each other in constructive ways. I didn't listen well. I thought I could change her, but it was too ingrained in the culture, at least for her. And, eventually, she left the project. The point is that while there are cultural differences that must be recognized, there are also personal differences regarding how strongly traditions are followed. When you are doing something that is new and different, you need people who are willing to be innovative and not rigidly wed to tradition.

Fitzpatrick: How was the team when it did work?

Wallis: If you're working with people who are in touch with one another, with tight feedback loops, there is a sense of personal and professional obligation or accountability. Vic was great at moving us along and giving timely feedback on our individual and team performance. Here's an example: In a conference call I was pretty frustrated with one of the other team members. When the call was over, Vic gave me a follow-up call saying, "Hey, you seemed to be a little out of it." This made me think, "I'm working with someone who understands me and wants to find out what's going on."

Vic brings a set of business skills to the process that academics are usually weak at. Either we think it's not appropriate to say something about the personal side of performance or we only treat it in the abstract as if there weren't a person attached to the work. What Vic and Carl did in terms of training the team to be a team was to give us permission to communicate more effectively with each other about trying to achieve team excellence. This included "tagging" or acknowledging behaviors that could undermine team effectiveness as they occur in the course of working together. Everyone understood *tagging,* so when we did it we also understood that it was being employed to improve the project and not to attack an individual.

Dukay: My own management style has been very open door. The whole purpose of having a team is to be able to make use of each individual's expertise and to share that expertise. I spent an immense amount of energy on personal phone calls with individual team members, especially the Tanzanians, at least once a week. Some of these calls were personal; some were professional. Just showing up on the phone and caring, not in a fake way, but being appreciative of what they have to do to get something done makes a real difference in motivating people and improving understanding. What takes me five minutes may take them two hours. We don't always appreciate that during a conference call their electricity is going on and off or their cell phone signal just fades out. The bottom line is that we need to approach each other with a warm heart. We need to assume that, like us, they are trying to produce an excellent project, but there are some real technical challenges involved that we in the United States don't always understand.

Wallis: We make assumptions in the United States about the process of knowledge production. We think it's largely a matter of technical expertise—applying the right tools. But when you're working across cultural boundaries, you have to think, "How do you know where they're coming from? How do I know what this means?" I'm working on a project now where I have great concerns. We're not talking enough, not challenging each other. We just think, "Well, we've got a great technical team and we will figure it out." But the work involved in "figuring it out" is not just technical, it's personal. It's about establishing communications that allow you to understand where someone is coming from when they challenge your assumptions and interpretations. Raising such challenges requires trust as well as technical expertise.

Dukay: Interpersonal relationships require two sets of expertise. One is technical, skills in the methods of evaluation, regression, sampling, and so on. The other set is just as important. It's the interpersonal skills set, emotional intelligence. How do you give feedback? How do you deal with conflict in a constructive way?

Fitzpatrick: Your team came from two quite different countries. Were there differences in your approaches to the evaluation across the countries of origin? What about differences across disciplines?

Wallis: The differences were more across different areas of expertise. I thought the Tanzanian social scientists were well trained, shared expertise and paradigms. But if you're dealing across disciplines, that's much more difficult.

Dukay: While I agree that getting across disciplinary differences is a challenge, the cultural differences are also there in the nuances. During the week of field worker training, many differences emerged concerning how you're going to get information from children in Africa. It's different than collecting information from children in the United States. Americans are pretty analytical. Being forced to make a choice (e.g., as in a Likert-scale question on the standardized instruments) is very foreign to the Tanzanian culture. If you look at the Swahili language, it is much more verbal than English. There are many words for what we might see as the same thing. So we tried using story telling as a technique to capture data, finger painting and music.

Fitzpatrick: What did you think those techniques would accomplish?

Dukay: We wanted to obtain a more in-depth understanding of what the children were experiencing. In the end, we didn't implement many of these because we felt that the cost of data analysis would be prohibitive. It's less traditional and the data are more difficult to analyze. The funders get nervous with that kind of data.

Fitzpatrick: This brings us to the evaluation. Let me ask you a bit about how it began. The evaluation team became involved in the project quite early on with a three-week visit to Idweli in September of 2005 after the Children's Center had opened in May. Allan, can you tell us a bit about that first visit there?

Wallis: It's important to realize that the team had worked in the United States on a preliminary selection of instruments that we thought might work in the field. So we brought a huge notebook of possible instruments. Then we worked a while together in Dar es Salaam before going to the village. Going to Idweli made me very aware of the contextual nature of the work. I realized that we needed to do some ethnographic work. We needed to understand that culture. And, in fact, we hired an ethnographer.

Being there created a lot more passion among people working on the evaluation. You were seeing the kids and wanting to help them. But also, we were realizing how rich the culture was and wanted to give a more robust description of it. We wanted the reader of the report to get a sense of what the village and culture were like.

Fitzpatrick: Was it helpful to be involved at that relatively early stage? Sometimes when you're involved with a program in the early stages, you become involved in program development. Did that happen in this case?

Dukay: Absolutely not. I made a clear distinction of what we were going to do from an evaluation perspective and what Africa Bridge, which was developing programs for the Center, was doing. From Day 1, we made the decision that we would not provide feedback to Africa Bridge but would make recommendations in the final report.

Fitzpatrick: Why did you want to do that?

Dukay: The first reason was that the Rockefeller Foundation asked us not to give feedback to Africa Bridge. However, I also wanted to separate myself from Africa Bridge for the evaluation. I had worked with Africa Bridge in the planning, construction, and opening phase, and I thought it would be very difficult to be an objective program director for the evaluation and simultaneously manage the program. It would be cleaner to have this separation.

Fitzpatrick: Did your previous role in planning and developing the Center help or hinder you in conducting the evaluation?

Dukay: It helped significantly. By actually working on the Center, spending three years in the village itself, I began to understand the culture and, more important, to develop friendships with key people in the village. As a result, trust was developed. They were very comfortable with allowing us to do the evaluation because they knew me.

Fitzpatrick: Moving more directly to the evaluation, I'd like to learn a bit about what prompted the evaluation. You cite several different purposes for the evaluation in the report: evaluating the initial, participative process used with adults and children in the village, identifying emerging best practices in caring for the burgeoning number of AIDS orphans in Africa, determining the impact of the Children's Center on the residents' psychosocial and physical well-being, and assessing the sustainability of the Center. Who was involved in identifying these purposes?

Dukay: The whole team decided on the purpose. Those of us in the United States came up with some initial purposes for the grant proposal, when we were writing it. When we got to Tanzania, we refined those purposes.

Wallis: I think the Rockefeller Foundation's own interest was more narrowly focused on measuring the psychosocial well-being of orphaned and vulnerable children. So the original proposal had to address that. But we were obviously interested in the questions "Does this Center work?" and, if so, "What does it say about developing similar hybrid institutions like this one?"

Dukay: I personally was not interested in evaluating one center in the middle of nowhere. My personal interest was in developing an evaluation protocol that at the end of the day would give NGOs some information on what works.

Fitzpatrick: Even though you had been so involved in the development?

Dukay: Yes, maybe that was part of the problem. I wanted something that could be used in other contexts, so we could influence even more children.

Wallis: Vic expresses the value difference between activists who want to get something done and academics who want to be shown that there is a "there" there. Fortunately, because Vic has a Ph.D. and is aware of the culture of research, there was a commitment to bridging those two cultures.

Dukay: Our passion was important. There are researchers who go into the field with much more money and less passion and don't pay attention to the details. And it's these details, like spending the time to understand the cultural context, that really enable you to understand what is going on.

Fitzpatrick: The Africa Bridge process for program development was quite participatory. Would you characterize the evaluation as participatory?

Dukay: No. I would characterize the vision and the building and operating of the Center as very participatory, but no, not the evaluation. We really did not interact with the villagers in designing the evaluation itself.

We are headed over to Tanzania soon to disseminate the findings from the evaluation. We will be making some of our presentations in the village to people who participated in the evaluation. We'll be sharing results. We'll be asking, "What do you think?" "What can we do with this information to improve things?" So we'll have significantly more participation in that phase than in the planning and data collection and analysis phases.

Fitzpatrick: Did you see the evaluation as mainly for external audiences, or did you see it as also providing information for program improvement? If so, how have you used it to revise or change program operations?

Dukay: It was really to serve both purposes because we had a lot of different stakeholders. Africa Bridge, the organization that is currently running the Center, is very interested in sitting down with us and learning how they might change what they're doing. The Minister of Health in Tanzania wants to use this to help them decide what to fund. Another whole group, major organizations that fund orphaned and vulnerable children programs, wants to learn how these tools can be used to better children's well-being.

Fitzpatrick: You did a tremendous amount of data collection and spent what must have been an intensive 3 months selecting or developing quite a few different qualitative and quantitative measures. You first chose to assess psychosocial and physical changes in the children at the Center, then moved to measure depression, some behaviors, social support, and school performance as well as children's general sense of well-being and the impact of the Center on previous caregivers. You used the BMI as a measure of physical change. Your choices seem pretty comprehensive. Let me ask first, how did you decide on these constructs or particular outcomes to assess?

Wallis: The chief concern of the Rockefeller Foundation was with psychosocial measures, but we felt measuring that alone wouldn't tell us all that much. Very early on, we thought of the three overarching areas—psychosocial, physical, and socioeconomic. What we learned from each would inform the others and give us a more complete sense of the whole.

Dukay: We actually developed those overarching questions in the conference room in Denver International Airport. We started talking early on about how we could go about defining *well-being*. Before we knew it, we had three circles: the physical, psychosocial, and the socioeconomic. This is basically the conceptual model used to define sustainable development. We then did the literature reviews and talked with other researchers and with funders.

Fitzpatrick: Were there other issues that you considered and rejected for the focus of the evaluation?

Wallis: We had some discussions about trying to elicit children's qualitative impression of what was happening in their lives. We were very fortunate in having a grants officer from Rockefeller, a pediatrician, who had a personal passion about this research. He was from South Africa and had adopted several AIDS orphans, some with HIV/AIDS themselves. He joined us for two days in Dar es Salaam and suggested having children draw and tell what they saw in the drawings. We thought these were intriguing notions, but we didn't know how difficult it would be or what exactly we would do with it. We wanted rich sources of qualitative data because quantitative data can be flat, but some of the more exotic seemed too unpredictable. I, for example, was keen on giving kids tape recorders to talk about their lives. We wanted to be creative, to give a three-dimensional picture of what was happening, but we wanted to be realistic about what we could do.

Dukay: It was a miracle that we did it all. That we actually completed the project as planned with high-quality data from the field. I think that it surprised the Foundation. That's why they gave us a second grant to support dissemination of our findings.

Fitzpatrick: Most of your quantitative measures were previously developed and used by others. What did you see as the strengths of these measures? Do you prefer using standardized measures?

Dukay: I wanted to use some standardized measures, ones that already had established reliability and validity. All of that was done so we wouldn't have to argue with the technocrats. It's very expensive to establish the validity of a new measure. At the same time we decided to triangulate those measures with data gathered through more qualitative and exploratory methods, including interviews with children.

Wallis: We wanted to do some things that were innovative, but we also wanted to use measures that would be immediately recognized by other researchers in the field. We were concerned with what you can do in the field. How costly and time intensive will it be? So it was important to have some instruments for which it would be fairly easy to predict how long it would take to administer them and analyze the data.

Fitzpatrick: Were you concerned with the extent to which these measures would validly assess these constructs in a different culture?

Dukay: Very! We relied quite extensively on our Tanzanian colleagues to review the instruments themselves and give us feedback on whether or not they would work. Then, we actually took the instruments into Idweli and did some pilot testing. We wanted to know if the questions were understandable and if they were capable of eliciting responses. After the pilot work, we came back and did some minor word changes.

Fitzpatrick: Other measures were developed specifically for this evaluation. Most of these were qualitative—for example, interview and focus group questions for children on their sense of well-being and for parents and caregivers on caring for the children. Was it difficult to develop interview and focus group questions for people from a different culture?

Dukay: One of the purposes of developing the open-ended qualitative questions was to mirror the quantitative questions. We felt that by triangulating what we were learning through the quantitative instruments with results from qualitative instruments, we would have the basis for a more robust interpretation. As part of this, the qualitative findings could help provide more of the cultural context for interpretation.

Wallis: I was involved in developing the focus group protocols. There is always a tension in developing the protocols. How many questions can we add? How reliable are the people going to be who facilitate the focus groups? We decided we had to be more parsimonious. There was a tension within the group between those wanting to have data on everything and those wanting less but making sure what we got was good. There weren't any gross disagreements, but we worked on figuring out how much time administering each instrument was going to take. We used a big chart trying to summarize what we were collecting and how long it would take to serve as a reality check.

Fitzpatrick: What role did the Tanzanian members of the team play in selecting and developing instruments?

Dukay: Two U.S. members of the team took the first stab at developing the focus group interview questions. Then they e-mailed them to the rest of the team for review.

There was continuing discussion with the field workers, during their training, trying to determine the appropriate Swahili word for different concepts. We talked about the differences in using these measures in a rural Tanzanian setting rather than in an urban setting.

Fitzpatrick: While the Tanzanian members of the team were, of course, knowledgeable about Tanzania, they were professors or physicians from Dar es Salaam and, thus, quite different from the villagers. Were they able to help you transcend some cultural differences but not others?

Dukay: Yes, one of the lead researchers was born and raised in a village right next to Idweli. So he had extensive experience there and his current research is around village life. A Tanzanian psychiatrist on the team was also very familiar with village life because he was from the village itself. We were always able to ask him, "Do you think your people would understand this?"

Fitzpatrick: Let's talk a bit about your data collection. You initially trained 10 Tanzanians in a weeklong program to collect data and ultimately hired 6 of them to conduct interviews and focus groups and collect other data. The report indicates that you oriented them to Idweli, so I assume they were not from the village. Did you consider using villagers?

Dukay: Three out of the six were from the region, so they were familiar with Idweli. We interviewed over 35 people. Only two from Idweli applied, and unfortunately, they didn't have the skill set that was needed. But even if they had, I probably would have been reluctant to hire them *because* of their familiarity. It could have resulted in problems with confidentiality. It was better to have outsiders who knew the village but were not a part of the politics.

Fitzpatrick: But, even after the training and selection, you found the field workers encountered problems in the interviews. Your report indicates that some children seemed to be trying to determine what the interviewer wanted to hear and, then, to respond in that way. Some interviewers departed dramatically from the interview protocol or actively guided children's responses. Fortunately, you had the tapes of the interviews and were able to screen out those interviews. But the conclusion of the report notes that the qualitative interviews failed to yield the rich descriptions of children's experiences that you had anticipated. Can you tell me more about the problems you encountered with the interviews?

Dukay: We don't have empirical evidence for what happened. Based on my observations of the training for field workers and then on follow-up with them in the field, I think the training was not sufficient. The training was originally designed to include practice with children in a nearby village. That never happened. And, at the end of the day, the field workers weren't trained as well as they should have been in interview techniques. For example, they were not good at probing. The field worker would ask a child, "How did you feel after your parents died?" And the child would say "Sad," and the field worker would fail to probe.

Fitzpatrick: Did you have concerns that the children's desire to please seen in the qualitative interviews may have affected the quantitative measures as well?

Dukay: To me, it's not a big issue. That desire to please would have been consistent across all sample groups, and our main interest with the quantitative measures was in comparing groups.

Fitzpatrick: Did the focus groups yield more rich information than the interviews?

Dukay: In general, focus group information was useful. We recorded them and then translated them into English for purposes of analysis. One thing that was very helpful in the focus groups was separating the men and women, which allowed the women to be more honest.

Wallis: We had one focus group with male elders and one with female elders. The women were much more in touch with the needs of children, whereas the men appeared to be giving more stock answers. When we first came to the village, there were women on the Board, but at village meetings, they weren't sitting at the table with the men. The fact that they weren't able to sit at the table gave a clear indication of the need to separate genders for the focus groups.

Fitzpatrick: You compared data from children living at the Center with orphans and non-orphans living in the village. To summarize many different analyses, your main findings were that orphans at the Center were significantly less depressed than the other two groups; voiced higher educational aspirations and liked school more; and were at least equivalent to the other two groups in social support, school attendance and performance, behavior, and BMI. Were any of these results surprising to you?

Dukay: Yes, I was surprised. I didn't think there would be such a huge difference between the children at the Center and the children being taken care of by extended family members on depression. I was shocked at how depressed children being taken care of by extended family members were, but I wasn't surprised that children at the Center were happy.

Fitzpatrick: Your qualitative data on the impact of the Center on the children were very positive. Caregivers and leaders from the town perceived children at the Center to be in a much better situation than orphans living with relatives, although they felt comfortable in admitting concerns about sustainability. Which qualitative data did you find most useful? What did it add to your study?

Wallis: I thought the most useful data came from the focus groups and interviews with people who participated in the process of identifying the need for a Center and developing it. One of the key factors in the success of the Center was that process. In the report, we argue that while Idweli appears to be successful, those findings don't mean build such centers all over. Instead, they mean use a similar process to let villagers identify their needs and solutions. We would not have as strong a foundation for that conclusion if we had not spent quite a bit of time interviewing key informants and people involved in the decision-making process.

This was very essential to tell the story. The participative process arose from our concern that they would feel outside white benefactors were bringing this idea. We felt it was important that the idea to build the Center was an outcome of the process.

Dukay: One of concerns of the funders was whether these hybrid interventions would be sustainable given the poor condition of the local economy. The funders were asking about how much support the community was providing and about the community's buy-in and sense of ownership. So getting opinions about a sense of ownership and buy-in through focus groups was very important.

Fitzpatrick: In your qualitative results, you indicate that many children are envious of the Center orphans. It must be very difficult to balance providing the Center orphans with care and support to improve their lives given the norms of the village. Is this issue a concern? In other words, can the Center do *too* much for the orphans?

Dukay: Yes, it's a difficult and constant balancing act. How do you give the kids at the Center what they need—keeping them healthy, learning—so they're not pulled down by the rest of the kids in the village but not segregating them either? This has come up so many times. I think they've done an adequate job because kids from the village come and play at the Center.

Fitzpatrick: One of your concerns in the evaluation that I haven't devoted as much time to here is the sustainability of the Center. Your results showed that village stakeholders felt quite involved in the planning of the Center but less so in its implementation. I encourage others to read your report on the planning process, which was fascinating. Why do you think villagers' feelings of collaboration and ownership changed once the Center opened?

Dukay: Many people from the village were involved in the visioning and the implementation phase. Once it was opened, it seemed like the funders just showed up and ended up dealing with a very small group of people, essentially the governing board of the Center and the Center manager. There weren't specific steps taken to continue to encourage the broader participation of the village. In the interviews, the villagers said, "We just thought the white folks were taking care of it and we didn't have to worry about it." There wasn't an active plan for how to involve them at this stage.

Wallis: Africa Bridge didn't really have a clear idea of the degree of involvement that was desirable for the project. It emerged through the process. Africa Bridge was a relatively new NGO, feeling its way along on this project, going into the village and facilitating talks, without a clear idea of their responsibility. On the other side, villagers were confused as well about their role and the role of the NGO. In retrospect, it would have been very useful if the roles and responsibilities for running the Center were clarified at the planning stage and if a discussion about transitioning responsibilities from Africa Bridge to the village over time were spelled out.

Dukay: Africa Bridge's original intention was not to build the Center. It was to come in and do leadership development training. But they never said to the villagers, "This is exactly what we're going to do for you, and then we're going to disappear and expect you to keep it up." One of our recommendations is to be clearer about roles and responsibilities.

Fitzpatrick: As you note, the Children's Center is a hybrid program. Unlike many institutional settings for orphans, the children at the Center attend school with other villagers and can visit family members. The Center offers preschool and after-school programs attended by village children. So integration between the community and the Center is occurring in these ways. Did children from the Center visit their past caregivers and family members as you anticipated? Did relatives come to the Center to visit them?

Wallis: There were mixed feelings on this issue. The volunteer nurse from the United States, who was very active in managing the Center, was critical of the extended family members for not bringing a cup of beans or something to help the Center when they came to visit. By contrast, our Tanzania team members who grew up in the village suggested that the village families are struggling to feed themselves. So the idea of bringing something to the Center probably seemed ridiculous to them. Many things were open to interpretation. I think it goes back to the lack of clear understanding of who would do what in sustaining the Center.

Dukay: I wish we had collected data on the number of times extended family members visited the Center. If you talk to the Center manager, he would say there were all kinds of visits. Then you talk to some other folks, and they say there have been no visits. My expectations around more support from the community have never been met. Those villagers are struggling, period. No one in that village is rich by any stretch of the imagination. And there were no discussions about expectations after the Center opened. If this had been done, I think there would be much more buy-in by the villagers.

Fitzpatrick: I know your final report is just coming out, but have you seen ways in which the evaluation is being used either in Idweli or among NGOs and others working in Africa?

Dukay: Yes, our objective in the upcoming dissemination phase is to get this information off the shelf and into the hands of key stakeholder groups who have the power to improve the lives of children. We plan to talk to the chief, who is the head of the main tribe in the village; the doctor for the Center; and the headmaster of the school to see how we can help them take this evaluation to make a difference in the school and at the Center. As I mentioned, the Tanzanian Ministry of Health is interested in the evaluation. There is an organization for orphaned and vulnerable children made up of different NGOs working with kids that is interested and has invited us to make a presentation. We have a commitment to talk with people in the federal government, Joseph Biden and others instrumental in making U.S. aid decisions.

We now have an incredible opportunity to influence some of the decisions made about U.S. aid to Africa. As of last November, there were no evaluations of what U.S. aid to Africa has achieved in terms of assisting those infected and affected by HIV/AIDS, especially orphaned and vulnerable children. So we're hopeful that our evaluation can provide a model for assessing impacts. All of our dissemination work is geared to getting the report on this Center into the hands of people working on policies concerning orphaned and vulnerable children in Africa.

Wallis: One of our hopes is that this evaluation will encourage more systematic, comparative evaluations of programs for orphaned and vulnerable children. That process will not just be a bunch of social scientists getting together and talking but getting many different types of people, including practitioners, involved.

Our dissemination plan has evolved. It's not just about getting the information out but about structuring dialogue. We need to start with Idweli and get their input—gain credibility and understanding—and then move up to national and international audiences, so that if we end up in a Congressional hearing room, we have support for our findings.

Fitzpatrick: What did you see as the most important results from the evaluation?

Dukay: The most important piece that I have learned, and it's important because it could affect the lives of kids, is that kids who are "institutionalized" can lead happy lives. So, from a policy perspective, these types of hybrids, ones created at the community level, should be funded.

Wallis: I'd like to reinforce that. The current literature is very strongly against "orphanages." I think they're throwing the baby out with the bathwater. From our perspective, the Idweli Center isn't an orphanage in the traditional sense. It is an institution of and for the village. That makes it a hybrid: something between an institution and extended family placement.

Fitzpatrick: Are there any other lessons that you learned about working in a cross-cultural context?

Dukay: We learned something when designing the study and then in evaluating its findings, but we also learned about cultural differences in the process of disseminating the results. The policy debate has become polarized around placing orphaned and vulnerable children with extended families or in orphanages. That polarization seems to preclude consideration of other options. We have found some organizations oppose the idea of the Center per se because it is perceived as a form of institutionalized placement, as an orphanage. We have found some people who want to dismiss the evaluation findings out of hand because they feel the Center is an orphanage. In short, it was hard to get people to understand the idea of a hybrid alternative, such as the Center.

Fitzpatrick: So differences across cultures continue to emerge in the dissemination phase. In this case, these different views of the Center, as a hybrid or an orphanage, influenced people's response to the evaluation. Thank you both for helping us understand more about the many different cultural differences that can emerge in conducting an international evaluation.

Fitzpatrick's Commentary

This evaluation provides us with a useful example of an evaluation conducted in another country, one quite different from the United States, Canada, or other Western countries. As such, cultural competence, an understanding of the culture in which the evaluation is to be conducted, is critical to the evaluation. Cultural competence is addressed in this evaluation in two ways: (1) Dukay's intimate knowledge of the Idweli village, its leaders and processes for decision making, and the creation of the Center and (2) the inclusion of several Tanzanian professionals with different areas of expertise, including knowledge of HIV/AIDS, OVC, and the region around Idweli, on the evaluation team. Dukay's work in Idweli on the Center and his familiarity with village leaders provide him with the access to conduct the evaluation, to interview villagers—caregivers, children, and village leaders—and to collect existing data from schools and medical professionals. Similarly, the Tanzanians on the evaluation team are available to provide advice on the culture and mores of rural villages in Tanzania, views of HIV/AIDS, and issues concerning data collection. They review instruments and provide feedback on what will work, although they do not take the lead in developing interview or focus group questions or in selecting instruments.

The strengths of the evaluation also present strains. Coordinating the work of an evaluation team from different countries and different disciplines requires skill and constant communication, as Dukay and Wallis indicate. Much of Dukay's time in managing the evaluation is devoted to these teamwork issues to ensure that the evaluation is able to benefit from the expertise of different team members. Differences between Tanzanian team members' and U.S. team members' perceptions concerning teamwork, input, feedback, and evaluation mimic the differences that Dukay and Wallis must encounter in collecting evaluation data from Tanzanian children and adult caregivers as compared with children in the United States or other Western countries. Dukay touches on these differences in describing Tanzanian children's difficulty with Likert-scale items and making a choice. Similarly, Dukay's three years in the village and experience with the Center provide him with a great depth of knowledge about the culture but could present a strain in distancing himself from the Center he had helped Africa Bridge develop. However, the evaluation is prompted by Dukay's and the Rockefeller Foundation's desire to develop an evaluation protocol that can be used by other organizations working with orphaned and vulnerable children, and this goal, evaluations beyond Godfrey's Children Center, helps Dukay maintain that distance.

Dukay's role in this evaluation is somewhat akin to Ross Conner's role with the Colorado Healthy Communities Initiative. Conner worked with the Colorado Trust early on to help develop the principles and model for the Initiative and as a facilitator with the stakeholders as they planned their programs, but a major purpose of his evaluation was to develop a template or plan that others using a healthy cities model could adopt to evaluate similar programs. Through these evaluations, both Dukay and Conner demonstrate the many hats an evaluator can wear during a long-term program and evaluation.

Evaluators can learn much from Wallis and Dukay's discussion of teamwork. They emphasize the need for frequent communication but also the need, even obligation, of each team member to give feedback and to let others know when they were not meeting their obligations. Although Dukay discusses the differences that occurred on this issue across cultures, the problem of how to handle team members who are not meeting their obligations can be a problem on any evaluation team. Their discussion and strategies suggest that evaluators could benefit by learning more about teamwork and ways to prompt each member to contribute ideas and feedback freely.

Wallis and Dukay both feel that the passion they and their team members had for the project and for working to help children in Africa orphaned by HIV/AIDS was an asset to their evaluation. This passion allowed them to recruit skilled, informed evaluation team members on a limited budget. And, they argue, it prompted them to pay more attention to the details, to the cultural context, because they really wanted to "understand what was going on." Passion is not something evaluators typically talk about, yet one can see passion in many of our interviews in different ways. Len Bickman is passionate about using evaluation to make a difference in the treatment of children's mental health. Jean King is passionate about building competency in evaluation in her school district. Certainly, passion can serve as a useful motivator in focusing our evaluation efforts, if we do not let that passion hinder our ability to look at results. James Riccio illustrates this when he accepts and actively disseminates results on welfare reform that are surprising to him and other experts—that is, that the program emphasizing immediate moves into the workforce, over education, had the best long-term effects.

Wallis and Dukay are unusual among those we interviewed in the lack of stakeholder involvement in their evaluation. Their funding source, the Rockefeller Foundation, is the major stakeholder and, in fact, asks them not to share information with local stakeholders until the conclusion of the evaluation. In this evaluation, the rather large, multidisciplinary, multicultural evaluation team of professionals serves almost like an advisory group might in a typical stakeholder evaluation—that is, reacting to ideas for the focus of the evaluation, methods and procedures for data collection, and interpretation of results. Since their primary purpose is to influence policy on solutions for OVC and provide templates for future evaluations, rather than serving formative or summative decisions regarding the Center in Idweli, stakeholder involvement from those connected with the Center is less essential. This evaluation is the most recently conducted in this book. Its results are just now being disseminated. More time will be needed to assess its impact and use, both internally at the Children's Center and externally by other NGOs.

Dukay, Wallis, and their team chose to use a mix of standardized measures, interviews, focus groups, and existing data. This mix gave them a fuller picture of the children's well-being. Some may question using standardized measures developed in the United States with children in rural villages in

Tanzania; however, many factors influenced this decision, and their choice demonstrates the difficult issues evaluators face in cross-cultural evaluations. Like others we have interviewed, they were concerned with the costs and time involved in developing new measures and wanted measures with established reliability and validity. Perhaps most important, they knew that these established measures would be more acceptable to other researchers and their funder. The Rockefeller Foundation's main interest was in measuring the psychosocial well-being of the children and identifying measures that could be used in evaluations of other OVC programs. Wallis and Dukay worked with Tanzanian colleagues to determine which measures would be most acceptable and pilot tested them in Idweli.

From this interview, we learn about some of the difficult choices evaluators make when conducting evaluations in countries whose cultures differ dramatically from our own. The difficulties are amplified when the audiences and potential users of the evaluation, in this case NGOs and others working to help OVC in Africa, want traditional research evidence. Wallis and Dukay are to be commended for initiating and completing this evaluation and for working to understand the values and culture of Idweli during the evaluation while meeting the needs of their stakeholders.

DISCUSSION QUESTIONS

1. What are the purposes of this evaluation? How are Wallis and Dukay's roles consistent with those purposes? How are their designs and measures consistent with those purposes? How are they inconsistent?

2. Contrast how Bledsoe in her evaluation in Trenton and Wallis and Dukay in their evaluation in Idweli work to establish cultural competence. How are they alike in their efforts? How do they differ? What do you see as the strengths of each of their efforts? The weaknesses? What would you have done differently?

3. One focus of the interview is on the working of the team, whose members come from two quite different cultures. One of their areas of emphasis is providing feedback to each other or feeling comfortable, even obligated, to give other team members feedback when they were not meeting their obligations. Have you worked with teams that are successful at doing this? What are

the obligations of a team member in evaluation? What do you see as the strengths and weaknesses of the team methods that Wallis and Dukay describe?

4. Contrast Wallis and Dukay's choice to use United States-based, standardized instruments to measure children's psychosocial well-being with a choice of developing new measures for the project that are more sensitive to the cultural norms of rural Tanzania. What are the strengths and weaknesses of each approach?

5. In this evaluation, the evaluation team members determine the focus of the evaluation. Contrast their role in making these decisions with Bickman's role in arguing with the funders over measuring children's mental health and with Henry's role in leading stakeholder groups to identify factors for the Georgia school report card. How do these evaluators' roles differ in determining the focus of the evaluation and the constructs to measure?

FURTHER READING

The complete evaluation report as well as a two-page summary are available at www
.lundy-africa.org/research_results.html

REFERENCES

Ainsworth, M., Beegle, K., & Koda, G. (2005). The impact of adult mortality and parents' deaths on primary schooling in northwestern Tanzania. *Journal of Social Development, 41,* 412–439.

Dayton, J., & Zimmer, Z. (2005). Older adults in sub-Saharan Africa living with children and grandchildren. *Population Studies, 50,* 295–312.

Foster, G., Levine, C., & Williamson, J. (Eds.). (2005). *A generation at risk: The global impact of HIV/AIDS on orphans and vulnerable children.* New York: Cambridge University Press.

Nyambedha, E. O., Wandibba, S., & Aagaard, J. (2003). Changing patterns of orphan care due to the HIV epidemic in western Kenya. *Social Science and Medicine, 57,* 301–311.

United Nations Children's Fund. (2004). *Children on the brink: A joint report of new orphans estimates and framework for action.* New York: Author.

United Nations Children's Fund. (2006). Africa's orphaned and vulnerable generations: Children affected by AIDS. New York: Joint United Nations Programme on HIV/AIDS and PEPFAR.

# PART V

ANALYSIS, INTERPRETATIONS, AND CONCLUSIONS

⊰ FOURTEEN ⊱

EXEMPLARS' CHOICES

What Do These Cases Tell Us About Practice?

Jody Fitzpatrick

———◦•◦———

his book is about the *practice* of evaluation, how skilled evaluators actually *do* evaluation. Thomas Schwandt (2005) has argued that "we need to restore the centrality of practice to evaluation" (p. 105), and this book is intended to be a step in that direction. Evaluators read and write about evaluation theories, approaches, and models—how evaluation *should* be practiced. We also read and write about the results of our studies and the methods we use to obtain those results. But evaluation practice is more than that. Evaluation practice, as any professional practice, is concerned with subtleties, nuances, or larger shades of difference in how evaluators *behave* during a study—what they consciously or unconsciously chose to do: in learning about the context of the program to be evaluated, the nature of the program itself and the stakeholders involved; in determining one's role in the evaluation; in choosing ways to interact with stakeholders; in deciding what to study and how to study it; and in other choices and challenges through each stage of the evaluation. There are no magic formulas or recipes for successful practice. Instead, the successful evaluator is observant, aware of the choices to be made and the need to consider the characteristics of the context, program, and stakeholders, just as a good teacher adapts his or her teaching strategy to the abilities and motivations of a student and the subject matter being taught.

The editors of this volume hope that, through these interviews, the reader has become aware of some of the ways in which a few successful, but quite different, evaluators approach practice in a particular setting. This chapter will highlight some of the challenges and choices that these evaluators faced through each stage of evaluation. In the sections that follow, several of the choices that evaluators make, and the challenges they face, will be examined, including

the role(s) evaluators play in an evaluation,

the factors or questions the evaluation addresses,

the ways evaluators interact with and involve stakeholders,

the methods they select, and

the strategies they use to encourage use.

These areas are selected to address major areas of practice and, to a certain extent, the sequence of the evaluation, although several stages overlap and iterate in actual practice. The reader will see different choices. In some cases, those choices reflect the context of the evaluation, including the characteristics of the program, its culture, and the stakeholders; in others, they reflect the proclivities and preferences of the evaluator. You have read the interviews and, in many cases, will have observed these choices. This chapter will highlight some choices that serve to illuminate commonalities and differences in practice that should prompt readers to consider and reflect further on the choices they make in practicing evaluation.

One qualification: Unlike Jennifer Greene's intensive case studies of decision makers' actions in conflict situations in the field (Chapter 3), the editors were not able to conduct interviews with others involved in these evaluations to verify the reports made in the interview. Instead, the interview provides the evaluator's own perspective. Each interviewer read evaluation reports and articles that provided her with a foundation to ask questions and probe. However, the interviewer's task was not to learn "the objective truth" concerning the conduct of the evaluation but, rather, to learn how the evaluator being interviewed perceived the choices, decisions, and challenges he or she faced in conducting the evaluation. In this chapter, I draw some conclusions about emphases and choices that come from the interviews themselves; however, those interviewed often chose to focus on different elements of their evaluations, sometimes in spite of the emphasis of the questions. They spoke about what was interesting and important to them, though their answers were generally responsive to the questions. As such, their choices concerning what to talk about are revealing of their priorities in the evaluation, and I draw some conclusions about those choices here. Moreover, the questions were targeted to the particulars of each evaluation, rather than using a common set of questions for each interview, to gain an understanding of *that* particular evaluation. It is possible that others followed similar practices and simply did not talk about those practices in their interview. The contrasts made in this chapter are to illuminate practice, especially the choices that practicing evaluators have made in the conduct of one evaluation. The contrasts are not intended to label or categorize any individual evaluator—we are, after all, focusing on only one of their many evaluations. Instead, the contrasts are designed to highlight elements of practice that might be of use to other practicing evaluators in guiding their choices and practice.

CHOICES CONCERNING ONE'S ROLE IN AN EVALUATION

A major choice made by each of those we interviewed, early in the process, concerned the role he or she would play in the evaluation. The role of an evaluator can be defined in a number of different ways. Rather than rely on traditional definitions of role as defined in the prescriptive or theoretical literature, I have examined the interviews to highlight some of the roles that emerged in practice.

Becoming a Part of the Team Versus Maintaining Some Distance

One element of the evaluator's role that emerged in the interviews concerned the extent to which the evaluator became involved with the program, in planning or improving the program or advocating for a particular stakeholder group, or, conversely, attempted to maintain a distance from the program as a "neutral" or "objective" observer. In many cases, this choice was influenced by the stage of the program. When a program was at an early stage, many evaluators chose to become involved with helping program staff or administrators in making decisions concerning the best ways to deliver the program and meet the needs of their clients. As such, the roles of evaluator and program planners become less distinct.

Debra Rog, Stewart Donaldson, and Ross Conner all took such roles. They became involved in their evaluations at the beginning of program development. As such, they defined their role as one of helping those involved in program planning, to consider how to plan and deliver the best intervention. Debra Rog describes the circumstances that led her to take this role (Chapter 6):

> The whole topic of homelessness among families was a new, emerging issue at that time. Homelessness was ill defined; there still was not a lot known about it. There was especially little known about homeless families—who they were, how many there were, what their needs, were, how they became homeless. But providers and others did not believe they could wait for the information before they tried to deal with the problem. Therefore, in our evaluation, it was critical that we try to obtain some of this information, focusing more on describing the participants in the program than we might otherwise, to help increase our understanding of these families.

While the Foundation and the federal agency funding the program felt that a systems approach, coordinating and providing available services to homeless families in a more accessible way, should serve as a guiding theory for their intervention or program, Rog realized that the systems approach to intervention was based on many implicit assumptions about homeless families that were untested. She knew that the lack of information on the clients to be served and the nature of their problems might stymie program success. She observed that the Robert Woods Johnson Foundation (RWJ) felt that the services homeless families needed existed but were not oriented toward families. Her data then found that some of those services, in fact, did not exist. Thus, she concludes, "The initial work with the families helped to refine and articulate a more detailed model." Describing her role, Rog says,

> I did feel that we were in a developmental, formative role. . . . It [the program] did not begin with an extremely explicit theory or with a very elaborate understanding of the needs and problems of families. Therefore, part of our role was to help develop these bases of knowledge and then, in turn, use this knowledge to help guide program efforts.

Conner and Donaldson, in different ways, describe similar efforts. Both begin work quite early with the funding foundation before programs or sites are even funded. In Donaldson's case (Chapter 9), he worked with programs, once they were funded, to develop their program theory and, as the programs began, gave continuous feedback for improvement. Conner's role (Chapter 11) appears to be even more as a program insider than Donaldson's. Conner worked with many different healthy community programs, each of which was encouraged to develop an approach appropriate to improving citizen's engagement and, ultimately, health in their communities. He helped communities develop their logic models, provided them with profiles of their communities, and, for these community stakeholders, enabled them to tell the story of what they accomplished. Both Conner and Donaldson bring their own proclivities to this planning stage, Conner with his interest in community-based evaluations and Donaldson with using program theory for planning, but the activities they undertake with stakeholders during the planning phase and their role, working as part of a team to develop the programs, are quite similar.

In contrast, other evaluators came into a new program and define their role somewhat differently. James Riccio, in his evaluation of the California GAIN program (Chapter 2), wanted to watch and describe what the different counties were doing, not to become involved in planning. He saw himself more as the "neutral" observer whose task was to describe what occurred. The California legislature was his primary audience, and he and they wanted to know which models worked best, but he allowed the programs to evolve in each county and, then, detailed what emerged and its effects. In a quite different way, Jennifer Greene, in observing the Natural Resources Leadership Program (Chapter 3), established communication with program managers and staff, whom she saw as her main audience, but she did not become involved in helping them plan the program. Instead, she provided feedback on how it was going, encouraging them to reflect on their purposes and actions. They made changes with her feedback as the program progressed, but she was not involved in program planning. She defines her primary role in this way:

> I think we saw as our job to develop a good understanding of, and to make some judgments about, the quality and effectiveness of the leadership institute. We saw the evaluation as helping to do things *better in the future* [italics added]. We hoped our work might inform the institute but were probably more oriented toward developing a good description of how this institute was implemented, the ways it succeeded, and how it fell short.

Although using very different methods and evaluating programs with a different focus and a different scope, both Greene and Riccio defined their role as describing the program and its outcomes, rather than becoming intimately involved with planning and program development.

Other evaluators dealt with a program that was at a mature stage and made different choices about their role. As with the evaluators described above, these choices reflect a mixture of the stage of the program and their own proclivities as an evaluator. Bickman and Fetterman fall into this category. Each was evaluating a well-established program. Planning had occurred in the distant past. Of all the evaluators interviewed, Bickman most clearly took the role of wanting to be a "neutral" observer (Chapter 4). He wanted to provide definitive answers to whether the systems of care approach to improving children's mental health actually achieved its goals. He was responding to the program developer's desire "for an objective evaluation of the systems of care demonstration." Like Conner, Donaldson, and Rog, he took a very active role in the evaluation, but in a quite different way. Instead of working with program administrators and funders in a client-directed approach, his approach was led by his own knowledge and beliefs concerning how to determine the effectiveness of a program. Although in the role of a "neutral" scientific observer, Bickman was hardly passive. He states, "It was a battle with the Army throughout the project to maintain the integrity of the design." But he saw his role as that: protecting the integrity of the design, conducting a study that will have credibility with policy makers—his primary audience—to make decisions about whether to expand the systems of care approach or to discontinue it. In fact, Bickman chose to distance himself from program staff to establish independence and to avoid losing the trust of policy makers.

Fetterman, too, evaluated a mature program, the Stanford Teacher Education Program (STEP; Chapter 5), and, like Bickman, chose his own preferred methodology, immersion in the program, as a way to judge that quality. In doing so, his methods and his interactions with program participants are almost the antithesis of Bickman's. Fetterman became heavily involved in *experiencing* the program, sitting in on classes, following the students' schedules, observing their days, chatting with faculty about student performance, observing faculty's approach and performance, and the like. But, like Bickman, Fetterman's role was to judge the quality of the program, as he saw his primary stakeholder's information need. As such, he reviewed the literature, attended conferences and talked with experts to learn the factors that characterize or describe a high-quality teacher education program. He then compared what he saw in STEP with research and advice from other experts.

Although Bickman's and Fetterman's evaluations of mature programs differed quite dramatically in methodology and in interactions with stakeholders, in each case, the evaluator did not become involved with program planning and improvement during the evaluation. Instead, they worked to understand what the program was intended to do and how it was to do that, through either developing program theory and/or learning about research in the field, and then, they collected information to determine if the program succeeded and to make a judgment about that success.

Developing an Evaluation System

Finally, some of those interviewed work with programs that are not so much programs as parts of an organization or institutions. In these evaluations, the evaluator defined a role quite different from those above. This was the case with Preskill's work in developing an evaluation system for training and development programs at Sandia Labs (Chapter 10), with King's evaluation of the special education program at Anoka-Hennepin School District (Chapter 8), and with Henry's development of a performance measurement system for Georgia Public Schools (Chapter 7). These "programs" are not only mature, they are not going away.

Henry's role is akin to that of Preskill in developing an evaluation system for Sandia Labs, though Henry was developing a performance-monitoring system for the state of Georgia, for varied stakeholders across the state to use in judging schools. With this task, he found himself in a different setting from his usual work, which is more focused on determining program effects using causal designs or models. Instead, in this case, he was working to describe schools on some important factors, in a nontechnical, succinct fashion that was accessible to parents and the public. And he demonstrated flexibility in responding to the task. He made use of research literature and surveys of citizens of Georgia to identify potential factors to include on the report. Thus, part of his role was evaluator led, to set the stage for important stakeholder groups to make decisions about the report cards. A key aspect of his role, like King's role, was facilitating groups' decisions. He established and worked with four groups of stakeholders—principals, superintendents, teachers, and community members—to "create the architecture of the accountability system." Having developed the system, he defined a role in helping others understand and use the system, using talks with everyone from the press to principals to parents and workshops with school personnel to help them learn how to use the report cards for their own needs. His role evolved as the report cards continued and his Center led their dissemination (Chapter 7).

Advancing a Special Method

Preskill and King both defined their roles through an approach that they personally champion, but in both cases the approach was compatible with the organization's culture. Preskill used appreciative inquiry (AI) to approach the development of an evaluation system for the training and development department at Sandia Labs, but the Lab was using AI in other parts of the organization (Chapter 10). She indicates that they were "very receptive" to AI. They "purported to be a learning organization" and "wanted to model open-mindedness and were willing to try new things." These factors helped her feel confident that an AI model could work well in helping them develop an evaluation system that succeeded for them.

In King's case (Chapter 8), the choice of model and role was a little more complex. King would appear to face a challenge in this evaluation that she describes as "the most overtly political environment I have ever worked in." The evaluation is political because it is prompted by parent complaints to the state department of education. A representative of the department monitors the evaluation. Reflecting the high-profile nature of the evaluation, King identified the School Board as the primary audience for the evaluation. However, the culture of the school district "focused on collaboration and data." She noted that "part of my charge as an internal evaluator was to foster evaluation across the district," so she chose a role in building capacity in this high-profile evaluation. Her responses in the interview focus not on the results of the evaluation but on the processes she used to build competency. That was her interest in this evaluation. Although she concludes that "building capacity was the obvious choice," this choice risks that the evaluation may not address the needs of the School Board or the State Department of Education. To build competency, King had the self-study group define the evaluation's purpose, identify methods of data collection, interpret the data, and draw final conclusions. As she noted, her role was more on the client-centered end of the continuum of client-directed versus evaluator-directed actions, and her clients were the stakeholders involved in the evaluation. Her process increased the evaluative thinking skills of those participating, and her role was facilitating that process. Preskill and King both are concerned that their participants, Sandia employees in

Preskill's case and school employees and parents in King's case, enjoy the process of evaluation. King, in particular, sees part of her role as setting the appropriate environment.

Reflections on Choices Regarding One's Role

Each of these evaluators' choices concerning roles was influenced by the context of their work—the stage of the program and its characteristics, the expectations and values of stakeholders, and the nature of the surrounding environment. However, each *did* make choices in defining their role. It can be useful for the reader to picture those differences. How would Bickman have defined his role in evaluating the Stanford Teacher Education Program? How would Fetterman have defined his role in the context of Sandia Labs or the Homeless Families Program? It is likely that these evaluators, to a certain extent, choose to evaluate in contexts that are compatible with their own proclivities and approaches. Would Greene choose to conduct the evaluation of the large GAIN program in California, serving a legislative, policy-making audience? Would Riccio choose to evaluate Bledsoe's Fun with Books program in Trenton? Readers of this chapter also make choices of the evaluations they seek and accept, but they should also be aware of the choices that they make, having stepped into an evaluation, in considering and defining their role. Finally, readers should be aware that roles change, as seen in many of the interviews (Donaldson, Greene, Conner, Rog, Henry). As Conner notes,

> I think as an evaluator in community-based programs, you wear a lot of hats and have to be ready to shift. You have to know where you stand and know the expertise that you bring. . . . An evaluator brings skills in asking and answering evaluation questions, in the pros and cons of research methods, and so forth; it's this expertise that starts the interaction and relationship. But what keeps you effective, as part of the relationship, are the sensitivities, the human skills—knowing when to push, when to hold back, when to be a devil's advocate, when to be supportive, when to talk, and when to listen. (Chapter 11)

Conner's comment highlights the final element of an evaluator's role and that is the extent to which those interviewed view themselves, consciously or unconsciously, as a supporter of the program they have evaluated, as a "neutral" observer, or as a devil's advocate or critic. It is useful to observe evaluators' language and their ways of talking about the programs they evaluate.

Some are comfortable with discussing failures or drawbacks of the program; they view that reporting and judgment as part of their job. Others are not. They view their job as supporters of the program, helping to nurture and improve it, to not only recognize but also applaud and highlight its accomplishments. This role, too, should be one taken consciously with careful thought concerning the evaluation's purpose and the evaluator's role.

CHOICES CONCERNING THE ISSUES
OR QUESTIONS THE EVALUATION WILL ADDRESS

Role and questions are, of course, interrelated, but just as the evaluators face choices in defining their roles, so too they face choices in deciding *what* to evaluate. I will highlight a few evaluations here that shed light on those issues and some interesting choices.[1]

Evaluator-Led Choices on What to Evaluate

The interview with Allan Wallis and Victor Dukay (Chapter 13) provides useful insight into an evaluation team independently defining the important issues to evaluate. Dukay is intimately familiar with Godfrey's Children Center, but the others had not yet visited it when they define the overarching factors that they will evaluate: children's physical and psychosocial status and the sustainability of the Center. To an extent, these are obvious outcomes, and because they wanted to examine the success of the program, studying these outcomes seems appropriate. Nevertheless, their interdisciplinary team, with some consultation with the Rockefeller Foundation, defined the outcomes independently, without consultation with program stakeholders. In this case, Dukay seems sufficiently familiar with the goals and activities of the Children's Center and the potential interests of foundations working in this area to make some informed judgments about the important issues to address. In working with his interdisciplinary team, he learned more about how to conceptualize these outcomes and how they might be measured, but their choices were to make these decisions with less interaction with other stakeholders than others we interviewed. Their large, interdisciplinary, and cross-cultural team was the source of their decisions.

They were, however, mindful of the concerns of the Rockefeller Foundation, and those concerns prompted them to consider psychosocial measures. Their own views and those of the Rockefeller Foundation also prompted them to recognize their purpose as helping to develop protocols for evaluations of other, similar interventions, and this focus influenced the issues they chose to evaluate. Wallis observed that he wished they had collected data on family visits, because this element of program operations emerged as a potentially important issue in the integration of the Children's Center into the community, but their early focus on outcomes, rather than describing the activities of the Center, did not prompt them to consider addressing that issue when planning the evaluation. They were also constrained by a very tight time frame for conducting the evaluation. Thus, we see how context—the need for a large, interdisciplinary team, the purposes and time frame for the evaluation—influenced their choices of what to evaluate.

Len Bickman, too, took a strong, evaluator-led role in choosing what to evaluate. We have noted Len Bickman's role in advocating for a rigorous evaluation. We will add a comment here, however, on his choice of what to measure. He is shocked that the Department of the Army considers measuring process and costs as sufficient to determine program success and argues vigorously for measuring mental health outcomes in children, the ultimate program goal. He fights to look at mental health outcomes in children, stating,

> I think not looking at clinical outcomes for services that are intended to affect those outcomes is poor evaluation practice. I did not know if the continuum of care would affect child and family outcomes, but I did know that was what the program claimed it would accomplish. If you're claiming to do policy-relevant research, you must look at what happens to people. (Chapter 4)

The factors that influenced Bickman are the tenets of social science research methodology, not the wishes or desires of funders or stakeholders. But this choice, and his advocacy for it, was consistent with his purpose of influencing policy, helping others make summative choices about whether to advance the continuum of care concept or to end it. As such, he saw measuring the ultimate outcomes as the only choice.

Finally, Fetterman's interview (Chapter 5) shows evaluator-led choices in what to evaluate, though, unlike Bickman and Wallis and Dukay, Fetterman chooses to focus on the process of the program much more than on its outcomes. Charged by the president of Stanford University with determining the quality of the Stanford Teacher Education Program and whether it met "Stanford standards," Fetterman reviewed the literature on teacher education, talked with experts in teacher education, and visited some of their programs,

but he does not mention discussing his choices with stakeholders. After reviewing the literature and talking with experts, he decided to focus on the process,
or actions, of the program and the extent to which they were consistent with
both the plan for the program and the characteristics of other outstanding programs in order to judge the quality of the Stanford Teacher Education Program.
This choice, to emphasize program description and its consistency with indicators of high quality, may have been influenced by the environment of higher
education, which is only just beginning to study outcomes and where accreditations and the like focus on the characteristics of the program—for example,
faculty research and reputation, admission standards, dropout rates, and so on.
It is likely that the choice was also influenced by Fetterman's own training in
anthropology and his related emphasis on immersion. Just as Wallis and
Dukay's team felt the obvious choice was to focus on outcomes, Fetterman felt
the obvious choice was to focus on process. He noted,

> We began by trying to understand what the model for STEP was—what
> insiders said it was *supposed to do.* Then, we wanted to look at what kind of
> compliance there was with the model. . . . It was a mature program, and we
> wanted to look at what it was doing—how it was operating. . . . In most
> cases, we had specific things we were looking for. We reviewed the literature
> associated with teacher education programs and internal program documents
> and then attempted to document whether program intentions were being
> actualized. . . . The idea was to describe, not to test. . . . [O]bservation in our
> case was really a series of hypotheses about how things should work, and
> then we used observation to test those assumptions or statements about pro-
> gram operations.

Fetterman's immersion methods provided a great deal of understanding
concerning what the student was experiencing, but his model for ultimately
judging the quality of the program is akin to Provus's (1971) discrepancy
model for evaluation—that is, how do program actions differ from the intent.
Fetterman is, however, committed to immersion as a central means of data collection, noting that "immersion is the *only* way to get the best-quality data. . . .
You can't see patterns without long-term immersion." Thus, Fetterman brought
a greater depth of description and understanding to his evaluation through his
use of immersion than a typical discrepancy evaluation study might.
Nevertheless, his choices for focus are on process and discrepancies with
existing models.

A Stakeholder-Led Example of What to Evaluate

In contrast, Ross Conner's choices (Chapter 11) appear to be very responsive to, even contingent on, stakeholders' questions. In this case, stakeholders' questions led him to focus on telling the stories of people and communities and examining some immediate outcomes of the program—complex studies of changes in community decision making and governance at individual and community levels—rather than examining ultimate, long-term program outcomes as Bickman argued to do. In explaining why he did not use the randomized model he had used in the earlier evaluation, Conner's response illustrates his client-focused role in choosing what to study and how to study it:

> In the case of the Tres Hombres program, the migrant workers with whom I worked really wanted to know if the program was making a difference. In this case, we had a control group design where we set up contrasts, because this is how we could best understand whether the program made a difference. The Colorado Trust program, on the other hand, had different evaluation questions. The funders knew that because of the complexity and diversity of the individual community projects, the program at best would be *contributing* to change, not solely causing it. They didn't want or need to spend the relatively large resources necessary for implementing a causal design.
>
> The common thread is that I am responding to the questions that are being asked for the evaluation and then adapting the evaluation design to those questions, the reality of the context, and the conflicts and restrictions presented.

Thus, in each case, Conner's choices about what to study evolve from conversations with key stakeholders about what is important for them to know. Like Wallis and Dukay, his focus on immediate outcomes comes about through his considerations about what the funder would like to know. At other points in his evaluation, he is influenced by what community members want to know.

Studying Those Who Might Succeed

Jennifer Greene's interview (Chapter 3) does not provide much background on whether the outcomes to be studied were evaluator led or client led, but she provides an interesting model in examining process and outcomes. Her description of the program was intended "to develop reasonably thorough portrayals of this program as designed and implemented." Not unlike Fetterman, some of her methods were designed "to anchor our evaluation in the lived experiences of those closest to the program." Her team's observations and her intensive case study permitted her to do that. One of her interesting choices about what to study emerged in her study of outcomes. Her choice to conduct mini-case studies on a sample of cases most likely to have an impact was appropriate to the nature of the program objectives and might be adopted more frequently by others. The goal of this series of workshops, which brought together people who work on different sides in forming environmental policy, was to help them work together better and, ultimately, improve environmental policy and the quality of the environment. Greene measured some immediate outcomes, changes in knowledge and skill in resolving conflicts, and collected data from all participants. But she also wanted to attempt to measure longer-term outcomes. In discussing what she decided to measure, she said,

> The emphasis on practical program outcomes [what happened when using the skills in the field] was an intentional focus of the evaluation from the out-set. Not only did our stakeholders want this information, but we thought it was important too. What we all know about training is that the real question is the "so what" question. Do people actually realize the intentions of train-ing in the field?

Thus, she and her team undertook mini-case studies, which were quite labor-intensive, interviewing the participant to identify dispute resolutions that occurred in the field *and* interviewing others involved in the resolution of the dispute to learn what the participant had contributed. Because some of the par-ticipants in the program did not have the authority or position to go back and "make things happen differently," she and her team decided to use their resources to study those who might have been able to do so. She notes, "The idea was not to be representative but rather to purposefully sample the best cases. We wanted to learn if, at its best, the institute had the potential to make a difference." Given the ultimate goals of the workshop and the reasonable recognition that each participant, even if he or she were in a position of author-ity, might not have the opportunity to use his or her conflict resolution skills to improve the quality of the environment—a pretty lofty, though certainly worth-while, goal—some evaluators might blindly take a random sample. Instead, Greene thought consciously about the purposes of the institute and her purpose, to determine whether the institute could have made a change in the best circumstances, and chose to study a purposive sample that was more likely to make the change. This is a methodological choice. She also, however, chose to use this outcome as her primary criterion in judging the success of the institute, even though the impacts she found were modest. She could have claimed stronger success for the institute by citing the attainment of immediate goals concerning changes in knowledge and skill with many participants. These choices emerge from Greene's recognition of the role of values in evaluation. She was conscious of her choices and values in this evaluation. She noted,

> We anchored our judgment in the observed instances of meaningful success. . . . We had strong evidence of knowledge, skills, and attitude change, but the outcomes in the field were the main criteria we wanted to use to judge the institute.

In these examples, we see evaluators making different choices about *what* to evaluate—process, immediate outcomes, or ultimate outcomes. Their choices are affected, again, by these factors: the nature of the program, their views of stakeholders' needs and expectations, and their own proclivities. We see them making a variety of choices about who to involve in this decision and the sources to consult. They differ in which stakeholders and resources they chose involve or use to make these choices and their conclusions about stakeholders' or intended audiences' needs and preferences.

CHOICES CONCERNING INTERACTIONS WITH AND INVOLVEMENT OF STAKEHOLDERS

Our interviews illustrate many choices and variations in working with stakeholders, including the depth and breadth of stakeholder involvement; the manner in which the evaluator works with stakeholders; and the ways in which stakeholders are involved, and their interests considered, in the evaluation.

Both Jean King and Ross Conner described evaluations in which there is a great deal of depth of stakeholder involvement. King's goal (Chapter 8) was to build evaluation capacity among the members of her 100- to 50-person self-study team, and in fact, the stakeholders on the self-study team made the major decisions about the evaluation. They defined the initial purposes of the study. They developed the survey items and interview questions. They interpreted the data and developed the final commendations and recommendations. As King states, "It was participatory from the beginning. . . . It was highly interactive all along." Although she acknowledged that the Evaluation Consulting Team played "a critical role" in ensuring that the self-study groups were using data to support their conclusions, the self-study groups actually *do* the evaluation, with only technical guidance (which appears to be asking them to prove that their conclusions were derived from the data) from the team. As such, the self-study groups must learn much about evaluation, achieving King's goal. Her interview provides useful guidance for an evaluator who wants to build capacity and involve stakeholders in that depth. Since participation in the self-study groups is voluntary, King describes how she made use of the setting, meals, and group interaction to make the experience pleasant, to get the participants to keep coming back. She discusses the problems and the actions they take to get parents, particularly minority parents, to serve in continuing roles in the self-study group. And, in fact, she measures her success by surveying self-study group participants about what they have learned and what they thought of their involvement. She observes that "the key was helping them [people on the self-study team] to be purposeful about the learning process. Part of that is demystifying evaluation for people." By having them look at actual data, and draw conclusions, and justify their conclusions with the data, she does "demystify" the process. She made them become comfortable and familiar with the data. Her process was very client driven. She reports that "The Evaluation Consulting Team purposely did not make separate analyses and have separate reports. . . . We were the technicians; we were preparing the data. But as far as analyzing the data and interpreting it, we didn't do that." Of course, preparing data does require some judgment, as does correcting "technical errors," but King's point is that the clients in the self-study group are doing the evaluation. That represents a huge depth of stakeholder involvement, and clearly, that is where her attention lies. Interestingly, the stakeholder group had power because they were conducting the evaluation, and yet, they did not make the initial decision to focus the evaluation on capacity building. That decision, and the means to build capacity, was made by King and the school district administrators.

Conner's evaluation (Chapter 11) also demonstrated a great depth of stakeholder involvement, though less than in King's capacity-building evaluation. He waited for areas of interest to emerge from stakeholders and then took them, developed them further using his expertise, and shared them with other communities in the project. In describing the emergence of the community indicators, one of the outcomes for which his evaluation is noted, he reported,

Upon reflection I would say that the desire to have something like a community indicators component existed and that the evaluation helped set a context for it to emerge. But it wasn't imposed. What one project was doing really intrigued people, and it gave me an opportunity to say, "Hey, this is a great way to have localized community measures."

Conner worked with the stakeholder advisory group to identify the evaluation questions for the study. Stakeholders were also involved in developing the survey, which he feared was too long, but he went with it. In the end, they had a very high response rate, and he attributed that rate to the involvement of community members in developing the survey. Conner and his evaluation team analyzed the data but sought feedback on results from stakeholders. While Conner and King both had a great deal of stakeholder involvement, Conner was *part* of the team, sometimes serving as a facilitator but at other times using his evaluation expertise to make decisions. Thus, he observes, "We [evaluators] know that certain ways of focusing on outcomes are better than others. Most people don't have that expertise. That's okay if we as evaluators bring it, working collaboratively." Reflecting on being a member of a team, he discusses sharing expertise: "The evaluator definitely brings certain kinds of expertise, but the community members do too. And, sometimes, they [the community members] lead us in a way that we might not anticipate, but we, the evaluators, have to be open to that." Conner was more concerned with the evaluation itself, and less with capacity building, than King. He wanted to involve stakeholders to learn their views, to gain from their knowledge of their community and, thus, improve the evaluation.

Other interviews provide fascinating detail about how to work with stakeholders in more evaluator-led evaluations. Donaldson and Preskill provide quite a bit of detail on how they work with stakeholders. Donaldson gives excellent examples of, and insights into, dealing with stakeholders. He and Preskill both comment that the evaluator doesn't need to teach stakeholders all the jargon of the field. In Donaldson's case, logic models are used to help the *evaluator* decide what questions to ask. Since program people often become bogged down in the details of the program, which are, of course, their day-to-day concerns, Donaldson recommends developing the logic model by starting at the end and moving backward. He begins with "How will this participant be different or change after completing the program?" Once that difference—the change the program hopes to bring about in the participant—is defined, the evaluator can move to immediate outcomes and, then, identify the program processes or factors that are intended to lead to those outcomes. Donaldson's style of working with stakeholders was more evaluator led than King's or Conner's style, but he interacted extensively with program staff. He describes the evaluation team as

> the facilitator and leader. We're not saying, "What do you want to do?" but "Here's what we could do. These are the things that are most feasible." Then, sometimes, others would say, "No, no, what about this?" (Chapter 9)

The interaction was there, but using his expertise in evaluation, Donaldson was telling stakeholders what the evaluation could do and listening to stakeholders' reaction and thoughts. Realizing that he was giving program staff feedback on what they do, Donaldson sought feedback from them about *his* performance each year and adapted to that feedback. Finally, Donaldson recognized the need for the evaluator to be open to receiving feedback, not to become defensive with feedback or questions but instead to "model" the behavior he hoped to see in stakeholders when he gave them feedback.

Hallie Preskill (Chapter 10), too, cautions not to explain too much. With reference to appreciative inquiry (AI), she observes, "I don't think you always have to teach participants what AI is. If you start by describing the underlying theories, it often serves as a barrier." Instead, she guided them in experiencing it. She then describes some of the specific exercises she used with Sandia Labs and their reactions to it.

For those evaluating a smaller-scale program, Katrina Bledsoe (Chapter 12) made some useful choices concerning involving stakeholders. In observing that she wanted her evaluation to stimulate use and organizational learning, she says "relationships are key." She was new to Trenton and knew that cultural competence was critical to her evaluation. Bledsoe got to know the community by driving and walking around the neighborhood and by reading about their history. She realized that knowing the context for the program was critical to her developing relationships. The team being new to Trenton was a major drawback. So Bledsoe went "where the people live." She spent time with people in the community and at the organization, noting "you have to get to know people to build trust." Bledsoe took the time to do that, meeting weekly with program people for four or five months to hammer out the theory for the program. Although she wanted to develop a relationship with program people, Bledsoe was aggressive in questioning them about their program model. But her style, questioning them but trying to work together, for example offering to draw her version of the model, did not appear to offend or distance the program staff. Her work to establish relationships had helped them see her as part of the team, though in an evaluator's role. She was bringing them new expertise that may help improve the program. In the end, the time Bledsoe spent with the organization, administrators and staff, and her desire to understand the program and its context allowed her to make suggestions that they were open to use.

Allan Wallis and Victor Dukay's evaluation (Chapter 13) of Godfrey's Children, Center in Tanzania illustrates other choices made by evaluators. Their concern was not so much to improve the existing Children's Center as to influence policy regarding the treatment of orphaned and vulnerable children in Africa. As such, and consistent with their desire for the study to have credibility with other NGOs and foundations working in this area, they chose to have little stakeholder involvement in their evaluation. Dukay had much knowledge and familiarity with the Center, and this knowledge helped him in conducting the evaluation. He notes that his three years of working with the Center helped him "began to understand the culture and, more important, to develop friendships with key people in the village. As a result, trust was developed. They were very comfortable with allowing us to do the evaluation because they knew me." But Dukay believes minimizing stakeholder involvement at the program level will improve the evaluation's credibility with outside audiences. Instead, as discussed, Wallis and Dukay used their large, bicultural evaluation team to make decisions and discuss choices in the evaluation. Their work with the team also involves choices, choices concerning the expertise of the team, how the team should work together, and the role of each member.

This chapter is about the practice of evaluation. A critical element of practice is the choices one makes concerning stakeholder involvement. Here, I have highlighted some of the choices that evaluators, consciously or unconsciously, make in that practice. In most of these interviews, the evaluators made their choices based on the context of the evaluation: Will greater or lesser involvement of stakeholders improve or detract from the purposes of this evaluation? King believed that the school district's efforts to improve evaluation capacity in the district was of primary concern in this evaluation and, thus, used the evaluation to enable members of the self-study group to learn some of the tools of the trade. At the other end of the continuum on stakeholder involvement, Wallis and Dukay believed that for their primary audiences to find their evaluation credible and valuable, they must separate themselves from the program and its stakeholders to retain the autonomy of their team and the credibility of their evaluation. In different ways, Conner, Donaldson, and Preskill saw involving stakeholders as critical to improving their evaluation work. In Conner's case, stakeholder involvement helped him learn what they wanted to know and to gain their support in survey returns. Knowledge of stakeholders' conceptions of program theory helped Donaldson develop a relationship with those stakeholders and learn what to measure and when to do it. Stakeholders' involvement in developing the evaluation system was critical to Preskill in using appreciative inquiry to develop a system that will be useful for the organization. The choices our interviewees made about stakeholder involvement were typically concerned with their perceptions of how such involvement would enhance or impede the purposes of the evaluation. Key examples here are King's evaluation, where she saw a depth of stakeholder involvement as essential to developing capacity, and Wallis and Dukay's evaluations, in which they viewed a separation from stakeholders during the evaluation as important in establishing credibility with their intended audiences. The theme for evaluation practice here is to consider your purpose and your needs and whether, and how, stakeholder involvement can assist in achieving that purpose.

CHOICES IN METHODOLOGY

The Influence of "Scientific" Values

Many people think that evaluation is all about methodology. These interviews illustrate the many other factors that influence evaluation. As Katrina Bledsoe (Chapter 12) notes, evaluation is "part science and part art. You can't get to the science until you've done the art." The previous sections have dealt with that art, but selecting a methodology involves some art and choices as well. This section will highlight a few of the factors that appear to influence methodological choices and some of the noteworthy choices and methods that emerged.

Several of these evaluators' methodological choices were influenced by their view of what their audience expected or valued. Specifically, quite a few of those interviewed argue that the methodology they used needed to meet the expectations of audiences whom they believe value "scientific" data. Wallis and Dukay (Chapter 13), for example, discuss considering several more "innovative" methods but are ultimately influenced by what they think their audiences, foundations and policy makers, will value. Dukay notes that they chose to use standardized measures "so we wouldn't have to argue with the technocrats." With positive feedback from their Tanzanian team members, they believed that these Western-based instruments can be used validly with rural Tanzanian children and saw the use of such standardized measures as critical to the credibility of their study with their wider audiences. Their short time frame also forced them to be practical about what they could do. Although a grants officer from the Foundation suggests "having children draw and tell what they saw," they ultimately rejected that idea and other more qualitative approaches. Wallis reports,

> We thought these were intriguing notions, but we didn't know how difficult it would be or what exactly we would do with it. We wanted rich sources of qualitative data because quantitative data can be flat, but some of the more exotic seemed too unpredictable. . . . We wanted to do some things that were innovative, but we also wanted to use measures that would be immediately recognized by other researchers in the field.

Wallis and Dukay's time frame and their desire for credibility with a "scientific" community, or those who value that type of data, led them to choose what they saw as safer measures. So they spent time working to facilitate the transfer of these measures, largely standardized in the United States, to use with children in rural Tanzania with their Tanzanian colleagues' support and assistance in this endeavor.

Katrina Bledsoe (Chapter 12) also raises the specter of "science" and how others' views of it can affect one's methodological choices. She notes that the stakeholders wanted "to have a program that was based upon 'scientific' concepts. . . . They wanted to say that 'science' drove their findings and, by extension, drives the program." As a result, she looked to the research literature, as well as talking with stakeholders, to derive the evaluation questions that guided her study. But her perceptions of the funding environment mirror those of Wallis and Dukay. She notes that

> "science" seems to be the battle cry of governments and funders, meaning if the program is supported by science, then it must be okay. I haven't been able to do one evaluation of late without having to address the use of science to drive the evaluation.

When it comes to selecting measures to use in her study, Bledsoe reports, "He [her colleague in developmental psychology] gave us some background in the area based upon his approaches and his research. We also explored the literature. What seems reasonable or similar to what we're exploring in the current situation?" As a result, like Wallis and Dukay, she selected some standardized measures to evaluate changes in the children's reading readiness. But she also chose to develop other measures tailored to the Fun with Books program. She indicated that in spite of the preference she saw in funding agencies for "scientific" measures, "since a lot of my work is community based, it [developing new measures specific to a program or setting] makes sense." She adds, "Communities can differ greatly from one another, and although there are universals that can be assessed with known measures across communities, some aspects cannot and need measures developed specifically for the situation and for the evaluation." For example, she wanted to measure children's social awareness and found no appropriate, existing measures, so she developed some items to tap this issue themselves. Bledsoe also talked with staff and learned that "they also wanted to be able to share their experience" and, so, designed interviews and meetings to tap those experiences. Because the interaction between parents and children was a critical part of the Fun with Books program, she chose to use videotapes to examine these interactions with more care. She found these videotapes to be "invaluable." They "allowed us to see the smaller picture—how the family interacted while reading, how kids responded to their parents and vice versa, and so forth." Thus, Bledsoe was influenced by her perception of the need for "scientific" findings but also moved on to develop some quantitative and qualitative measures that are specific to the program.

The Use of Experimental Designs

James Riccio and Len Bickman are the only evaluators to choose traditional experimental designs in their evaluations, using random assignment to conditions to test the causal effects of the programs they evaluate. Both of their evaluations were highly visible with prominent audiences, and this visibility probably played a role in the choice of design. Riccio notes that "a few important legislative staff" pushed for the program to be "subjected to a rigorous, independent evaluation." Similarly, Bickman says that "we had no choice in the design. That was given to us." Perhaps something as controversial as random assignment, especially to programs concerning critical outcomes such as work and personal income and children's mental health, can only come about through strong political action or support from outsiders. Riccio notes

(Chapter 2) the advantages of a randomized design on a highly politicized issue. He reports,

> When we're able to use a random assignment research design, as in the GAIN study, it's hard to dismiss the evidence as simply "political." Almost anyone can look at the basic results of the study and see whether the program group did better in terms of employment and other outcomes than the control group. It's difficult to run from that kind of evidence, and you don't need to be a statistician to understand it. . . . [U]sing randomly-assigned control groups helped us enormously in establishing our credibility.

Given their experimental designs, Riccio and Bickman made similar decisions concerning the need to avoid "a black box" study—that is, not knowing what caused the program successes or failures. Both chose to devote a large amount of resources and time to describing program implementation. Bickman (Chapter 4) chose to examine both program implementation and the quality of program delivery using the logic model for the program as a guide. He states, "I wanted to know that the program was delivered with fidelity—to know that if the program failed to produce effects, it was because it was a theory failure." He saw his job as testing the continuum of care, and first, he wanted to know if the continuum of care was actually delivered. A strength of his evaluation was his decision to assess program quality as well as implementation, and he recognized the role of judgment in determining that quality.

In contrast, Riccio (Chapter 2) decided to measure implementation because, in fact, the legislature expected the counties in California to adapt and change the model provided in the state legislation for welfare reform, and he wanted to be able to describe the changes counties made. Riccio did not develop a logic model for the program; he only had the legislation. But his remarks emphasize the importance of describing implementation. He states,

> Local implementation turned out to be very important. Although it was expected that the counties' programs would vary somewhat, no one quite anticipated the ways in which they would vary. Perhaps most striking was how the counties could all operate the same basic program model yet provide such different messages to recipients about work and welfare. Thus, recipients in different counties had different program experiences.

His observation is true for many programs. One logic model or program theory can lead to many different styles of implementation. Ultimately, county variations in implementing GAIN led to different outcomes across counties in welfare clients' incomes and movement into the workforce. Without Riccio's efforts to carefully study variations in implementation, the differences in outcomes would have been difficult to explain and the policy recommendations emerging from the study would have been much more limited.

Both Bickman and Riccio choose to use extensive qualitative and quantitative measures, observations, interviews, surveys, and existing data to describe the programs in delivery. These are massive studies but illustrate the ways in which evaluators can use different types of data to inform. However, the choice of what to measure and how, and the interpretation of the results, requires careful examination and thought by the evaluation staff. Riccio notes,

> The field research [observations, interviews] complemented the survey data in important ways. It helped us understand better what we thought we were measuring with the staff survey and allowed us to illustrate some of the important differences in staff practices across the counties.

In other words, evaluation staff's observations of GAIN orientations, workshops, staff-recipient meetings, and day-to-day program operations helped them realize that Riverside County was giving a work-first message. They saw what staff were saying and doing.

Choices Concerning Using Observation

David Fetterman, Jennifer Greene, and Ross Conner all made use of observation as an important tool in their evaluations, but they made different choices about how to conduct those observations. Both Fetterman and Conner talk about using observation to "tell people's stories." Fetterman and Greene emphasize wanting to know "what it was like to be a participant in the program" (Greene, Chapter 3) and "to understand what students were experiencing" (Fetterman, Chapter 5). But they chose somewhat different approaches to their observation. Fetterman became an active participant as he and his staff immersed themselves in the Stanford Teacher Education program. He argues, "You have to be part of the culture, to help clean up the lab, to understand the extra work and the pressures of their [students'] personal lives." Although he says, "Most of the time we simply listened," he talked with teachers about students and shared his opinions, as a fellow teacher, about students with supervising teachers in the program. He and his staff used digital photography and rotation across classrooms to share what they had experienced and to discuss whether they reached the same conclusions.

In their intensive case study of the first round of the Institute, Jennifer Greene and her two colleagues observed the workshops together, using a one-page observation guide to help them focus on areas of importance and, though they talked with participants at breaks, seemed to be in the role of observers more than that of participants or advisors to the trainers. Like Fetterman with his graduate students, the three evaluators in Greene's study talk with each other after the sessions about what they observed and their perceptions. Because the colleagues came from different backgrounds—conflict resolution, leadership, evaluation, they sometimes observed different things and their conversations helped clarify those differences.

Ross Conner studied many communities and assigned evaluation staff to each community to observe community meetings and project-related activities (Chapter 11). He reports that he "looked for diverse research assistants because I wanted the evaluation team to look like the communities." Conner's staffs' observations appeared to be more like the methods used by Greene, though without the colleagues for discussion. He indicates that they were "quiet participants" who did not take notes but would write a report after the meeting using "a rough frame of topics and issues to watch for." Conner feels that he is "fortunate to have good people as research assistants who were accepted right into the community," and elements of Fetterman's immersion emerge as he notes that each got to know their community quite well "from the 'coffee shop' perspective." Because a large part of Conner's purpose was to describe changes in the community, his research assistants were both watching the program and observing outcomes and changes. These observations helped them tell the story of the community. Although the observations used in these three evaluations are more similar than different, the nuances are useful. Fetterman's observation made them part of the program and, often, a large part (Chapter 5). He reports that classroom teachers "were very enthusiastic about having us there" and even gave them "a little award at the end of the summer as a way of recognizing how important we were as part of their lives." Conner and Greene are less well known to those they observe because they are more concerned with quietly fitting into the environments they are observing.

Choices Concerning Group Composition: Deliberative Democracy?

Another choice about methods concerns how to compose groups for planning the evaluation or collecting data. Jean King and Gary Henry make some different choices in composing their stakeholder groups. King put her self-study group participants in smaller groups to review and analyze data or to discuss issues in a focus group format (Chapter 8). The composition of these groups varies, but they are generally mixed by role. That is, principals, teachers, and parents could be in the same group. The table teams, the permanent teams that reviewed, analyzed, and interpreted data at each meeting, consisted of the people who sat at each table at the first meeting. Although King planned to change these groups at each meeting, participants wanted to stay with their first group, and she went with their preference. For her focus groups, teams were sometimes people with the same role—for example, teachers, parapro-fessionals, and parents. Other times, she reports, "we'd mix people up to get cross-role conversation." How does this composition of groups reflect her pur-pose? How does it affect the validity of the data collected or its interpretation by table teams? In her evaluation of the special education program, King was concerned with "bringing many people to the table during the study, especially those whose voices often went unheard in the district." She, and others on the evaluation team, worked to recruit and retain parents of color, who were under-represented in the self-study group, but they were unsuccessful and, ulti-mately, conducted telephone interviews with parents of color to make sure that their views were not neglected. But parents of color, who are recruited but not retained, did not gain the knowledge of evaluation and special education department activities that those in the self-study group did.

Gary Henry made a different choice in composing stakeholder groups for the planning and development of the Georgia school performance monitoring system (Chapter 7). He made use of four stakeholder groups: superintendents, principals, teachers, and community representatives. Their participation was, at least in part, motivated by the wishes of the Council for School Performance. Henry notes that they "were very emphatic about extending stakeholder status to members of the community in a highly inclusive way—including parents and others in the community." Like King, Henry worked with the groups for a long time, almost a year, to develop "the architecture of the accountability system." He reports that turnout for the meetings was high throughout the process. But he chose to compose groups of like members, that is, teachers with teachers, community members with community members, "to reduce the influence of preexisting power relationships on the deliberations." With King and Henry, we see quite different choices for similar purposes. Each knows his or her envi-ronment well. Perhaps King felt that her stakeholders had few concerns about communicating with others, across groups with different power. As King notes

about the parents, "These were special-needs parents. They were very committed. They weren't shy. They were advocating for their children and working to
make the system better for all kids." She observes, "In the table teams, democracy lived. People got to know each other as people. People got to know each
other and feel comfortable" (Chapter 8).

House and Howe (1999) have cautioned evaluators to be conscious
of power differences and to recognize their role in creating a "deliberative
democracy." As such, the evaluator can play an important role in making sure
that people with less power are able to have a voice in the evaluation. King
hoped to do that by establishing group norms that were developed by participants at the first meeting of the self-study group and included giving everyone
the right to speak, welcoming conflicting ideas, and speaking your truth. She
saw the groups "leaning in" and concluded that the mixed composition in
groups worked. Henry chose another route, establishing groups with like
people and hearing each of their views. Teachers did not have to be concerned
with what superintendents or administrators would think of their ideas. Parents
could speak without fear or anxiety about how their remarks might influence
the treatment of them or their child by teachers or administrators. Henry's and
King's choices reflect two different views, emphases, and beliefs about ways
to achieve "deliberative democracy."

Involving Stakeholders in Methodological Decisions

Debra Rog's interview (Chapter 6) gives us some insight into relatively
small, but important, issues in evaluation—that is, the conflicts that can arise
among program people, and others, about collecting certain types of data. A
major conflict arose across the administrators and program staff at different
sites over collecting data on "violence directed toward the homeless mom."
Rog had made the collection of such data optional because of the opposition,
but one site thought the data could be important and felt strongly that all sites
should collect it. She brought the sites together and let the program directors
argue the issue rather than arguing for the data collection herself. Rog reports
that the Portland project director, who favored the data collection, "was persuasive. The sites finally reached consensus, having all the domestic violence
questions included in the family assessment interview." In the end, these data
are important in revealing "extremely high rates of violence overall and even
severe violence in the lives of the mothers," and Rog used the data to make the

case for mental health service needs for these families. But by empowering the project directors to discuss and make decisions concerning data collection, she may have won the battle. The project directors knew their families and their staff. They could communicate, and persuade, each other about what was appropriate for their clients in a more effective way than Rog, who had less knowledge of the clients.

On another data collection issue, Rog demonstrated her ability to listen and respond to program case managers and, in so doing, developed a better instrument to describe case managers' activities. A few case managers thought that Rog's original form failed to capture what they did and created one with a different format. Rog reports,

> With the new format, we got more data than we had originally planned! The next time I came to visit, the case managers said, "You *did* change it." They were pleased that they had been heard. We bought a lot of credibility with that. The form became one of our most important tools. We got them to buy in, and thus, we got better data.

Rog made methodological choices here that reflect flexibility and stakeholder involvement and that, ultimately, led to more cooperation and better information.

Evaluations to Influence Future Evaluations

Most evaluations focus on the program being evaluated. Two evaluations in these interviews, however, are at least partially concerned with developing a protocol for future evaluations of similar programs. Ross Conner's evaluation (Chapter 11) received part of its recognition for developing community indicators that could be used by other programs hoping to improve the health of communities. Conner reports that people with the World Health Organization "had been calling for evaluation [of these types of programs] for many years, but not much had ever occurred. This, I believe, was the first attempt to do this systematically and comprehensively." The Colorado Trust reached out to Conner because of their interest in learning whether this strategy, a community-based approach to health beyond the particular program he was evaluating, was working. Conner observes that other foundations, communities, and researchers at universities were also interested in the issue and, thus, his description of how he conducted the evaluations and how the community indicators were used made a contribution to future evaluations.

In a quite similar vein, the Rockefeller Foundation reached out to Wallis and Dukay (Chapter 13) to test ways to evaluate interventions in Africa for orphaned and vulnerable children. Dukay was inspired to initiate the evaluation, and seek funding for it, by his encounter with the chief epidemiologist from the World Health Organization, who expressed his disappointment at the paucity of evaluation on HIV/AIDS programs in Africa designed to help children. Dukay's main interest was in developing evaluation methods that others can use, and their dissemination was, and continues to be, targeted toward that use. Conner and Dukay were aware of these purposes as they planned and conducted their evaluations and made choices to help their evaluations extend beyond the particular program they were evaluating. Conner, for example, took care to describe how he and his staff conducted the evaluation so that others can replicate it. Wallis and Dukay selected standardized measures to help them, at least partially, transcend the specifics of the Children's Center they were evaluating and to test the viability of using these psychosocial measures with orphaned and vulnerable children in Africa.

Views and Ambivalence on Objectivity

In closing this section on methodological choices, I would like to briefly explore the issue of "objectivity." People and organizations often contract with evaluators in order to obtain an "independent," "objective" assessment of a program. The word *objectivity*, or *objective*, is frequently used by program people and funders to cite the advantage of conducting an evaluation. However, those in the evaluation field, have different views concerning "objectivity" and the degree to which it is possible to achieve that in making a judgment about a program, regardless of the methodology. I begin this section by noting how several of those interviewed were influenced by stakeholders' desire for "scientific" evaluations and how these views affected their methodological choices. Here, I am concerned with describing how the evaluators themselves view objectivity. King, for example, describes one aspect of her role as that of an "objective technician," correcting "errors" that the self-study group made in interpreting the data. Others refer to the objectivity of their role and actions that may threaten it. For example, Bledsoe indicates that if an evaluator takes on certain advocacy roles, "a level of objectivity is compromised." Henry notes that the independence of the Council on School Performance, being separate from schools of education and state departments of education, "enhanced its ability to provide an objective analysis of educational performance data." Donaldson, in describing their decision to go against the foundation and include certain information in a report, observes that "we were able to retain our objective, independent view of things." In these remarks, King, Bledsoe, Henry, and Donaldson, like funders and program administrators, are acknowledging the values of independence and objectivity that evaluators bring to studying a program.

Others question the concept of objectivity. Conner, in response to a question from Christie about how he responds when people ask about the objectivity of his approach, says, "Ah, is anybody really objective? I tend to put objectivity in quotes these days." Jennifer Greene notes, "You [the evaluator] know you have a viewpoint and that your data are colored by your own lens." David Fetterman reveals some of the ambivalence evaluators feel about objectivity. He indicates that he is able to maintain "objectivity" as an internal evaluator, stating, "I didn't have any problem with approximating some form of objectivity or independent judgment." But in reference to a question on objectivity in data collection, Fetterman mirrors the remarks by Conner and Greene, stating

> There is no real or absolute objectivity. We approximate concepts of this nature. We hold ourselves up as models of it. Science and evaluation have never been neutral. We always bring our own lens. Most people have a very naive idea about what objectivity is. It's a nice concept, but it's not real. If we delude ourselves with it, we're just perpetuating a myth. We are *all* wearing a lens when we observe or judge something.

As noted, people and organizations hire evaluators for their objectivity and use the word frequently, so it is not surprising that many of our evaluators also use the word in discussing their performance. Yet these interviews reveal many choices, choices that can change the direction and results of a study. We are aware of the need for "objectivity" and "independence," but we must be aware of the fact that our values and views do affect our evaluations.

CHOICES CONCERNING USE
AND DISSEMINATION OF RESULTS

Our interviews showed extensive use of evaluation results. These included direct, instrumental use of results as program staff and administrators made changes in programs to improve the achievement of their goals and as foundations, government, and policy makers made decisions about funding programs. What knowledge about practice can be gained from reading these interviews? How did these evaluators work to encourage use of their findings? Two trends emerge: (a) reporting results about what works, and (b) extensive and creative networking both during the evaluation and after the results are completed to make stakeholders aware of the results and how they can use them.

Reporting the Successes

Preskill introduced appreciative inquiry to help her clients, in designing an evaluation system, consider what has worked well in their organization in the past. But, similarly, other evaluators recognized the value of letting clients know what has worked well, what they were doing right. Both Donaldson and King noted the value of this approach and used it. Donaldson adapted his reporting strategy to report first what was going well, after receiving feedback from program administrators and staff that they wanted the reports to also tell how they were succeeding. King began their report with "commendations" before proceeding to recommendations for change. These commendations highlighted what was working well in the special education program.

Extensive Networking and Outreach to Stakeholders

Others achieved a great deal of use through extensive networking and reporting. James Riccio's work with legislative staff and the State Department of Social Services prompted the state legislature to revise GAIN regulations in order to emphasize the county model Riccio's evaluation had found to be most successful. His work with counties inspired some county officials to modify their processes with clients even before the changed legislation. These instrumental uses of the evaluation results came about at least partially through Riccio's extensive work in involving these stakeholders in the results and the reporting process. He asked key state and county welfare administrators and legislative staff to review draft reports and says, "Their input helped increase the accuracy and fairness of reports, and in that process, they became intimately familiar with the findings." So his sharing of these draft reports not only gave him input but also encouraged often busy people to learn more about the results. As he notes, it is "fascinating testimony to the power of evaluation to influence public policy as it is practiced on the ground." He acknowledges that he and many others working in welfare reform were surprised by the results. They did not think that the work-first emphasis would show the best results. "But that's what we found, and it changed opinions." He believes part of what is important to achieve use is having one's results trusted. One of the ways he achieves that trust is by working to be direct and clear about evaluation findings—what program elements worked and which ones did not, what is very clear from the evaluation and what is more ambiguous. He notes, "[W]e tried to be clear on what we knew with a lot of certainty and what we knew with less certainty. . . . Being honest about the level of certainty that different findings and observations enjoy is critical if evaluators want to maintain their credibility."

Stewart Donaldson observes that they "killed a forest" with all their reports, required by the funding source. He, too, achieved much use, particularly in the planning stage, in helping programs that were less well thought out to carefully consider the steps to take to achieve their goals. But Donaldson thinks that "written reports slow down the communication process" and recommends oral communication, whether through telephone conference calls, if distance is an issue, or face-to-face meetings. Bledsoe, in her smaller-scale evaluation, was able to make use of face-to-face meetings to suggest changes to program administrators and staff. Many of her recommendations were implemented, from specifics concerning changing the length of the program to achieving greater consensus on program goals. One of the most important effects of her evaluation was making the program administrators aware that other programs like their's existed and they could learn from them. Bledsoe says that she achieved use by framing her recommendations in terms of what was feasible to the organization and suggesting that the organization was moving in the direction of the recommendations already. Although she believes that the program administrators "were primed for utilization" and just needed "evidence to corroborate their perceptions," in fact, her results are quite different than initially anticipated by program administrators, who viewed Fun with Books as their "flagship program" and just wanted results to show that and help them obtain more funding. Instead, her evaluation suggested many changes to achieve success, but her close work with the program seems to make those results palatable. The results are not a surprise, probably because she was priming them for what the evaluation could show all along.

Gary Henry developed something different, an ongoing performance-monitoring system for schools, but he and his organization did not stop with just publicizing results. He considered every potential audience. He recognized that just placing the report cards on the Web would not necessarily result in use: "The key to making this dissemination strategy work was that we placed a great deal of effort in notifying the press that these reports were out there. So every year we did some analysis to emphasize a theme for the press when we released the school reports." He met with reporters and editorial boards. He encouraged reporters to use the report cards when they were writing a story on education in their area. He and his staff conducted workshops with school districts to help them learn how to interpret and use the data. He personally responded to calls from principals, superintendents, and parents.

The activities of these evaluators say much about what is required to get evaluation results used. The dissemination phase can take as much time and energy as the study itself. The evaluator needs to consider who will be using the evaluation and consider their information preferences, needs, and values. And the evaluator must prepare these stakeholders for use by developing relationships with them, seeking their input, and making them aware of "surprises" that the data may show so that the final results are accepted.

LESSONS LEARNED FOR THE PRACTICE OF EVALUATION

What do we learn from these examples of evaluation practice by exemplary evaluators? A primary lesson that transcends each stage is for evaluators to be aware of the choices they have. One should make those choices consciously, considering the context of the program, its stage, and stakeholders' information needs and expectations and, given the evaluator's knowledge and expertise in evaluation, what is appropriate and feasible to accomplish in the evaluation. Even experienced evaluators make unconscious "choices" or fail to recognize when a choice is available. Below, I have summarized some of the strategies that emerge from the interviews.

The Evaluator's Role

Should evaluators attempt to be "neutral" observers or work closely with program staff for program development or improvement? A major consideration is the stage of the program to be evaluated. Is the program a mature one or a new, emerging, or changing program? New programs should not be rushed to judgment unless egregious harm is being caused. Most social programs are complex and need to make changes to adapt to the real world of the field or to a new context, new clients, or new staff. In the early stage of a program, stakeholders are likely to need evaluators for planning or to provide information for program improvement. But as time passes, evaluators may need to change their role from a formative one, working closely with program staff and administrators for improvement, to working to judge a now mature program and to prepare the stakeholders, and themselves, for that change.[2] In contrast, mature programs often, but not always, are ready for judgment and may need the evaluator to play a more "neutral," distant role to establish credibility with intended audiences. This role, too, can change if the evaluator identifies problems or weaknesses in the program that need improvement if the program is to continue.

Another consideration concerns one's personal style. How comfortable are you in giving feedback that is disappointing in a clear way? In acknowledging program failure? Are you more comfortable doing that in writing, or can you do that in a face-to-face meeting? How comfortable are you in defining your role in a way that differs, strongly or slightly, from that expected by your key stakeholders? Or, alternatively, how responsive do you believe you need to be to stakeholders' concerns? We all have strengths and weaknesses, proclivities and preferences, and things we would rather avoid. Evaluators should not put themselves in the position of taking on a role they will not be able to carry out effectively. Instead, one might choose a partner for the project who can carry out this role and, perhaps, model some behaviors for you to learn.

Evaluators should consider the expertise they bring to a particular evaluation. That expertise may include traditional evaluation tools, such as defining evaluation questions, developing or identifying measures for data collection, analyzing and interpreting results, and communicating technical findings. But the expertise may include other areas: helping stakeholders develop objectives, program descriptions, or program theory; knowledge of scholarly or research literature on the program content or ability to find it and communicate it; helping stakeholders identify what they want to know and how they might use it; and considering ways to communicate results. Evaluators should consider the ways in which it is appropriate to share such expertise in each evaluation. How does it affect one's role? Can stakeholders cope with changes in the evaluator's role? How can the evaluator educate and prepare them for those changes? Alternatively, what are the stakeholders' areas of expertise, and how can they contribute to the evaluation? How will the evaluator gain from their expertise? How can the evaluator establish lines of communication to share that expertise to better the project or the evaluation?

Evaluators should remember to seek stakeholders' input on how they are doing. What do stakeholders think of the evaluation and the evaluator's role and actions? In long-term evaluations, how do stakeholders foresee the evaluation and the evaluator's role changing? Then, as Donaldson suggests, evaluators should model the behavior they would like to see in stakeholders by receiving their suggestions without defensiveness and making suggested changes if appropriate.

Stakeholder Involvement

This issue, in some ways, overlaps with the evaluator's role discussed above, but there are some distinct areas of difference that will be addressed here. Who are your primary stakeholders? What are their interests? To achieve their interests, and to accomplish an evaluation that will benefit the stakeholders, the program, and society at large, what level and types of stakeholder involvement are appropriate? Evaluation is intended to have an impact, to be used in some fashion, whether that use is by distant policy makers who may adopt the program, or discontinue it, in other locations or by program administrators and staff. Therefore, considering use is one element of determining the level and types of stakeholder involvement that are appropriate. In some cases, as seen in the evaluations conducted by Bickman and Wallis and Dukay, distance may be appropriate to establish credibility with more distant audiences.

But in most cases, as demonstrated in our interviews, stakeholder involvement is important. If such involvement is the choice, consider both the breadth and the depth of stakeholder involvement that is appropriate: Which groups might be considered for involvement? What role could each group play that will enhance the evaluation and/or longer-term needs of the organization (learning, capacity building, equity)? What is the most appropriate way to involve that group to achieve the intended goal? It can be critical to involve stakeholders in defining evaluation questions, in reviewing results, and in considering the best ways for using those results and for disseminating them to others. However, stakeholders can be invaluable in developing data collection strategies and procedures, as seen in several of the interviews here.

Methodological Choices

Many authoritative textbooks are written on how to design and conduct the methodological portions of evaluation. This book is not intended to fill that need. Instead, it is intended to focus on your choices. As these interviews illustrate, good evaluations make use of mixed methods, collecting various types of data to illuminate our knowledge of the program. The key is matching data collection with the purpose of the evaluation and the questions to be asked.

The discussion of methodological choices, however, reminds readers that methodology in evaluation is not restricted to design, development of measures, procedures, and the traditional steps of research. The good evaluator often considers methodology as a way to involve stakeholders, whether through developing measures, interpreting data, or considering use. Such involvement can improve your data collection measures and results, as seen in Rog's and Conner's work with stakeholders, as well as improving their use of the results.

The interviews also demonstrate the importance of getting to know, and describing, the program you are evaluating. Consider the extent to which you want to become immersed in or observe the program, but certainly know what you are evaluating.

Finally, make conscious decisions about which outcomes you choose to study. Are immediate outcomes appropriate, or should you study long-term outcomes? When research indicates that immediate outcomes generally lead to the desired long-term outcomes, choosing to measure the immediate outcomes can be a more cost-effective and practical choice. In other cases, the importance of the long-term outcomes, or the uncertainty of their being achieved, can make it critical to measure those desired outcomes.

Use

As the interviews illustrate, use is not achieved through neglect. If you want stakeholders close to the program to use the evaluation results, you must develop relationships with them to help them be receptive to the results. To make feasible recommendations, you must get to know the stakeholders and the organization, its culture, and what will be feasible within that culture.

But use occurs in many different fashions. Long-term use requires careful consideration of audiences. Consider ways to make your evaluation known within the organization as well as to distant users. Think about the ways each of these potential users are most likely to receive and use information. Use meetings, presentations, and informal conversations to encourage others to be familiar with the results and reflect on how they can use them. Use comes through talk and conversation with many potential stakeholders.

To facilitate use, remember to tell program staff and administrators, and other stakeholders, what is working well. The evaluator's job is recognizing the good and describing why it is good, as well as identifying what is not working so well and, as appropriate, making recommendations for change.

Our final words of advice are to consider your choices carefully, be aware of them, and be flexible in areas where change is important. Poor evaluation choices, as with any choice, often occur because we are not aware of the choices. We fail to recognize our choices because we are not open to change. We hope these interviews have illustrated the wide variety of options that evaluators have and the choices they can make that are appropriate for their context and the evaluations they are conducting.

Notes

1. Several multiyear evaluations addressed many different issues as the focus of the study changed. These evaluators faced fewer choices and were, ultimately, able to choose to describe program actions at different stages and measure immediate and long-term outcomes. See, for example, the interviews with James Riccio (Chapter 2) and Debra Rog (Chapter 6).

2. Donaldson provides a useful discussion of this transition in his evaluation.

REFERENCES

House, E. R., & Howe, K. R. (1999). *Values in evaluation and social research.* Thousand Oaks, CA: Sage.

Provus, M. M. (1971). *Discrepancy evaluation.* Berkeley, CA: McCutchan.

Schwandt, T. A. (2005). The centrality of practice to evaluation. *American Journal of Evaluation, 26,* 95–105.

FIFTEEN

ANALYZING THE PRACTICE OF EVALUATION

What Do These Cases Tell Us About Theory?

Christina A. Christie

———◆◆◆———

The interviews presented in this book provide valuable insight into the different ways leading evaluators choose to approach and execute an evaluation study. It is evident from these interviews that no two evaluations are the same and that the practice of evaluation can look quite different from one study to the next. This variability is common knowledge (i.e., observed in practice and discussed in the literature), yet rarely empirically tested. The interviews, while not originally intended for this purpose, are well suited for a post hoc, multiple-case-example examination of practice.[1]

In the previous chapter, the challenges and choices that interviewees faced through each stage of evaluation were described and analyzed for what they tell us about evaluation practice. In this chapter, an analysis of the practices described in the interviews is provided, specifically how they illuminate some of our conceptual notions about evaluation theory. This analysis, however, is not independent from the discussion offered in the previous chapter, which describes some of the more concrete decisions made by evaluators in a specific study context. Indeed, it is meant to complement and connect what we have learned about evaluators' practice to the theoretical and empirical literature on evaluation, where possible. This chapter begins by briefly describing the call for research on evaluation, a context for the analysis offered here. What follows is an examination of the interviews in relation to Alkin and Christie's (2004) evaluation theory taxonomy, which is then followed by a separate discussion of what we have learned from the interviews in relation to the existing conceptual and empirical literature on evaluation methods and, then, evaluation use. The specific questions addressed in this chapter include the following: Do the interviews support Alkin and Christie's assertion that evaluators' values about the primary purpose of evaluation influence the approaches and procedures evaluators' choose to use? For the individuals interviewed who are also positioned on Alkin and Christie's theory tree, do the interviews support their placement on the tree? In the evaluations presented in this book, how do notions of evidence influence method selection by interviewees? How did the interviewees use program theory in their evaluation practice? How do the interviewees describe the use of their evaluations and findings? What types of use are mentioned?

THE CALL FOR RESEARCH ON EVALUATION

Evaluation theorists have written extensively on how they believe evaluation should be conducted. The literature is also full of examples of evaluations that have been conducted, often including commentary on what might have been done right or wrong during an evaluation study or as a means of illustrating how an evaluator might use a particular kind of study design or method during an evaluation study. While this literature is useful, there is relatively little published *research* on evaluation practice in spite of repeated calls by evaluation scholars to develop a substantial empirical knowledge base for evaluation (e.g., Cousins & Earl, 1999; Henry & Mark, 2003; Stufflebeam & Shinkfield, 1985). Henry and Mark (2003) note, "There is a serious shortage of rigorous, systematic evidence that can guide evaluation or that evaluators can use for self-reflection or for improving their next evaluation" (p. 69). However, over the years, this appeal for increased empirical study of evaluation practice has been met with only a tentative and sporadic response.

The call for more research on evaluation began early in the development of the field (e.g., Worthen & Sanders, 1973), with evaluation scholars arguing for increased empirical knowledge of evaluation, based on the notion that such knowledge is necessary to explain the nature of evaluation practice (e.g., Cousins & Earl, 1999; Stufflebeam & Shinkfield, 1985; Worthen & Sanders, 1973). The benefits of empirical study of current evaluation practice include, but are not limited to, the following: the generation of information necessary to refine current practice and develop alternative approaches to evaluation (Smith, 1993), the advancement of conceptions about the connection between theory and practice, and an increased understanding of the influence of context on the nature of evaluation practice.

There are several possible explanations for the scarcity of research on evaluation practice. One, perhaps, is that designing and conducting studies of evaluation practice can be difficult. Research related to human behavior and decisions in other fields, such as psychology, can be conducted in labs with college students. Evaluation practice, however, is situational. Each context offers unique constituents, programmatic elements, and bureaucratic hurdles, to name a few. Therefore, when designing studies of evaluation, conditions can be more difficult to predict and control. Furthermore, many who conduct evaluations have not completed formal academic training in evaluation (Christie, 2003), perhaps because there are relatively few comprehensive training programs. By and large, formal research is conducted in the university setting; thus as a discipline, evaluation lacks a critical mass of students pursuing research on evaluation.

Because of the repeated call for and challenges related to conducting empirical studies on evaluation practice, the interviews presented in previous sections of this book are useful for an analysis of evaluation practice in the context of theory. More specifically, Alkin and Christie's (2004; Christie & Alkin, in press) taxonomy of evaluation theorists as well as some of the more recent empirical studies of evaluation practice will provide the context from which the interviews will be analyzed.

EXEMPLAR INTERVIEW COMPARATIVE ANALYSIS: INSIGHTS REGARDING CONCEPTUAL NOTIONS OF EVALUATION PRACTICE

Comparative studies of evaluation practice often attempt to compare a set of practices across contexts or, alternatively, examine how practices might vary given similar contexts. Henry and Mark (2003) note that some of the more obvious examples of comparative research on evaluation practice include "survey studies of evaluators examining the contingencies present in their evaluations and the impact of these on evaluation choices, and comparative case studies examining several evaluations as they unfold to learn about decisions made and why" (p. 74). Others have offered comparative analytic assessments of evaluation practices, a kind of content analysis, devoid of primary data collection. Stufflebeam (2001), for example, compared the usefulness of evaluation models, or theories, against a commonly accepted set of standards for evaluation practice to assess which models are most valuable in practice.

Alkin and Christie (2004) developed a taxonomy of theorists' perspectives, depicted in the form of an evaluation theory tree, based on a comparative analysis of theorists' writings on the primary purpose of evaluation. Beyond the content analysis conducted to derive and argue the "tree," there is no empirical support for this conceptual framework. Because the theoretical perspectives of several of the interviewees for this book are represented on this theory tree, the interviews can lend some empirical insight into Alkin and Christie's conceptual work.

A Description of Alkin and Christie's Theory Tree

Evaluation theories, more appropriately referred to as persuasions, frameworks, or organizers, are intended to *guide* practice (rather than explain phenomena). They are almost exclusively prescriptive, offering a set of rules, prescriptions, and prohibitions that specify what a good or effective evaluation study is and how an evaluation study should be conducted. Theories address the focus and role of the evaluation, the specific evaluation questions to be studied, the evaluation design and implementation, and the use of evaluation results. They emphasize, prioritize, and combine a range of evaluation procedures. As such, theories help evaluators frame their evaluations and make decisions about which stakeholders to involve at what stage of the evaluation and for what purposes, as well as the methods used for data collection, the procedures implemented to encourage use of the evaluation and its findings, and how evaluation information is communicated.

When considering the various theories of evaluation, it can be helpful to have a framework for understanding how they are related. As mentioned previously, Alkin and Christie (2004) developed one such framework, called an "evaluation theory tree." Alkin and Christie posit that all prescriptive theories of evaluation must consider issues related to (1) the *methods* used in an evaluation, including the study design; (2) the manner in which data are to be judged and valued and by whom, and the underlying *values* used to accomplish this; and (3) the *use* of the evaluation effort. Alkin and Christie also argue that theories differ in the particular emphasis placed on one or another of these dimensions, represented by the branches of the theory tree. Thus, theories can be categorized based on the primary emphasis of the theory (methods, values, or use).

A primary principle of Alkin and Christie's (2004) framework is that one's beliefs about the ultimate purpose of evaluation will greatly influence the choices an evaluator makes during an evaluation. The core set of values the evaluator holds about evaluation and what it is intended to accomplish helps us understand which procedures or methods an evaluator may or may not be willing to compromise (and why), in light of the given contextual restrictions and influences. Understanding the evaluator's core values offers a context for understanding the choices an evaluator makes given the constraints of any particular evaluation situation.

The aim of the theory tree is to identify which one dimension of evaluation practice (use, methods, or valuing) is most central to a theorist's thinking rather than the connections among the three dimensions of evaluation practice. Thus, Alkin and Christie ask, "If given only one chip, on which 'branch' of the evaluation theory tree would the evaluator place that chip?" That is, on which of the three basic principles or dimensions of evaluation is the evaluator least willing to compromise? The act of assigning theorists to a branch according to the dimension of evaluation practice most prioritized (i.e., forced choice) is an acknowledged limitation of our analysis—of any categorization schema, but simplification is a necessary function of developing clear taxonomies. The conceptual analysis accompanying the theory tree is intended to illuminate and legitimize our rationale for placement of each theorist based on a theorists' complete body of theoretical writing. Thus, it is important that we do not dismiss the analysis of a body of work based on what an evaluator did in one study (one data point). The analysis of the interviews can help explore empirically the theory tree taxonomy and provide an opportunity to consider the interrelatedness of the three branches in each theorist's evaluation practice.

Alkin and Christie classify 29 different evaluation theorists and position them on the theory tree in a manner that reflects some combination of history and/or influence. The most recent version of the theory tree (Christie & Alkin, in press) is presented in Figure 15.1. A previous iteration was published in Alkin's *Evaluation Roots* (2004), which also includes chapters by each theorist included in the framework commenting on their placement on the tree as well as describing what influenced their thinking about evaluation.

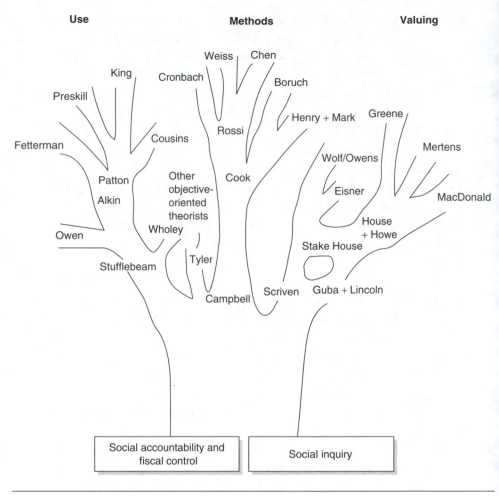

Figure 15.1   Evaluation Theory Tree Reexamined

Several of the evaluators interviewed for this book are included in Alkin and Christie's categorization system—Greene, Preskill, King, Henry (with Mark), and Fetterman, indicating that they have been identified in the evaluation literature as embracing a particular theoretical approach. Other intervie-wees are not included in this particular evaluation theory taxonomy but are still known for their theoretical writings on a particular approach (Donaldson, Bickman, Conner); other evaluators interviewed are not as strongly identified with any one model or approach in the evaluation theory literature (Riccio, Rog, Bledsoe, and Wallis/Dukay), yet based on their practical work and other writings, we might expect to see their work fit into one of the three categories presented. For example, Rog is well known for conducting high-quality evaluation studies rather than for being a proponent of a particular theoretical approach. However, from her practical work, we might expect her to conduct a study that would be closely associated with a methods focus approach rather than, for example, a values focus.[2]

Alkin and Christie's theory about theories has yet to be empirically examined in the context of actual practice. Because several of the interviewees in this book are included on the theory tree, this analysis offers an opportunity to systematically examine some of Alkin and Christie's presumptions. For example, Preskill, King, and Greene discussed evaluations that were intended to illustrate their approaches in action and as such are quite suitable for examination. Preskill's interview, in particular, calls into question some of the presumptions made by Alkin and Christie given her newer focus on appreciative inquiry (AI) in evaluation. Others were less suited for this analysis. For example, Henry developed a performance-monitoring system to be used for evaluation purposes, not an evaluation study per se; thus, it is a bit more difficult to use his interview for an analysis of Alkin and Christie classification. But the interviews do offer more general insights into evaluation and practice in the context of the taxonomy.

Use-Focused Interviewees. Reading from left to right, the first branch of the theory tree is the use branch. Use theorists are most concerned with the use of the evaluation itself, be it instrumental use, process use, or capacity building. Fetterman, King, and Preskill are each placed on the use branch of the evaluation theory tree, suggesting that each is most concerned with evaluation use, especially when juxtaposed with methods or values. This argument, however, is challenged by our analysis of the interviews, particularly when examining Fetterman's and Preskill's evaluation studies. Fetterman is best known for his body of work on empowerment evaluation. This approach intends to increase the capacity of program stakeholders to plan, implement, and evaluate their own programs (Fetterman, 1994). Fetterman explains that he chose *not* to use an empowerment evaluation model to guide the Stanford Teacher Education Program (STEP) evaluation study because, he argues, this approach was not appropriate given the evaluation situation presented to him. When asked why he did not use an empowerment model, Fetterman responds (Chapter 5),

> There's a rational basis for my decision. . . . The rational part of my decision was very simple: The president of Stanford requested the evaluation. His request was more like the traditional accountability focused evaluation.

> There are multiple purposes for evaluation: development, accountability, knowledge. Empowerment falls more into the development purpose rather than into traditional accountability. If I truly believe that, that means I must abide by those distinctions and use the traditional approach when it is more appropriate.

Unique in his deliberate departure from the model with which he is identified, Fetterman, nevertheless, seems to remain rather connected to his training as an educational anthropologist. His attention to a key decision maker's (Stanford's president) information needs are discussed during the six-month planning phase, and although implicit, it appeared that the president requested of Fetterman information concerning whether the STEP program was meeting the high standards required of an educational program offered by Stanford University (the value judgment). Fetterman states, "The directive from the president and provost was absolutely clear. This was a Stanford program. They wanted to know if it met that criterion. Was it up to Stanford standards?"

The decision to be made by the president was whether to continue the STEP program. Once given this directive, however, Fetterman does not discuss actively engaging the president in the evaluation process, which is a clear divergence from what he prescribes for the empowerment evaluator. His procedures for this STEP study, instead, were quite focused on developing an in-depth picture of how the program was operating through immersion and other ethnographic techniques and strategies drawing on his training in anthropology. For example,

> We spent every moment in the summer with STEP students—from 7 in the morning until noon at the public school where they practiced teaching and in Stanford classes until 7 at night, and then sorting data at night like students doing their homework. You ended up being more accurate by being immersed in the culture. You're much more sensitive to the nuances and realities when you live the life you are evaluating. When put to the test, you're better prepared to confront fundamental program issues because you have a better insight into what people think and believe.

In Fetterman's interview, we see a clear emphasis on methods, rather than on evaluation use. This is important to note for two reasons in particular. First, in his chapter *in Evaluation Roots*, Fetterman (2004) maintains that his work could be represented accurately on any of the three branches of the tree and that being designated to only one dimension offers a limited representation of his work as an evaluator. However, he does concede that his empowerment evaluation work is the most influenced by evaluation use. The approach Fetterman took in the STEP evaluation offers support for his position that his placement on the tree may tell only part of his evaluation story and demonstrates his strong identification with other evaluation emphases. This may also be true for others on the tree, and it points to the shortcomings of category systems more generally, and this one in particular, with respect to the rather narrow view they offer of a person's work. Taxonomies are useful in that they take complex information and classify it so that the underlying relationships can be studied. However, the simplification required to create a taxonomy is not well suited for generalization across specific and unique situations. In other words, there are always going to be exceptions to the rule. Fetterman's departure from the empowerment evaluation approach for this particular evaluation and his emphasis on qualitative methods, more than use, supports his assertion in the *Roots* book that he could be placed on other branches. Alternatively, it may simply represent an unusual instance of departure from the taxonomy's reach. The interview does appear to provide evidence that Fetterman is willing to adjust his emphasis according to the context of a given evaluation.

In contrast to Fetterman, King and Preskill chose to describe evaluation studies that they believe serve to illustrate their conceptual ideas in practice. Both maintain that the evaluation context provided an opportunity to implement their particular model. In her study of a special education program, King argues that her capacity building approach was "the obvious choice" (Chapter 8). She reflects,

> In this politically charged environment, we couldn't do a traditional formal evaluation and have it be of great value. . . . So we thought, let's do a really good job of involving people and create an ongoing, inclusive evaluation process so that from that point forward, evaluation issues can always be addressed collectively. Not only are you getting the results of the study, but you are putting in place a structure for continuing the work.

The "obviousness" of her choice is further supported by the fact that the district was looking for someone specifically to build a culture of capacity building and data-based decision making.

Preskill describes her first attempt at using AI in an evaluation context, specifically to develop an evaluation system for the Corporate Education Development and Training (CEDT) at Sandia National Laboratories. AI is described as a method for assisting organizations in identifying areas of strength (Cooperrider, 1986) and to promote organizational learning and development (Hall & Hammond, 1995; Preskill & Catsambas, 2006). Preskill had become interested in using AI as an evaluation method for promoting organizational learning and saw the CEDT as an opportunity to apply AI in this way (Chapter 10). She states,

> For a while, I had been thinking about what an "evaluation system" would look like in an organization. . . . As we talked . . . it became clear that we would need to not only understand what kinds of data they were collecting and how but that we would need to be very clear as to what would work in their particular context. Conceivably, that meant talking with a large number of employees. Given that our time and resources for this project were limited, my business partner and I decided that in order to design the "ideal system," AI would be an appropriate strategy for the six-hour Needs Analysis Meeting. . . . And we were very excited. It was an opportunity to do two things: one, to develop an evaluation system for an organization and, two, to use AI for this purpose. I knew it would be a learning experience for all of us but that it would also test what I believed about the potential for AI in evaluation.

And so, both King and Preskill's interviews offer an opportunity to examine their more recent thinking about what they each believe to be the primary purpose of evaluation and how this relates to Alkin and Christie's notions about their work as represented in the theory tree. In their studies, King and Preskill both had the specific goal of promoting organizational learning and building organizational capacity. As evidenced in their interviews, many evaluators concerned with organizational learning and capacity building view evaluation as a tool for fostering systematic learning by guiding stakeholders through the evaluation process, a learning-by-doing model for which the evaluator serves as the teacher, coach, or mentor. But King's work is quite different from Preskill's: King's role is more reflective of someone informed by theories of evaluation use, while Preskill is informed more by the constructivist theories represented on the valuing branch of the tree.

King first describes herself as an "objective technician" because she uses data to support evaluative conclusions and notes that this was at least part of the rationale for the district hiring her (Chapter 8). This is evident in King's description of the participatory data analysis process she facilitated. She reflects,

> They [professional educators, community members, and other staff] really learned over the course of the study. They got better at data analysis, so our role was more comparing and contrasting the results across tables. People at

the tables would write the claims and identify the data that they thought supported them. If different tables produced similar claims using similar data, that was great. We would look at the different versions of the claim and pick the best one, editing it if need be. If there were different claims supported by the data, we brought those back to the group for discussion the following month. Remember, our role was to ensure the accuracy of the claims.

One gets the impression from King that the process of building evaluation capacity is frequently a lengthy endeavor. When describing a case study with a school district on building evaluation capacity, she repeatedly describes the process using the term "over time." In this particular case, King (2002) worked with the school district for two years (p. 63). The long-term commitment of evaluators to a site in King's capacity-building approach is also evident in King and Volkov's (2005) description of the three areas of focus in evaluation capacity building. They are

(1) organizational context, including internal and external factors; (2) resources, including access to evaluation resources and sources of support for evaluation in the organization; and (3) structures, including an oversight mechanism, a formal ECB [Evaluation Capacity Building] plan, core ECB principles in policies and procedures, infrastructure to support the evaluation process, purposeful socialization, and a peer learning structure. (p. 23)

The third of the three focus areas requires a serious commitment to an organization to make systematic changes within the organization or program to support evaluation processes. The ongoing nature of King's relationships with stakeholders underscores her emphasis on stakeholder participation in the evaluation process and, as an extension, on process use. This lends support to Alkin and Christie's argument for placing King on the use branch of the theory tree.

Preskill's process for promoting organizational learning offers an interesting contrast to King's work. King engages in an ongoing process, over time, with stakeholders. Preskill, on the other hand, spends one day with her large stakeholder group, facilitating a process during which positive perspectives emerge. If we take King's work as an example of capacity building with a primary focus on use, Preskill's approach suggests a shift away from a heavy emphasis on use to one that is more focused on stakeholders' values related to successes. Preskill comments,

For the CEDT evaluation team, we put together a couple of handouts, described the process, and then answered their questions. They got it right away; for some people, it intuitively makes sense. And it's in line with the culture they are trying to create—a collaborative culture, one that is focused on success versus problems. You're usually willing to believe that you can solve problems by describing and discussing success.

Preskill's approach includes facilitating a group process designed to explicate varying perspectives on what is working well, with an emphasis on what the participant values about what is being done and what might be accomplished. Alkin and Christie placed Preskill on the use branch of the theory tree. Her work in the area of evaluation and organizational learning were used to inform this choice, and Preskill (2004) has validated this positioning. However, her work in the area of AI, as described in the interview for this book, is more reflective of a value-focused approach. This is evident in how she describes her role (to facilitate the identification of what people believe is working), as well as in the questions she poses to participants about what they value, and then the process she engages in to move the group to identify and agree on a common vision of what they imagine the best situation to be. As described, Preskill's procedures reflect constructive values of inquiry and are intended to focus the evaluation on explicating (positive) values and using these values to offer insights about the evaluand.

Methods-Focused Interviewees. The middle branch of the theory tree is the methods branch and grows from the social inquiry "root." The primary focus of those placed on this branch is on developing models for evaluation practice grounded in and derived from social science research methods. Theorists' models are mostly derivations of the randomized control trial (RCT) and are intended to offer results that are generalizable and have a focus on "knowledge construction."

Both Bickman and Donaldson maintain that they used a "theory-driven" approach to guide their evaluations. *Theory-driven evaluation* uses the underlying program theory to guide the evaluation. A program theory is a specification of what must be done to achieve the program's desired goals, the important impact that may be anticipated, and how these goals and their impact would be generated (Chen, 1990; Donaldson, 2007). The evaluator uses this theory to guide the evaluation activities and as a benchmark for determining program effectiveness. This is distinguished from Fetterman's use of a program model (what STEP intended to do) and a program theory. Fetterman's program model appears to be a descriptive one, focusing on program actions, rather than a program theory that by definition links program actions to outcomes.

In the tradition of postpositivist[3] approaches to evaluation (depicted primarily on the methods branch of Alkin and Christie's tree), of paramount concern for Bickman is the maintenance of the methodological integrity of his evaluation, even under political pressure to modify and, in his mind, weaken his study design. This is of primary importance to Bickman, which he highlights as a success of his work (Chapter 4):

> Another thing I am proud of is that we were able to keep the integrity of the study design and the measures throughout the study while under considerable political pressure. The studies that had been done in the past had not even looked at clinical outcomes. They had only examined cost and the amount of services. . . . The Army people I negotiated the contract with were not used to dealing with research. . . . They . . . wanted to be able to comment on anything we published, which I explained was not under their control.

Bickman's belief about the primary purpose of evaluation as an activity intended to generate the most methodologically sound knowledge about a program's effects (Bickman & Reich, in press) and outcomes is clear in his arguments with the funders over outcomes, measures, and sampling. In focusing the evaluation, he illustrates how the evaluator often has to balance his values about evaluation with the needs of stakeholders. When asked how he decided to focus the evaluation, specifically on the concept of continuum of care, Bickman responds,

> I did not make a decision on that focus. That's the disadvantage of program evaluation. You're given a program, a focus. But I did push for examining outcomes. Most studies of mental health treatment in the community (as opposed to university laboratories) do not show that they are effective. I think not looking at clinical outcomes for services that are intended to affect those outcomes is poor evaluation practice.

Bickman's focus on methods and rigor not only illustrates his emphasis and concern for methods in this particular study but is also illustrative of methods-focused evaluations more generally. Thus, Bickman's study offers an effective practical example of the theoretical work of many on Alkin and Christie's methods branch.

Donaldson was candid about the struggle between what local stakeholders thought should be the focus of the evaluation and the funders' request for a particular evaluation study focus. In his interview, Donaldson describes how the California Endowment, which supported the evaluation, wanted to implement and test an existing program theory that had been established and tested in Michigan, while local stakeholders grappled with whether it might be best to adapt the program theory so that it would better address the needs of those in California. Donaldson facilitated the dialogue between the funder and local stakeholders to finalize the focus of the evaluation (Chapter 9):

> A central issue that came up was whether they should adapt for California residents or try to remain true to the original model. There were some different views on that, to the point that the decision was made to do it only in English, which, in California, cuts out a significant portion of the population. For the most part, the Foundation supported the Michigan team's view that sites should strive to remain true to the model. A question for the evaluation became "If you deliver the program as it's supposed to be delivered, do you get the immediate outcomes?" . . . So the real issue was "Would this work with an ethnically, educationally, and occupationally diverse population?" These were the questions that emerged. The developers saw this as a relatively robust program that should work across the world. Journals had published much on the success of this model. But some of the people in California felt they needed to give it a California flavor.

From the tone of this comment, Donaldson was seemingly willing to compromise the research emphasis (i.e., generalizability) of the study to improve the program for participants in California. And, with perhaps some skepticism, he moves forward with testing the social science model presented to him, at the request of the funder. Thus, we see the sometimes unavoidable tension between the evaluators' and stakeholders' preferences for practice and how the evaluator may indeed compromise on procedures in response to funders' political pressures.

As mentioned in his interview, Conner studied under Donald Campbell, a postpositivist social psychologist who authored the seminal manuscript on experimental and quasi-experimental designs (Campbell & Stanley, 1966) and serves as the "anchor" of Alkin and Christie's methods branch. Although it does not appear that Conner has abandoned the principles and ideals of impartiality, he does admit that he now sees his role as an evaluator more broadly than that of an experimental researcher. He describes the evaluator as someone who helps "people create their story," as a facilitator and teacher, and as a part of the overall program "family," bringing to the table an expertise in evaluation design and methods. This is not dissimilar from how King described her role in the evaluation process. When asked about his views on objectivity, Conner's reply further highlights his more pragmatic views (Chapter 11):

> Ah, is anybody really objective? I tend to put objectivity in quotes these days. We, along with those involved in the study, need to set the standards so that they make sense and are real for them [the program stakeholders]. There are certainly outside standards that are recognized and brought in. . . . [In the Colorado Trust evaluation, the] theories of change and the principles served as benchmarks, again, in a way that would be adaptable to the different communities that were going to be involved in this. It wasn't a recipe but rather a general instruction people would follow. That provided enough objectivity— to know where to look. We continued to look at other things, but it provided the right kinds of anchors.

Conner's study was guided by a community-based participatory research framework (Kisira & Conner, 2004; Lantz, Israel, Schulz, & Reyes, 2006) and had a notable emphasis on stakeholder participation. Like Donaldson, Bickman, and Bledsoe, Conner began his work with the Colorado Healthy Communities Initiative, an emerging program, by developing a logic model with the "main stakeholders" and then a "shell of on an evaluation plan." Conner talks explicitly about how the evaluation questions drive his study designs. He comments,

> I believe that the questions need to be the anchor. Then, we have a variety of designs, which can be used to answer the questions. In the Colorado Trust's case, the questions were about process and about short-term outcomes and some indication of whether this was beginning to move down the path toward impact.

Both Donaldson and Conner offer evidence of stakeholder and use focus in their more methods-focused work. Indeed, it could be argued further that Conner's study places greater emphasis on use and stakeholders' values than on methods. Taken together, Donaldson and Conner's interviews offer evidence of the interconnections between the three branches of the theory tree and the influence that each dimension may have on the other two. In contrast, Bickman's interview offers an excellent example of an evaluator with a strong commitment to methods with a clear emphasis on one of the three dimensions of evaluation described by Alkin and Christie.

Henry (with Mark) is also on the methods branch (see, e.g., Henry, Julnes, & Mark, 1998), and he too spends a significant amount of time working with stakeholders to ensure that he can offer the most methodologically rigorous accountability system that can be used by a variety of stakeholders, including teachers and parents. Particularly of late, Henry has been an outspoken proponent of methodological rigor (e.g., Henry, in press). There is little argument regarding his placement on the methods branch. So to some, it may be surprising that there is considerable focus on use, within the evaluation context he discusses in his interview (Chapter 7). For example, at the conclusion of the interview he states,

> In this project, we were less concerned with causal attribution than with getting an accurate description to large numbers of people. . . . evaluators can fill a very important role when they provide accurate information that allows parents, the public, and elected officials to answer the question about whether public objectives for improving social conditions have been achieved.

In all stages of the evaluation, Henry considered the end user, from the evaluation-planning stage, where stakeholders (e.g., principals, superintendents, teachers, and community members) were involved in creating the "architecture of the accountability system" to the dissemination of the results in a manner that encourages use (e.g., an accessible two-page report with condensed critical pieces of information; considering the best way to publicize the results to the media; answering telephone calls from principals, teachers, and parents; and workshops on how to interpret and best use the data). In Henry's own words,

> One of the things that I think I developed was a broader view of evaluation and the activities that constitute an evaluation. My understanding of evaluation expanded from working on a performance measurement project. Essentially, we're trying to describe the immediate outcomes of schooling. In this project, we're less concerned with causal attribution than with getting an accurate description to large numbers of people. We want to inform people about how the students are doing and whether schools are getting better or worse.

Henry's emphasis in this particular study appears to be on use. Although he is concerned with finding valid measures for the performance-monitoring system, his primary emphasis is on developing formats that stakeholders can understand and working with the media and many stakeholders to make the results known and used. Like Fetterman, who is placed on the use branch of the tree but whose context prompted him to focus on methods, Henry's actual practice in this individual study is concerned primarily with use. Bickman's focus continued to be one of methods, as he is placed on the tree, but Donaldson's study shows the merger of a methods and a use focus. Donaldson was willing to continue the attempt to replicate the Michigan model, illustrating his allegiance to methods, but he was concerned with this decision and took many actions in working with stakeholders during the formative stages of the evaluation to increase use of his results. As in other cases, the interviews concerning an actual, single evaluation demonstrate the influence of context on evaluators' choices and the connections and blending of the different branches of the tree in actual practice.

Values-Focused Interviewees. The "valuing" branch, to the right of the "methods" branch, focuses on those theorists for whom the process of placing value on the evaluation is the essential component of an evaluator's work. This includes theorists who advocate for the evaluator to systematically facilitate the determination of value by others, informed mostly by the notions related to the constructivist paradigm.[4]

Greene is the only interviewee whose theoretical work reflects constructivist views of science and inquiry and the only interviewee on the valuing branch of the theory tree. She argues in her writings that evaluation should be used to determine value, specifically by developing a consensus around a set of criteria to be used to determine the value of a program. Greene describes what she calls a value-engaged approach to evaluation, which incorporates elements of responsive evaluation (Stake, 1975, 2005) with principles from democratic evaluation (House & Howe, 1999). She identifies her evaluation of the National Resources Leadership Program as one that serves to exemplify the principles of this approach in practice. In her interview (Chapter 3), Greene briefly describes her theoretical views:

> Some of my work has highlighted the intertwining of values and methodology. . . . This study had many of the characteristics that I try to implement in evaluations. . . . [E]valuation tries to become attuned to the issues and concerns of people in the context of this program. And these issues are always ones about values. Second, my methodology is inclusive in that multiple diverse perspectives, stances, and concerns are included in the evaluation. Finally, and I want to underscore this, the methodology is reflective. That is, in this particular evaluation, throughout the process of the three-year study, there was a continuing cycle of reflection and analysis.

Greene goes on to describe her role as an evaluator as "a partnership, a collegiality with the stakeholders. We were not members of the program team, but we were not outsiders. We actually sought to be collegial with the program staff."

When determining the evaluation focus, we see Greene's emphasis on values and the use of values in the evaluation process. She explains,

> I think we saw our job as to develop a good understanding of, and to make some judgments about, the quality and effectiveness of the leadership institute. . . . The key challenge is determining the basis or criteria for making the judgment. In addition to criteria informed by [evaluation] team expertise, we were trying to be responsive to stakeholders' criteria and to what we understood as the Foundation's priorities.

Perhaps to ensure that the evaluation team incorporated the values of and multiple perspectives on what makes good training programs good, Greene's evaluation team included an expert in leadership development. She was the only evaluator who mentioned deliberately including a "content" expert on her evaluation team for this purpose, thus underscoring her constructivist orientation and emphasis on values. Bledsoe talks of relying on her collaborating colleague for insights related to child developmental theory; however, she does not suggest that this developmental psychologist was included as part of the evaluation team, specifically for the purpose of serving as a content expert. Others, such as Riccio, are known for their work in the substantive focus area of the program. Bickman mentions that he was new to children's mental health at the time he started this study, though certainly, psychology is his field of study.

Greene's interview seems to offer a practical example of her theory at work (e.g., Greene, 2000, in press). Most of the procedures she describes are what we might expect to see from someone with her theoretical emphasis and position on Alkin and Christie's theory tree. She explains her choice of methods with an eye toward inclusion; for example, she decides to collect survey data because it was one way to increase inclusion of and hear from a broader group in the evaluation study. She also explains how she integrates her own values related to the program into the final evaluation report.

General Insights. Using the interviews as a vehicle, we gain some insights into Alkin and Christie's framework as well as the relationship between theory and practice more generally. A few important points emerged. First, the interviews offer some evidence to substantiate the premise that evaluators' beliefs about the primary purpose of evaluation influence practice. Nevertheless, we see that there are serious limits to using one evaluation study to illustrate the complexity of a theorists' complete work because the specific approach taken by a theorist in a given study can, and should, be influenced by the contextual demands of the stakeholders and the program to be evaluated. A second, related point that emerged in this analysis is that evaluators will depart from their beliefs about the primary purpose of evaluation if the context calls for a different approach. The interviews, by providing much in-depth information on the choices evaluators make in practice, demonstrate the moderating effects that context may have on evaluators' theoretical preferences. In fact, the situational demands of a particular evaluand sometimes have a greater impact on the specific choices made by an evaluator than the influence of theoretical conceptions. An evaluator's theoretical stance may, however, be a better predictor of the kinds of evaluation studies a theorist chooses to conduct. That is, while theorists are open to using different procedures to best respond to the evaluand, they are not likely to conduct evaluations that diverge dramatically from their primary beliefs about the purpose of evaluation. Last, we found that the dimensions of Alkin and Christie's tree are more related and fluid in practice than is suggested by the categorization system.

As described previously, Alkin and Christie's framework attempts to reflect the overall emphasis of a theorists' body of theoretical work, and the analysis of our interviews highlights the difficultly of exploring empirically a broad body of theoretical work using just one practical example. As described in the previous chapter, this may be because good evaluation work requires the evaluator to be responsive to the political and contextual complexity of a given evaluand. Additionally, theorists' notions often change over time. And a theorist may draw on theoretical notions put forth at any point in time over the course of his or her career, past or present, to inform current practice. This helps articulate the difficulty of studying evaluation practice more generally; from our interviews, the Fetterman and Preskill studies explicate these points particularity well.

Fetterman's interview offers the most obvious example of how, when presented with a particular evaluation context, theorists may chose an approach different from the one for which they are best known. Admittedly, Fetterman deliberately chose not to use an empowerment approach. It is surprising how little evidence there is in this study of the empowerment evaluation principles that are grounded in evaluation use. This might be an extreme case, an outlier.

Nevertheless, it suggests that we explore the utility of categorization systems beyond descriptive commentary. Because the theory tree is designed to explain theories in the context of three general dimensions of evaluation practice, our analysis of the interviews calls attention to the complexities of different theories and how they may be diluted by broad descriptions of prescriptive evaluation models. It is important to note this limitation of category systems more generally, and Alkin and Christie's tree more specifically, because evaluation theories are indeed intended to offer some specificity related to practice. Consequently, categorization systems should not be misjudged and presumed to be comprehensive frameworks that reflect the complexities and nuances of evaluation theories.

In a related point, both Fetterman and Preskill's interviews point to the possible incongruence between what one might be writing about theoretically and what one might do in practice, at a given point in time. That is, one's current theoretical publications may not be what a theorist draws on for a particular evaluation study. Indeed, as seen in the interviews, theorists draw on their current as well as previously published work. And Alkin and Christie's category system does not reflect the evolution of a theorist's work over time, again because it is intended to reflect the broader notions of theorists' work and the work for which they are best known.

For example, in Fetterman's STEP study, some theoretical ideas he had written about prior to his work on empowerment evaluation are evident. Thus, his interview better reflects his earlier theoretical writings on using educational anthropological methods in evaluation practice (Fetterman, 1988, 1989) than his more contemporary writings on empowerment evaluation, illustrating how theorists may draw on any of their theoretical notions when deemed appropriate for a specific evaluation context. Preskill's interview also offers evidence of how theorists' views change over time and how this evolution may not reflect a more general shift in theorists' focus. In her interview, Preskill describes her first attempt at using AI in the context of her evaluation work. This reflects a progression of theoretical ideas and the development of what is likely to be a new line of theoretical work. For both Fetterman and Preskill, shifts in theoretical thinking did and will indeed affect their placement on Alkin and Christie's tree. If the tree had been developed in the early 1990s, it is likely that Fetterman may not have been placed on the use branch of the theory tree but rather, with careful examination, would have been categorized on either the methods or the values branch. Preskill was placed on the use branch, reflecting her focus on use and organizational change through evaluation. Her notions related to AI might be better suited for placement on the values branch. These two interviews, then, offer some evidence of how theorists' practice is a dynamic reflection of one's overall thinking about evaluation that is often not restricted by or to the theoretical writings of the moment—and how one's evolution in thinking may influence a more general analysis of one's work.

Examining the interviews in the context of Alkin and Christie's tree also points to a movement between the general and the specific, where theoretical ideas offer more general principles for practice and the evaluand shapes the specifics of what the evaluator actually does in any given study. Starting from the more general, categorization frameworks are one step removed from prescriptive evaluation theories, reflecting more general thoughts about evaluation theory. Prescriptive evaluation theories are one step removed from evaluation practice, reflecting more general thoughts about evaluation as a practice (Scriven, 1983). The responsive nature of good evaluation practice requires that the evaluator use the more general notions offered by evaluation theories to guide practice, rather than as a formula for the procedures one should use in a specific evaluation study.

Each of the interviewees was responsive to the evaluand, and the complexities of the context shaped the specific evaluation designs and procedures chosen. And although we see that a theorist may shift focus in response to the specifics of a given evaluation situation, when taken together, we find that theorists choose to conduct studies that reflect more general beliefs about the primary purpose of evaluation—that is, more general notions about evaluation practice. It is these more general ideas that seem to shape the overall career trajectory of an evaluator, rather than the actual step-by-step procedures one implements during an evaluation study. In this way, evaluators choose to work on particular studies that are aligned well with their values related to inquiry or, conversely, won't work on studies that aren't consistent with their values. Thus, it is unlikely that Bickman would respond to a call for proposals to conduct an AI for an organization, just as it would be doubtful that Preskill would conduct a federally funded, randomized, experimental, five-wave longitudinal design study. Indeed, King comments that she was hired specifically to continue the district's capacity-building activities. She argues explicitly in her theoretical writing that increasing evaluation capacity is essential for promoting and ensuring evaluation use and that stakeholder participation is a requisite for achieving this goal (Christie & Alkin, 2005). Thus, it is no surprise that she would be selected to do this work for a school district with a similar focus. Of importance here is that the evaluators either chose or were chosen to conduct their studies because the evaluation context and need reflected their values about inquiry or, at the very least, did not conflict with those values.

Last, the interviews with Fetterman and Preskill as well as Henry, Donaldson, and Conner, point to the interrelationships between the three dimensions of Alkin and Christie' s tree, an important complexity that is not necessarily or obviously captured by the categorization framework. Attention to or emphasis on more than one dimension of evaluation practice does not suggest that the primary interest is being ignored. Rather, it stresses the multiple dimensions of evaluation practice and how evaluators can and often do attend to each of the three dimensions identified by Alkin and Christie. Thus, we see in Henry's study, considerable attention to methodological rigor and also to evaluation use by various stakeholder groups. In Donaldson's interview, the influence of stakeholders' information needs to test the intervention in a different context directs the focus of the study, again highlighting a fluid relationship between evaluation methods and use. This does not contradict the basic premise of Alkin and Christie's argument; indeed, they argue that all three dimensions of practice might be present in an evaluator's work. Distinctions are emphasized in their frameworks so as to distinguish and categorize theories. So our interviews lend support for the presence of each of the three dimensions of evaluation practice, but the distinctive and exclusive influence of one dimension over the other two was less evident in the interviews.

EVALUATION METHODS

Christie (2003) conducted one of the more recent comparative studies of evaluation practice. This study examines the relationship between evaluation theory and practice and offers a comparative understanding of the similarities and differences of eight theories of evaluation practice when applied. Using multidimensional scaling procedures, theorists' data were analyzed to ascertain and describe their practices. A two-dimensional solution resulted, and the dimensions were found to represent the constructs scope of stakeholder involvement and method proclivity. Of importance is the clear emergence of a strong postpositivist methods emphasis on the methods dimension of the solution, suggesting that this dimension of practice, when evident, is a power-ful predictor of an evaluator's practice. This also suggests that theories of knowledge (e.g., postpositivism, constructivism) indeed influence an evalua-tor's practice choices.

Recent arguments about what constitutes credible evidence in evaluation have resurfaced, a result of several federal policy changes instituted by the Bush administration (Donaldson, Christie, & Mark, in press) that identify the randomized control trial (RCT)[5] as the ("gold standard," if you will) design for generating credible "scientific" evidence of program effectiveness. The identification of a particular research design as *the* design that decides what should and should not be considered an "evidenced-based" practice or pro-gram has angered many in the field of evaluation and has sparked debate among respected colleagues and friends. Beliefs about evidence and what con-stitutes credible evidence often translate into methods choices, as suggested by Christie's research (Christie, 2003; Christie & Masyn, in press).

Some other kinds of research on evaluation have also identified methods as a distinguishing feature of evaluation practice. For example, Alkin and Christie (2005), in a guest-edited issue of the journal *New Directions for Evaluation*, developed a systematic structure for analyzing, comparatively, how theorists apply their approach in practice. The editors provided a sce-nario for which an evaluation was required and asked four prominent evalua-tion scholars known for their theoretical writings (Donaldson, Greene, Henry, and King) to describe how they would design and conduct an evaluation of this program. Thus, they developed a comparative picture of how different evaluators might evaluate the same program. Alkin and Christie analyze the theorists' evaluation plans, which resulted in the development of a schema depicting similarities and differences of reported proposed practices that included depth versus breadth of stakeholder involvement, emphasis on the particular type of evaluation use, use of program theories, attention to social justice, and methods.

All the theorists in their exercise acknowledged the importance of under-standing program theory as a part of the evaluation. However, differences in the emphasis placed on the role of program theory in the evaluation process emerged. For example, the cornerstone of Donaldson's approach was the development of a program theory. Once developed, he looked to the program theory to prescribe and order the questions that the evaluation will address. Henry used the program theory as a means for determining the connections between program processes and outcomes, but he was most concerned, however, with examining program outcomes and did not see it as necessary to connect each program outcome to a program process. Differing from Donaldson, Henry identified the primary questions for the evaluation prior to program theory development. Program theory was not the focal point of Greene's approach to evaluation. Yet a concern for "understanding the conceptual rationales" of the program was a part of her approach. Her strong attempt at understanding the school context adds light to her consideration of the program's theory. The distinctions, then, lay in whether the theorist considered program theory a primary, secondary, or perhaps even tertiary focus.

In sum, related to methods, current literature suggests that an evaluator's notions of evidence, specifically what makes for credible evidence in an evaluation, is an issue worth exploring through the interviews. Additionally, the use of program theories is becoming more evident in the evaluation literature and, thus, also warrants more systematic examination. The interviews presented in this book offer an opportunity to examine the issues related to evaluation methods so as to better understand when and how they might be used.

Evidence and Methods

The influence of the evaluator's beliefs about the nature of inquiry was most obvious in the choices made about which methods they chose to use. Perhaps this should be of little surprise given how closely linked method choices are with views about inquiry. Yet an analysis of methods that simply categorized the methodological approach used by these evaluators might have overlooked some of the more interesting nuances about method choice afforded by an analysis of the interviews.

Let's begin by pointing out that all interviewees designed mixed-method studies—that is, studies that incorporated the use of both quantitative and qualitative data collection methods. Few evaluators, however, designed studies using a balance of methods from each paradigm, such as those described by Tashakkori and Teddlie (2002). In other words, by and large, interviewees placed greater emphasis on methods from one paradigm over the other, reflecting their phenomenological approaches to evaluation.

Method choices bring to the forefront a fundamental issue facing evaluation practice today—evaluators' beliefs about what counts as sound evidence for decision making. Not surprisingly, postpositivist evaluators were more likely to, first, design studies that measured program outcomes and impact and, second, use quantitative methods to do so. The postpositivists interviewed, in particular Riccio and Bickman, appreciate the explanatory power and contributions of the qualitative data collected in their studies. Bickman comments, "In a comprehensive evaluation, we need to know how the program was implemented to learn why it was or was not successful." Yet he goes on to say, "First, we need to be able to measure outcomes" (Chapter 4). Riccio's comments about methods echo Bickman's when he argues,

> The field research complemented the survey data in important ways. . . . It helped us understand better what we thought we were measuring with the staff survey and allowed us to illustrate some of the important differences in staff practices across the counties . . . [yet] using randomly assigned control groups helped us enormously in establishing our credibility. (Chapter 2)

Yet Riccio suggests that the descriptive components of his study were quite important, more so than Bickman did, a distinction between Riccio and Bickman worthy of note.

Greene offers a contrasting example of how constructivists choose to measure program outcomes (Chapter 3). In her evaluation, Greene uses a mini-case study approach to address the question, "At its best, can the institute . . . bring about a change in how people make decisions on contested environmental policy?" She chose to sample practicum projects that were considered to be the best products, as selected and nominated by program directors. The analysis of each project and the interviews with all those affected by the project that accompanied each analysis were rather extensive. Distinguishing Greene's outcome study from the others, however, was the sample used to examine program outcomes, which she described as being investigated at a "broad" level. Like others that examined program outcomes, Greene's unit of analysis was the individual; but she chose to examine a small select sample of participants. Other interviewees examined program outcomes using the entire sample from which data were collected and used quantitative measures to accomplish this. For example, Bickman searched for and used what he thought were the best extant measures of psychopathology and family functioning, which he lamented were "not too good." Similarly, Bledsoe used existing research measures, such as parent–child interactive inventories, to measure her program outcomes, although she argues that because of problems with attrition, her qualitative interviews and observations yielded the most meaningful information about the program.

Not all evaluators examined program outcomes as a part of their work. Specifically, Preskill and Henry did not conduct an evaluation of a program, but rather their work focused on the development of data collection systems to be used for evaluation purposes. Henry's school performance measurement system relied heavily on the integration of existing quantitative data for the purpose of providing stakeholders with solid information from which sound judgments about school performance could be made. In contrast, Preskill's approach was predominantly qualitative and focused on the sharing of positive experiences and values about the current methods used by CEDT to internally evaluate programs. Preskill describes the first phase of the AI process during which participants conduct paired interviews guided by three core questions, two of which are "values questions" (Chapter 10). She remarks, "Here, interviewees are asked to describe what they value most about the topic of inquiry as well as what value they bring or add to the topic of inquiry." Indeed, we see a constructivist emphasis in Preskill's work, particularly related to values and her methods used to bring them to the center of this project.

Donaldson and Rog offer examples of more balanced mixed-methods studies. Their emphasis on quantitative methods was less prominent than seen in Riccio and Bickman's studies. Although they each placed significant value on the insights offered by their qualitative data, Donaldson and Rog relied far less on observation and emersion in the program setting than Fetterman. Nevertheless, Rog maintains that some of the "more poignant stories came through our analysis of the qualitative data" (Chapter 6), where they learned about the histories and stressors of homeless mothers. Greene also spoke of the use of qualitative methods as a way to know what it was like to be a program participant. Similarly, Donaldson emphasizes the value he places on program observation as a means for getting "a realistic view of what's happening" (Chapter 9). Nonetheless, neither Donaldson nor Rog are comfortable measuring program outcomes using strictly qualitative measures. Rog explains that because her study was primarily descriptive, she collected more data with the intent of increasing the explanatory power of her study than she might have if she had conducted a causal study. Donaldson's views on evidence perhaps come closest to the pragmatist paradigm,[6] as evidenced in his comfort with his appreciation for the use of both quantitative and qualitative methods. He maintains, "It's the interplay between the quantitative and qualitative that is really informative."

Program Theories

In Alkin and Christie's (2005) exercise, described above, in which four theorists were asked to design a proposal to evaluate the same program, the use of program theories emerged across all four proposals. Each theorist, however, had a unique take on what a program theory was and how it might be used in their evaluation study. This suggests, as with other evaluation procedures, that the term *program theory* may mean different things to different people and, thus, may also be used differently.

To Chen and Rossi (1992) and others with more postpositivist leanings, a program theory is "a specification of what must be done to achieve the program's desired goals, the important impact that may be anticipated, and how these goals and their impact would be generated" (Chen, 1990, p. 43). Chen and Rossi (1992) advocate deriving program theories from existing social science theory, cautioning that key stakeholders' views about a program's theory can be biased and subjective. However, as long as social science theory serves as the foundation for formulating the program theory, most theorists do not object to the inclusion of key stakeholders' views in formulating the program theory. Lipsey (1993) in his seminal article on program theories, republished in a recent issue of *New Directions for Evaluation* (where significant articles were reprinted in a single issue), advocates deriving theories from conversations with stakeholders and program planners, just as Bledsoe, Donaldson, and Bickman do in their interviews, signifying that the field has moved to seeing this as a legitimate process for developing program theories. By and large, the interviewees who discussed developing or using program theories stayed true to the definition offered by Chen and others and engaged in a process reminiscent of what these authors have described in their writing. Note, however, that with the exception of Fetterman, the evaluators who chose to discuss the use of program theories in their interviews are by and large postpositivists or postpositivist-leaning pragmatists. The evaluators who were interviewed engaged stakeholders using program theories during different stages of the evaluation process, depending on the focus of the evaluation study. Bickman, for example, worked with stakeholders early on in the evaluation process to finalize and then test the program theory. Rog, on the other hand, used the information gathered throughout the evaluation process to help develop a program theory toward the end of her evaluation.

Bledsoe describes, in some detail, the iterative process she undertook with stakeholders to develop a conceptual model for the Fun with Books program. In this case, Bledsoe was attempting to articulate a program theory for an existing program. Because the program had been operating, stakeholders seemed to have strong feelings about its impact as well as its conceptual model. Getting stakeholders to suspend their beliefs about the program required a rather extensive stakeholder engagement. She met weekly over the course of four to five months with the program director, the CEO of the organization, the external consultant, and some of the staff members. Bledsoe describes her process (Chapter 12):

> People would say, "We *know* this works!" . . . And we would counter, "Okay, but what do you want them to walk away with when they leave the program at night? Reading skills? What's the long-term outcome?" . . . They would often answer the latter part of the question with the statement "We know the literature." I would counter with the question "What literature? There's a lot of literature out there." They would say, for instance, "Well, cognitive stimulation is important in encouraging children to read." And I'd say, "What does cognitive stimulation look like?" . . . So that's how we developed the models— talking with administrators and staff in the organization and using the literature to validate their assertions. . . . We went through about five iterations, and we could have gone through more, but at the time, the model we decided upon seemed to demonstrate what we thought was a realistic program process, considering no model had been articulated prior to this exercise.

Donaldson talked most extensively about the development and use of program theories, in part because his interview was intended, by design, to focus on program theory development, as he is known for conducting exemplary theory-driven evaluation studies (Chapter 9). In his interview, Donaldson emphasizes the importance of developing a "fairly parsimonious model," one that is not bogged down in excessive detail, which he argues, "tends to be a real hindrance in an evaluation." He clarifies what he sees as the purpose of developing a program theory (as opposed to a logic model) as he explains, "You're trying to consider whether the paths leading into this outcome have any chance at all of accounting for a significant portion of the variance in the desired outcome."

Donaldson's postpositivist description of the purpose of a program theory helps distinguish this type of program theory from the more descriptive program theory Fetterman used in his STEP evaluation. Fetterman explains (Chapter 5),

> We began by trying to understand what the model for STEP was—what insiders said it was *supposed to do*. Then, we wanted to look at what kind of compliance there was with the model, but from a consumer perspective. That is, we came up with the basic program theory and then looked at it to see if the action linked up with the plan. It was a mature program, and we wanted to look at what it was doing.

From this statement, it seems that Fetterman and his evaluation team developed the program theory with little stakeholder involvement. His process of program theory development seemingly departs from what was described by the more postpositivist evaluators, which is important to note. I would suggest, however, that what Fetterman describes to be "program theory" might be quite different from what Chen and others describe. Here, instead of highlighting the difference in practical approach, we might have identified an occasion of definitional or conceptual confusion related to the use of the term *program theory*.

General Insights

Gathering credible evidence is a key component in an evaluation study. The Centers for Disease Control (www.cdc.gov/eval/) identifies *gather credible evidence* as the fourth of six steps in their widely used evaluation model. Patton (1997) and others argue that for evaluation findings to be used, they must be accurate and credible. And *accuracy* is one of the four primary standards for evaluation practice (Joint Committee on Standards for Educational Evaluation, 1994). Consequently, gathering credible evidence is indeed one of the most important jobs of the evaluator. Yet evaluators may have differing ideas about what constitutes credible evidence, which are likely shaped by phenomenological beliefs and knowledge of theories.

As seen in the interviews, and an important point to highlight, all evaluators chose to design mixed-method studies, although each study design reflected a preference for one paradigm over the other. With the occasion to examine more than 10 exemplars of evaluation practice, the point that all evaluators designed mixed-method studies is indeed noteworthy. In the literature, mixed-method designs are argued to offer the evaluator the opportunity to integrate the merits of experimental and nonexperimental designs. Presumably, few would dispute this more general point. However, when asked to identify the feature of a mixed-methods study design that is intended to get at program impact—that is, whether this program worked, paradigm preferences emerged. For example, Greene chose to answer the program impact question by using mini-case studies of program successes. Fetterman chose to immerse himself and his evaluation team in the program context to determine if the STEP program was working. Alternately, Bickman and Riccio used experimental designs to measure program impact. And so it seems from our interviews that when answering the program impact question, we find evidence of paradigm preference. The methods chosen to address this question then, may serve as a key predictor of paradigm allegiance and commitment to particular kinds of evidence. In this vain, those such as Bickman (e.g., Bickman & Reich, in press) or Rog[7] (e.g., Julnes & Rog, in press), who support the use of RCTs more generally, would argue that without some measure of causality, a reliable measure of impact cannot be obtained, while those on the other side of the debate, such as Fetterman (e.g., Fetterman, 1988, 1989) and Greene (e.g., Greene, in press), tend to deemphasize causality as the central factor in determining program impact. Thus, notions about what credible evidence is, may be related not only to design and methods but also to how the evaluator conceptualizes "impact."

It is fair to say that the evaluators interviewed for this book would likely agree that there will always be limitations to evidence. As seen in the interviews, where they disagree is on whether we can—and how we should—control for or intervene in an attempt to strengthen our evidence. Again, Fetterman and Bickman offer us two of the more extreme illustrations of this point, where Bickman attempts to control for variance using systematic procedures and methods planned at the outset of the evaluation design and Fetterman chooses to get in and stay close to the program and its "actors" to describe and judge program quality, with little regard for controlling the environment he was studying but rather to understand it fully. But it should be noted that Fetterman does not, in fact, measure program impact the way Bickman does. Rather, his conceptualization of *impact* is to describe the program and compare its quality of delivery with that of other programs. He chooses to focus on program actions, not outcomes.

Disagreements about whether conditions in evaluation studies can be controlled stem from and are informed by notions about truth. Thus, arguments about credible evidence call into question our basic notions of truth and science and the ways in which we perceive the world around us. And while this was not directly observed in the majority of our interviews, it can be inferred from some of the comments made by the interviewees.

Shifting from evidence to program theories, the definitional confusion that emerged around the use of the term *program theory* warrants acknowledgement and some further elaboration. Fetterman's description of a program theory and how he uses it in this STEP evaluation, though admittedly limited, was different from Chen's description of a program theory. This discrepancy points to the degree to which social researchers and evaluators use a set of common terms and assume that we all apply roughly the same meaning to them. To be sure, such blending and confusing of terms is part of language use, professional or otherwise. But, given the applied nature of evaluation, and given that our terms are frequently communicated to those unfamiliar with the field of evaluation, we wonder whether there should not be more explicit discussion in the field about the language we use. Furthermore, understanding that there may be definitional problems among some of our leading evaluation scholars leads us to wonder what kind of definitional confusion or overlap one might find in a diverse field of practice. Inquiry focusing on the study of the language of evaluation would have both theoretical and practical benefit.

EVALUATION USE

Mark argued in his 2006 American Evaluation Association presidential address that we should consider the consequences of evaluation in several areas: consequences of there being an evaluation, consequences of the evaluation process, consequences of evaluation findings, and consequences of the professional organization of evaluation, and last, the relationship that evaluation has to other organizations and processes (Mark, 2007). Generally, the first two are related to evaluation process use and the third, evaluation findings use, highlighting the still ever-present focus on use as a fundamental issue in evaluation.

Evaluation use is one of the few evaluation issues that have been studied rather well. Henry and Mark (2003) refer to the period during which the majority of these studies were conducted as the "golden age" of evaluation research. Most of the existing research on evaluation examines the relationship between specific evaluation procedures, contexts, and conditions that affect evaluation use. These studies (e.g., Alkin, Daillak, & White, 1979; Patton et al., 1977) were incited by the belief that evaluations were not being used in the ways they were intended, a great concern to those conducting evaluation studies and considering evaluation theory. On reflection, it is clear that data from these studies meaningfully influenced both evaluation theory and practice.

In 1986, Cousins and Leithwood examined the research on evaluation utilization conducted during the previous 15 years. The authors reviewed 65 studies and purport that they "exhausted the empirical literature about evaluation use for this period" (p. 332). They identified different types of uses (e.g., discrete decision making, policy setting) and factors influencing use (e.g., evaluation quality, credibility, relevance). From this review, the authors also identified the conditions that optimize use. Overall, evaluation use is evident when evaluations are appropriately designed, users are involved and committed to the evaluation process, users consider the information reported relevant, and outside information does not conflict with evaluation findings.

Several ways of thinking about the various types of use, which led to a class of evaluation theories that focus on use, emerged from this period of empirical work. The newly developed theories aim to ensure that evaluation has an influence on the program. The different types of evaluation use identified include enlightenment, instrumental, and process use. *Enlightenment use* describes the occasion where evaluation results change the way stakeholders think about the program, organization, or policy being evaluated even when the results do not immediately change the program, organization, or policy. This kind of use is described by Weiss (1998) as general "enlightenment" surrounding social science research work that is generated from evaluation studies. *Instrumental use* occurs when evaluation results are used to make relatively immediate decisions about a program, organization, or policy. *Process uses* are changes in procedures, practices, and culture that result from the conduct of an evaluation, as participants learn from their involvement in the evaluation. Any or all of these types of use can occur during, or as a result of, the evaluation process. Theories about how to build evaluation capacity have also grown by framing evaluation in the process use literature. For an evaluation to have an impact, it must be used. Each of the three primary types of use is evident in the interviews, and evaluators expressed concern for promoting at least one of these types of use.

Both Bickman and Riccio offer examples of enlightenment and instrumental use in the policy sphere and illustrate how evaluation research can be used in practice. To demonstrate enlightenment use, Riccio comments, as a welfare reform expert, "Many of us were surprised. Like many people following the welfare reform debates, we didn't think the Riverside approach . . . would be the one that performed better. But that's what we found, and it changed opinions" (Chapter 2).

He used a variety of strategies, including briefings with federal, state, and local policy makers and the media to ensure that the findings from his study of a highly politically-charged program were disseminated widely. Riccio's findings were also used more directly (instrumental use) by California policy makers, who revised programs in other areas of the state to resemble the Riverside County program which was shown to have a significant impact on the well-being of participants. Like Riccio, Bickman describes enlightenment use as a result of his study—changing how policy makers think about children's mental health to focus on treatment as well as systems change. Bickman also mentions how the National Institute of Mental Health (NIMH) used his findings instrumentally by increasing the funding available to support mental health programs for children.

Fetterman's study was clearly intended to assist in the decision making about the STEP program. And although Fetterman's study was designed to respond to the specific informational needs of the university president, one of the key findings from his evaluation, that there was a lack of unity about the purpose and vision of the STEP program, was said to have influenced teacher education training programs across the country. This suggests that studies designed specifically for instrumental use in a specific program context can indeed have an impact beyond the particular program context.

Bledsoe's study (Chapter 12) offers another example where instrumental use of study findings is emphasized and the organization has taken almost all the recommendations from the evaluation and revised the program accordingly. When asked about use, she reflects,

> The organization has changed the length of the program in the manner we recommended, making it longer in terms of number of weeks offered. Additionally, they are in the process of developing school readiness measures. They have also divided up the zero-to-six age range. Now, they do a zero-to-three program. We suggested they identify the program strategy, and they have done that by hiring a person to fully *develop* a program strategy. They also spend more time with volunteers to orient them to the purpose of the program and to the clients. They also developed an internal evaluation team, as we suggested. That evaluator has now been there a couple of years.

Although process use is more difficult to describe and observe than instrumental use, interviewees did offer evidence of process use as a result of participation in their studies. For example, as a means of promoting buy-in to the evaluation process as well as rigorous data collection, Rog trained providers in data collection strategies and created data collection instruments that would be useful for instrumental use at the local level. Such procedures are evidence of an attempt to promote process use. This strategy may have also helped promote the instrumental use of her findings at the community sites. She, too, is concerned with enlightenment use, as she states early in her interview that one of the goals of her study was to develop an understanding of homeless families.

Greene discusses her team's ongoing evaluative conversations that facilitated both process and instrumental use throughout the evaluation. She facilitates ongoing dialogue by developing what she describes as one "team" that includes her key program stakeholders. This team, as it was described in the interview, is different from what the literature describes as a participatory evaluation team, where program stakeholders become involved in several of the data collection and analysis activities. Rather, the goal of Greene's team was to foster trust and buy-in to the evaluation process, as a way to promote an open dialogue about the successes and shortcomings of program activities. This was accomplished in a multisite, multistate evaluation, through extensive interactions with key program stakeholders and consistent exchanges of information. These interactions did not necessarily occur in person due to resource limitations; rather, Greene describes a process by which she engaged key stakeholders through virtual and phone communications.

Donaldson also describes an ongoing dialogue with stakeholders to promote formative instrumental use. His process, however, is distinct from Greene's in that he uses more formal meetings and briefings to foster use. Riccio also describes intentional procedures, similar to those used by Donaldson, to build relationships and foster ongoing communication with key stakeholders to promote instrumental use.

Distinguishing King and Preskill's procedures to promote capacity building was the involvement of primary intended users (those whose informational needs the evaluation was designed to address) in the capacity-building activities. Preskill's primary intended users helped coordinate and organize the "Big Day Meeting." King's primary intended users, the school board, were not included in the monthly self-study team meetings, where capacity-building activities such as data analysis transpired. This suggests that capacity building, as King states in her interview, can be an outcome of the evaluation, irrespective of, and distinct from, the instrumental use of findings. Her primary goal, however, was process use: changing the knowledge and beliefs of those on the study team through their involvement in the evaluation.

Quite different from the capacity building described in King's interview, Henry did indeed engage in strategies that were intended to promote instrumental use and capacity building. Specifically, to promote instrumental use and to build evaluation capacity in the schools, Henry trained teachers, principals, and others to use the accountability system he developed for the state, conducting workshops on how to use multiple indicators to make judgments about school performance. In developing a state-level accountability system, Henry's work was intended for making decisions at the policy level, as well as at the school district and school levels. This is distinct from King, who engaged in capacity-building activities with the intent of changing organizational culture around evaluation and to increase stakeholders' ability to think "evaluatively." Thus, there is evidence of instrumental use (e.g., parent calls to Henry) and perhaps even enlightenment use as a result of this work.

General Insights

Through our interviews, we found that evaluators can and do design studies with the intention of promoting specific kinds of use. Each interviewee was concerned with whether the findings would be used and took deliberate steps to help secure a "future of use" for their findings. Additionally, the interviews offer examples of use beyond findings use, including capacity building, and provide at least some detail about the different procedures an evaluator may employ to promote specific types of use.

Our interviews demonstrated, however, that the evaluator often has little control over use once the study has concluded. Indeed, as was evidenced in the interviews, evaluators can never be sure about who might use the information generated from our studies. Weiss argues this point in a rather well-known debate with Patton and maintains that because of this, evaluators should design the most rigorous and robust studies possible, as we never know when someone might be looking to use our results (Patton, 1988; Weiss, 1988a, 1988b). This points again to the important and fluid relationship between evaluation methods and use and underscores the importance of these two evaluation issues and dimensions of evaluation practice.

To help ensure use, many of the interviewees described establishing a formal or organized group of stakeholders with whom they interacted regularly. This emerged as an important strategy for increasing instrumental use and is an instance where we have evidence to support some of our more general theoretical ideas about stakeholder involvement, specifically as it related to promoting evaluation use. Yet we also found that in some instances, such as in Fetterman and King's studies, the "primary users" of the evaluation findings had very little involvement in the evaluation process. And these are two evaluators who we expect to have heavier primary user involvement, based on their theoretical writings. This suggests that we need more current studies of the role of stakeholders in the evaluation process as it relates to evaluation use so that we can better understand when and why primary users are indeed active participants in an evaluation.

Speaking more generally about program impact and the limitations of use, some of the studies that were designed to determine if a program was "working" found that, indeed, important aspects of the programs were not working. This was the case in Bickman, Rog, Fetterman, and Bledsoe's studies. Greene says that her team found some cases where the program had an impact on the desired outcomes but that this was the exception rather than the norm. Henry mentions that at the time of the interview, the accountability system he developed had not yet influenced any major policy decisions statewide but that it had brought attention to the large proportion of very low-performing schools in the state that "no one is doing anything about." Riccio, by and large, found that Greater Avenues for Independence (GAIN) produced modest (significant), rather than dramatic, impacts on program participants. Riccio explains how the findings from his study were used to revise, and presumably improve, welfare program practices and activities across California and the country. Yet, not unlike Henry, he claims that the findings from his study did not have a direct influence on the development of the new federal welfare legislation enacted in 1996. Thus, our interviews not only demonstrate how evaluations can be used but also highlight some of the important limitations of the use of evaluation studies in making decisions about programs and policies.

CONCLUDING THOUGHTS
AND LIMITATIONS OF THE ANALYSIS

A goal for this chapter was to highlight various themes that emerged in the interviews that relate to some of the broader philosophical and theoretical ideas presented in the evaluation literature. Through this analysis, we have discovered that some of the theoretical propositions about practice that seem so clearly delimited in the literature are not as neatly defined in practice. In this way, this analysis serves as a practical test of some of our theoretical ideas.

As mentioned earlier in this chapter, most of our research on evaluation examines issues related to evaluation use, and much of that research was conducted in a wave about 20 years ago. Although the field has not seen a resurgence of research on any one particular aspect of evaluation, smatterings of more recent studies of evaluation practice have been published. Mark, Henry, and Greene are examples of evaluation scholars who have been particularly influential in advocating for and conducting research on evaluation. For example, Greene (2001) investigated the effect of stakeholder views of the technical adequacy of an evaluation's methods as well as the extent to which ideas and constructs from the philosophy of social science and evaluation theory influence evaluators' practice decisions. Henry, Dickey, and Areson (1991) studied the influence of stakeholder attitudes on an evaluation, whereas Campbell and Mark (2006) developed an experiment to test the benefits of alternative ways of framing stakeholder dialogue.

Occasionally, when evaluations are conducted, narrative accounts are composed or data on evaluation practice are collected from which we can learn about evaluation practice. However, these case examples are often limited to reflections about practice, supported only by data collected during a particular evaluation (Christie & Barela, 2005; Christie, Ross, & Klein, 2004; Fetterman & Wandersman, 2005) rather than studies conceptualized a priori and designed specifically to investigate some aspect of evaluation. Another kind of reflective case example that can inform practice, and could be thought of as a particular type of study of evaluation practice, are the interviews published in this volume. Like other case examples, those presented in this book offer important insights into evaluation theory and practice; however, there is only limited opportunity for understanding practice beyond the particular case discussed when examining each interview separately. Examining the interviews collectively, however, offers us an opportunity to examine qualitatively a data set on evaluation practice.

Our analysis suggests that evaluators' values about what evaluation is are, indeed, evident in the procedural choices made by evaluators. However, some of the theoretical ideas about the primary emphasis of particular evaluation scholars, Fetterman and Preskill specifically, as described by Alkin and Christie, were not strongly supported when practices were analyzed in the specific evaluation they described. Insight into how evaluators use mixed methods and the influence of theories of knowledge on methods choices are illuminated through the interviews, as well as the various ways people use program theories in practice. An area of confusion related to theoretical language was identified. And theoretical notions of evaluation use as they were evident in the studies conducted by the interviews offer insight into how evaluators promote different kinds of use and how evaluation use may occur beyond the specific evaluation context.

Research on evaluation has increased our understanding of both evaluation theory and practice in notable ways. Yet much more research is needed. While the current study was developed using interviews that were not originally intended for systematic study in this way, we hope that the analytic approach used will offer new insights into evaluators' reported practices and stimulate future research on the topic. We want to remind readers that our interviews were initially intended to be case examples illustrating the choices made in a particular evaluation study rather than a qualitative analysis conceptualized and designed specifically to investigate evaluation practice. Thus, interview questions were designed to build on the evaluation itself, and the answers provided by the interviewee, rather than to develop a systematic comparative look at evaluation practice. The interviews are not a representative sample of evaluation studies, and thus an analysis of them is not intended to offer a comprehensive or conclusive study of practice. Yet as a field that has repeatedly called for and is in need of systematic examinations of evaluation practice, we thought it worthy to offer an analysis of the practices discussed in the interviews. Taken together, the systematic look at these interviews presented in the two chapters in this section of the book is intended to serve as an inspiration for more extensive studies of evaluation practice.

Notes

1. This analysis is, of course, restricted to the information presented in the interviews, and therefore, if an interviewee was not asked or did not choose to talk about a particular practices or issue, we cannot assume that it was not addressed or incorporated into the evaluation procedures.

2. By and large, interviewees did not set out to design studies to exemplify the model or approach for which they might be known but rather designed studies that best addressed the evaluation questions or issues at hand. It should be noted that some evaluators—Donaldson, Preskill, and Greene—were interviewed with the intent that they would describe a study to illustrate the model or approach for which they are best known. Other evaluators describe studies using designs that are different from those they frequently discuss in the theoretical literature.

3. The postpositivism ontological position argues that there is a single reality that can be studied objectively; however, there is no way to understand reality in its totality,

and thus, full understanding of truth can be approached but never reached. Postpositivists have a strong preference for quantitative methods and deductive reasoning. However, in alignment with the notion of "approaching" truth rather than "capturing" it, postpositivists would not argue that quantitative methods or deductive reasoning should be used exclusively, just predominantly. The approaching truth ideal extends to views on causality as well. It is believed that causation is observable and that over time predictors can be established, but always some degree of doubt remains associated with the conclusion. As for axiology, values and biases are noted and accounted for, yet the belief is that they can be controlled within the context of scientific inquiry (excerpt from Christie and Fleischer, 2007).

4. The constructivist ontological position argues that there are multiple realities. These multiple realities are subjective and change according to the "knower," who constructs his or her own reality using past experiences and individual contexts to perceive what is "known." This type of realism is referred to as "ontological relativism." In the constructivist paradigm, the knower and the known are interrelated, unlike positivist epistemology, where they are considered independent. Inductive logic is the rule, which means that particular instances are used to infer broader, more general laws. Of notable distinction, inquiry is considered value-bound rather than value-free. It is the constructivists' position that it is better to acknowledge and consider bias than to attempt to ignore or control it. Qualitative methods are used most frequently within the constructivist paradigm because they are thought to be better suited to investigate the subjective layers of reality. Generalizability is not nearly as important as local relevance. Cause and effect are thought impossible to distinguish because relationships are bidirectional and thus everything is influencing everything else at one time (excerpt from Christie and Fleischer, in press).

5. RCTs require the random assignment of individuals into a treatment group (the group receiving the intervention or program) or a control group (the group not receiving the intervention or program). Random assignment is argued to reduce most threats to internal validity (e.g., selection bias, maturation, history), and the use of a control group provides data to determine the relative performance of the treatment group, helping answer the "compared with what?" question when measuring program impact (Azzam & Christie, 2007).

6. Pragmatists embrace objectivity and subjectivity as two positions on a continuum and believe that both quantitative and qualitative methods are legitimate methods of inquiry and that the decision of what method to use is based on the nature of the study question. Pragmatists also argue that deductive and inductive logic should be used in concert. Pragmatists are more similar to postpositivists with regard to notions about external reality, with the understanding that there is no absolute "truth" concerning reality. More in line with constructivist thought, however, pragmatists argue that there are multiple explanations of reality and at any given time there is one explanation that makes the most sense. In other words, at one point in time, one explanation of reality may be considered "truer" than another. Pragmatists are again similar to postpositivists in that they believe that causes may be linked to effects. However, pragmatists temper this thinking by providing the caveat that absolute certainty of the causation is

impossible. In contrast, pragmatists are more similar to constructivists in that they do not believe that inquiry is value-free and they consider their values important to the inquiry process (excerpt from Christie and Fleischer, in press).

7. Rog argues in her interview, however, that an RCT was not necessary in her evaluation. Rather, the final post-only measures were so dramatic that no further evidence was necessary to establish causality. Her choice in this study is an interesting example of adapting to context.

REFERENCES

Alkin, M. C. (2004). *Evaluation roots.* Thousand Oaks, CA: Sage.

Alkin, M. C., & Christie, C. A. (2004). An evaluation theory tree. In M. C. Alkin (Ed.), *Evaluation roots* (pp. 12–65). Thousand Oaks, CA: Sage.

Alkin, M. C., & Christie, C. A. (Eds.), (2005). *Theorists' models in action* (New Directions for Evaluation, No. 106). San Francisco: Jossey-Bass.

Alkin, M. C., Daillak, R., & White, B. (1979). *Using evaluations.* Beverly Hills, CA: Sage.

Azzam, T., & Christie, C. A. (2007). Using public databases to study relative program impact. *Canadian Journal of Program Evaluation, 22,* 57–68.

Bickman, L., & Reich, S. (in press). Randomized control trials: A gold standard with feet of clay? In S. I. Donaldson, C. A. Christie, & M. M. Mark (Eds.), *What counts as credible evidence in evaluation and evidence-based practice?* Thousand Oaks, CA: Sage.

Campbell, B. C., & Mark, M. M. (2006). Toward more effective stakeholder dialogue: Applying theories of negotiation to policy and program evaluation. *Journal of Applied Social Psychology, 36,* 2834–2863.

Campbell, D., & Stanley, J. (1966). *Experimental and quasi-experimental designs for research.* Chicago: Rand McNally.

Chen, H. (1990). *Theory-driven evaluations.* Newbury Park, CA: Sage.

Chen, H., & Rossi, P. H. (1992). Introduction: Integrating theory into evaluation practice. In H. Chen & P. H. Rossi (Eds.), *Using theory to improve program and policy evaluations* (pp. 2–11). Westport, CT: Greenwood.

Christie, C. A. (2003). *What guides evaluation? A study of how evaluation practice maps onto evaluation theory* (New Directions for Evaluation, No. 97, pp. 7–36). San Francisco: Jossey-Bass.

Christie, C. A., & Alkin, M. C. (in press). Evaluation theory tree re-examined. *Studies in Educational Evaluation.*

Christie, C. A., & Barela, E. (2005). The Delphi technique as a method for increasing inclusion in the evaluation process. *Canadian Journal of Program Evaluation, 20*(1), 105–122.

Christie, C. A., & Masyn, K. E. (in press). Profiles of evaluators reported practice: A latent profile analysis. *Canadian Journal of Program Evaluation.*

Christie, C. A., & Fleischer, D. (in press). A context for the debate on credible evidence. In S. I. Donaldson, C. A. Christie, & M. M. Mark (Eds.), *What counts as credible evidence in evaluation and evidence-based practice?* Thousand Oaks, CA: Sage.

Christie, C. A., Ross R., & Klein, B. M. (2004). Moving toward collaboration by creating an internal-external evaluation team: A case study. *Studies in Educational Evaluation, 30,* 125–134.

Cooperrider, D. L. (1986). *Appreciative inquiry: Toward a methodology for understanding and enhancing organizational innovation.* Unpublished doctoral dissertation, Case Western Reserve University, Cleveland, OH.

Cousins, J. B., & Earl, L. M. (1999). When the boat gets missed: Response to M. F. Smith. *American Journal of Evaluation, 20*(2), 309–317.

Cousins, J. B., & Leithwood, K. A. (1986). Current empirical research on evaluation utilization. *Review of Educational Research, 56*(3), 331–364.

Donaldson, S. I. (2007). *Program theory-driven evaluation science: Strategies and applications.* Mahwah, NJ: Lawrence Erlbaum.

Donaldson, S. I., Christie, C. A., & Mark, M. M. (in press). *What counts as credible evidence in evaluation and evidence-based practice?* Thousand Oaks, CA: Sage.

Fetterman, D. (Ed.). (1988). *Qualitative approaches to evaluation in education: The silent scientific revolution.* Albany: State University of New York Press.

Fetterman, D. (1989). *Ethnography: Step by step.* Newbury Park, CA: Sage.

Fetterman, D. (1994). Empowerment evaluation. *Evaluation Practice, 15*(1), 1–15.

Fetterman, D. (2004). Branching out or standing on a limb: Looking to our roots for insight. In M. Alkin (Ed.), *Evaluation roots* (pp. 304–318). Thousand Oaks, CA: Sage.

Fetterman, D., & Wandersman, A. (2005). *Empowerment evaluation principles in practice.* New York: Guilford Press.

Greene, J. (2000). Challenges in practicing deliberative democratic evaluation. In K. E. Ryan & L. DeStefano (Eds.), *Evaluation as a democratic process: Promoting inclusion, dialogue, and deliberation* (New Directions for Evaluation, No. 85, pp. 13–26). San Francisco: Jossey-Bass.

Greene, J. (November, 2001). *Introduction to the panel on understanding evaluators' practice decisions: The influence of theory, philosophy, values, experience, and individuality.* Paper presented at the American Evaluation Association Annual Conference, St. Louis, MO.

Greene, J. (in press). Evidence as "proof" and evidence as "inkling." In S. I. Donaldson, C. A. Christie, & M. M. Mark (Eds.), *What counts as credible evidence in evaluation and evidence-based practice?* Thousand Oaks, CA: Sage.

Hall, J., & Hammond, S. (1995). *The thin book of appreciative inquiry.* Plano, TX: Thin Book.

Henry, G. (in press). When getting it right matters: The case for high quality policy and program impact evaluations. In S. I. Donaldson, C. A. Christie, & M. M. Mark (Eds.), *What counts as credible evidence in evaluation and evidence-based practice?* Thousand Oaks, CA: Sage.

Henry, G., Julnes, G., & Mark, M. (Eds.). (1998). *Realist evaluation: An emerging theory in support of practice* (New Directions for Evaluation, No. 78). San Francisco: Jossey-Bass.

Henry, G. T., Dickey, K. C., & Areson, J. C. (1991). Stakeholder participation in educational performance monitoring. *Educational Evaluation and Policy Analysis, 13*(2), 177–188.

Henry, G. T., & Mark, M. M. (2003). Toward an agenda for research on evaluation. In C.A. Christie (Ed.), *The practice-theory relationship in evaluation* (New Directions for Evaluation, No. 97, pp. 69–80). San Francisco: Jossey-Bass.

House, E., & Howe, K. (1999). *Values in evaluation and social research.* Thousand Oaks, CA: Sage.

Joint Committee on Standards for Educational Evaluation. (1994). *The program evaluation standards: How to assess evaluations of educational programs* (2nd ed.). Thousand Oaks, CA: Sage.

Julnes, G., & Rog, D. (in press). Evaluation methods for producing actionable evidence: Contextual influences on adequacy and appropriateness of method choice. In S. I. Donaldson, C. A. Christie, & M. M. Mark (Eds.). *What counts as credible evidence in evaluation and evidence-based practice?* Thousand Oaks, CA: Sage.

King, J. A. (2002). Building the evaluation capacity of a school district. In C.A. Christie (Ed.), *The practice-theory relationship in evaluation* (New Directions for Evaluation, No. 93, pp. 63–80). San Francisco: Jossey-Bass.

King, J. A., & Volkov, B. (2005). *A grounded framework for evaluation capacity building.* Unpublished manuscript, University of Minnesota, Minneapolis.

Kisira, S., & Conner, R. (2004, December). Community-based monitoring and evaluation: Benefits, challenges, and recommendation. In *Proceedings of the third conference of the African Evaluation Association*, Cape Town, South Africa.

Lantz, P., Israel, B., Schulz, A., & Reyes, A. (2006). Community-based participatory research: Rationale and relevance for social epidemiology. In J. M. Oakes & J. Turner (Eds.), *Methods for social epidemiology.* San Francisco, CA: Jossey-Bass.

Lipsey, M. (1993). Theory as method: Small theories of treatments. In L. B. Sechrest & A. G. Scott (Eds.), *Understanding causes and generalizing about them* (New Directions for Program Evaluation, No. 57, pp. 5–38). San Francisco, CA: Jossey-Bass.

Mark, M. (2007). Building a better evidence base for evaluation theory: Beyond general calls to a framework of types of research on evaluation. In N. Smith & P. Brandon (Eds.), *Fundamental issues in evaluation* (pp. 111–134). New York: Guilford Press.

Mark, M. M. (2006, November). *The consequences of evaluation.* Presidential address at the American Evaluation Association Annual Conference, Portland, OR.

Patton, M. Q. (1988). The evaluator's responsibility for utilization. *Evaluation Practice, 9,* 5–24.

Patton, M. Q. (1997). *Utilization-focused evaluation.* Thousand Oaks, CA: Sage.

Patton, M. Q., Grimes, P. S., Guthrie, K. M., Brennan, N. J., French, B. D., & Blyth, D. A. (1977). In search of impact: An analysis of the utilization of federal health evaluation research. In C. H. Weiss (Ed.), *Using social research in public policy making* (pp. 141–163). Lexington, MA: Lexington Books.

Preskill, H. (2004). The transformational power of evaluation: Passion, purpose and practice. In M. Alkin (Ed.), *Evaluation roots* (pp. 343–355). Thousand Oaks, CA: Sage.

Preskill, H., & Catsambas, T. T. (2006). *Reframing evaluation through appreciative inquiry.* Thousand Oaks, CA: Sage.

Scriven, M. (1983). Evaluation ideologies. In G. F. Madaus, M. Scriven, & D. L. Stufflebeam (Eds.), *Evaluation models: Viewpoints on educational and human services evaluation* (pp. 229–260). Boston: Kluwer-Nijhoff.

Smith, N. L. (1993). Improving evaluation theory through the empirical study of evaluation practice. *Evaluation Practice, 14*(3), 237–242.

Stake, R. (1975). *Program evaluation, particularly responsive evaluation* (Occasional Paper No. 5). Kalamazoo: Western Michigan University Evaluation Center.

Stake, R. E. (2005). *Multiple case study analysis.* New York: Guilford Press.

Stufflebeam, D. (2001). *Evaluation models* (New Directions for Evaluation, No. 89). San Francisco, CA: Jossey-Bass.

Stufflebeam, D. L., & Shinkfield, A. J. (1985). *Systematic evaluation.* Norwell, MA: Kluwer-Nijhoff.

Tashakkori, A., & Teddlie, C. (Eds.). (2002). *Handbook of mixed methods in social and behavioral research.* Thousand Oaks, CA: Sage.

Weiss, C. H. (1988a). Evaluation for decisions: Is anybody there? Does anybody care? *Evaluation Practice, 9,* 5–19.

Weiss, C. H. (1988b). If program decision hinged only on information: A response to Patton. *Evaluation Practice, 9,* 15–28.

Weiss, C. H. (1998). *Evaluation* (2nd ed.). Upper Saddle River, NJ: Prentice Hall.

Worthen, B. R., & Sanders, J. R. (1973). Evaluation as disciplined inquiry. In B. Worthen & J. Sanders (Eds.), *Educational evaluation: Theory and practice* (pp. 10–39). Worthington, OH: Charles A. Jones.

APPENDIX

Other Categories for the Interviews

---◆◆◆---

Clarifying the Evaluation Request
Chapters 4 (Bickman), 6 (Rog), 7 (Henry), 11 (Conner)

Developing Program Theory
Chapters 4 (Bickman), 9 (Donaldson), 12 (Bledsoe)

Examining the Political Context
Chapters 2 (Riccio), 4 (Bickman), 5 (Fetterman), 12 (Bledsoe), 13 (Wallis and Dukay)

Internal Evaluation
Chapters 5 (Fetterman), 8 (King), 13 (Wallis and Dukay)

Stakeholder Involvement Issues, Strategies, and Concerns
Chapters 6 (Rog), 8 (King), 9 (Donaldson), 10 (Preskill), 11 (Conner), 12 (Bledsoe)

Planning and Managing an Evaluation
Chapters 2 (Riccio), 3 (Greene), 5 (Fetterman), 6 (Rog), 9 (Donaldson), 13 (Wallis and Dukay)

Reporting and Use of Results
Chapters 2 (Riccio), 3 (Greene), 7 (Henry), 9 (Donaldson), 12 (Bledsoe)

Data Sources and Methods
Chapters 2 (Riccio), 3 (Greene), 6 (Rog), 7 (Henry), 12 (Bledsoe), 13 (Wallis and Dukay)

Using Observation
Chapters 3 (Greene), 5 (Fetterman), 11 (Conner), 12 (Bledsoe)

Process/Monitoring Evaluations
Chapters 2 (Riccio), 3 (Greene), 4 (Bickman), 5 (Fetterman), 6 (Rog), 11 (Conner), 12 (Bledsoe)

Randomized Field Experiments
Chapters 2 (Riccio), 4 (Bickman)

Performance Monitoring and Establishing Evaluation Systems
Chapters 7 (Henry), 10 (Preskill)

Examining Program Impact
Chapters 2 (Riccio), 3 (Greene), 4 (Bickman), 6 (Rog), 9 (Donaldson), 11 (Conner), 12 (Bledsoe), 13 (Wallis and Dukay)

INDEX

ABOUT THE AUTHORS

———•◦•———

Jody Fitzpatrick is Director of the Masters in Public Administration Program and an associate professor with the School of Public Affairs at the University of Colorado Denver. She is the author of *Program Evaluation: Alternative Approaches and Practical Guidelines* (with James Sanders and Blaine Worthen; 3rd ed., 2004). Dr. Fitzpatrick's interests include evaluation practice, ethics, and education policy. Dr. Fitzpatrick has many years of experience conducting evaluations, first as an internal evaluator in Appalachia and New York and then as an external evaluator in a variety of settings. She has published in *Evaluation Review, American Journal of Evaluation*, and *New Directions for Evaluation* and has served on the board of the American Evaluation Association and as Associate Editor of the *American Journal of Evaluation*.

Christina Christie is an associate professor, Director of the Masters of Arts Program in Psychology and Evaluation, and Associate Director of the Institute of Organizational and Program Evaluation Research in the School of Behavioral and Organizational Sciences at Claremont Graduate University. Christie has received funding from a variety of sources to evaluate social, education, and health behavior programs targeting high-risk and underrepresented populations. She cofounded the Southern California Evaluation Association, a local affiliate of the American Evaluation Association, and is the former Chair of the Theories of Evaluation Division and current Chair of the Research on Evaluation Division of the American Evaluation Association. Christie is a section editor of the *American Journal of Evaluation* and on the editorial board of *New Directions in Evaluation.* She is also an editor of the forthcoming book *What Counts as Credible Evidence in Evaluation and Evidence-Based Practice?* (with Stewart Donaldson and Melvin Mark; Sage). In 2004, Dr. Christie received the American Evaluation Association's Marcia Guttentag Early Career Achievement Award.

Melvin M. Mark is Professor and Head of Psychology at Pennsylvania State University. A past president of the American Evaluation Association, he has also served as Editor of the *American Journal of Evaluation*, where he is now Editor Emeritus. Dr. Mark's interests include the theory, methodology, practice, and profession of program and policy evaluation. He has been involved in evaluations in a number of areas, including prevention programs, federal personnel policies, and various educational interventions. Among his books are *Evaluation: An Integrated Framework for Understanding, Guiding, and Improving Policies and Programs* (with Gary Henry and George Julnes; 2000) and the recent *SAGE Handbook of Evaluation* (edited with Ian Shaw and Jennifer Greene; 2006, Sage), as well as the forthcoming books *Credible Evidence* (with Stewart Donaldson and Tina Christie, Sage) and *Social Psychology and Evaluation* (with Stewart Donaldson and Bernadette Campbell).